Yuletide in Dixie

Yuletide in Dixie

SLAVERY, CHRISTMAS, AND SOUTHERN MEMORY

Robert E. May

UNIVERSITY OF VIRGINIA PRESS
Charlottesville and London

University of Virginia Press

© 2019 by the Rector and Visitors
of the University of Virginia

Printed in the United States of America on acid-free paper

First published 2019

1 3 5 7 9 8 6 4 2

Library of Congress Cataloging-in-Publication Data

Names: May, Robert E., author.
Title: Yuletide in Dixie : slavery, Christmas, and Southern memory /
    Robert E. May.
Description: Charlottesville ; London : University of Virginia Press,
    [2019] | Includes bibliographical references and index.
Identifiers: LCCN 2019002096 | ISBN 9780813942148 (cloth : alk.
    paper) | ISBN 9780813942155 (ebook)
Subjects: LCSH: Slaves—Southern States—Social conditions. | Slavery—
    Southern States—History. | Christmas—Southern States—History. |
    Collective memory—Southern States. | Southern States—Social life
    and customs—1775–1865. | Southern States—Social life and customs—
    To 1775.
Classification: LCC E443 .M39 2019 | DDC 306.3/620975—dc23
LC record available at https://lccn.loc.gov/2019002096

For my daughter, Heather,
and her passionate commitment
to racial justice in America

The correct thinker . . . hears with a scorn too bitter for words that the slave dances and sings and gormandizes during a Christmas fortnight . . . and that he is fat and sleek and merry. To give the smallest value to suggestions of this nature, the humanity of the black man must be dogmatically denied.

The Independent (New York), June 4, 1863

CONTENTS

ILLUSTRATIONS

ACKNOWLEDGMENTS

This book has benefited from the advice of many people, none so more than my wife, Jill, and my daughter, Heather. Jill, a former professor of children's literature at Purdue University and an insightful reader who has come to the rescue of my manuscripts many times since we first joined marriage with academia, encouraged my initial interest in the intersections of slavery with Christmas and has continued to encourage this pursuit since my retirement from teaching a few years ago. She has long claimed the field as my strictest and most helpful copyeditor, and this book, like all my previous ones, has been greatly improved by attention to her objections and suggestions. Our daughter, Heather, associate professor of Theatre at Hobart and William Smith Colleges in Geneva, New York, wrote her dissertation on a nineteenth-century cross-dressing U.S. minstrel performer, and has been absorbed with issues of race and gender for decades as well as an activist for racial justice. She has also read this book in manuscript form, and provided me with extremely valuable advice about both content and navigating issues of race.

One of my very first "contacts" in the profession, Howard Jones, University Research Professor Emeritus at the University of Alabama, who participated in a conference session with me when I was just "learning the ropes" of being a professional historian, has remained a considerate and always generous friend for many years and characteristically provided very helpful corrections and suggestions regarding this book after reading the entire manuscript. George C. Rable, Charles G. Summersell Chair of Southern History Emeritus at the University of Alabama and one of the country's finest Civil War historians, another longtime friend, provided me with a very close reading of my chapter on Christmas in the Confederacy as well as a number of very useful research leads. Wanda Hendricks, professor in the Department of History, University of South Carolina, another long-standing friend, gave my final chapter and epilogue close readings, and provided additional writing suggestions and some great research tips. The author of a fine study of an important early twentieth-century black activist (*Fannie Barrier Williams: Crossing the Borders of Region and Race*), Wanda among other things alerted me to an important story Williams published related to Christmas and slavery that I discuss in chapter 7. Further, she connected me with some of her contacts in the public history field—Fielding Freed (director of Historic House Museums in Columbia, South Carolina), Robert R. Weyeneth (professor of history at the University of South Carolina with specializations in public history, historic preservation, and African American heritage preservation), and John Sherrer (director of cultural resources for Historic Columbia)—who provided me with additional leads and suggestions. They led me to Elizabeth L. Laney, park interpreter, Redcliffe Plantation State Historic Site on Beech Island, South Carolina, and Christian J. Cotz, the director of education and visitor engagement at James Madison's Montpelier. Both provided me with valuable internal documents illuminating Christmas themes at their respective sites. One discovery brought another in a kind of spiraling research quest, and I cannot imagine my epilogue, which goes into depth into treatments of slave Christmases at modern historic sites, without their collective insights.

I would like to thank the Purdue interlibrary loan service for prompt handling of my many requests. They've been in my corner for as long as I can remember. John David Smith, Charles H. Stone Distinguished Professor of American History, University of North Carolina at Charlotte, helped me work through an interpretive issue about Christmas gifts to slaves and provided further feedback as a critical reader of the manuscript for the University of Virginia Press. I'm likewise greatly indebted to Charles Dew, Ephraim Williams Professor of American History at Williams College, for his suggestions as another of the press's readers. Brandon Ronald Byrd of the Department of History, Vanderbilt University, answered my queries about Christmas programming at a southern historical site he visited and offered suggestions for this book's treatment of public history treatments of slave Christmases. Brian J. Cuthrell (electronic access archivist at the South Caroliniana Library at the University of South Carolina), Louisa Hoffman (archival assistant, Oberlin College Archives), Emma Parker (graduate research assistant, Louis Round Wilson Special Collections Library, University of North Carolina), and John McClure (director of library and research services, Virginia Historical Society) also provided help. Neal A. Harmeyer (digital archivist, Purdue University Archives and Special Collections) was especially generous in terms of time and sharing his expertise, making superb scans from Purdue library collections of several of the images used in this book. Alan Mehringer, newsletter editor for the Camp Tippecanoe Civil War Round Table, with which I have been affiliated for decades, alerted me to helpful digital research sources that I probably would never have stumbled across without his guidance. Jessolyn Larry, a decades-long close family friend and executive director at St. Louis Public Schools, read sections of the book manuscript and gave me the benefit of her reactions. Fortuitously, Frederick (Tom) Sparrow, Professor Emeritus of Industrial Engineering at Purdue, dropped a casual lead over lunch with me at the local Irish pub, and it turned into gold. I'm greatly in his debt as well.

Finally, R. Douglas Hurt, head of Purdue University's Department of History, has supported this book with administrative resources, despite my recent retirement. I am very appreciative of his continuing commitment to my research and writing.

Yuletide in Dixie

Introduction

It would be easy to ignore the remark, merely a passing allusion in a 416-page futuristic novel. Shortly before the Union began dissolving in 1860, the elderly Virginia planter, agricultural reformer, and proslavery fanatic Edmund Ruffin published *Anticipations of the Future.* Using the artifice of letters supposedly written by a *London Times* correspondent, Ruffin's book spun the tale of an imagined "southern confederacy," something he had craved for a long time. Unsurprisingly, history would prove wrong many of Ruffin's predictions, most obviously that his southern nation would win its war for independence and that it would take less than a year to do it. Still, Ruffin's *Anticipations* correctly approximates how the Civil War would actually start: South Carolina's secession causes a North-South rift over conflicting federal and state claims to sovereignty over U.S. forts at Charleston Harbor.

And it is within this context that Ruffin's story makes a fleeting allusion to Christmas that inadvertently is so damning about slavery that it deserves reflection. Ruffin's lapse occurs in the context of his correspondent's "Letter XXI" dated Washington, D.C., January 21, 1868, around the time the first six slave states, all in the Deep South, leave the Union to establish a new nation. In his dispatch, Ruffin's newsman recounts the events of recent weeks, including actions that the governor of South Carolina has taken to secure the military posts that the U.S. government controlled in Charleston. The chief executive had planned to seize Fort Sumter in the harbor and challenge the federal grip on Fort Moultrie opposite it to the north on nearby Sullivan's Island on the night of December 24. Knowing he needed to mobilize troops without tipping off Union officials that something sinister was afoot,

the governor had purposely chosen that particular night for his operations because such assemblages were "not unusual at Christmas." After
all, in recent years there had almost always occurred at Christmastime
"false and foolish rumors" of slave insurrections necessitating militia
mobilizations. Given this history, the governor calculated, Union officials would suspect nothing if militia were called out. The governor's
clever plot, the correspondent reports, has worked flawlessly. He has
had twenty volunteer militia companies assemble at nightfall without
incident, employing some of the troops to put Fort Moultrie under
siege. He also has dispatched some denizens of the city to visit the sole
Union sergeant occupying Fort Sumter under the guise of a Christmas
social call, and they have succeeded in taking the unsuspecting officer
into their custody. By sunrise on Christmas morning, 500 South Carolina militiamen had lodged themselves at Fort Sumter.[1]

Ruffin's allusion to Christmas slave insurrections commands our
attention not just because it amounts to a confession by one of the stri-
dent proslavery intellectuals in the Old South that many white southerners assumed their slaves were discontented enough to revolt but
also because it flies in the face of one of the most persistent tropes, or
myths, in southern history and memory—that slaves were happiest at
Christmas, a holiday that held far more importance in the South than
in the North during America's early history.

Though the overwhelming percentage of European settlers in the
thirteen English colonies was Christian, not all Christians regarded
Christmas similarly. The Puritans who settled and dominated New
England in the 1600s suppressed Christmas celebrations, regarding
them as obstacles to their mission of purging or *purifying* their English
homeland's official Anglican Church of offices, practices, and extrav-
agances, including holidays, that distracted adherents from understanding God's word as expressed in the Bible. In 1658, the General
Court of the Massachusetts Bay Colony (the colonial equivalent of
today's Massachusetts legislature) passed a statute saying that anyone
"found observing any such day as Christmas, or the like" by feasting
or refusing to labor or in "any other way" should pay a five-shilling fine
to the colony for each infraction. Though anti-Christmas prejudices
waned in the 1700s as New England became more pluralistic, they lingered in some rural parts of the North until the Civil War. In Michigan
and the New England countryside, people worked on Christmas Day;
country stores, taverns, and offices remained open, and parents sent
their children to school as usual.[2]

In contrast, Christmas-approving Anglicans dominated early settlement in England's colonies in the South, giving the Church of England official status and supporting with taxation what many whites, especially the elite, considered a sacred date on their annual calendar. Landon Carter, one of the richest landowners and slaveholders in colonial Virginia, underlined in his diary a self-instructing reminder one Christmas Eve that Christmas was the day for him to reflect on "*the Nativity of our Lord & Saviour Jesus Christ.*"[3] As a result, Christmas got a head start in the southernmost colonies that arguably persisted long after Anglican disestablishment during the age of the American Revolution.

Indeed, antebellum white southerners remarked on regional distinctions between North and South when it came to Christmas, considering them revealing cultural markers. Daniel R. Hundley, a native Alabamian from a slaveholding family living in Chicago when he published *Social Relations in Our Southern States* just before the Civil War, insisted Christmas was a time "of much greater renown in the South than in the North" because the original thirteen English colonies had been settled by distinctively different peoples from the mother country—Puritans in what became the North and so-called Cavaliers in the South. In the free northern states where Puritans had once lived and where slavery had been abolished, he elaborated, "there is not in them that general *abandon,* that universal merry-making which always characterizes Christmas in the Slave States." Hundley's certainty was widely shared throughout the South. In fact, a southerner writing a rather critical review of his work for *De Bow's Review,* a New Orleans commercial magazine, agreed that in Dixie, the "festivals and merrymakings of Christmas" showed that southern whites kept more of the customs of their transatlantic cousins in England than did northerners.[4]

Though historians have long since debunked the simplistic notion that the American Civil War came because dissenting Puritans settled the northern colonies while Cavaliers (supporters of the monarchy during the English Civil War of the mid-1600s) dominated southern ones, Hundley and his reviewer were right that antebellum southerners and northerners passed their Christmas seasons differently and that these distinctions held significance in the sectional divisions between North and South that would bring on the Civil War. As this book shows, varying regional Christmas traditions bore on the slavery question dividing North and South that lay at the heart of Civil War causation. After Appomattox, recollections of prewar southern

Christmas experiences became central to how slavery was remembered in the era of Jim Crow.

According to southern legend, during the "antebellum era" (approximately 1830 to the beginning of the Civil War in 1861), kindly masters not only reveled through the holiday season but also allowed slaves to share fully in their joyous celebrations. They gave slaves a week off from labor and bestowed so many generous gifts, lavish feasts, and travel privileges on them during this festive season that slaves could only conclude they were lucky to be owned and cared for by kindly white folk. Slaves chose Christmastime for their weddings, had reunions with relations normally too far away to see, ate delicacies until their bellies were too full for another bite, drank booze to their hearts' content, and danced, sang, and otherwise partied all night if they so desired.

Consider in this respect one of the most ambitious propaganda salvos by southern whites before the Civil War to justify their labor system against Yankee abolitionist assaults, William J. Grayson's epic fifty-four-page poem of 1854 entitled *The Hireling and the Slave*. Grayson, who had served in his state's legislature and the U.S. Congress, hailed from coastal South Carolina's Beaufort District, an area of sea island cotton production and vast slaveholding estates, and owned plantations and many slaves himself. Upset by the negative portrait of slavery in Harriet Beecher Stowe's best-selling *Uncle Tom's Cabin* (1852) that was roiling the country and much of the Atlantic World at the time, Grayson authored a literary rebuttal in heroic couplets that compared southern slavery as he understood it to the North's free labor system, or, more precisely, the lot of the slave worker in the South to that of the North's paid but mistreated industrial worker, "the hireling." Grayson's portrait of plantation Christmases, in this context, could not have been more idyllic, conveying slavery at Christmastime in the mellowest language imaginable. Who would not want to be enslaved on such a joyful, munificent, mirthful occasion? Who would not want to join their exuberant, uninhibited dances?

> Around the slaughtered ox—a Christmas prize,
> The slaves assembling stand with eager eyes,
> Rouse, with their dogs, the porker's piercing cry,
> Or drag its squealing tenant from the sty;
> With smile and bow receive their winter dues,
> The strong, warm clothing and substantial shoes,

Blankets adorned with stripes of border red,
And caps of wool that warm the woolier head;
Then clear the barn, the ample area fill,
In the gay jig display their vigorous skill;
No dainty steps, no mincing measures here—
Ellsler's trained graces—seem to float in air,
But hearts of joy and nerves of living steel,
On floors that spring beneath the bounding reel;
Proud on his chair, with magisterial glance
And stamping foot, the fiddler rules the dance;
Draws, if he nods, the still unwearied bow,
And gives a joy no bearded bands bestow;
The triple holiday, on angel wings,
With every fleeting hour a pleasure brings;
No ennui clouds, no coming cares annoy,
Nor wants nor sorrows check the Negro's joy.[5]

Such accounts of slave holiday bliss as Grayson's, standard fare in popular understandings of Christmas in the South before the Civil War, had staying power afterward. Prior to the Civil War, southern whites commonly deluded themselves into thinking that the seeming happiness of their enslaved people at Christmastime testified to their suitability for bondage. Assumptions of slave contentment at Christmas gave the lie to abolitionist critiques of what white southerners possessively dubbed their "peculiar institution" and contributed to the region-wide defensive mentality that helped produce southern secession from the Union in the winter of 1860–1861.[6] How could Yankees, prejudiced by a visceral hatred of slavery in the abstract, truly grasp what really transpired in the intimate relationship between a master or mistress and his or her human property on a day-to-day basis? If abolitionists could only witness the slaves' joy at Christmas, southern whites widely assumed, they would cease their critique of coerced labor. As the historian William Freehling has noted in his magisterial study of southern secession from the Union, the ostentatious conferring of holiday presents by masters to their slaves amounted in slave owners' eyes to a reaffirmation of their deservedness to command labor for free—or, as Freehling put it, "annual paternalistic reelections."[7]

Such conceptions about slave Christmastime contributed to southern secession from the Union in 1860–1861, and persisted after Appomattox, informing the South's so-called Lost Cause and the battle over

Civil War memory that characterized the post–Civil War decades. To a good degree they also percolated through other parts of the country as much as they did the South. As David Blight observed in his pathbreaking book *Race and Reunion,* in the late nineteenth century the defeated South, desperate for a "new religion of nationhood" to justify itself in the wake of a horrific defeat, began construing a "mythos" of a "pleasing past" in which the rationalization of slavery imparted an important component. If their prewar labor system had been benign, southerners hardly deserved censure for leaving the Union to protect it, causing the Civil War with its attendant horrors. Nor could they be blamed for resisting northern occupation and the enfranchisement of former slaves after the war ended, or subsequently creating a full-blown system of racial segregation once they overthrew Radical Reconstruction. During these decades, southern white writers like Thomas Nelson Page, himself the product of a childhood plantation upbringing, created, in Blight's words, a literary world populated by "Southern gentlemen," "gracious [white] ladies," "Negro mammies," and "unwaveringly loyal bondsmen," a world in which ex-slaves in dialect fondly reminisced about the happy, carefree days they had experienced before the war left them impoverished and rootless.[8]

Though Blight says nothing about Christmas in his study, post–Civil War southern commentators like Page paid homage to joyous slave Yuletide celebrations in their campaign for the American imagination. Take Unc' [Uncle] Edinburg, the elderly onetime slave driver in a fifty-three-page story that Page published in 1889, who much preferred the Christmases of slave times to postwar holiday times, when "free-issue niggers" did not "know what Christmas is." During the particular antebellum Christmas in Page's story, Unc' Edinburg and his master visit the Braxton place. There, slaves not only celebrate the holiday with a dance at the washhouse but also enjoy a fancy meal in the carpenter's shop—a setting that their master had thoughtfully decorated for the special occasion, as noted by our appreciative protagonist:

> Oh, hit . . . beautiful! . . . big silver strandeliers [chandeliers] out de house . . . an' some o' ole mistis's [plantation mistress's] best damas' [damask] tablecloths, an' ole marster's gret bowl ful o' egg-nog . . . flowers out de greenhouse on de table, . . . Oh! oh! nuttin warn too good for niggers dem times.[9]

Such imagery of slave ecstasy at Christmastime lingered into the twentieth century, reinforcing white Dixie's racial mores, even after the civil rights movement brought segregation and racial discrimination under sharp attack in the 1950s and 1960s. As the New Orleans preservationist, author/travel writer, and southern romanticist Harnett Kane put it in a book published four years after the Supreme Court's 1954 *Brown* decision integrating the schools, Christmas before the Civil War was a day when slaves received gifts and spiked eggnog from their masters before feasting in their quarters on spareribs and other delights. There they joked around in a state of "hilarity and good will," held an evening dance, and roasted popcorn for their children over "crackling fires." Sometimes their masters showed up at their Christmas dinner to exchange toasts, and it was common for the master's entire family to appear for the slaves' holiday dance, where they were accorded "places of honor" in the front so that they could best observe their slaves' exuberance. Or so Kane asserted.[10]

Squaring popular pastoral southern Christmas images with Ruffin's admission about persisting white southerners' fears about Yuletide servile insurrectionism is no easy matter, since ample historical documentation seems to substantiate every element of the story that Grayson, Page, and company related. Diaries and letters of southern slaveholders, the observations of travelers to the Old South, newspaper accounts, and even some antislavery publications attest that slaves feasted, danced, received presents, rested and relaxed, held family reunions, and got married during the Christmas season. Northern writer Metta Victoria Fuller Victor for example, intended her fast-selling dime novel *Maum Guinea* (1861) as a critique of slavery; she made a seething, angry plantation cook its central character and explored how enslavement wrecked the family lives even of slaves owned by kindly masters. Still, her plot conceded to white southerners that slaves got a full-week's Christmas work hiatus when they gained immunity from punishment and care; and she described how enslaved people radiated happiness over their hoe-cake and molasses holiday breakfast and grand roast hog holiday barbecue, and how they fiddled, sang, and danced away holiday hours when they were not gorging themselves.[11]

Then, too, as we shall see, surviving African American documents, including many escaped slaves' autobiographies and the now widely consulted Federal Writers' Project interviews with slaves that occurred during the Great Depression of the 1930s, confirm that such scenes truly occurred. As the elderly ex-slave Charlie Sandles put it to one of those interviewers,

CHRISTMAS EVE FROLIC—*Page 17.*

Frontispiece in Metta V. Victor, *Maum Guinea and Her Plantation "Children"; Or, Holiday-Week on a Louisiana Estate: A Slave Romance* (New York: Beadle, 1861). (Widener Library, Harvard University)

On Christmas, boy did we have a time, yes sir, Maser he would have a big eggnog on Christmas morning, then he would give all the slaves some kind of present—fireworks, candy, nuts and the best of all, was that dinner Christmas day . . . just anything a man could want to eat. On that day the slaves he had was free to go anywhere they wanted or do anything they wanted to do.[12]

Indeed, though many southern masters gave slaves holidays other than Christmas, most commonly Easter and the Fourth of July, and sometimes threw feasts on other occasions like "corn shuckin'" time, Christmas was unarguably the most important slave holiday, the season they took ownership of as "peculiarly their own" in the words of a pre–Civil War Mississippi newspaper editorial. Charles Joyner, a leading expert on the Gullah culture of South Carolina and Georgia slaves, decreed Christmas the slaves' "most popular holiday," a conclusion echoed in William H. Wiggins Jr.'s study of black emancipation celebrations and many other accounts. Wiggins deemed Christmas "the longest and most universally observed slave holiday during . . . the slaves' calendar year." And its significance transcended the food, liquor, and gifts lavished on slaves at that time of the year. Paradoxically, it gave slaves the relief from daily labor demands to better hone their own customs and beliefs, some of them based on African survivals, even as it drew them socially into temporary spatial proximity with their masters since Christmas was the only time on many slaveholdings when slaves were encouraged to visit the "Big House," as their owners' residences were often called.[13]

Still, there is another side to Christmas in the Old South, a darker story that is only hinted at in Ruffin's concessionary remark about slave insurrection rumors at holiday time. Consider, for instance, the nuanced take in Frederick Douglass's first autobiography, *Narrative of the Life of Frederick Douglass, an American Slave*. Here, the famous black abolitionist speaker and editor and onetime Maryland bondman invited his readers to ponder the insidious effects of the holiday on slaves, no matter how generous a particular master seemed to be at holiday time, by highlighting his own experience as a rented slave on Edward Covey's farm in 1833. Recalling that the slaves got the entire Christmas–New Year week off from labor other than for tending to the master's stock, Douglass noted that slaves were allowed to visit distant family members over the holiday; work on improvements to their quarters by making mats, corn-brooms, and other useful items; hunt raccoons, rabbits and opossums to supplement their diets; engage in sports like footraces and wrestling; and dance and drink whiskey. His account seems an endorsement of his temporary owner's paternalism—until Douglass adds that southern masters actually wanted their slaves to get drunk over Christmas, sometimes betting on which slave could hold the most whiskey (to encourage their chattels to drink competitively). Further, they considered any slave *not* getting inebriated "a disgrace." Why was this? Because drunkenness, Douglass observes, allowed slaves to vent frustrations over their plight in less subversive ways than challenging the peculiar institution itself. Christmas drinking amounted to a safety valve releasing "the rebellious spirit of enslaved humanity" in ways harmless to the master's vested interests. Douglass's indictment is searing, as he explains how the master's copious liquor succeeded in making slaves feel so debased by their own drunkenness that they wound up believing they were unworthy of freedom!

> The most of us used to drink it down, and the result was just what might be supposed—many of us were led to think there was little to choose between liberty and slavery. We felt . . . that we had almost as well be slaves to man as to rum. So, when the holidays

ended, we staggered up from the filth of our wallowing, took a long breath, and marched to the field. . . . Their object seems to be, to disgust their slaves with freedom, by plunging them into the lowest depths of dissipation.[14]

Yet though Douglass's account of Christmas is profoundly disturbing, it insufficiently captures the totality of slaves' holiday experiences, and no more represents the story than the ecstatic polemical and literary accounts of Christmas in the Old South that have prevailed in the white American literary imagination. Arguably as informed about slavery as anyone living in the United States in the early1840s when he began constructing his autobiography, Douglass nonetheless centered his account of Christmas on the Covey place. His text is ambiguous about whether his experiences were typical or atypical for slaves at other farms, even in his own neighborhood much less in other parts of the South like the cotton plantations of the Black Belt or the sugar estates in Louisiana's bayou country, or in the region's factories and cities. As a result, while Douglass's story powerfully conveys the psychological price slaves paid for conforming to their masters' expectations over the holiday, he nonetheless lets stand common understandings of master Christmas paternalism—the copious largesse conceded to slaves by their owners over the holiday season. And this is unfortunate, since a surprising number of documents show masters playing Scrooge rather than Santa over the holiday season.

Not all masters gave slaves extended holidays off from work. Some gave their workers very abbreviated releases; others planned or fantasized about eventually ending Yuletide holidays altogether; and some initiated cutbacks, both on the length of the season and the distributions to workers and their families of presents and food. Even as their own children hung up stockings on their mantels on Christmas Eve, slave owners engaged in whipping, buying, and selling human property. Meanwhile, some slaves capitalized on their masters' relaxed vigilance during the holiday to run away. Most revealing, as Edmund Ruffin mentioned in his novel, southern whites suffered acute anxiety year after year that their slaves might choose Christmas to rebel and kill them. Though no general slave uprising ever occurred at Christmas during the antebellum period, a disproportionate number of the Old South's slave revolt panics occurred at Christmas. Many southern slaveholdings conformed to polemical and literary stereotypes; others did not. And that is the ambiguity that invites this book.

Yuletide in Dixie suggests that the time is overdue for Americans to divest themselves of all romantic illusions about Christmas in slave times, not only because they distort history but also because any quasi-justification of human bondage—the "slavery-wasn't-all-that-bad" trope—hampers racial reconciliation today. If Christmas made slavery tolerable, then celebrating the Confederacy, its leaders, and its flag becomes less offensive to modern sensibilities. Some years ago the historian Michael Tadman cautioned against the trap of assuming on the basis of the kindly treatment and privileged status that some masters afforded a few of their favorite and most important slaves (Tadman called them "key slaves") all year round, that most slaves received humane treatment.[15] In the same spirit of skepticism, we need to beware of conceding master decency at Christmastime. Master giveaways to slaves were only part of the holiday story, and it is important to recover the missing elements of the narrative. If Christmas traditions indeed made yearlong slavery tolerable, masters would have had scant cause to fear slave uprisings on December 25.

Using a wide variety of documents, this book takes a kind of "horse's mouth" approach to evidence—that is, although slave autobiographies (or "narratives") like Frederick Douglass's and Work Projects Administration (WPA) interviews of elderly slaves in the 1930s provide rich material for this text, I've found the most damning sources about master behavior at Christmastime, ironically, are the surviving letters, plantation journals, and diaries of slave owners themselves. These sources, along with newspaper reports, travelers' accounts, and fugitive slave advertisements, disclose how far the realities of Christmas in the southern states diverged from what white southerners claimed was the norm. Close readings of such documents expose the parameters and limitations of master generosity, or what many historians call slaveholder paternalism. How many days off at Christmas did slaves actually get? Was master gifting as selfless as slaveholders liked to think? Were slaves as free to do what they wished at Christmas as commonly believed? Were slaves appreciative or resentful of their masters' holiday largesse? Necessarily, too, *Yuletide in Dixie* examines slave Christmastime resistance primarily with documents that southern whites generated themselves. Was there any genuine basis for master paranoia about Yuletide rebellions? Did Edmund Ruffin know better when he dismissed Christmas insurrection rumors as unfounded?

Although this book is hardly the first work to apply critical perspectives to the interplay between Christmas customs and southern slavery,[16] *Yuletide in Dixie* assesses this interplay more broadly than is customary in most literature about Christmas in the Old South. As might be expected, my narrative, like most studies of the holiday in Dixie, foregrounds southern Christmas plantation traditions, partly because of the richness of sources about the holiday on the region's larger landed estates (well-educated elite planters kept infinitely more written records than did semiliterate white farmers on middling land-holdings) but also because of the centrality of plantation life to the antebellum South's culture, economy, and politics. Still, plantations were hardly the whole story. *Yuletide in Dixie* additionally probes the holiday's meaning for slave-master relations in towns, cities, and factories, while emphasizing tensions between master abuse and slave agency in all settings. Though their means for resistance were limited, slaves struggled to control their own destinies over Christmas by making escape attempts under the cover of relaxed master supervision and by making *demands* on their owners and other whites for extra holiday presents during games of "Christmas Gif'" and performances known as "John Canoe," the latter a tradition that tells us much about lingering African survivals amid the hardships of southern racial repression.

Yuletide in Dixie also differentiates itself from most prior works on Christmas and slavery by fully integrating the Civil War into its narrative. While the fighting raged, wartime shortages and other circumstances made it difficult for masters to confer the kinds of feasts, presents, and other privileges that slaves were accustomed to receiving over the holiday. The evidence suggests that transformations in holiday observances contributed to the disintegration of slavery that occurred during the war, as hundreds of thousands of slaves ran away from their masters, with about 140,000 of them joining the Union army while additional thousands enlisted in the Union navy. While it would be absurd to claim that curtailments of Christmas bounty sparked the slaves' exodus, the holiday transformations contributed to these defections, in turn hastening Union victory in the war by strengthening Washington's military establishment while depriving the Confederacy of needed black manpower on farms and in other labor capacities. A significant part of this study, therefore, is devoted to illuminating what happened on Christmas Day during the Civil War, and what we can learn both about slavery and southern race relations from wartime Christmas practices. This is an important story, as is the matter of southern Christmas mythology during the heyday of segregation in the late nineteenth and early twentieth centuries, which draws the attention of *Yuletide in Dixie*'s seventh chapter. Did southern whites and blacks continue, forego, or transform biracial Christmas practices forged in slave times? How did Christmas mythologies play into the Lost Cause ideological underpinnings of southern segregation? Was the antebellum southern Christmas romanticized after the war, as one scholar has suggested, to "help bury the racial tensions of Jim Crow society" and "navigate" the dislocations of postwar modernization sweeping through the South,[17] or was the antebellum holiday manipulated in postwar print to justify Jim Crow? And what happened to the southern Christmas romance in the wake of the civil rights movement of the 1960s? Do vestiges of this mythology survive today? Such inquiries draw the attention of the epilogue, which focuses especially on Christmas's salience in modern southern plantation tours.

Finally, a word on what drew me to this topic. Years ago, when researching my book *John A. Quitman: Old South Crusader*—a biography of an American war hero and Mississippi governor who became the Magnolia State's most radical pre–Civil War secessionist[18]—I became intrigued by how many Quitman family letters and diary entries referenced the role of household servants in Christmas celebrations at Monmouth, the family's mansion in the outskirts of the Mississippi river town of Natchez. After telling my wife, Jill, a professor of children's literature at my institution (Purdue University), about my curiosity regarding this fascinating material, she not only encouraged me to pursue the topic of Christmas and slavery in its own right but also to involve a Ph.D. student we were jointly mentoring, Shauna Bigham, in the project. Shauna and I subsequently collaborated on an article that we published about the subject in 1998,[19] before each going on to other projects. Over the next fifteen years, though, I remained intrigued by the topic of Christmas in the slave states, publishing an article about its Civil War implications in the magazine *North & South* and giving public talks about the subject throughout Indiana.[20] I therefore owe a great debt to both Jill and especially Shauna for launching me on this quest. Many of the themes pursued in *Yuletide in Dixie* were sketched out, in a preliminary fashion, in the article that Shauna and I researched and wrote together. I doubt I would have ever embarked on this new journey without that prior spadework under my belt.

1

Time and Punishment

Arguably, the most famous photographic image of a southern slave concerned a Christmas whipping during the Civil War. In its Independence Day issue in 1863, the popular northern illustrated publication *Harper's Weekly* carried a story titled "A Typical Negro" with three engravings based on photographs of a Mississippi slave named Gordon, who had made his way to Union lines and freedom at Baton Rouge, Louisiana. The one farthest left depicted Gordon in the clothes he wore upon arriving at Union positions. The one on the right showed Gordon armed and smartly attired in uniform after being enrolled in the Union army. The image in the center, over twice as large as either of its companions, showed Gordon seated from an angled rear perspective, his back heavily scarred, just above a caption reading "Gordon Under Military Inspection." The accompanying story explained that the slave's back showed "the traces of a whipping administered, on Christmas-day last." Subsequently, this same image, reproduced in small carte de visite photographs as "The Scourged Back," circulated as Union propaganda in Great Britain and the North. Since then, the image has reappeared in numberless books and articles about slavery and related subjects as a way of depicting the peculiar institution's cruelty.[1]

Gordon's scarring raises some important issues for consideration. Had this "Typical Negro" received atypical treatment the previous Christmas? Or was his story representative of other southern slaves who were punished rather than feted by their owners at Christmas? Many? And if so, what does this do to common narratives about

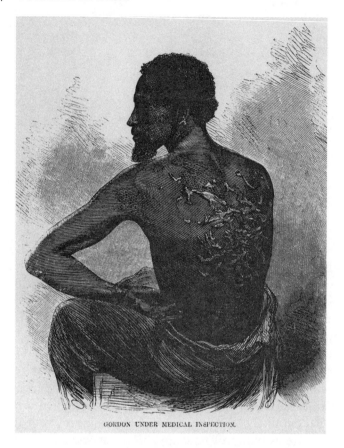

GORDON UNDER MEDICAL INSPECTION.

Scarred slave from Christmas whipping in *Harper's Weekly*, July 4, 1863, p. 429. (Purdue University Library)

Christmas in the Old South being a magical time warp for master and slave alike, when expected behaviors for both parties lapsed and slaves passed their holiday seasons rollicking for days on end?

Just as it is impossible to separate slavery from southern history, so is it impossible to separate human bondage from the history of Christmas in the American South. Starting in colonial times, southern slaveholders granted their enslaved peoples holiday privileges, and by the Civil War, Christmas seasons held profound meanings for masters and slaves alike.

It should hardly be surprising that southern masters gave slaves time off for Christmas, since precedents for slaveholders doing so date at least to the Middle Ages. During the 1600s and 1700s, such concessions spread throughout slave societies in the Western Hemisphere, as in the French West Indies, which came under King Louis XIV's *Code Noir* (1685); the sixth article of this set of rules for slave governance warned of fines and other penalties for masters working their bondpeople on any Catholic holidays, which of course included Christmas. In some cases, Christmas work breaks resulted at least partly from pressure by slaves. In 1701, after a slave owner in the British Caribbean sugar-producing colony of Antigua compelled his bondpeople to labor over the holidays, his angry workers murdered him, apparently in reprisal. Eventually Antigua's legislature accommodated such tensions, passing a special act in 1723 guaranteeing all slaves (except those performing "necessary" duties in white households) their Christmas off, noting that slaves had committed murders in the past because masters withheld the privilege. A half-century later, Antigua's lawmakers clarified that slaves should get a labor break from Christmas Eve to dawn on December 28. In Jamaica, British authorities passed a law in 1807 fining slaveholders five pounds should they deny slaves their "usual" Christmas break, implying that such holidays were already the custom there.[2]

England's colonies on North America's South Atlantic coast conformed to this pattern, though it is difficult to pinpoint when the custom took hold. In 1727, a statute of colonial Virginia's General Assembly alluded to a tendency by "negroes" to make "unlawful concourse" during Christmas and other holidays since they were "usually exempted from labour," suggesting that Virginia slaves were getting holiday work breaks at least by a century after settlement in the colony began. Similarly revealing is a later remark by a "Northern Neck" Virginia plantation owner that his black hands would be getting an entire week off for Christmas "according to custom," which conceivably alluded to his own practices in previous years but likely reflected contemporary community standards where he lived. In 1790, a former merchant and planter who had resided in colonial South Carolina and Georgia before the American Revolution recalled that slaves there had "a few holidays . . . entirely at their own disposal" during Christmas, apparently meaning that slaves in those rice-producing colonies got several days off from work each time it rolled around, without indicating how long this custom had existed.[3]

Whenever they started, Christmas concessions by masters to slaves reflected what the historian Joyce Chaplin describes as enslaved laborers' creolization process, the gradual adaptation or accommodation over time of their African linguistic patterns and customs to those of their owners and other southern whites. When interacting with creolized slaves, southern whites, as Chaplin puts it, came to recognize "people much like themselves" who were beginning to attend Christian churches, spoke English, and generally "behaved much as did Euro-Americans." Indeed, encouraging enslaved people to attend church on Christmas Day was one particular manifestation of acculturation in South Carolina's early colonial history. Well before 1730, missionaries of the Anglican Church's Society for the Propagation of the Gospel in Foreign Parts who were resident there reported that "Negroes" attended services and were baptized on Christmas. Meanwhile, by the 1700s some southern slaves went by the name "Christmas," further suggesting the holiday's special meaning for them and their masters, though it is not always clear who chose the name or whether the choice indicated a Christmas day of birth. One liberal-minded Virginia master purposely selected the Christmas when favored slaves "came of age" as the appropriate time to manumit them, another indication of acculturation's holiday manifestations.[4]

Nothing illustrates this process better than the diary notations of Philip Fithian—a children's tutor from New Jersey residing before the American Revolution at the Tidewater Virginia Nomini Hall estate of the wealthy slave owner Robert Carter III. Fithian's holiday season entries in 1773 indicate that Christmas celebrations must have been pervasive among white families in his vicinity. Indeed, he wrote there was so much excitement in the air beforehand that all people could talk about was the upcoming holiday. Everyone anticipated the balls, camaraderie, entertainment, and fox hunting that Christmas would bring. When Christmas Day finally arrived, he sat down with Mrs. Carter and five Carter daughters to the most "elegant" dinner he had experienced in his life. His jottings also indicate that local folk fired off guns on both Christmas Eve and Christmas Day to mark them with noisemaking. On the day after Christmas, which that year fell on Sunday, Fithian accompanied Mrs. Carter and her daughters Priscilla and Nancy to church, where the minister's sermon quoted the book of Isaiah about the birth of Jesus, limiting his sermon to a "fashionable" fifteen minutes, as Fithian put it.[5]

Though silent on the role the Carters' slaves surely played in preparing the Christmas meal he so enjoyed, Fithian did notice that the "Negroes" there suddenly seemed "inspired with new Life" as Christmas Eve arrived, probably relating to their getting holiday relief from normal work responsibilities. In fact, Fithian's Christmas Day diary entry recorded how he spent all Christmas morning handing coins to a parade of Carter's family servants, who expected special tips for chores they had done for him in the past and that very morning:

> Nelson . . . was early in my Room, drest only in his shirt and Breeches! He made me a vast fire, blacked my Shoes, set my room in order, and wished me a joyful Christmas, for which I gave him half a Bit.—Soon after he left the Room . . . the Fellow who makes the Fire in our School Room, drest very neatly in green, but almost drunk, entered my chamber with three or four profound Bows, & made me the same salutation; I gave him a *Bit,* and dismissed him as soon as possible.—Soon after my Clothes and Linens were sent in with a message for a Christmas *Box,* as they call it; I sent the poor Slave a Bit, & my thanks. . . . I gave Tom the Coachman, who Doctors my Horse, for his care two Bits, . . . I gave to *Dennis* the Boy who waits at Table half a *Bit*—So that the sum of my *Donations* to the Servants for this Christmas appears to be five Bits.[6]

Clearly, Carter's house domestics regarded Christmas as an opportunity to improve their material condition, and aggressively capitalized on their momentary advantage.

As the acculturation of black laborers in the South gained momentum in the years before the War of 1812, which Congress abetted by outlawing the African slave trade as of 1808 (sharply curtailing the fresh arrival of Africans who did not speak English), white southerners made Christmas increasingly inclusive of their enslaved population. Charles Ball, a slave in Maryland and then in Georgia around the turn of the nineteenth century, later remembered that slaves in the former state got a week off for Christmas, and that although the hiatus was much shorter in Georgia, slaves there did get a meat dinner for the only time all year plus either a distribution of winter clothing or a "small gratuity." Slave servants at William and Mary College in Williamsburg, Virginia, got monetary bonuses for Christmas, while at ex-president Thomas Jefferson's Poplar Forest property, slaves benefited from a work break of about five days and special holiday clothing distributions.[7]

Some of the best evidence of Christmas as an acculturative process for slaves comes from two accounts of South Carolina estates over the holiday during the period. When New Englander and newly minted Yale College graduate John Pierpont turned up as the newly hired tutor at William Alston's Monjetta plantation in time for Christmas in 1805, he quickly learned that slaves throughout the state received a three-day Yuletide break when they could visit relations at distant places if they so chose. Additionally, Pierpont observed that Alston provided his own slaves on Christmas Day with copious amounts of a rum concoction served from tubs; that morning, moreover, he had twenty-one bulls butchered to ensure that all his laborers got a rare meat meal by day's end. Besides feasting and imbibing, Alston's slaves spent much of their three-day holiday making music with their drums and violins, dancing to hand clapping, and engaging in running about and other physical exertions, all of which culled up in Pierpont's imagination "the bachannal feasts and amusements of antiquity." All day long, Pierpont was hailed with "Merry Christmas" greetings from Alston's slaves, revealing evidence of their familiarity with expected Anglo-American norms of behavior. Even more suggestive testimony, though, comes from a traveler who, a few years earlier, had spent Christmas at a South Carolina estate about forty miles north of Charleston. This observer later confirmed that South Carolina slaves at the time of his visit got a three-day work holiday and a provision of beef for Christmas, and that they celebrated the season with dancing and fiddling. Most intriguingly, the visitor mused that over the holiday slaves were permitted "latitude . . . in their intercourse with their superiors" disallowed at other times, and that some of the slaves were even welcomed into the hallways and rooms of the master's mansion residence. There they gazed wondrously at the sight of unfamiliar furniture, carpet, and mirrors, while those "negroes" on the place who hailed from "various tribes and nations of Africa" lingered at the doorway and engaged outside in "sports and gambols" learned in their homelands.[8]

In granting their enslaved people Christmas feasts and gifts as well as time off, southern slaveholders conformed to practices already prevalent in slave societies throughout the hemisphere. During Spain's colonial control of Peru, for instance, Jesuit inspectors told hacienda administrators to provide slaves with new sets of clothing every Christmas. Similarly, special Christmas distributions to slaves were commonplace in Britain's sugar colony of Jamaica. Englishman Thomas Thistlewood, who arrived there in 1750, regularly recorded in his diaries the rum and extra food like herring he gave slaves on

Christmas Day. At the island's Worthy Park plantation in the 1790s, oxen were specially slaughtered to give the slaves a feast at Christmas. In 1796 alone, Worthy Park slaves got 922 gallons of rum for their celebration. Around the same time, in Britain's Barbados colony, planters specially rewarded female slaves who bore children, expanding their workforces, with Christmas bonuses. In Portuguese Brazil, a militia captain reported from the Recôncavo region in the colony's northeast that on "those said Holy days of Christmas" slaves came together to dance, play, and drink together long into the night.[9] Christmas and slavery, in other words, had a long-comingled history crossing cultures and boundaries.

But granting Christmas privileges to slaves, it must hastily be added, came at a psychological cost for southern masters. Long before American independence, southern masters already confronted the paradox Edmund Ruffin acknowledged ever so fleetingly in his Civil War novel *Anticipations of the Future* about the South becoming an independent nation: that giving enslaved men and women freedom from work also gave them disposable time to plot resistance to their masters' control over them. Taking such possibilities in hand, the Virginia colonial assembly's 1727 measure mentioned above called for special patrols of whites during Christmas to ensure that slaves temporarily excused from labor did not get out of hand. Similar apprehensions also applied farther down the Atlantic coastline. South Carolina's initial slave code of 1712 included a provision for special Christmas Day policing by Charleston's constable and deputies for the purpose of taking into custody slaves using the holiday to assemble together for drinking, fighting, cursing, and other "wicked designs and purposes"—the last phrase implying that by the early eighteenth century, masters feared what their slaves' holiday carousing might lead to.[10]

Intriguingly, in the 1740s an English official in Georgia, a colony where slavery had been banned since its founding, cited the very potential for Christmas insurrections in neighboring South Carolina as evidence that the trustees in England who ruled Georgia should keep the ban in place, despite the aggressive demands of petitioning settlers who wished the Georgia colony opened to slavery. Carolinians were "so continuously apprehensive of their Rising" at festivals like Christmas, he reported, they mounted horse patrols to regulate slaves from traveling about and assembling together. For a time, the trustees must have concurred, since they retained the ban. But caving to persistent pressure from materialistic Georgia settlers, the trustees in 1751 reversed course and opened the floodgates to human bondage as well as the Christmas paranoia inevitably accompanying it. In 1770, Georgia's General Assembly passed an act stipulating that all church wardens, deacons, and selectmen be required at Christmas, Easter, and at least twelve other times annually to inspect militiamen attending services, to enforce regulations that they be armed on such occasions with guns and ammunition for the purpose of defending the colony from insurrections.[11]

Over time, southern white fears of servile Christmas insurrections would only worsen. Indeed, as we will see in chapter 5, white southerners would eventually fall into the habit of pinning this danger on northern antislavery agitation, contributing to the climate of grievance that led eleven southern states out of the Union in 1860–1861 and into the Civil War that followed.

Although, as we have seen, the story of southern Christmases has its roots in colonial and post-Revolutionary times, regional mythologies about the holiday almost exclusively concern the "antebellum" period before the Civil War, roughly 1830–1860. This was when southern cotton became the world's "white gold" and, along with other slave labor–intensive crops like rice, tobacco, and sugar, enriched the pockets of southern masters, making the wealthiest of them among the richest people in the United States and enabling them to throw lavish Christmas celebrations for family, friends, and slaves alike. By the Civil War, southern slaves not only cultivated about two-thirds of all the world's raw cotton, but they represented a worth of approximately $3 billion, nearly 50 percent more than the value of all U.S. manufacturing and railroads at the time. In fact, in 1860 all eight of the wealthiest U.S. states in terms of wealth per white capita were southern slave states.[12]

Some of the most affluent of the South's nearly 400,000 slaveholders on the eve of the Civil War amassed fabulous riches for their day and enjoyed distinctively lavish lifestyles that often included extended European travel and vacations to northern cities and resorts. The native South Carolinian rice magnate Robert F. W. Allston owned several plantations on the Pee Dee River and 631 slaves in 1860; he could easily afford what some people regarded as the finest home in Charleston as well as the hiring of private tutors from the North and Europe for his children and overseers to superintend his plantations. He owned so much silverware that he could serve nearly fifty people at a dinner party. Georgian James Hamilton Couper, who held about 1,500 slaves, maintained a magnificent three-story mansion at his Hopeton plantation with over twenty rooms and graceful gardens outside.[13]

Given how much white southerners had already embraced Christmas in colonial times, it was hardly happenchance that southerners led the parade of American states making Christmas into a legal holiday in the antebellum period. In 1809, Maryland's lawmakers foreshadowed this trend by legislating that Christmas and Sundays would be the only days in the year when convicts in the state penitentiary near Baltimore would be excused from labor. Arkansas, Alabama, and Louisiana made Christmas a formal state holiday in the 1830s, and Florida's territorial governor followed suit for his jurisdiction in 1842. According to Alabama law, the state's treasurer and comptroller of public accounts could only close their offices in the state capital on Christmas, the Fourth of July, and Sundays. In South Carolina, similar legislation specified that several state officials as well as the "ordinary" of the Charleston district (an official charged with the disposal of property belonging to persons dying intestate) could take Christmas off without penalty.[14]

Almost everywhere in the slave states during the antebellum years, whites of all social classes exuberantly embraced Christmas, though class distinctions set some parameters for how they went about it. A traveler passing through South Carolina in the early 1840s at Christmastime noted that although affluent low-country rice planters elaborately prepared for the holiday, upland planters seemed "too poor to make a show."[15] Still, most white southerners embraced Christmas exuberantly enough to persuade witnesses that the region far outpaced the North in its observances of the occasion.

Undoubtedly, one of the characteristics most distinguishing southern Christmas holidays from Yankee ones was that the slave states' citizenry marked the Yuletide's arrival with such rambunctious noisemaking—especially the discharging of firearms—that some observers thought the sound level there alone distinguished Christmas in the South from how it was observed elsewhere. As early as Christmas Day 1804, the mayor of Richmond complained to Virginia's governor that despite a prohibitive city ordinance, many residents were following "an old established custom" of shooting off "what is called Christmas Guns," and such practices only worsened over time. Harvard Divinity School graduate John Pierpont Jr. was stunned by the holiday's cacophony after moving to Savannah, Georgia, in 1852 to minister to a Unitarian congregation there. On December 26 the following year, with cannons booming and firecrackers popping as he penned a note to his father (now a minister in the Boston area), John Jr. related that the explosions had also occurred on Christmas itself and described Savannah as "in the midst of the excitement of Christmas, which, you know, is differently observed here from what it is at the North." Indeed, Savannah's celebration seemed so rowdy that John Jr. thought it mocked "the Prince of Peace" rather than affirmed him.[16]

Elsewhere too in the South, the earsplitting sounds of guns and "poppers" anointed the holiday. In Austin, Texas, a newsman mused that the town's juveniles exploded enough powder to wage a small battle of Waterloo. Staying in Natchez, Mississippi, where he owned a cottonseed crushing plant, Georgia planter James Hamilton Couper wrote his wife that the "firing of guns around reminds me that it is Christmas Eve." In the small river town of Batesville, Arkansas, a German immigrant named Charles Heinrich adjusted over Christmas to the "fiering [firing] of guns, pistols and little firecrackers." And when the visiting British geologist Sir Charles Lyell attended Episcopal services in Charleston, South Carolina, on Christmas Day 1845, he became annoyed when street boys just outside the church discharged pistols and exploded fireworks throughout the service. That same year, up in Wake County, North Carolina, where it was customary for town youths to begin firing their guns an hour before dawn on Christmas Day, inventive poor boys who could not afford gunpowder reportedly found ways to compete with firecrackers by hitting heated coal pieces resting on smooth wood logs with the backs of their axes. Explosions rocked plantations too.[17]

Invariably, the uproar inaugurated extended days of socializing among the elite and middling classes with special events like elaborate meals and eggnog and masquerade parties, accompanied by so much drinking and dancing that an unimpressed young New England woman of strict Baptist upbringing who served as a tutor on a Virginia plantation described the reveling as "wild" and bordering on "dissipation." The plantation diary of a Florida girl is suggestive of how completely elite white southerners immersed themselves in visitations over the holiday. Noting that her entire family would dine at her place on Christmas, she added that "the next day we go to Live Oak; the next day we spend with Uncle Richard and Aunt Nancy; the next day we go to Uncle Tom's; the next day we spend in town with Aunt Sue and Uncle Arvah and then we go to Walnut Hill, to Uncle William and Aunt Mary." Similarly enlightening are the records of the South Carolina Ravenels, owners of several plantations. Two days after Christmas in 1850, Thomas Ravenel mentioned that about "30 or 40 young folks of the neighborhood" had just attended a dance at Pooshee, a family plantation in the low country. Another year, Thomas's brother Henry, a prominent botanist, recorded in his diary that fifty-two guests (apparently most of them extended family) had shared the Christmas Day dinner he held at Pooshee.[18]

Sometimes, southern aristocrats reached across class lines to entertain their less fortunate white neighbors for the holiday, as a way of binding their society together. Susan Dabney Smedes, author of a post–Civil War memoir about Old South elite Christmases, recalled that on Burleigh, the Mississippi plantation where she grew up, one night of the holiday season was reserved for an eggnog celebration to which virtually all whites living in the vicinity, including "plain neighbors," were invited. Invitations to "yeoman" neighbors, however, were no guarantee of attendance. South Carolina planter-politician James Henry Hammond's Christmas outreach to middling white neighbors one year bombed, possibly because of his own snobbishness. On Christmas Day 1837, he ruefully admitted he had invited "a large party to dinner & only three came—curse these low bred country folk." Perhaps Hammond's poorer neighbors were busy with their own holiday affairs. North Carolina teacher-farmer Basil Thomasson reported a middling-class Christmas in his diary some years later, mentioning that he had gone to a big family affair at his aunt's where, sitting at a table with a "clean white [table] cloth" (hardly typical table-covering for a middling southern family's meal), he enjoyed a "sumptuous dinner" and the first vinegar pie of his life, followed by a buggy ride with family members and a guest and a "Christmas-eve romp."[19]

At Christmas, southern villages, towns, and cities pulsated with holiday excitement, though Charleston, one of the region's most important urban centers, lacked many of its wealthiest residents at holiday time since it was a local custom for rich resident slaveholders to retire to their country plantations for the seasonal celebrations. Arriving in little Fayetteville, Alabama, to make his way in life, the youthful Reuben Davis, later a Mississippi congressman, discovered streets packed with "country people" on hand to "celebrate the holiday." A Macon, Georgia, newspaper branded Christmas a "joyous season" when "good feelings" prevailed and townspeople patronized the opera, horse races, and balls while business grinded to a halt; they also threw tea parties and visited back and forth. In the southern trading hub of New Orleans, according to a *New Orleans Crescent* correspondent, coffeehouses on Christmas Day filled with "nog and toddy convivialists," and people crowded the city's shops and streets, children clinging to their "newly bought toys." Every nook of the Crescent City witnessed people enjoying "famous dinners" and reunions, while some locals attended the show of a circus troupe or a minstrel performer. From Batesville, Arkansas, the immigrant Charles Heinrich recorded a two-week Christmas season of "balls, private parties, storm parties, ladies' fair, suppers and dinners, Masonic processions, theatre . . . and dances"; and in Savannah, musicians took to the streets for the holiday, males threw flaming cotton wads around for sport, and young costumed men self-dubbed the "Mysterious Fantasticals" made it a Yuletide tradition to thunder down city streets on their horses and intimidate pedestrians.[20]

"Storm parties," when groups of young people turned up uninvited at someone's residence expecting to be welcomed and given a bash, also occurred across the Mississippi River in Mississippi. A student at the all-male state university in Oxford wrote his sister just before Christmas in 1857 that the boys there had just pulled off a storm party at the Union Female College, a woman's academy in the same town. Probably storm parties were common in Mississippi, since this young man did not bother to explain them in his letter. There is reason to suspect, however, that most hosts of storm affairs were tipped off in advance, to ensure that invaders got a green light upon arrival at their destinations. The mistress of the Forest Place cotton plantation in Carroll County explained to her daughter a few days after Christmas that storm parties had been occurring throughout the month and the family place had been "stormed Friday night by the people of Middleton and Shongalo," noting that they "were invited" and that she had a week to prepare the food, including cakes and oranges, and otherwise ready herself for the occasion. She related how the crowd danced throughout the night. Meanwhile, the family had themselves been "invited" to an upcoming storm affair.[21]

Rural southern white men, if they were wealthy, incorporated recreational hunting outings in their seasonal amusements. In 1833, an acquaintance contacted South Carolinian plantation magnate James Henry Hammond to express his appreciation of Hammond's "very kind letter inviting me to join you and friends in a hunt, and to dinner on Christmas day." Louisianan Bennet Barrow's Highland plantation diary reveals that outdoor activities punctuated his holiday routine. Just before Christmas in 1836, he recorded that his mare had raced against a colt and a Mexican horse and that his entry had won by doing the "best 3 in 5 mile Heats," enabling him to sell her off after the race for $1,000. Barrow mentioned going fox hunting on Christmas Day 1837, and he probably did so most holidays. In 1843, he reported two days before Christmas, "[W]ent Fox hunting this morning"; then on Christmas Day—"Dr King & several went out with me this morning Fox hunting." James Battle Avirett, who later authored a memoir about his boyhood on Rich Lands, a turpentine plantation in the piney woods of North Carolina, claimed that fox hunting was "indispensable" to Christmas on his father's place. Less wealthy rural southern males also hunted on Christmas, seeking game for their table. North Carolina teacher-farmer Basil Thomasson spent part of one Christmas Day hunting rabbits.[22]

A glance at the surviving correspondence and other records of the John and Eliza Quitman family of Natchez, Mississippi, helps illuminate the importance antebellum white southerners, especially the elite, placed upon Christmas. "Pd. for Christmas presents for children," the Natchez lawyer and politician John Quitman—who owned cotton and sugar plantations besides his mansion Monmouth on Natchez's outskirts—recorded in his daybook four days before Christmas in 1839, noting that he had spent $23 on the gifts. Absent from home the next Christmas, Quitman got a report from his eldest daughter, Louisa, about how she had spent the holiday while visiting at her great-uncle's country estate. It was an occasion, she said, for walks, backgammon games, horseback riding, and drinking eggnog. In November 1849, when John and Eliza's son Henry was attending Princeton College in New Jersey, Eliza urged her son not only to return home for Christmas but also to get there in time to attend a Christmas Eve children's ball. In November 1852, an entry in daughter Annie Rosalie Quitman's diary announced that for her brother's "Christmas gift" she was busy embroidering a sweater.[23]

Some members of the slaveholding elite chose Christmas as the date for their weddings, layering extra celebration upon an already momentous event. John Quitman, for instance, and his very well connected bride (of about half his age), Eliza Turner, tied their knot on Christmas Eve 1824. When the thirty-three-year-old coastal Georgia planter John Hamilton Couper crossed the age gap, marrying his sixteen-year-old fiancée Caroline Wyllys of the Village plantation on St. Simon's Island at her place on Christmas night 1827, the excitement began with afternoon dancing in the Wyllys house and later moved out to the lawn, lighted by fire stands, because there were too many guests on hand to continue indoors. A 7:30 p.m. wedding ceremony was followed by a late supper at 11 p.m. in the dining room and on the piazza, featuring all kinds of meat and fish, breads and cakes, with ample syllabub— a drink concoction involving cream or milk and wine or cider. Though the newlyweds left after midnight toasts, guests were invited to stay into the morning hours, and those who remained were treated to a breakfast of waffles, fresh fish, preserves, and much more.[24]

Christianity, clearly, was secondary to socializing in antebellum white southern Christmas calibrations, though devout sectarians considered "the nativity of our Blessed Saviour," as one Mississippian phrased it, a transcendent aspect of the holiday's appeal. Religiously inclined southerners regarded attendance at Christmas services as mandatory, turning out in sizable numbers even during inclement conditions. "There was a service at Black Oak Church," noted Henry William Ravenel on Christmas Day in 1859, "& a large congregation notwithstanding the severity of the weather." When illness or other circumstances precluded attending Christmas services, devout southerners could become anxious over their limitations. Louisa Maxwell Holmes Cocke, the wife of a prominent central Virginia planter, for instance, envied "others hurrying to the sanctuary to commemorate the Blessed Redieming [sic] Nativity" when she was unable to attend church on Christmas Day 1840. Still, an Alabama editor mused that people might be observing the holiday more from habit than because they felt a compelling need to commemorate the date of Jesus's "supposed" birth, an observation that speaks to what might be called the passively Christian perspective of most antebellum white Christmas celebrants in the Old South.[25]

Well before the Civil War, on the other hand, Christmas was already considerably commercialized throughout the southern states. In a seasonal letter from Natchez, one young man described the town as "crowded with people from the country buying things for Christmas." By the late antebellum period, the region's newspapers filled their December columns with Christmas advertising from local merchants. "CHRISTMAS IS COME! Again, with its time-honored attendant SANTA CLAUS," proclaimed a Savannah merchant's copy in 1851, adding that his store on Congress Street now contained "the most suitable varied assortment of Toys that ever realized juvenile hope of a MERRY CHRISTMAS."[26]

By then, Santa Claus had infiltrated slave-state culture, reaching southerners by way of the free states. New York, earlier a Dutch colony, had provided the originating point for America's modification of the European Saint Nicholas into Santa Claus. Washington Irving packed his *Knickerbocker's History of New York,* published in 1809, with some twenty-five allusions to Saint Nicholas. The next year, the New York Historical Society initiated an annual Saint Nicholas Day dinner on December 6, the day Nicholas supposedly had died. Famously, in 1823 the popular Saint Nick–focused "Night Before Christmas" appeared in a Troy, New York, newspaper, ensuring that Santa Claus would become a fixture in U.S. Christmas observances. A few years afterward, the European tradition of taking trees into private homes for the holiday, especially popular with the Pennsylvania Dutch, began spreading through major Atlantic coast cities. Explaining Christmas's triumph nationally, one historian reflects that Yuletide traditions provided Americans with a "symbol of non-denominational Protestantism" that helped to bind together their nation of many faiths.[27]

Years before the Civil War, southerners hung stockings on Christmas Eve, which were generally filled later in the night with modest gifts of things like oranges and raisins, shells, slippers, small dolls, and peppermint candy. Serving in the U.S. Army during the War with Mexico in 1846 and far distant from his Arlington estate in Virginia across the Potomac River from Washington, Robert E. Lee nonetheless took some moments on Christmas Eve to muse about the presumably wonderful gifts from "good Santa Claus" his children were extracting from their overburdened stockings, and allusions to Santa Claus are easy to find in documents originating throughout the region. Mahala Eggleston Roach, a married woman living at a country estate near Vicksburg, confessed in her Christmas 1852 diary entry, for instance, that the day brought as much excitement "as when I was a believer in 'Santa Claus'" at a younger age. Other southerners, though, referenced Kris Kringle, a derivative of the German name for Christ child (*Christkindl*), for (as a New Orleans newspaper put it) "the patron saint of happy childhood" who unloaded a wagon at every household fireplace and went from roof to roof to go up and down chimneys. Annie Rosalie Quitman, who went dancing up the stairs of her family's Natchez mansion on Christmas Eve 1853 reciting "'Twas the night before Christmas," jotted in her diary a few years later, "[a]nother season of Kriss Krinkle" and noted that her younger sister Fredericka had been disappointed that year because her bags (presumably stockings) were "but thinly filled" due to "stinginess" by the gift-giver. Fredericka, however, had done better than Rose, who quipped to her brother Henry, then residing on the family sugar plantation Live Oaks in Louisiana, that Kriss Krinkle had apparently deemed her too old for stocking gifts and withheld the usual "candy & juvenile gratifications."[28]

Possibly, Ada Bacot's home had a Christmas tree, an item that many elite southern residences had by the late 1840s and early 1850s, often decorating them with food, candy, and small hand-crafted items. On Christmas Day 1851, Mahala Roach recounted how she "made a Christmas tree" for her household's children on the basis of what she had learned from some German tales she was reading and that the adults on hand had "said it was something new to them." One southern girl described in her diary how her governess taught the household's children to color pine cones with flour, fasten them to her tree with fine wire, and then attach candles to the mounted cones with melted wax. According to one historian, antebellum Texas house owners commonly adorned their trees with strings of popcorn and cotton balls. Meanwhile, Christmas trees began appearing in public spaces. When reporting that the mayor of Charleston had given a speech at the Christmas Festival in the city's Hibernian Hall on Christmas night 1856 to a large crowd, the *Charleston Mercury* took note of the Christmas tree there and how "toys and presents were displayed in tempting profusion." Mahala Roach noted in a Christmas 1860 diary entry that the Episcopal Church in Vicksburg had its own tree.[29]

Although Christmas took considerable advance planning in southern urban households, readying slaveholding plantations for Christmas festivities required especially herculean efforts and major outlays of funds, not only because planters and their wives had to plan for their own often very large families and their guests over the holiday but also because they needed to butcher livestock and go on shopping excursions for whatever they planned to offer their scores, hundreds, or in some cases thousands of slaves in the way of feasts, presents, and other perks. Roxana Chapin Gerdine, a native New Englander married to a Mississippi plantation owner, told her sister just after Christmas 1859 that during December she—using a sewing machine—and the "seamstresses" (presumably household slaves) had sewn "one hundred and sixty-five garments for negroes . . . consisting of woolen coats, pants, dresses and cotton under garments, besides thirty white bordered aprons I made for their Christmas gifts." Georgia slaveholder James Hamilton Couper one year bought 2,710 pounds of beef for Christmas.[30]

Post–Civil War southern memoirists dwelled on the meticulous planning that went into Christmas celebrations on their places. James

Avirett emphasized how "methodical" preparations for Christmas began as soon as the fall harvest was over. Then the work of butchering hogs and bulls; stockpiling wood for Christmas fires; dispatching wagons to New Bern and Wilmington to bring back purchased candy, nuts, fruits, and other items; sending roasting hogs and large turkeys to friends in town (who reciprocated with boxes of oranges, figs, wine, and other goodies); sewing greenery onto the borders of tablecloths; sending out invitations for a Christmas week cotillion party; and much more began in earnest. Avirett claimed that the house often filled with "company from the neighboring towns, friends of the old planter's children . . . who had come out to enjoy an old-fashioned plantation country Christmas." Similarly, Esther S. Reynolds, who as a child regularly visited her grandparents' Mulberry place near Camden, South Carolina, for the holidays, recalled how days before crowds of relations arrived at the three-story, twelve-bedroom mansion for Christmas, hogs were slaughtered and the plantation kitchen stirred with activity as sausages, cheeses, and pigs' feet were prepared and fruit cakes, mince and cranberry pies, and other desserts were baked.[31]

What did all this planning, in the end, mean for slaves? One way to comprehend Christmas's impact on the millions of African Americans doing forced labor in the Old South is to linger on the third syllable of the compound word *Christmastime*. We need to ask, in the strictest literal sense, how many days southern slaves get off from work to celebrate Jesus's birth? Pre–Civil War southern newspapers claimed they got quite a few, with the New *Orleans Daily Crescent* specifying that the "general jollification" of the "negro Christmas" began Christmas Eve and lasted "until after the 1st of January." Similarly, southern humorist Thomas Bangs Thorpe, in a piece for *Frank Leslie's Illustrated Newspaper* entitled "Christmas in the South," generalized that slaves used the entire "last week of the expiring 'annual'" for their time of "boisterous mirth and physical enjoyment." No one stated the case more categorically than the Nashville, Tennessee, master who not only told a New York editor that "all the slaves throughout the entire South have from Christmas to New Year's as a holiday week" but also boasted that southern slaves enjoyed far more happiness over that period than did free northern factory operatives.[32]

After the Civil War, some white southern memoirists perpetuated notions that antebellum slaves got a week off at Christmas. Felix Gregory de Fontaine, a northern journalist who had served as a correspondent for a Charleston newspaper during the conflict, made such a claim decades later, and so did Hillary A. Herbert, secretary of the navy during President Grover Cleveland's second administration in the 1890s. The latter, who grew up on a South Carolina plantation, told a reporter that his family's thirty or so slaves had enjoyed a week of Christmas "merry-making." Similarly, South Carolina memoirist Elizabeth Pringle, the daughter of a prominent planter-politician, recalled that slaves got three days off at Christmas and another three at New Year's. James Avirett specified that slaves experienced holiday-time from Christmas to January 2, and Maryland's John Williamson Palmer recollected that "rollicking darkies" spent a "happy" Christmas week dancing and singing "corn-songs" in slave cabins and "great house" alike as they passed from plantation to plantation. Unsurprisingly, the later southern romanticist Harnett Kane agreed that many plantation owners insisted on slaves receiving "six or seven full days of rest, starting on Christmas Eve" in the contracts they negotiated with their overseers. (One wonders how many such contracts Kane actually read. South Carolina rice planter Plowden C. J. Weston's printed rules for overseers specified that slaves got Christmas and two days after off, nothing more.)[33]

Such claims might be dismissed as southern propaganda to rationalize slavery were it not that some non-southerners temporarily resident in the Old South or visiting the region on their travels confirmed the week standard. Abigail Mason, a New Englander serving at Christmas 1832 as governess on a place near Richmond, Virginia, that had some 100 slaves, said that "every negro" had the week entirely off. Charles Lanman, an anti-abolitionist northerner visiting a plantation in South Carolina's interior, reported in his travel account that on the morning of Christmas Eve day slaves began an "accustomed holiday" that lasted "until the close of the year." A New York City resident on his first trip south of Philadelphia discovered that it was customary throughout the slave states for masters to give their laborers "full liberty from Christmas to New Year." *New York Times* correspondent–travel writer Frederick Law Olmsted, later the landscape architect who helped design New York City's Central Park, discovered on his travels in Virginia that field hands enjoyed release from labor for the entirety of the Christmas to New Year's period, though house servants did not.[34]

Some ex-slaves and abolitionists also conceded the point. Frederick Douglass and George L. Knox, the latter a Tennessee slave who escaped to Indiana during the Civil War and became an important Indianapolis businessman and public figure, recalled in their autobiographies that southern slaves were free from labor Christmas to

New Year's. So did the escaped Missouri slave John Anderson, the famed late nineteenth-century and early twentieth-century black leader Booker T. Washington, and the antislavery novelists Mary B. Harlan and Richard Hildreth (writing respectively in their tales about Kentucky and South Carolina). Washington claimed that during "the old slave days" in Virginia where he spent his boyhood, Christmas lasted "a week, sometimes longer." Thirty-four elderly ex-slaves told WPA interviewers in the 1930s that they had enjoyed a week off for Christmas during their years in bondage. Former Virginia slave John Washington elaborated that slaves were allowed on Christmas Day to retreat to their cabins once they received their presents at the "great House" and take a holiday for the following six days.[35]

Given such testimony, some historians allow that giving slaves a week off for Christmas was standard practice.[36] But others are more guarded,[37] and we should be too. Slaveholders' journals, diaries, and letters, as well as other documents, were frequently very precise about the number of days slaves were relieved from labor at Christmas, especially on the large plantations where the great majority of slaves lived and worked (in 1860, about half of the South's slaves belonged to masters owning twenty or more of them[38]), and these sources are infinitely more reliable than hasty impressions of visitors to the slave states, claims in the southern press, or the later reminiscences of either masters or slaves.

Despite all the accounts implying or outright stating that every southern slave got a week's vacation at Christmas, only a minority of slaves appear to have received that much time off from work, though slaves rented out to southern industries and other business concerns may have come closest as a cohort to the standard. Since hired slaves generally left their home farms and plantations to work elsewhere, often in urban and industrial settings, they required extra time to travel at Christmas in order to reunite with family members over the holiday and/or to make labor arrangements for the coming year if their masters allowed them the privilege of choosing their coming employers.

Hiring agreements often provided that slaves would begin their labors for a particular employer on January 1 or 2 and stop working just before Christmas. In a contractual arrangement dated January 1, 1858, the University of Alabama hired a slave named Paul from one W. J. Hays, promising to return him to Hays "if alive, on the 25: of next December" and stipulating that if Paul died in the interim the

Promissory note from George Benagh, University of Alabama, Tuscaloosa, Alabama, to W. J. Hays, January 1, 1858. (University of Alabama, University Libraries, Special Collections)

university would pay for the part of the year he had labored on a pro-rated basis, while Hays would assume responsibility for nursing him if he fell seriously ill during the year. Such arrangements left a year's-end labor gap of about a week for vacation time, minus time allocated for travel to and from the home place to see relations. Thus Natalie De lage Sumter, who lived on a South Carolina plantation and leased out slaves for railroad construction, entered in her diary on December 27, 1840, that she had "talked to all my negroes & dispatched them for the rail road" carrying a new suit of clothes, meaning that they were already on their way. Still, the point is that hired slaves typically had far more time to themselves at Christmas than at any other time of the year, a tradition insinuated in an Austin, Texas, ordinance that prohibited masters from allowing their slaves to be at large for more than one day to hire their own time, but did allow them to do so over the Christmas season.[39]

Returning slaves to their masters' places was common in the iron industry in the Upper South. A youthful Ohioan arriving in Mount Sterling, in northeastern Kentucky, just before Christmas a few years before the Civil War, noted in his journal how a line of black iron-workers arrived in town on Christmas Eve, led by a couplet-singing captain: "Oh Lord have mercy on my soul / De hens and chickens I has stole." As early as 1815 at the Etna blast furnace in Botetourt County, Virginia, according to the historian Charles B. Dew, operations for Christmas shut down early enough so that hirelings could make it home to spend Christmas with their families, as it was almost impossible to get slave workers to stay on without significant compensation to them. In the 1830s, Virginia ironmaster William Weaver paid an extra $5 each year to every hired teamster at his works who remained on site over Christmas. Revealingly, Jordan, Davis & Company, running Weaver's Bath Iron Works, near Lexington, informed Weaver in November 1830 that though the firm's managers originally intended "blowing through the Christmas holy days and going on as long as possible," they had developed second thoughts about keeping the blast furnaces operating since "the most part of the blacks will be going home and the few remaining not willing to be closely confined." Given these conditions, a short Christmas shutdown seemed in everyone's best interest.[40]

Similar dynamics operated for the many slaves hired out for hemp and tobacco production, as well as railroad construction work. In Virginia, for example, in 1849 the hiring agent of the Richmond and Danville Railroad Company took on three slaves owned by Nottoway County farmer Frances Epes to work in a different county for a $200 rental charge, promising to return them by the next Christmas with new clothing, a blanket, and a hat. Urban tobacco factories in Virginia sometimes shut down days before Christmas to allow their slave laborers time to reach their families in the countryside or simply relax in town. For several years preceding the Civil War, chartered steamers called at the port of Savannah, Georgia, a few days before Christmas to board—at the expense of their "owners and employers"—slaves employed at railroad construction in Florida and Georgia and convey them northward along the South Atlantic coastline to Wilmington, North Carolina, so that they could enjoy the holiday at "their old homes" in the latter vicinity.[41]

It would be misleading, however, to jump to the conclusion that all hired slaves automatically got Christmas–to–New Year breaks, much less slaves under the direct supervision of their owners. One 1852 hiring contract specified, for example, that a slave named Jim could be absent from his employer "twice during each year for the space of three days each time (once in early July and once at Christmas) to go see his wife." Obviously Jim's Christmas break amounted at the most to three days, at least on paper. That same winter, the South Carolina planter-politician James Chesnut *hoped* that his slave Abram, then being tutored by a trainer of thoroughbreds on another place, could be reunited with his wife for Christmas, but was only willing to authorize Abram's return if he had made enough progress in his training to justify suspending it for the holiday. Some employers of hired slaves denied them vacation time as punishment for what they considered bad behavior or poor work; thus, five slaves laboring on dredge boats on the Savannah River were denied their customary holiday work break one Christmas for disciplinary infractions. Additionally, slaveholders occasionally instructed persons leasing their laborers to keep the hirelings over the holiday because it would be an inconvenience to deal with their temporary returns. Telling a renter of slave turpentine laborers simply to retain them over Christmas, one master rationalized that such a policy made sense given how few days net vacation his slaves would wind up spending at their home place, while implying that the slaves would not even have a good time if they returned because of the "unpleasantness" of weather at Christmas.[42]

In general, plantation masters lagged behind their industrial counterparts, though there were exceptions. Some plantation masters indeed gave field hands the Christmas–to–New Year week off or even more. There were no legislative limits maximizing Christmas slave holiday lengths in a society dedicated to enshrining masters' discretionary powers over their own slaves. Since each master made his or her own rules for slave governance, variance was natural. The Louisiana cotton and sometime sugar planter Bennet H. Barrow recorded in his journal on New Year's Day 1841, "Yesterday being Friday Negros still have Holliday, 12 days." A year earlier, Barrow logged that his slaves had received an "Eleven days Holliday." Obviously Barrow made it a practice to give his slaves extended holidays. Others undoubtedly matched his liberality. Andrew Pickens Calhoun, who ran a cotton plantation in Marengo County, Alabama, funded largely by his famous father, John C. Calhoun of South Carolina, informed the latter on December 30, 1840,

> We finished gathering our crop some time since, and have been
> following the usual train succeeding that event. As we have been
> so constantly on the move for two years, I have slacked off with

the hands, and have done but little more than right up things for two weeks, and this week they have to themselves . . . to put them into condition for the winter work.[43]

Solomon Northup, the free black New Yorker kidnapped into slavery in Louisiana (and the subject of the 2013 award-winning film *12 Years a Slave*, based largely on his later autobiographical account), conceded that some slaves got nearly a week off at Christmas, recalling in the narrative he wrote after being liberated that while his master gave laborers three Christmas days off, "others allow four, five and six days, according to the measure of their generosity."[44]

But notice that Northup never suggests that *most* slaves got six days off, much less seven or more. The point is that Barrow, Calhoun, and the six-day providers Northup mentioned were *atypical*, not that they were unique. Planters' diaries and journals show that *for slaves getting more than Christmas Day alone,* breaks almost universally included Christmas Eve and mostly ranged from two-and-a-half days to four days, with their specific lengths varying yearly, depending on the master's mood and financial situation, whether the weather was suitable right before or after Christmas for outdoor labor, or whether December 28 fell on a Sunday (in which case slaves sometimes got an added day's bonus since they generally had Sundays off anyway). Throughout the South, slaves were far more likely to return to work on December 28 than January 2, as reflected in this very explicit entry in a Mississippi planter's diary for December 28, 1852:

> I have recommenced work to day. I called all hands up last night, told them the work we had before us compelled our holidays to close & made a few remarks to them as to their duties the following year.[45]

Southeastern Louisiana's sugarcane parishes were the main exception, not because the slaves got less or more time off for their winter's holiday than slaves did elsewhere but because the nature of sugar production in the bayou country meant they sometimes got different time off. Because sugarcane required a ten-month growing season as well as harvesting in mid or late October to escape the occasional frosts of southern Louisiana's subtropical climate, production sometimes overlapped Christmas. Unprocessed cut cane spoiled in less than two days. This meant that if Louisiana's sugar magnates wished to get their entire large crops into production without rotting, once they began harvesting they had to keep their equipment operating continuously, approximately a two-month process since so much sugarcane was grown on most of the large Louisiana sugar estates. During grinding or "rolling" seasons, whether Christmastime or not, these sugar masters made their slaves work frenetically for as much as eighteen hours a day, assigning them multiple production responsibilities and often whipping them more than customary since the stakes were so high: slaves cut and gathered wood (often pulled from swamps and rivers) to fuel the steam engines running mill machinery, cut leaves from cane stalks, loaded the stalks onto conveyor belts leading to the mill machinery, and fed the cane into mill rollers so that it could be crushed into juice. And slaves were hardly off the hook once the crop was milled. Sugar required January planting to ensure a ten-month growing time for the next year's crop. So if mill production ended late enough in December, landowners often transitioned immediately into planting, further deferring the slaves' holiday, sometimes until late January.[46]

Some sugar planters allowed their slaves breaks either on or nearly on Christmas Day. Maunsel White, a former New Orleans merchant who became one of southern Louisiana's larger sugar planters with more than 200 slaves on his Deer Range estate, on the day after Christmas one year gave "all the People . . . several gallons of wine for their Comfort & the whole of the evening for recreation." But the plantation journal of Octave Colomb, who owned a sugar estate in St. Jones Parish, Louisiana, shows that sugar slaves could expect almost anything regarding when Christmas celebrating occurred and how long it lasted, depending on the year. In 1851, Colomb gave slaves December 23–25 off for the holiday, but on December 26 he reported his slaves were busy working on drains for his cropland. Two years later, he kept his slaves "sugar making" December 23–25 and did not give them a three-day break until January 21–23. In 1854, the "Negroes Holidays" came December 29–31, while in 1855 the slaves got an extremely short break for Christmas itself. Slaves did no work after finishing cleaning up his sugarhouse on December 24 until the hands were put to work shelling corn on December 27, though he noted on December 26: "Put away last sugar, otherwise no work done." In 1856, his hands planted cane on December 24 and 26 and worked on ditches and cutting wood on December 27, but did get Christmas Day itself. In 1857, slaves on his place did such chores as cutting wood, cleaning out ditches, pulling out corn stalks, and using mules to drag logs out of the river on December 24 and 26, but again received a pass from labor on Christmas

Day. A similar story occurred in 1859, but in 1860, just months before the Civil War, Colomb explained that after finishing boiling his sugar at midnight on December 25, he gave his slaves the next two days off.[47]

Many sources reveal the typical holiday rhythms on plantations that produced other crops than sugar, collectively confirming that slaves with a full week off at Christmas were the lucky ones. The New England–to–South Carolina transplant Caroline Gilman's *Recollections of a Southern Matron* timed what she called the Christmas plantation "festival" at three days, and another southern woman in a public letter put the slaves' Christmas "jubilee" at three to four days, a schedule exactly mirrored in slave-owning magnate James Henry Hammond's plantation manual stipulation that each "Christmas a holyday of three or four days is given commencing on Christmas day." The journal of Richard Arnold, master of two plantations in Bryan County, Georgia, noted on Christmas Eve day 1847 that his slaves were still cleaning out drainage ditches in his rice fields and doing other chores. Then Arnold inserted this combined entry for Christmas and the two days following: "These three days Holy days killed three Boars for the people & had Dancing at W Hall all the time" (almost certainly meaning that the laborers at his White Hall plantation had that period entirely off). David Rees's plantation on Louisiana's Atchafalaya River, at least in 1832, followed a similar timetable. Rees's journal on December 24 noted that his corn harvesting (surely involving slave labor) had finished up that day. Then, after simply noting "Christmas Day" for the 25th and leaving December 26 blank, he jotted "Grinding corn & C." on the 27th.[48]

The "Record Book" of Natchez, Mississippi, planter John Nevitt shows parallel patterns. His slaves worked Christmas Eve day in 1827, 1828, and 1829 but got that day off in 1830 and 1831. Generally, Nevitt let his slaves take off from work the two days after Christmas in addition to the holiday itself, though in 1827 he noted on December 27 that "all hands went to work except Old Edmund" and that his slaves had pressed six cotton bales that day. On the other hand, in 1829 Nevitt noted on Sunday, December 28, that his "negroes still keep up holyday." Another surviving plantation record, covering Christmas 1850, noted not only that slaves on the Bonaventura rice plantation did not finish threshing rice until sometime on December 24 but also that vacation did not last long. "Holliday over" read the entry for December 27.[49]

Sometimes masters in a given area colluded so that all the slaves in their neighborhood enjoyed the same break, probably from concerns that slaves at the short end of the stick might become irritated if they learned that slaves on nearby places got longer vacations. Consider, in this regard, the diary of a South Carolina slaveholder named John Peyre Thomas. Thomas seems to have usually had his slaves back to work on December 28, jotting in his diary entries for that day comments like "The Holy days expired last night" and "The Negroes commenced work this morning." In 1833, he reported, "The Negroes all appeared & were put to clean up the new ground given them to plant." Still, he kept his eye on what nearby planters were doing, and it is possible that he always followed local convention in setting his calendar. In 1829, he observed in his December 27 entry, "Every one in this neighborhood commences work tomorrow, & so do I." Two years later, similarly, he noted on December 28, "Every one in this part of the world had ordered the Negroes to go to work to day." Even aberrations seem to have been by consensus. On December 29, 1839, he noted, intriguingly, "we all in this neighborhood gave the Negroes all the week." But this hardly meant that the week had become the neighborhood's standard. In 1843, Thomas's slaves were back at work on December 28, though his diary neglected to mention whether his neighbors were following suit.[50]

The difference between two-and-a-half days and a full week demands emphasis for the obvious yet easily overlooked reason that the former break was only about one-third as long as the latter and the typical three-day holiday was less than 50 percent of a week's break. All we have to do is consult Solomon Northup again to grasp that the difference was hardly trivial so far as slaves were concerned, especially since there is no evidence that slaves receiving shorter breaks got more in the way of gifts and feasts than slaves with longer ones. Northup emphasized that Christmas was "the only time" all year that slaves looked forward to "with any interest or pleasure." Given such attitudes and since there was no trade-off between quantity and quality, it is safe to assume that virtually all slaves would have greatly preferred a week off over two or three days. They could have enjoyed extra days of rest and more time to visit with relations and friends on other slaveholdings or in southern towns and cities. In fact, slaves sometimes pressured their masters to lengthen their holidays or grumbled when masters curtailed their holiday sooner than they wanted. A South Carolina slave owner noted one December 28 that his hands did "not like to go to work so soon but they have to do it," mentioning that earlier in the day he had assigned them labor on his fishpond. Even the seemingly liberal

Bennet Barrow ran into resistance from slaves wishing longer Christmases. On Friday, January 2, 1846, Barrow admitted being pressured by slaves who wanted him to lengthen their holiday until the coming Monday. Perhaps here it is wise here to remind ourselves of Abraham Lincoln's entirely obvious if simplistic rumination that even the stupidest slave knew he was "wronged" by forced labor and that no one ever heard of a man pining to be a slave.[51]

Then again, not all slaves even got a two-to-three-day break, much less a week off. The historian Eugene Genovese argued that very few masters ever entirely deprived slaves of their Christmas holidays and that the "especially brutal ones" who only gave slaves a day or two off were "outnumbered by those who gave a longer holiday than the average—five days, a week, or even more." I am not at all certain that his estimate is accurate; rather, I believe he gives more credence to southern "Yule log" traditions than he should. Genovese explains that some southern masters calibrated their slaves' holiday by the time it took a specially selected and slow-burning log to be consumed, having the slaves pick the log. But did any planters really abide by Yule log standards for slave down time?[52]

The problem is the dearth of Yule log allusions in the diaries, journals, and letters of southern slaveholders. Antebellum southern newspapers occasionally mention Yule logs, to be sure, but almost invariably in the context of Christmas feature articles briefly treating the hallmarks of "ye olden tyme" in England that had died out in North America, including wassail bowls and boars' heads. Similarly, the prolific southern novelist William Gilmore Simms alludes to a Yule log in his 1847 serialized tale about a Carolina plantation called "Maize-in-Milk" (named, Simms tells us, for "Indian corn not yet ripe, but ready in the *ear* for the table") during two Christmases spaced three years apart, but he fails to explicitly connect its burning time to the length of the slaves' holiday season or mention that slaves chose it. Rather, Maize-in-Milk's Yule log is "brought in" by unidentified persons on Christmas Eve day and lit with remaining fragments from the previous year's log.[53]

Antebellum southern Yule log allusions, in other words, generally referenced an English labor custom (letting servants and tenants eat at landlords' tables so long as Yule logs burned)[54] without specifying that regional slaveholders had benevolently extended this tradition to their own laborers and intentionally allowed their workers to rig the system. As a result of this paucity of documentation, we should be skeptical that slaveholders subscribed to Yule logs scheduling their slaves' holidays.

Possibly, southern Yule log mathematics—the pegging of slave time off to the burning of immense, water-saturated logs—represents the projecting of *postbellum* Yule log tales about plantation holidays backward onto pre–Civil War Christmases. The northern children's magazine *Youth's Companion,* for example, gave a very detailed iteration in 1887, even specifying that in Mississippi in slave times the log of choice came from holly trees. White Louisiana local color author Ruth McEnery Stuart's 1891 story for *Lippincott's Monthly* placed a smoldering Yule log at the main house to help set her tale about Christmas on the fictional Sucrier plantation. That same year, Rebecca Cameron, the granddaughter of a southern rice planter, rendered her own personal remembrance of how the annual Yule log, known on her place as the "back-log," was selected, prepared, and burned on Granddad's place. She identified the cut of wood, explained in intricate detail the time of day the log was "carried into the great holly-wreathed hall," and described how it always lay on a bed of wet ashes prepared ahead of time. Then, in *Yule Log,* a 1900 memoir of her own childhood Christmas experiences in eastern Virginia, LaSalle Corbell Pickett, third wife and hagiographer of the famed Confederate general George E. Pickett (Pickett's charge at Gettysburg), had a slave servant pronounce in dialect that Christmas lasted as long as "dat faifful ole Yule log" burned.[55]

Eventually, Harnett Kane boldly pronounced without a shard of proof that slave-cut Yule logs were "an essential part" of Christmas throughout the South. Kane even took the liberty of claiming that when the holiday ended southerners typically conformed to English tradition by preserving the last bit of the Yule log to be starter wood for the next year's fire. Possibly Kane got his material on this from Rebecca Cameron's memoir, since she mentioned how when the Yule log burned in two, a slave would carry one of the two chunks out, extinguish it, and store it the next day in the woodhouse to ignite the next year's Yule log. If so, he apparently took her claims on faith.[56]

One wonders, too, about more modern and seemingly authoritative Yule log pronouncements. In 1999, the site manager for the preserved two-story home and birthplace of North Carolina's slave-owning Civil War governor Zebulon Vance reportedly claimed, according to a newspaper reporter, that the burning of "a yule log—in the back of the large fireplace" had always governed the timetable for Vance Christmas celebrations. Apparently the reporter took on faith everything the site manager said, as there is no indication in the article of what sources survive about Christmas at the Vance place in the nineteenth century. The park interpreter of a modern southern plantation site whose hand-outs to tourists bluntly state that "Christmas in the Quarters lasted as long as the Yule log did" admits when pressed that the site lacks a scintilla of evidence for that assertion and depends on what "other sources" have said about the holiday elsewhere.[57]

Admittedly, a few former slaves rendered their own accounts of Yule logs years after the Civil War. Tuskegee Institute's African American president Booker T. Washington, who certainly had a keen skill at couching slave times in a soft glow, recalled that the South's "coloured people" used to get a Christmas holiday "as long as the 'yule log' lasted" when their break was not automatically set for a week. More colorfully, ex-slave Tom Wilson told a Federal Writers' Project (FWP) interviewer in the 1930s that at Christmas, his master was accustomed to sending "one er de cullud mens out to git a log an' say, 'Now long as dis log burn, y'all kin have offin wuk'—co'se us'd hunt de biggus' gum log an' den soak hit in de stream so hit wud burn on a long time." Much more recently, a long-time black native of an isolated Arkansas Ozarks community told a newspaper reporter that his grandmother passed on to him Yule log tales passed down to her from her own father, who had been a slave. A few such tales, however, hardly prove the commonality of Yule log holiday scheduling in the Old South.[58]

Just as Genovese almost certainly paid too much heed to Yule log tales, he probably understated the number of masters who either gave no days off for Christmas or Christmas Day at most. Lewis Clarke, who fled enslavement in Kentucky in 1842 on rumors he was to be sold off to Louisiana and dictated his autobiography a few years afterward, claimed the norm in Kentucky was a six-day Christmas break for slaves; but he also reported that although some masters there gave slaves an even longer holiday, others granted "less, some *none,* not a day nor an hour." Similarly, some slave interviewees of the FWP debunked the stereotype that all slaves got long Christmas holidays. Former field hand Lewis Evans related, "Marster Major give us Chris'mas day and a pass to visit 'bout but we sho' had to be back and report befo' nine o'clock dat same day." Other slaves either explicitly stated that Christmas only lasted one day or implied as much. The latter interpretation possibly explains Peter Clifton's clipped "They give us Christmas Day." But Sam Mitchell was blunt enough, insisting, "Slaves had only one holiday in de year. Dat Christmas day." His master, though, was apparently more liberal than Frances Patterson's. Patterson recalled, "Christmas an' New Years day like any other day wid us—we worked jus' de same unless day come on Sunday."[59]

When it came to holiday scheduling, in fact, southern masters sometimes played Scrooge more than Santa, reserving the right to deprive their enslaved people of vacations for what they deemed due cause. Charles Ball was sorely disappointed to learn, after enduring the domestic slave trade and marching overland from Maryland to South Carolina, that the overseer of the cotton plantation where he was beginning work in 1805 had decided to withhold an intended three-day Christmas break from the slaves on his judgment that their laziness in cotton picking had left too many plants still unpicked in the fields to justify a work stoppage. The best he could do for the holiday, he announced, was a dram of liquor and a meat dinner for each field worker. "We went to work as usual the next morning, and continued our labour through the week as if Christmas had been stricken from the calender [sic]," Ball added, mentioning too that all clothing and shoe distributions were deferred until New Year's Day. Enforcing similar discipline at his rice plantation in the same state, a slaveholder formally incorporated into his instructions for his overseer provision for withholding time off from slaves who failed to complete their work assignments or misbehaved.[60]

More suggestive is evidence that slaveholders would have scaled back the holiday time they did grant slaves had they felt that they could get away with it without angering their workers or irritating neighbors who followed more liberal schedules. We have already seen that John C. Calhoun's son took a pretty lackadaisical approach to slave time off at Christmas, at least in 1842. But Calhoun's son-in-law Thomas G. Clemson, who helped manage the senator's home Fort Hill plantation, was hardly happy about the Calhouns' laid-back approach, complaining about the overseer's policy at that place,

> We are in the midst of Christmas vacation. The hands recommence work on Wednesday next. Considering the quantity of work to be done, four days is rather much but Mr. Fredericks said it was customary to give that time & it was given.

An editorial for a Florida newspaper took an even more extreme view than Clemson's. It suggested that since wintertime was when slave labor was least demanding because of short days and weather conditions that restricted work outdoors, it would be best for masters and slaves alike if long Christmas breaks—"of no good on earth, either to negro or owner"—were traded for holidays at times in the year when they were more in need of rest. A slaveholder contributing to a southern farming magazine with advice for "Management of Negroes" trafficked in similar logic. Under the pseudonym "Tattler," this agriculturalist proclaimed in the *Southern Cultivator* that giving slaves a week off for Christmas, facilitating their "strolling about," was "productive of much evil." On his own place, therefore, slaves were compelled to resume their work assignments on December 26, with their week off postponed until July when the crops were laid by.[61]

Unsurprisingly given these reservations, many southern masters exhibited relief when slave vacationing was over, evidencing that they would have preferred it not last as long as it did. North Carolina slave owner Ebenezer Pettigrew told his sister on December 29, 1840, "Christmas is over (blessed be the Lord) and tomorrow we go to work," with the personal pronoun "we" alluding to slaves under white supervision. South Carolina coastal cotton planter Thomas Chaplin, something of a poster child for grumpy masters, complained in his diary on December 27, 1848, "Last day of the holidays & I am glad, for then the Negroes will go to work & something for me to do." In 1850, he even expressed disappointment on Christmas Day itself that his slaves were not laboring, as he griped, "I only wish the Negroes were at work." Then, on December 27, he celebrated, "The last day of the holidays, and I rejoice at it." Showing a diarist's talent for redundancy, he virtually plagiarized himself in 1852, recording, "This is the last day of the Negroes' Christmas holidays, & I am really glad of it. I hope now we will have some good weather for ginning." Surely, no southern planter summed up the case better than Georgia rice planter Louis Manigault, who reflected during the Civil War's first winter, "it is always a God-Send . . . when that Holyday is over and we all resume our quiet plantation work."[62] Virtually unknown, at the other extreme, are expressions of guilt by slaveholders about not giving their slaves enough break time!

We are not quite finished with time. A final point needs attention, which becomes obvious if we reconsider from a different perspective how Andrew Pickens Calhoun explained his Christmas slave labor policies in 1840 to his father, John C. Calhoun. Andrew told his father, it might be recalled, that the work of his hands had *slacked off* and that their only work for about two weeks had been to *right up things*. What did he mean?

Most likely, he meant that his slaves had been doing light work of some kind over the preceding days, probably a variety of small tasks that only bore tangentially on crop production. The tasks themselves could have been almost anything—repairing fences comes to mind as an example. One rice plantation physician, in answering an official inquiry from the state of South Carolina about management and labor conditions, responded that female slaves on a 100-slave rice plantation were expected to devote one of their Christmas holiday days to scouring their cabins with soap, while the menfolk either worked on gathering fuel (presumably wood for winter fires) or tending to their own gardens.[63] But Calhoun's phrasing alerts us that Christmas for slaves rarely boiled down to two options: either work as usual or no work at all. There were always things that could not be postponed entirely until after the holiday, most especially tending to stock. Slaveholders' farm animals represented a considerable investment, a responsibility that could not simply be ignored for spans of up to a week. Animal care could hardly be deferred until Christmas holidays ended, and slaves were the obvious candidates to do it.

Possibly for a majority of slaves in the Old South, Christmas reduced to a question of work as usual versus light or partial work, rather than to no work at all, despite the many claims that slaves got Christmas completely off. Elizabeth Pringle admitted as much in her memoir *Chronicles of Chicora Wood*. Pringle casually noted that over their holiday "negroes" never did "a stroke of work . . . except feeding the cattle, pigs, and sheep, and horses." Similarly, Esther Reynolds not only mentioned that for Mulberry plantation field hands the only work required of them during a three-day Christmas break was attending to stock but also noted in an aside that house servants (who got their three-day break after the holiday was over) remained on call, with the dining-room waiters donning special holiday broadcloth suits of dark blue to make the white family's Christmas afternoon feast seem more festive. Frederick Douglass explained in his autobiography that during the Christmas–to–New Year's interval, slaves where he lived "were not required to perform any labor, more than to feed and take care of the stock." When the northern traveler Charles Lanman reached a South Carolina plantation, he observed how house servants and those field hands "as think their services may be needed" purposely approached their master and mistress on Christmas morning so that they could do whatever work was required of them. He also noted how later that Christmas week the slaves traded off tasks with each other so that "the necessary labor of the plantation" might be continued despite the seasonal labor force reduction.[64]

For some slaves, tending stock was but one of several "light" tasks compromising their holiday "freedom." According to a study of Texas plantations in antebellum times, not only were slaves expected to feed livestock for the entire Christmas–New Year's holiday, but they also had to gather eggs and do the milking, with chores around the master's residence rotated among the servants so that each could get "some days off." All sorts of other documents confirm that slaves got imperfect relief from their labor responsibilities at Christmas. Former slave field hand Madison Griffin not only claimed that Christmas was limited to a one-day holiday on his place but also that during their day off slaves still had to "grind our axes." White memoirist Samuel Escue Tillman, who grew up on a plantation in middle Tennessee, recalled that throughout Christmas week the "preparation of properly cut firewood and the feeding of all the stock was the only work" required of his father's slaves, "the culinary operations excepted," leaving open the possibility that his father's household domestics were still expected to handle the cooking and other matters attending the preparations of meals for their master's family, including cleanup. South Carolinian Ada Bacot reflected in her diary toward the end of Christmas Day 1860 that during the day she had "tried to make the work as light as possible for the servants." After their early dinner, she had dismissed them and made the tea, bread, and toast herself as well as set her own table. Was she implying that most of the day her domestics had been under her beck and call doing odd chores? Probably.[65]

To be sure, some Christmas work was paid work. Mississippi planter William Ervin recorded in his journal on the last day of the year in 1843 that he owed his slaves money "for Christmas work picking cotton," and onetime Mississippi slave Louis Hughes recalled in his autobiography that when planters tried to get a head-start on preparing their fields for the next year's crop by getting cotton stalks chopped over Christmas, they paid slaves fifty cents for every day's labor required of them. Other documents suggest such customs were hardly limited to Mississippi or to labor on crops. A northerner sojourning in Georgia claimed that when masters truly needed slaves to work on crops over Christmas, they always paid them for such work out of respect for the inviolability of the slaves' holiday time off, and the diary of Marylander John Blackford shows that he allowed his Ferry Hill plantation slave Will to make money by hauling wood for Blackford and other whites on Christmas Day 1838. He even outfitted Will with straps to facilitate the endeavor. A Yankee arriving in St. Augustine, Florida, one Christmas season immediately discovered that so long as the holiday lasted, slaves would only help "keep the system in motion of his master's household" as a "special favor" out of "real love" for his master, or for "large pay."[66]

Comparable practices applied in southern industry. While in Virginia at Christmas, Frederick Law Olmsted encountered slaves lying on the ground near a smoking charcoal pit and learned from their master that the slaves were "burning charcoal for the plantation blacksmith," getting paid by the bushel as a means of earning "a little money for themselves." Another northerner, coming upon slaves laboring in a turpentine forest one holiday season, found out that their master's policy was to give them "'half tasks'" at Christmas and to pay them for it "as if they were free." Similarly, salt manufacturers in western Virginia allowed both owned and rented slaves special monetary compensations when they kept furnaces operating over Christmas.[67]

Unfortunately, it is impossible to quantify or even guess the percentage of slaves getting paid for doing such chores over Christmas. When onetime slave Addie Vinson told an interviewer in the 1930s that her mother did washing and weaving for "de white folkses'" over Christmas, she failed to indicate whether it was paid for. Many other documents about slave labor at Christmas are similarly ambiguous. But, of course, even bringing up the pay issue begs the real question: *Why* did atypical remuneration persuade slaves to do Christmas chores? Was it really from loyalty to their masters, or was it because they had been so deprived all year long that they desperately craved the material goods a little pay might allow for themselves and their families? And there is a related issue. Could slaves say no? Presumably, some slaves would have been whipped if they had outright refused to do requested chores over the holiday.[68]

So we return to this chapter's starting point, the Christmas whipping. In late 1852, an antislavery doctor from Maine, Charles Grandison Parsons, who had been involved in organizing the abolitionist Liberty Party of the early 1840s, traveled southward to investigate slavery firsthand. In recounting his experiences, he told about the reaction of the proprietor of the Marshall House hotel where he lodged in Savannah when a favored slave servant boy, "Johnny," had the misfortune to spill what was likely whale oil on the proprietor's daughter's silk dress, ruining it. Infuriated on learning of Johnny's carelessness, the proprietor stormed through the hotel looking for him. Finding the unfortunate youth, he grabbed "the boy by the throat, exclaiming, 'Now you scoundrel, I'll pay you for spoiling C's dress!'" According to Parsons, the proprietor hurled Johnny to the floor, "jumped on him with his big hard heeled winter boots, and stamped on his breast and face" until the boy ceased movement. Parsons claimed that although the boy recovered, he disappeared from the sight of hotel guests for some time and reemerged three weeks later with half of his face still showing the bruises and with his spirit broken.[69]

Of course, one could protest this incident was conceivably fabricated, since it originated in an unabashedly abolitionist work. Additionally, Parsons had a monetary incentive to make his account as dramatic as possible, since he was trying to crack a highly competitive antebellum literary marketplace; readers had many other options if they sought inflammatory critiques of slavery.[70] In fact, none other than Harriet Beecher Stowe, the author of *Uncle Tom's Cabin,* certainly an expert at tugging on readers' emotions, wrote the introduction to Parsons's *Inside View of Slavery.* Still, Parsons named the hotel where the beating occurred, the proprietor/slaveholder, and another witness (a fellow Yankee from Maine who had preleased the hotel as of early 1853). Additionally, he claimed he would provide additional information to readers wishing to personally confirm his story and in a prefatory note emphasized the book was a factual account of things he had personally observed and learned. If we are to rule out sources like these on the grounds of authors' biases, we need to similarly exclude from the historical record the many reminiscences by planter families that have so influenced historical accounts of the Old South. Surely slaveholders were just as biased as their critics.

The odds are far more likely that the incident Parsons related occurred than that it did not. All sorts of anecdotal evidence suggest that southern masters and public authorities in the antebellum period physically abused slaves over Christmas, despite mythologies about the holiday season being blissful for the entire slave community. It is illuminating that Virginia planter Charles Friend's surviving plantation records reveal a prohibition on the whipping of children on his place over Christmas and that Georgia cotton planter Joseph Tooke followed similar practices, not allowing any child to be whipped during Christmas week. Left unsaid in both cases, of course, was the reserved option to lash over Christmas any adult slaves that Friend and Tooke believed deserved it. There were additional slaveholders who never even surrendered their right to whip children at holiday time, like one "mean" master who took out his anger on a nine-year-old slave boy who failed in his responsibilities of tending his cows. According to another slave on the place, the boy's lapse occurred when he became so distracted by children nearby who were setting off holiday firecrackers that he joined them. While so engaged, the now unsupervised cows trampled his master's wheat field. Infuriated, the latter lashed the boy so vigorously that the youth began bleeding from his mouth. Carried off to bed, the boy never recovered and died later in the week.[71]

At Christmas, enslaved people in the Old South aroused their masters' wrath for all kinds of labor shortcomings, as the cases of Johnny and the nine-year-old boy exemplify. Additionally, slaves also incurred punishments for a host of other perceived sins of omission or commission, and sometimes their supposed misbehaviors were opaquely defined. Former slave Matthew Gaines, who served as a senator representing Washington County in the Texas legislature during Reconstruction, recalled that while he had been enslaved before the Civil War he had been promised "a whipping Christmas to make me a good negro the next year." Onetime Richmond, Virginia, slave Richard Toler recalled how his mistress had threatened him with a whipping on Christmas Eve simply for daring to ask her for additional flour for bread, but then had mysteriously fallen over dead on Christmas Day before rendering it. On one South Carolina plantation, a slave named Sibby incurred her master Davison McDowell's wrath for miscarrying a pregnancy. He decided to withhold her usual "holiday treat" in punishment and to "lock her up" in the belief that she had miscarried purposely.[72]

Unsurprisingly given the various motives impelling enslaved people to steal things, some Christmastime punishments of slaves concerned suspicions of thievery in either the literal or figurative sense. A tavern owner in an Alabama village in the late 1820s reportedly brutalized a slave so badly one Christmas over a contested "piece of old carpet" that the slave died from being whipped repeatedly and punched, hit with a stake, and mangled by dogs. An infuriated eastern Virginia master, believing his slave shoemaker was "making more money" for himself than he should have, chose Christmas Day to abruptly confiscate his tools, and then hired him out to a man known locally as the "worst" master around with instructions, all but telling the renter to whip his new employee. Virginia ex-slave Isaac Williams remembered his last whipping in bondage as punishment "for stealing corn for bread for

Christmas" to supplement the daily meat slice and weekly one-and-a-half peck of corn meal his master allowed him for meals. At one of his South Carolina plantations one Christmas, master Robert F. W. Allston postponed seasonal partying, apparently until at least January 14 the next year, until his slaves identified the two thieves of a hog from his pen; then he made Cupid and Thomas, the fingered pair, "run the gauntlet," probably meaning that he had them rush between lines of his other slaves trying to hit them with sticks or possibly other implements.[73]

Anecdotal evidence suggests, however, that southern slaveholders and public authorities reserved many of their most vicious Christmastime chastisements for truancy, perhaps because such absences amounted to immunity from the very condition of being enslaved. In the fall of 1849, a northern antislavery paper told of a Tipton County, Tennessee, slave household carpenter named Jack who had been given 300 lashes over Christmas by his owner. As related to a friend by an Ohioan named John Heighton (witness to the incident), Jack had worked frantically "day and night" for two months to complete a house for his master by Christmas, so he would be allowed the time to visit his wife during the holiday. Unfortunately, Jack still had a week of construction work remaining when Christmas arrived. Desperately wanting to visit his wife (she had been sold away previously, and he had not seen her for two years), Jack announced his intention to set out anyway, a decision his master summarily rejected. Deciding to punish Jack for even contemplating an infraction of his work responsibilities, the offended master took him to the barn and laid on the brutal whipping despite protests from both his own wife and Heighton.[74]

Jack's case was hardly unique. The escaped slave John Brown related how a man on the Georgia plantation where he labored, a free black from South America named John Glasgow who had been jailed on arriving in Savannah port on an English vessel and had subsequently been committed illegally to bondage, was given a bucking and whipping because his master did not approve of Glasgow's marrying off the plantation and trying to visit his wife on Christmas Day without permission. Similarly, according to a prison journal kept by one Jonathan Walker, a shipwright from Massachusetts interned in Pensacola, Florida, for involvement in a failed plot to help slaves escape bondage, a slave was committed to that same jail in January 1845 "for going out of town at Christmas, and staying [beyond his master's control] too long." In a later journal entry, Walker elaborated that this slave's absence had resulted from wishing to spend extra holiday time with his wife and children who lived elsewhere, and that he paid dearly for this lapse. Not only had authorities unsuccessfully tried to sell him in both the Mobile, Alabama, and New Orleans slave markets (which would have removed him further from his family and likely prevented him from ever seeing them again); on his return to prison, his mistress had appeared at the jail "in a rage" where she had him flogged. Walker failed to indicate the cause of her anger, but, since her husband had recently sold off his plantation and moved to Pensacola, it probably had more to do with this slave's inability to bring a price in the market than his abusing his Christmas pass. The point, though, is that slaves took extreme risks in failing to strictly abide by the terms of their Christmas passes or neglecting to procure passes in the first place. Maryland planter John Blackford flogged his slave Aaron for being absent one Christmas Day without his permission. In 1856, a "slave patrol"[75] in Mississippi's Natchez District thrashed two slave women from a plantation who had gone to a party at a neighboring place without carrying passes from their master.[76]

Even more likely to incur a master's wrath than a slave abusing his Christmas leave privileges was one apprehended in an actual freedom bid over the holiday. A recent Yale graduate and missionary to western Indians was stunned during a stay in New Orleans one February when, during a hospital visitation, he encountered a horrifically disfigured and iron-collared male African American with a rotting leg, and found that his condition was the result of an unsuccessful freedom bid during cold Christmas weather. Upon being captured, he had been punished by confinement in his sugar plantation's cane house, with no source of heat and little clothing. "In this situation, his foot had frozen, and mortified," his horrified interrogator reported in his journal, before noting later on the same page that he had returned to the same hospital that very night only to discover that the sufferer had died in the interim. Bennet Barrow, who noted in his diary that he would "rather a negro . . . do any thing Else than runaway," recorded on December 24, 1839, that he had decided to punish his slave Dennis, captured just the previous day, by exhibiting him "during Christmas on a scaffold in the middle of the Quarter & with a red Flannel Cap on." Barrow followed this up on Christmas Day by reporting that Dennis had now been jailed. In 1858, slave owner Francis Terry Leak spent part of his Christmas Eve instructing one of his business agents to "whip Horace when he gets hold of him," alluding to a slave who had escaped on November 30.[77]

The point here is not that a majority of southern masters spent their Christmas holidays whipping slaves, or even that many did. Rather, what we need to consider is the extent to which traditional mythologies about antebellum southern Christmases have *entirely* erased such incidents from the historical record, and that virtually all slaves passed their Christmases with the potential of incurring a whipping or other punishment hanging over them. Slaveholders voluntarily relinquished much of their authority over slave labor and life over Christmas, but always retained the power, as such cases illustrate, to punish slaves if they so chose, and for whatever reason they wished. Enslaved persons, in turn, found it difficult to erase from their consciousness their masters' power to inflict corporal punishment, even amid the fog of Christmas inebriation and partying.

It is worth pondering, in this respect, the chilling discovery of Virginia native and physician William Holcombe, when visiting a plantation on Lake Concordia, Louisiana, for a Christmas holiday in the early 1850s. On New Year's Eve, Holcombe heard what he could only describe as puzzling "moanings and lamentations" arising from the slave quarters. On New Year's morning, he learned its cause from the plantation cook: slaves on the place shared a common superstition that if any slave child misbehaved on New Year's Day, all slave mothers there would be held accountable and be whipped excessively during the entire year to come. To avert any such possibility, then, on New Year's Eve slave mothers ensured that their children would remain submissive and stupefied the next day by turning down the covers of "their sleeping little woolly heads" and beating them frightfully with rods.[78]

2

Purchased at Little Cost

Ex-slaves like Junius Quattlebaum served history poorly. Speaking to a Federal Writers' Project (FWP) interviewer named Henry Grant in the 1930s about Christmas on the Saluda County, South Carolina, plantation where he lived in his youth, the eighty-four-year-old Quattlebaum effusively praised the generous and loving, even egalitarian, ways his master and mistress had behaved on Christmas toward the people they owned. Quattlebaum's heartwarming holiday morning scene placed slaves literally within their master's family circle, where they not only appreciatively received gifts and treats from the people who claimed to own them but also shared communal prayer:

> I can see missus so plain now, on Christmas mornin', a flirtin' 'round de Christmas trees, commandin' de little misses to put de names of each slave on a package and hang it on de tree for them. She was always pleased, smilin' and happy, cause she knowed dat . . . she would make somebody else happy. She tried as hard to make de slaves happy as she did to make her own white friends happy, it seem lak to me. Close to de tree was a basket and in dat basket was put in a bag of candy, apples, raisins and nuts for all de chillun. Nobody was left out.
>
> Christmas mornin', marster would call all de slaves to come to de Christmas tree. He made all de chillum set down close to de tree and de grown slaves jined hands and make a circle 'round all. Then marster and missus would give de chillun deir gifts, fust, then they would take presents from de tree and call one slave at a time to step out and git deirs. After all de presents was give out,

missus would stand in de middle of de ring and raise her hand and bow her head in silent thanks to God. All de slaves done lak her done. After all dis, everybody was happy, singin', and laughin' all over de place."[1]

What do we make of Junius Quattlebaum's wonderfully mellow Christmas vignette with its intimations of biracial inclusivity within an antebellum South Carolina slaveholding household, surely as much the peculiar institution's heartland as any southern state? Were most southern white slaveholders as committed as Quattlebaum's owners were to treating paternalistically over the Yuletide the very people they claimed as property the rest of the year, exemplifying the holiday goodwill to all and peace among men that we still invoke when speaking of Christmas's promise today? Did other southern masters feel a sacred obligation to honor their Yuletide with gifts to their laborers the way the family that claimed Quattlebaum's labor apparently did? If so, did slaves commonly accept their presents from their masters in the receptive spirit that Junius Quattlebaum described? Or is it possible that Quattlebaum's recollections misrepresent? As we shall see in this chapter, Christmas gifting by masters to their enslaved people was a complicated, often highly scripted process with all sorts of psychological meanings and consequences for both parties to these transactions. Further, the gifting involved far more than tangible items. Ultimately, we will also uncover some rather disturbing aspects to the many special privileges that southern masters accorded their enslaved people over the Christmas season. Or, to put it another way, we will test the limits of what historians often label master paternalism.

On the cautionary side, we need to keep in mind that FWP slave interviews like Quattlebaum's occurred during America's Great Depression of the 1930s, a dire time when recollections of slavery's daily minimum benefits of shelter and provisions, and especially its Christmastime excesses of food, drink, and partying, might perversely hold allure for struggling African Americans. "We lived a lot better then than we have since," one former slave who discussed Christmas in bondage informed her interviewer, "even if the government does give me a pension." "Dem wuz good ole days," another ex-slave confirmed. "A person could get er mess of good meat an' not hab to pay all dey made in a week for hit." Prince Johnson, who was born on a plantation in Yazoo County, Mississippi, and served as a houseboy in his younger days, noted right after saying that "Christ'mus was de time o' all times on dat plantation" that "Dey don't have no such as dat now." Certainly the text of Quattlebaum's interview suggests how standard-of-living relativism possibly tainted his memories, since interviewer Grant took notice that his subject was "partially capable" of supporting himself from produce and work he picked up "around" a city market. Likely, Quattlebaum was marginally self-sufficient at best around the time of his interview.

Maybe, too, Quattlebaum framed his responses to harmonize with what he thought Grant either expected or wanted him to say. If so, Quattlebaum was hardly the first interviewee ever to repress his real feelings to play to a questioner's prejudices. Consider that this former slave was being interrogated in South Carolina during the heyday of segregation. He surely gauged the odds that critical remarks about his former white owners would upset his interviewer, possibly leading to some kind of economic or physical reprisal against himself. In the 1930s, at the time of the ex-slave interviews, although lynching was in decline in the United States, assertive southern blacks still risked serious retribution for challenging the racial mores and expectations of whites in their communities. The text of Quattlebaum's responses suggests, in fact, that pleasing his interviewer influenced the substance of his remarks. The very first remark Grant attributed to him begins, "Well, sir, you want to talk to me 'bout them good old days back yonder in slavery time, does you?" Had Grant, presumably a white man since Quattlebaum called him "sir," literally put those words into Quattlebaum's mouth? Was Quattlebaum afraid of offending Grant?[2]

Still, far too many ex-slaves similarly exulted about Christmas in bondage to reject Quattlebaum's account as improbable. Frank Gill, a teenage slave servant before the war who waited tables, tended horses, and fetched mail, described "Christmas time" as "de bes' ob all" because of all the presents and the big dinner that his master gave slaves on the occasion, a remark much like ex-slave Carrie Hudson's comment that Christmas provided slave children with "deir bestes' good times" because their masters provided chicken, turkey, cake, candies, and "just about evvything good" over the holiday. Documents generated by southern masters, moreover, provide additional evidence that Christmas was the time of the year when slaves were best provided for. "Cloth the Negroes well, do not stint them. . . . Do not spare the Beef," one slaveholder wrote his manager as the holiday approached. Behind gifting and provisioning lay the primary goal of making slaves happy over the holiday, a purpose masters' and mistresses' emphasized in their letters, diaries, and instructions. Mississippi planter Everard

Baker on Christmas Day 1852 hoped to make "my negroes joyous & happy." Wade Hampton II of South Carolina informed his daughter in 1855 that he wished his slaves a "glorious Xmas." He had ordered presents for all his "people" and would "do anything to keep them in good spirits" during holiday time.[3]

Yet generalizations about the Christmas benevolence provided by southern masters are problematic, partly because they erase from the historical record Scrooge-personality types among slaveholders who hardly indulged their slaves at Christmas but also because they obscure the complex intentions explaining master benevolence in the first place. Some slaveholders gave their human property little or nothing at all for Christmas; many provided Christmas payoffs to slaves less from Yuletide goodwill than to channel potential slave discontent into acceptable behaviors and to incentivize harder labor from slaves in the future, an insidious process dubbed "intensely political" by one recent historian. As North Carolina state supreme court chief justice Thomas Ruffin put it shrewdly in an 1849 decision touching Christmas practices, masters would be well advised to let their slaves seek "the exhilaration of their simple music and romping dances" over the holidays because they indicated on the slaves' part "vigor united to a vacant mind." Read between Ruffin's lines and one realizes he was all but stating that partying slaves did not spend their Yuletide yearning for freedom or devising ways to resist their masters. Their exuberant Christmas celebrations, from Ruffin's perspective, served beneficial purposes of social control. Slaves who appreciated Christmas distributions and party opportunities from their owners were less likely to try to escape, more likely to identify with their owners' welfare, and more inclined to work harder in the future.[4]

Christmas master benevolence, in other words, requires contextualization, including recognition that unsentimental calculations inspired many Christmas giveaways, something rarely conceded in southern mythologies about excessively generous masters motivated by affection for their black servants and field hands. An advice manual for masters published in Charleston in 1851 clarifies this point, by instructing that voluntarily granting slaves "little rights and privileges" at Christmas ensured that servants would perform "their duties" cheerfully the rest of the time. So did the southern white overseer who told his employer that he had slaughtered twenty-eight head of cattle "for the people's Christmas dinner" because he could accomplish more "this way" than if he tanned the same cattle hides into whips—an argument that boiled down to getting harder labor out of the slaves he supervised with one day of kindness than with a series of lashes.[5] This was not exactly altruism run amuck.

And what of the seeming behavioral servility of southern slaves like Quattlebaum over the holiday? Slaves seemed *so* appreciative of the gifts they got at holiday time; *so* giddy about their special holiday priv-ileges, their feasts and parties. As in the case of the ex-slave who told an interviewer that the black children spent their Christmas mornings in bondage getting up early and "lookin' up de chimbly for Santa Claus,"[6] it was Christmas's mass consumptive elements that enslaved persons best remembered years later, dwarfing whatever sacred ele-ments the day held for them.

True, many thousands of southern slaves belonged to Christian churches, especially Baptist and Methodist denominations, before the Civil War, and ample contemporary testimony attests to slave re-ligious activity—either at white churches or as part of their own infor-mal black churches—over the holiday. A visitor to a South Carolina plantation one Christmas morning in the 1850s, for instance, noticed how the elderly slave women "and others who are religiously disposed" drove a wagon to a nearby church. Proslavery southern propagandist Mrs. Henry Rowe Schoolcraft, in contrast, emphasized how a segment of the southern plantation force passed much of their Christmas free time in "religious exhortations," prayer, and psalm-singing at special prayer meetings, a claim that accords with what antislavery novelist Mary Harlan apparently witnessed in Kentucky. In her story *Ellen; or the Chained Mother . . . Drawn from Real Life* (1853), Harlan claimed that over Christmas the "more pious" slaves attended religious services, preferring those held among people of their "own color."[7]

Whether slaves expended much thought about the connection be-tween Jesus's birth and the holiday they were celebrating, however, is another thing entirely. A visitor to a South Carolina plantation in the early 1840s reported slave girls singing a Christmas morning hymn with the lines "Cradled on his bed of hay, JESUS CHRIST was born to-day. Let a merry Christmas be, Massa, both to me and thee!" And for-mer tobacco field slave Jake Terriell recalled during his interview in the 1930s that each Christmas his master laid "a babe in the horse trough" and told the slaves that the baby's birth was to save them if they were honest. A onetime South Carolina slave remembered still in the 1920s how his mistress explained to his uncle the connection between Jesus and Christmas. But slaves' spirituals, with one possible exception, entirely ignored Jesus's birthday and only 6 of the 494 Fisk University and FWP interviewees who mentioned Christmas in their accounts of slave life had anything at all to say about Jesus in connection with the holiday—a pittance compared, say, to the 36 who mentioned eggnog, the 35 who recalled the whiskey, and the 153 who mentioned gifts from their masters. We should probably give credence to the recollections of the late nineteenth-century southern black minister Irving F. Lowery about his own days in bondage, even if he way overstated the biblical ignorance of the typical slave. As Lowery put it, few slaves on the place where he resided understood "the historical significance of Christmas," since their inability to read or write left them without access to "sacred" knowledge. That was why, Lowery elaborated, they alluded to their three-day Christmas breaks starting Christmas Eve day as the first, second, and third days of Christmas. December 25, in their cosmology, had no more significance than the 24th or 26th. Along similar lines, an ex-slave who had spent his boyhood enslaved in Tennessee claimed that though his peers on the Hoggatt plantation "certainly enjoyed" Christmas, they seemed to know nothing of Christmas's "real meaning," nor had they heard about Santa Claus.[8]

Did the slaves' graciousness in accepting presents from their masters and their professions of joy throughout the holiday, though, illustrate in any way that the Old South's peculiar institution amounted to a mild system of labor control? Southern apologists for slavery, of course, trumpeted that it did. After Harriet Beecher Stowe's *Uncle Tom's Cabin* became a runaway best seller, the Norfolk, Virginia, writer Martha Haines Butt answered it with her own novel, *Antifanaticism: A Tale of the South,* which used slave Christmas contentedness as a narrative tool to expose what she claimed in her preface was Stowe's malicious deceit that southern slaves were "mangled or cruelly tortured" by their masters. Butt related that all slaves much anticipated Christmas gifts from masters "who never fail to remember them." And on the particular Yuletide in the middle of her tale, two masters owning separate plantations generously and happily agree to free a male and female slave so they can get married and live together (and the master of the male slave allows him to keep his cabin gratis as a newlywed residence). Neither master cares an iota about taking a financial loss by freeing a slave; both are only concerned about the black couple's happiness. Naturally, the slaves' wedding occurs over Christmas, when slaves are allowed to sell off poultry they have raised in the market and there is feasting and banjo playing.[9]

Undoubtedly, Butt and other southern polemicists were right that slaves typically appreciated their masters' Christmas gifts. But she failed to probe that appreciation. We should ponder what options slaves had when it came to master gifting, which was often done in the presence of the entire plantation or household community, black and white. Could they openly spurn their masters' Christmas outreach on principle or seem ungrateful for the parties and gifts that masters gave them? What would that have accomplished? Southern masters were quite capable, at any time of the year, of whipping slaves for seeming surliness; they also sometimes sold off blacks in the domestic slave trade if they considered them troublemakers, even if it meant separating them from their families. Although some slaves, as we will see in chapter 5, mustered the courage to commit acts of resistance over Christmas, most played along with their masters' expectations at holiday time not only for their own benefit but also for the stability of their families and the slave community. For countless numbers of slaves, Christmas was the time of year demanding their best play-acting. Trapped in an untenable situation, they wisely performed rituals of humility and thankfulness to delude self-indoctrinated owners into believing they were a simple folk with simple needs who accepted, indeed welcomed, their own enslavement. They had every reason to do so.

Like Junius Quattlebaum's master and mistress, the great majority of antebellum southern slaveholders gave gifts of one kind or another to their slaves at Christmas, with the manner of their distribution and reception holding as much meaning as the substance of the gifts themselves. The Yankee native and Mississippi plantation mistress Roxana Gerdine told her sister that she put slaves' gifts of rag-babies, aprons, tobacco, and oranges on a Christmas tree in her parlor without explaining whether any special ceremony occurred when slaves got them off the tree, but many slaveholding masters bestowed their gifts ceremoniously as a conscious means of conferring gravitas on the process. By distributing presents ritualistically, masters enticed enslaved laborers into desired prescriptive behaviors that reinforced hierarchical parameters for bondage. Anything good coming to slaves, by this rendering, came from their masters' beneficence and charity, not the slaves' will. Teenager Annie Rosalie Quitman recorded in her diary on Christmas in 1857 that she went around her family's Natchez, Mississippi, mansion with a servant holding a basket of gifts like collars and ribbons following her, and gave them out as she ran into the various other servants. The next year she recorded distributing socks, handkerchiefs, cravats, pipes, and other items to the various servants, including perfume to a male slave whose body odor the Quitmans disliked. Her diary entries are valuable not only for itemizing the things given but also for describing the performances slaves play-acted in accepting their handouts, "the grins & bows of the dusky receivers" that rewarded the Quitmans for their magnanimity. "All the servants seemed happy & pleased with their gifts," she reported with obvious satisfaction in one diary entry. In another, she noted how when she gave her mammy a Christmas gift the slave's "eyes filled with tears as she wished us a 'Merry Christmas.'" Other documents convey similar images of servile humility when accepting their masters' gifts. "When the slaves came up to their masters and mistresses . . . the men would take off their hats and bow and the women would make a low courtesy [curtsy]," one South Carolina ex-slave remembered.[10]

On many large plantations, Christmas morning gifting upon field slaves amounted to a scripted process, with the laborers proceeding together from their quarters to the yard of the owner's mansion, where they became passive but very happy supplicants awaiting their master's ritualistic display of generosity. A slaveholding mistress wrote in her diary on a snowy Christmas Day that in the morning "the negroes" had "all come in for Christmas gifts & a right merry time have they had"; and one ex-slave later told an FWP interviewer how the slaves would "goes ter de big house ter celebrate an' ter git our gif's" each Christmas morning.[11]

Much later, Louisiana native Ruth McEnery Stuart's 1891 story "Christmas Gifts" would totally romanticize the lead-up to these Christmas morning rituals as well as the distribution of presents themselves. According to Stuart, on Christmas morning the slaves donned their finest Sunday clothes and waited together around the benches fronting their cabins for the plantation's bell to be rung, signaling the time for them to approach the master's residence for their "Christmas packages." As they milled about a grove of China trees surrounding their abodes, a couple of slave musicians respectively played a banjo and fiddle, while youthful slaves flirted with each other and other slaves good-naturedly reparteed about what "old marster" was likely to give them (surely trousers for the bow-legged slave Joe would require cutting out with a circular saw). Finally the bell clanged, causing the crowd to proceed "up to the house." Upon arrival they made a line some fifty feet from the back veranda's steps. Stuart has her slaves excitedly dancing forward when their names are called. Then they accept their gifts, curtsy, and dance back to their line.[12]

McEnery's account, so over-the-top in portraying enslaved workers as psychologically in thrall to their masters' whims, nonetheless conforms substantially to other accounts about Christmas morning southern plantation rituals. Take, for example, Louisianan Eliza Ripley's recollections of how the holiday passed on the "old plantation" in 1859. Ripley recalled how the "field negroes" were "summoned to the back porch of the big house, where Marse Jim, after a few preliminary remarks," gave them their presents. Cornelia Branch Stone contributed an essay to the *Confederate Veteran* in 1912 about her "golden days" growing up on an "old plantation," where slaves strummed "sweet memories on banjoes and pickaninnies danced" in the moonlight by their cabin doors. Christmas morning, slaves rose early and thronged around the master's residence expecting gifts. Further verification derives from a brief notation by a southern girl a few years before the Civil War remarking that family slaves on the plantation assembled in the backyard on Christmas morning to receive their gifts. And one will not find contradictions in Irving F. Lowery's published remembrances of his own boyhood experiences in bondage. Lowery confirmed many of the details and certainly the spirit of McEnery's story by telling of slaves going together to the "Big House" on Christmas morning. There they whistled and danced in the front yard with "smiling faces and joyous hearts" as they eyed the stacks of clothing earmarked for them on the master's piazza, each pile individually marked with a tag for its intended recipient. Not only did the slaves experience a momentary thrill when their names were summoned to advance forward to take their pile, but they seemed "as happy as angels" exiting the gate and returning to their quarters.[13]

Indeed, many ex-slave accounts echoed Lowery's, while showing that practices varied from place to place. Ex-slave Annie Stanton recalled that for Christmas her overseer simply summoned the slaves and distributed presents, and William Towns remembered the Christmas dispensations as a time when "we'd go to de Big House an' git our present." Prince Johnson put a humorous gloss on these gifting ceremonies in his remembrances:

> Ever' chil' brought a stockin' up to de Big House to be filled. Dey all wanted one o' 'de mistis' stockin's, 'cause now she weighed nigh on to three hund'ed pounds. Candy an' presents was put in piles for ever' one. When dey names was called dey walked up an' got it.

John Washington recalled that at the place near Fredericksburg, Virginia, where his mother had been hired out, slaves were "Summoned to the 'great House'" on Christmas, where the men and women received enough molasses, flour, sugar, whiskey, and other items (with larger families getting extra) to party at their cabins for the next six days.[14]

Process, of course, was not the whole story. What of the presents themselves? What were these generous gifts that masters selected for their unfree laborers? Since planters' journals and advice publications often mentioned the requirement of including slaves' "allowances" of basics like molasses, rice, and salt in their Christmas distributions, it is clear that much gifting involved food, which in turn partially represented a case of using the holiday as an expedient for distributing cooking supplies that owners would have needed to provide sooner or later, though sometimes masters included non-essentials. "On Christmas morning, each family would receive ten pounds of flour," recalled Tennessee ex-slave John McCline. One former slave griped to an FWP interviewer that the extra *amount* of food and drink provided at Christmas in such instances amounted to "nothin' extra or diffunt" to its recipients. William Holcombe, the Virginia native and physician who visited a Lake Concordia, Louisiana, plantation in the early 1850s, explained that slave families there received a "liberal" Christmas morning distribution of cranberries, tobacco, apples, molasses, sugar, flour, and coffee that was "sufficient to last them for a week or two." Just what did he mean to imply? We can assume that slaves there got two extra weeks of supplies for Christmas that they otherwise would never have received. But there are other possible readings of Holcombe's statement.[15]

Still, the overall impression is that typical slaveholder Christmas food distributions exceeded what we might dub as minimum sustenance requirements. Ex–Mississippi slave Louis Hughes, for example, mentioned slaves on his plantation getting a special flour ration at Christmas—a seemingly trivial item from a modern perspective, but one that Hughes emphasized held special importance to slaves since they generally lived on a corn-based diet. With flour, Hughes remembered, slaves could cook themselves biscuits—or "Billy Seldom"—a rare treat whose nickname testified to its unavailability most of the year. Similarly, John McCline added that in addition to receiving flour distributions, his family each Christmas got "two pounds of white sugar, called in those days, loaf sugar, which was scarce and considered a luxury." McCline noted that his grandmother would typically use this sugar to make candy for the boys in their family.[16] These explicit differentiations between the norm and the uncustomary are telling details about slaveholder Christmas food gifting.

As the historian Kathleen Hilliard perceptively notes, it was the very point when masters' holiday food offerings crossed the line from more of the usual to supplements like cheese, syrups, butter, rich deserts, and meat rarely received the rest of the year that plantation Christmas feasting won many slave recipients' genuine appreciation. Probably Hughes's companions got some kind of meat, fowl, or fish for Christmas in addition to the white flour; many southern planters' records highlight such distributions. On Christmas Day 1828, for instance, John P. Thomas recounted in his diary giving his workers "their usual supply of whiskey, some Tobacco, & the large Hog I killed a few days ago." Virginia planter John Selden recorded on Christmas Day 1858, "Gave my negroes . . . as much fresh meat as they wanted for their Xmas." According to the records of yet another plantation, every slave got three pounds of pork at Christmas. North Carolina planter John W. Milliken's Mulberry plantation journal for Christmas Day 1854 simply stated, "gave people extra allowance of rice and molasses—also killed a beef for them." A Maryland female slaveholder remarked that each household of her "People" was provided a turkey, other meat, and a barrel of cider. Naturally, many ex-slaves emphasized these Christmas meat distributions in their remembrances of plantation days; usually they got very little of it or none of it. Former Alabama slave James Williams claimed in his 1838 narrative that although slaves on his own plantation where he labored were well fed all year long on diets that included ham, slaves on a neighboring plantation awaited Christmas as the *only* time all year when they got meat to eat. A onetime Texas slave specified that Christmas gifting on the place where he labored entailed an allotment of one hog for every four slave families plus a present.[17]

Besides copious supplies of meat, other foods, and liquor, many masters liberally provided slaves with clothing at holiday time. A few days before Christmas one year, for instance, a slaveholding mistress from Mississippi entreated her husband to purchase "winter clothing for the house servants," and although she did not specify it was for Christmas presents, we can assume that likelihood given the timing. Cotton planter Thomas Chaplin's journal the day before Christmas in 1849 was more precise, mentioning his acquisition of "Negro shoes" from Beaufort that he had then given out for the holiday. Similarly, the day after Christmas in 1850, Wade Hampton II wrote to his South

Carolina family from the Walnut Ridge plantation he owned in Mississippi that on Christmas Day he had given each slave there fancy pants, a blanket, a pair of stockings, a hat, a handkerchief, a checked apron, a calico dress, and a fine bleached shirt.[18]

A large number of ex-slaves confirmed the frequency of Yuletide clothing handouts in their remembrances of Christmastimes. "At this time every man on the place was given a suit of clothes, consisting of coat, shirt, a pair of trousers, and a pair of shoes," John McCline remembered, adding that boys large enough to do outdoors work also got clothing and that slave women got shoes and "cloth enough to make dresses for themselves and their children." Customarily, Frank Gill's "Ol' Massa" "gib de women calico dresses an' shoes, an' de men shoes an' hats." Former South Carolina slave Mary Scott recalled her family *only* receiving clothing for Christmas, and ex-slave John Washington explained that Christmas was a time when slaves got "their new cloth Hats or Caps Boots and Shoes." In his reminiscence "Christmas Days in Old Virginia," Booker T. Washington recalled that "a new suit of clothes, or a new pair of shoes" was what slaves might expect to receive during the holiday at the small Virginia farm of his youth.[19]

Christmas outfitting, however, presents an interpretive challenge. Some of the clothing masters distributed to slaves over the holiday involved apparel of fine fabrics that slaves hardly needed for their labors, and therefore hardly ever received. But a white man who practiced carpentry on a slaveholding estate near Wilmington, North Carolina, said that the slaves where he worked received a Christmas allowance of clothing "for the year" including "coarse shoes, and enough coarse cloth to make a jacket and trousers," suggesting that many, perhaps most, of the clothes masters gave slaves at Christmas amounted to necessities rather than presents. Boston native Mary Livermore, tutoring on a Virginia plantation two decades before the Civil War, likewise noted Christmas clothing distributions to slaves were expected to go the year, and formerly enslaved people sometimes reported similarly in their recollections. The remembrance of Kentucky slave Bert Mayfield that each Christmas his master had his slaves line up for distributions of clothing made from hemp and flax the slaves themselves had cultivated reinforces such impressions, as does the recollection of ex–Kentucky slave Harry Smith. Smith described a former master who allocated one pair of shoes per year per slave, and added that the shoes were made by an "old colored man" on the place and distributed one day before Christmas. In case readers missed the obvious, Smith emphasized that this pair of foot wear, which he differentiate from normal shoes by saying they were "flat-downs" sewn by heavy twine, had to last until Christmas came around again. Ex–South Carolina Sea Island slave Sam Polite similarly explained that each "Christmas month you gits four or eider fibe yaa'd cloth 'cording to how you is," with the expectation that out "ob dat, you haffa mek your clote" to wear until the same time the following year.[20]

In such instances, masters gave their enslaved people clothes for Christmas that they had to provide sooner or later. Slaves, after all, could not run around naked the whole year and remain healthy and profitable. Undoubtedly, masters shelled out extra money for such slave clothing at Christmas, but whether the master's bottom line took a significant hit because of these expenditures is another matter entirely. If the costs had been too extreme, they would have given up slave ownership. When the famous Virginia politician John Randolph gave his hundreds of slaves Christmas presents of bedding, hats, coats, and other clothing to "last them the whole year," as a newspaper correspondent observed, he expended funds, presumably, that he would have had to part with anyway throughout the year if he had not done so then.[21]

On the other hand, since not all master Christmas gifting amounted to essential distributions of food and clothing, it would be misleading to regard all the presents masters gave slaves as self-serving, except in the simple expectation that happy slaves would work harder in the future than resentful ones. Over the holiday, some masters not only gave slaves fine apparel but also items like pipes, tobacco, and charms, and especially candy and toys for slave children. James Hammond, for instance, gifted his male slaves with pipes and tobacco. Ex-slave Peter Clifton told an FWP interviewer that on the place where he labored, each slave "woman got a handkerchief to tie up her hair" and that slave girls got ribbons, slave boys got barlow knives, and adult male slaves received a bill of paper money each. Among the most intriguing items that show up in slave remembrances is the Webster's "blueback spelling book" mentioned by a onetime Georgian slave "on the dole" at the time of her interview at the age of eighty-six. Despite prescriptions against slave literacy, an estimated 5 percent or more of all slaves achieved an ability to read and write through one means or another. This Georgia slave's mistress made a point of teaching her bondpeople their ABCs, probably as a way of introducing them to the Bible since some of their lessons came in the form of catechism.[22]

Also worth attention—given that slavery was premised on assumptions that labor should be unreimbursed—are indications that many slaveholders, like Peter Clifton's master, included money in their holiday distributions. Some money "gifts" represented, in reality, payback for produce provided from slave plots or the overtime slaves put in during the previous year, practices resembling the "settling-up day" that post–Civil War sharecroppers experienced on many southern estates. During Christmas, some masters assembled their laborers and then carefully doled out bills and coins based on ledger accounts of sums owed to particular slaves. But Christmas monetary gifting took other forms too. Some documents mention white holiday visitors to plantations throwing coins to slaves awaiting their arrival at plantation gates; others mention Christmas gratuities to slaves for special services either at holiday time or for services rendered earlier in the year. One holiday, for example, legendary Texan William Barret Travis rewarded a slave girl with a dollar for delivering a letter for him. One slaveholder simply threw quarters, nickels, and dimes for slave children to gather on Christmas Day, and, according to the records of a Virginia plantation, Christmas distributions to slaves included rattles, coffee mills, lace collars, and money. Annie Rosalie Quitman noted in her 1853 Christmas Day diary entry that after breakfast she went upstairs and gave her mammy a two bit piece, and a handkerchief and a small table respectively to two of the other house servants. The abolitionist James Redpath learned during his travels in North Carolina before the Civil War that "some owners" of plantations gave $10–$15 at Christmas to their slaves.[23]

One rice planter told a correspondent shortly before the Civil War that rather than conform to the local norm of allowing slaves to cultivate their own gardens year-round, he simply gave the slaves on his Savannah River place $5–$10 each for Christmas to compensate for his deviation, pointing to the diverse purposes monetary distributions served for slaveholders and their carefully calibrated capitalist perspectives. Giving slaves money instead of gardens, he maintained, saved him from worries that his slaves would exchange their produce with local traders for liquor, which in turn would lead them into "wickedness" like petty theft. Perhaps this planter had read and was following the model laid out in an advice column on progressive plantation management in De Bow's Review several years earlier. There, a self-proclaimed but anonymous "Mississippi Planter" had explained that rather than follow the practice of peers who allowed slaves to maintain their own garden patches to raise produce for local sale at Christmastime, encouraging them to add to their potential sales by stealing from their owner, he avoided such losses and possibly having to whip slaves for theft by giving them $5 each Christmas and sending them off to spend it in town, so long as they did not spend it on alcohol. If they did and he found out about it, he would deprive them of the $5 the next time Christmas came along.[24]

These two advice pieces remind us that not all slaveholders wished their enslaved people inebriated at Christmas. Like the Savannah River and Mississippi planters, other southern masters discouraged slave liquor consumption at holiday, sometimes as much from their own abstemious value systems as from a desire to ward off slave misbehavior. Though we tend to identify antebellum "reform" movements with the North, the South had its share of temperance proponents, and many of them so opposed slaves getting inebriated that they withheld completely or drastically limited liquor in their Christmas gifting. Martha Bradley's master gave his slaves "all the lemonade us could drink" rather than liquor for Christmas. "Befo' dinner," ex-slave Frances Lewis remembered about her Yuletide experiences, "there was a big eggnog and we all had a glassful. It had whiskey in it but not enough to make you drunk." Irving Lowery remembered that his temperate South Carolina master violated neighborhood norms of giving a dram of alcohol to each slave on Christmas morning, but made his slaves happy anyway with his Christmas gifting.[25]

More typically, however, masters fostered slave inebriation, including possibly that paragon of Enlightenment rationalism Thomas Jefferson, who apparently included whiskey distributions in his Monticello slaves' Christmas benefits well before 1800. New Englander Abigail Mason, while employed as governess on a Virginia plantation, reported to her half-sister that the slaves over Christmas had been "drunk every night with whiskey as they well can be yet dancing with all their might." "Lots of dem no count niggers got drunk" over Christmas, remembered one ex-slave from Alabama. An ex–South Carolina slave recalled slaves getting "partly drunk" after their masters ceremoniously doled out concoctions of whiskey and sweetened water from large pails.[26]

Some masters built work incentives into Christmas giving, a practice specifically endorsed in a North Carolina Supreme Court decision, in which Chief Justice Richmond Pearson upheld the practice of the administrator of a will to give the five hired slaves on the estate bonuses upon their return at Christmas. Pearson justified drawing upon the estate for the small amounts of money involved on the logic that such gratuities had become standard "usage in that community" for obedient and faithful slave behavior. South Carolina rice planter Robert F. W. Allston was a believer in such positive reinforcement of slave cooperation: he gave extra rice portions to field hands at his estates who had been fit for work every day the past year. South Carolina planter Henry Middleton monetarily rewarded slave seamstresses at his Weehaw estate for "well made" articles. Middleton additionally gave bonuses to slave nurses if the infants in their charge lived. Louisiana sugar planter John Hampden Randolph not only regularly gave Christmas bonuses to slaves, but he increased them in the winter of 1853–1854 at a time when his production was spiraling upward after he introduced a complex system of vacuum pans into his processes. John P. Thomas one Christmas gifted his slave workforce four Dutch ovens to share as a reward for picking more cotton per hand than in previous years.[27]

Some bonuses, rather than rewarding workers' contributions to production, instead recognized slaves simply for avoiding negative behaviors during the year that might have harmed output. Thus one rice master inspected slaves' tools on Christmas Day and awarded bonuses to laborers who were not "defaulters" in their upkeep. In 1842, a contributor to the *Southern Agriculturist* explained how he had curtailed slave thievery on his place for the last four or five years by a carefully calibrated system of positive and negative Christmas incentives. On the one hand, every year when Christmas arrived, he gave each worker a bonus of a barrel of corn or its value in cash. On the other, he made significant deductions from all the distributions if there had been thievery or the loss of tools on his estate over the year, unless the slaves themselves implicated the culprit. The writer estimated that this system of peer pressure saved him up to ten times the value of the Christmas corn bonuses he distributed.[28]

James Hammond promoted a rather different type of slave behavior with his Christmas bonus system, at least in 1832, by specially singling out all slave women giving birth during the year to receive a calico frock. Hammond recognized, of course, that slave infants who evaded mortality would in not too many years become a pool of potential laborers he would never have to pay. Left unsaid, also, was Hammond's presumed assumption that other slave women would covet the frocks and be more likely to become pregnant or maintain their pregnancies in the years ahead in order to earn their master's favor.[29]

Along with all this gifting, masters, especially those owning large staple-producing estates, often threw their slaves an excessive holiday culinary event accompanied by a large dance. The transplanted former slave Louis Hughes vividly described his first impressions of Christmas on the Mississippi place where he wound up after having been a slave in Virginia. After breakfast, he ventured into the yard, where he saw a cook scuttling about and met more slaves than he had ever seen in one place in Virginia. "I shall never forget the dinner that day," he added, calling the "bill of fare" a feast worthy of a king for its variety and lavishness. At Joseph Tooke's 3,000+-acre cotton plantation in central Georgia, it was customary at noon every December 25 for the slaves to assemble at tables Tooke set up in the yard for a feast of fruit and turkey. Solomon Northup, who played the violin for the Christmas dances on the Louisiana place where he was enslaved, recalled fondly that slaves and their guests from other plantations enjoyed a table in the open air loaded with meat and fowl (including duck, turkey, roasted ox, and pork) as well as vegetables, pies, tarts, and other goodies. The rich food and the time spent flirting and dancing over Christmas, Northup explained, caused their faces to light up in "ecstasy" with bursts of laughter and giggling.[30]

This festive atmosphere not only provided opportunities for slaves to socialize with each other to a degree impossible most of the year but also to fraternize with their masters far more than at other times. In fact, in Perquimans County, North Carolina, a slave patrol once broke up a party on Christmas night at a slaveholder's place, whipped black participants on the spot, and initiated legal action against the master for the very reason that the patrollers thought the holiday interracial intimacy had gone further than societal norms allowed.[31] But such countermeasures were rare. Southern whites generally considered Christmastime racial intermingling as unthreatening to community mores and almost always allowed such parties to proceed unimpeded.

Over Christmas, slaveholders intermingled with field hands and domestics in countless ways. Edmund Ruffin's Christmas diary entries for 1859 include an intriguing allusion to his "negroes" (presumably his servants) joining white children for a magic lantern (slide projection) show at Marlbourne, his mansion in Virginia's Pamunkey River valley.

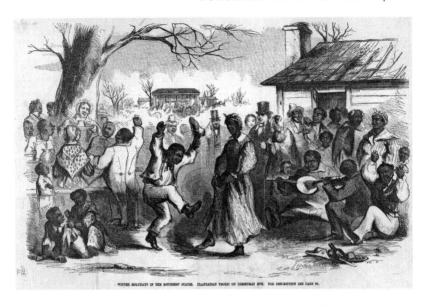

Slanted caricature of happy, well-fed slaves dancing at Christmas in *Frank Leslie's Illustrated Newspaper,* December 26, 1857, p. 64. (Library of Congress, Prints and Photographs Division)

Ex-slave Sarah Wilson recalled hanging Christmas stockings in "de big house" and remembered how her master let any of his slaves who so wished decorate his Christmas tree with popcorn strings holding kernels they grew in their own garden patches. Particularly revelatory was the Christmas toasting that occurred in 1856 at Chicora Wood, Robert Allston's home plantation. Allston's wife reported to their son following the holiday how the "negroes" had arrived at the mansion on Christmas morning "as usual" to wish "Merry Christmas and the compliments of the Season" to their owners, a custom that held special meaning that year since Robert Allston had just been elected governor of the state. "They made a great noise and drank the Governor's health in many a stout glass of whiskey," she related, describing the slave force as in "good spirits."[32]

According to Susan Dabney Smedes, it was customary at her family's Mississippi plantation during her childhood for slaves to come up to the "great-house" over Christmas, filling the doors and porches and watching their white owners and guests dance through half the night. Slave musicians apparently provided much of the music at these dances as well as for the weddings of the estate owners and their families occurring during the season. When the young Georgia rice planter James Hamilton Couper married his bride on Christmas night in 1827, the slave musician "Johnny" provided white attendees with tunes on his bagpipes, fiddle, and clarinet (while slaves took to the lawn to perform gymnastic acts). Former slave Louis Cain recalled that come Christmas night "all the slaves what could" brought "banjoes and fiddles and played for the white folks to dance all night."[33]

Just as Christmas summoned field hands to the "big house," it also enticed masters to their slave cabins, often to watch the seasonal social affairs they funded and authorized. While on site in the "quarters," masters could watch their laborers dance, feast, and—in the lingo of slaves and their owners alike—"frolic" in frenzied behaviors that allowed slaves to temporarily obscure in sweaty, uninhibited festivities the severity of their own yearlong uncompensated toil. As Solomon Northup recalled, Christmas gave slaves their one "respite from constant labor" and their only chance for "a little restricted liberty," which they took full advantage of by passing the holiday in "feasting, and frolicking, and fiddling." Consciously and subconsciously, slaves committed themselves fully to the partying their masters enabled, undoubtedly often hoping to drown their sorrows in complete exhaustion from overeating, overdrinking, and frenzied dancing. As one visitor to the Georgia Sea Islands put it, slaves were "completely done up with eating, drinking, and dancing" by the time their Christmas break ended.[34]

Slaveowners fostered this partying not only with copious supplies of barbecue and feast food and liquor but also by enabling the slaves' music and dancing. Mississippi slaveholder John Nevitt recorded in his diary one December 27 how he "gave" his slaves "a frolic at night" and the next year noted on December 26 how he had thrown them "a ball" that evening. One ex-slave recalled his master hiring musicians from another plantation if no one on his place could play for the slaves' dancing. Slaves probably made most of the banjos and drums they used at plantation dances since these instruments derived from West African antecedents, but they apparently depended on their owners for their fiddles because violins were alien to pre-1800 West African musical culture. "Application has been made to me by the principal musician to treat them to a violin for the amusement of the people this Christmas," one plantation manager reported to his employer, noting that such instruments were available for $5–$6. Years after the Civil War, the memoirist James Battle Avirett recalled his parents buying strings for the fiddle and banjo players on his place.[35]

According to Peter Clifton, an ex-slave interviewed in South Carolina at the age of eighty-nine, "Us always have a dance in de Christmas," and one gets the sense that such dances were as crucial to the slave Yuletide experience as the feasts were. Ex-slaves could not have made the point stronger than they did. "My, you should see de dance on de day after Christmas," ex-slave Ezra Martin told a reporter for the *Baltimore Sun* in 1898, recalling his experiences on a James River, Virginia, plantation. "On Christmas we had all we could eat and drink and after that a big party," ex-slave Will Adams recalled, adding that the dancing was liberating: "you ought to see them gals swingin' their partners round." When former slave James Boyd told an FWP interviewer that slaves got dances from their owners "on Christmas and sometime in de summer," he highlighted the Yuletide as a special dancing opportunity. Ezra Martin implied the connection between Christmas dancing and holiday courtships, telling his interviewer that the "purtiest black piccannanies you ebber laid yo' eyes on" turned up at the slaves' Christmas dances.[36]

It would be difficult to overstate the importance of black musicians and dancing to the entire slave Christmas experience. In 1841, South Carolina rice planter Robert Allston's wife, Adele, noted a month before Christmas that the servants on her place already had "a fiddler going and are dancing at a great rate in the wash kitchen," preparing, she assumed, for the upcoming holiday festivities. A Christmas visitor to a Georgia plantation not only observed a dance with tambourine and fiddle but also a parade of a slave band, including fiddles, drums, triangles, tambourines, and fifes. Decades after the Civil War, Hillary Herbert recalled the "old darkey" Giles on his father's Alabama plantation who would sit on a platform at the "negro quarters" and fiddle faster and faster throughout the night.[37]

For many slaves, dancing held especial spiritual significance since it offered a vehicle to preserve residues of cultural traditions derived from their West African ancestry. During the time of the international slave trade, West African dance was characterized by open-air performances involving complex rhythmicality as well as gymnastic and exhausting movements, often to the beat of percussion instruments and hand-clapping of observers. Such dancing could pit two performers in competition. Much slave Christmas dancing in the Old South replicated such patterns. White observers of antebellum southern black dances invariably recorded witnessing what they considered exotic elements rather than steps imitative of European dancing styles. This was, naturally, most true during the early nineteenth century, before the U.S. ban of the African slave trade in 1808 put the percentage of native-born Africans on American slaveholdings into precipitate decline. When one New Englander visited a South Carolina estate at Christmas in 1805, he described slaves on the place dancing on the portico to fiddle music but also noticed "native Africans" on the place doing dance moves that involved "distorting their frames into the most unnatural figures" to the beat of hand-clapping.[38]

Even as the years passed, however, many acculturated slaves clung to what they learned of African customs from their parents and others in the slave community and expressed those traditions over Christmas. Traveler Charles Lanman, observing blacks dancing to fiddle and banjo in the streets of a Florida town at Christmastime, emphasized how the "patting of Juba" (highly complex rhythms that slaves beat out by patting their thighs and knees and clapping their hands) seemed universal among the crowd that had gathered and that the dances demanded considerable endurance by the performers. Two dancers, he noted, competed on boxes of dry goods to see which one could dance longer without pause. Roxana Gerdine, attending a Christmas slave dance at her husband's Oak Grove cotton plantation in 1859, witnessed "funny antics," a condescending remark to be sure but one that nonetheless suggests the chasm separating slave dance from the way their masters and mistresses moved about a dance floor, and hints at why many southern slave owners enjoyed watching their slaves dance in the first place. Few slaveholders, we can be fairly confident, ever ventured the "turkey-buzzard dance" that one tall slave reportedly invented and performed regularly at South Carolinian James Hammond's place, though its exotic character undoubtedly intrigued white onlookers. Just as northern urban theatergoers patronized the "pornutopia" of blackface minstrelsy for its very violation of emerging middle-class codes of repressed sexuality—minstrelsy's dwelling on absurdly oversized clothes, childhood bodily functions, suggestive motions like sucking on sugarcane, and genital "amusement"—so southern slaveholders engaged in "erotic consumption" of "the Other" when they slummed in the quarters.[39]

Once the appointed party day arrived, slaveholders and their families commonly patronized the celebrations they enabled, as one planter revealed by noting in his journal, "I went to see the Negroes dance this evening, for the first time this Christmas." Hillary A. Herbert recalled that as a boy he spent hours during Christmastime "at the quarters" watching the slaves dance, and counted those moments as among the most joyous in his entire life. "Such fun—such scrapping—much music!" he exclaimed, adding how the hearts of those "dear souls" seemed to overflow with "goodness and with simple rapture." White holiday visitations to the quarters in turn, whether to watch the dancing or for other reasons, left quite an impression on the slaves, many of whom recalled these appearances long afterward. An ex-slave living in South Carolina told an interviewer in the 1930s that folks in the "big house" had "brung us" red candy sticks at Christmas. Another ex-slave remembered how at Christmas the slave children would play a card game with the white youths on her place, with the winner smudging the loser's face with smut from the fireplace. Former Mississippi slave James Lucas recalled how it was customary for "de white folks" to decide which slave was the best dancer when they watched their workers' Christmas Eve dances. Lucas remembered his master and mistress laughing hysterically at the "capers" slaves performed while they danced.[40]

Unfortunately, given their susceptibility to racial stereotyping, few masters teased more than superficial meanings from the exuberant slave behaviors they witnessed during these holiday encounters. Tellingly, Eliza Ripley, remembering a slave marriage at Christmas 1859, remarked that when her husband gave advice to the newlyweds during the service, he kept his messaging simple since the "darkey mind" would hardly comprehend sophisticated instructions. Ripley recalled how family "custom" had brought her father and the entire white household down to the quarters to witness the wedding of "quarter bride" Nancy Breckenridge to the younger slave Aleck in a ceremony conducted by the plantation's slave preacher, Lewis, the latter sporting an uncomfortably tight swallow-tail coat (a formal wear covering with a long, rounded tail) lent to him by her father to add dignity to the occasion. Eliza's father took advantage of his master's privilege by appropriating the wedding sermon from the presiding preacher, when he paternalistically reminded both slaves to remain faithful to each other and otherwise fulfill their marital "duties."[41]

Allusions to slave Christmas weddings percolate through surviving slaveholder documents. For the single Christmas that Robert F. W. Allston kept a diary, he listed seven slave marriages under "Xmas-Marriages." One Mississippi slaveholder sent his wife a letter saying that his slaves were pairing up, adding they wanted to know whether he expected them "to wait till Christmas" before getting married. Natalie Delage Sumter's diary entry for December 26, 1840, noted that all of her house servants and "every negroe in the yard" but one had gone off to the "fine wedding" she had thrown for a slave named Venus. Several years later, slaveholder Richard Arnold had his own slave Venus married Christmas season to a slave named Jim (who would be plowing for him just a few days later). Southern humorist Thomas Bangs Thorpe informed readers in a piece for *Frank Leslie's Illustrated Newspaper* that it was common in the southern states for "marriages among the 'upper circles' of ebony life" (meaning house servants) to happen during the Christmas season while the field hands watched. Emphasizing that slave marriages involved the entire plantation community, whites and blacks alike, Thorpe explained that young white women visiting a plantation for the holiday took great joy in choosing the right ribbons for a slave waiting-maid being married.[42]

According to one study, far more slaves in southern rice- and cotton-producing areas married in December than in any other month of the year, and there is no reason to doubt either that this pattern held for most of the South's geographical subregions or that most of these December marriages occurred over Christmas. In rice and cotton realms, over one in five slave marriages occurred in December, far more than the month's closest competitor (August at 15.63 percent). Statistics for the South's sugar regions would show a different pattern, however, since seasonal holidays were often deferred to January. On John Quitman's Live Oaks sugar plantation in Louisiana's bayou country, Quitman's son and manager, Henry, presided over a January 10, 1857, slave double marriage on the residential front gallery followed by a banquet and jigs and speechmaking in the sugarhouse, decorated for the occasion with a large American flag and palmetto leaves (with reminders of labor routines like kettles hidden temporarily from sight). According to the condescending language of Henry's sister Rose, who was on hand for the weddings, when the ceremony ended one of the slave grooms sealed his vows with a kiss "on the dusky cheek of his bride" to the "tittering" of all the bridesmaids and groomsmen who tried to conceal their immature reactions by hiding their mouths with white handkerchiefs. Apparently white involvement in Christmas season slave marriages occurred frequently in the Old South, though no standard procedures governed it. One northern visitor to a southern plantation told her father that the Christmas slave bride and her bridesmaids had all been dressed "grandily" in white, with the bride having a garland of flowers on her head.[43]

Southern Christmas mythologies about gifting in slave times fail on several counts, the most obvious being that in the process of implying universality for master liberality, they erase from historical memory the minority of masters who either gave their slaves no parties or gifts at all for Christmas, or very little. Such masters clearly existed, as Booker T. Washington revealed possibly unintentionally in an easily overlooked aside in his remembrance of the holiday in antebellum Virginia. "The master who gave no present to his slaves was looked down upon by his fellow-masters," Washington recalled, emphasizing that such slave-holders were deemed "unworthy" of aristocratic legitimacy by their peers. Since Washington began his paragraph on gifting with statements that each slave for Christmas got an extended holiday and present and finished it by alluding to presents conferred on slaves during the Civil War, it is very easy to miss his qualification.[44]

A bit of probing exposes Scrooge-personality types within the Old South's master class, persons invisible in traditional, stereotypical treatments of Christmas in slave times but needing spotlighting for a full rendering of what the holiday was like for the South's millions of slaves. Even slaveholders like South Carolinian Henry W. Ravenel, who appears to have genuinely cared about his slaves, privately admitted the modest parameters of his own holiday gifting to them by remarking in his diary, immediately after listing the pans and other presents he had just distributed, that they amounted to "pleasant gratification purchased at little cost."[45] Other slaveholders sometimes resented the giving itself.

One South Carolinian, for example, confided dreading "the Negroes peculiar festival" in a note to her father and expressed regret that she had to pay off slaves over Christmas for their own production at a time when money was tight (even though they had earned the payments). Likewise, Thomas Chaplin resented the Christmas generosity that societal norms imposed on him, allowing his frustrations to seep through his diary. When his wife one Christmas threw a lavish meal for their two maids who got married over the holiday, Chaplin bailed on attending the event, regarding it as "tomfoolery" because it wrongly allowed slaves to temporarily assume the personas of "ladies of quality." From his perspective, such pretentiousness by slaves was grossly inappropriate. Another year he noted on Christmas Day that all he had given to his slaves for the holiday were "a few turnips," and that though his workers seemed to enjoy the holiday, he did not. One Mississippi slaveholder gave money payments to his slaves for Christmas presents because they had become accustomed to them, while remarking "Christmas is anything but fun for me" because of those very distributions.[46]

When the northern abolitionist James Redpath queried one slave he encountered near the railroad tracks south of Petersburg, Virginia, about how his master treated him, and the slave complained about having a "bery hard" master, Redpath followed up: did his master at least give him Christmas presents? "No, mass'r," the man responded, "not a cent. Some bosses do 'low someding at Christmas; but not my boss. He doesn't even gib us 'bacca [tobacco] to chaw." In a similar vein, an escaped slave confided after reaching the North that although some slaves were accustomed to getting between $1.50 to $5.00 for Christmas in the Richmond, Virginia, area where he had labored, his own master, a farmer, "would never give me anything." Sometimes even normally generous masters came up with little for their laborers at Christmas. Louisiana planter Bennet H. Barrow recorded in his journal in 1842 that the times were so hard he could only afford to give his slaves lots of food and liquor over the holiday, nothing more in the way of gifts. As for James Hammond's Christmas bonuses, they proved a double-edged sword. One Christmas he admitted that although he had thrown a Christmas barbecue for his workers and given his workers tobacco, he had "not given much to them for Christmas" since they had "not worked well latterly." Hammond was hardly unique in this regard. Davison McDowell, who owned two plantations in South Carolina, revealed in his journal that he simply denied Christmas holidays to slaves who ran away, committed thievery, or, in the case of one female slave, caused herself to miscarry. The loss of slave progeny, of course, represented a diminution of potential future profits.[47] Incentives cut two ways.

Even in the hard times of the 1930s, when many FWP slave interviewees put a positive spin on their experiences in bondage, some indicted masters who gave them little or nothing in the way of presents and food at holiday time. "Us nebber know nutting 'bout Santa Claus 'till Freedom," insisted ninety-three-year-old Sam Polite, and a bitter Texan ex-slave asserted that the "only Christmas I got was what mammy giv' me." Gordon Bluford, a ninety-two-year-old onetime plantation slave domestic, claimed that his master distributed liquor so slaves could get drunk for Christmas but provided no special dinner. Yet another ex-slave, who said she had been separated from and never saw again two brothers and two sisters who had been sold off in the domestic slave trade, recalled that "Christmas never meant no more" than "any other day" to her in slave times since all her mother got was sorghum and shorts to bake gingersnaps. Yet another testifier knew of slaves with "rough" masters who said their Christmas bounty amounted to "a little flour."[48]

By erasing stingy masters from the historical record, southern Christmas mythologies misrepresent variances in the slave experience. But they mislead in other ways too. They obscure the price slaves paid when compelled during Christmas to submit to holiday pressures from their masters into behaviors like drinking that they otherwise might have resisted. As seen in the introduction to this book, Frederick Douglass resented slaveholders who manipulated alcohol distributions to their slaves' disadvantage. How many other enslaved people felt aggrieved by pressure from their masters to get drunk over the holiday but decided it safest to submit is anyone's guess, but it is likely that drinking contributed to an upsurge in violence in the quarters during the holiday. Statistical analysis by the historian Jeff Forret reveals a significant average annual uptick in black-on-black homicide cases in the South each January as compared to the previous month (fifteen in January; nine in December), because murders over Christmas holidays generally came to trial in January. Although Forret stops short of directly attributing the jump in homicides to master-provided holiday booze, he does document a serious fracas at a Christmas slave dance in South Carolina's Anderson District, an inebriated slave's death during a Christmas dispute with another slave over a woman both men claimed as a wife, and murder threats at a Christmas dance by a slave named Primus because other slaves made fun of his wife's dance movements (while also acknowledging that some masters tried to repress slave fighting because it put their investment in human bodies at risk).[49]

Undoubtedly, many slaves were complicit in their own drunkenness, but surely others felt like Kentucky house slave Francis Fedric, who escaped from bondage and authored a narrative about his experiences. Fedric excoriated his former master for keeping his slaves in "the most beastly intoxication" over the entire Christmas period by forcing them to drink huge quantities of whiskey. After making the slaves continue drinking even when they protested they were sated,

Fedric's master conducted an insidious sport of psychological war on them, converting their own debasement into a rationale for their own continued enslavement:

> He would then call them together, and say, "Now you slaves, don't you see what bad use you have been making of your own liberty? Don't you think you had better have a master, to look after you, and make you work, and keep you from such a brutal state, which is a disgrace to you, and would ultimately be an injury to the community at large?"

Then Fedric explained what followed, describing a scene that could hardly better illuminate the fawning behaviors fostered by masters' powers: "Some of the slaves, in that whining cringing manner, which is one of the baneful effects of slavery, would reply, 'Yees, Massa; if we go on in dis way, no good at all.'" To Fedric, the irony of slaves putting a seal of approval on their "own servitude" exposed the insidiousness of their master's strategy.[50]

Drinking, of course, was but one of several problematic slave behaviors encouraged (and sometimes compelled) by masters over Christmas, and these master expectations become salient in any analysis of slave Christmastimes in the Old South. Did the former slave Will Adams, who when describing slave happiness at Christmas told an FWP interviewer that "massa" would have "two niggers" wrestle each other while he and his family watched from seats on the gallery, really mean to suggest that slaves welcomed the chance to fight each other for their masters' gratification? Possibly. But it is entirely possible that Adams and similarly situated slaves resented such expectations but knew it was safer to conform to their owners' prurient interests than to irritate them by refusing.[51]

When ex–South Carolina plantation slave Jacob Stroyer declared in his post–Civil War narrative that masters compelled slaves with religious scruples against dancing to dance for their amusement anyway if they wanted to get gifts, he indicated such demands caused anxiety, mentioning the "intense emotion" among slaves when trying to please their mistresses and masters. Campbell Davis did not state outright that his own master each Christmas night made "de darkies sing songs for de white folks," but possibly there was implied compulsion at play. After all, Davis told his interviewer that this same master lashed slaves whenever "dey need whippin" for not working hard enough. Would Davis have dared tell his master that he disliked singing for him? In

1849, a Mississippi newspaper published a story about slaves on an unnamed plantation who resisted their master's demands for a Christmas toast with the liquor he provided them. Each slave answered with a snicker, "I don't know how to do dat, massa," according to the very possibly fabricated report. But a lead cotton picker held up his glass "with ludicrous gravity," apparently thinking he was too valuable to punish, and said, mockingly,

> The big bee flies high
> The little bee makes the honey.
> The black folks makes the cotton
> And the white folks gets the money.

Perhaps this incident occurred, but accepting "one's 'place,'" as one scholar has put it, was an intrinsic element in learned slave behavior on southern plantations. What would have happened had Campbell Davis looked his master in the eye and sullenly refused to sing? It is not difficult to guess the outcome in most such cases.[52]

The third flaw with stereotypes about master Christmas paternalism concerns processing the massive documentary evidence that slaves were appreciative for the gifts, feasts, and parties masters provided them over the holidays. To be sure, slaves smiled and bowed timidly in the rituals of accepting their gifts, in scenes reenacted in southern white households every Christmas year after year. "I am engaged in giving out supplies of meat, sugar, & coffee to the people," Wade Hampton wrote his wife the day after Christmas in 1853, adding how his slaves in turn were dancing "& seem quite happy." "I gave out this morning pans, spoons & fish to all the negroes here for Christmas presents—all happy & delighted," Henry W. Ravenel remarked in his diary three days after Christmas in 1859.[53]

These were the very behaviors that months and years of enslavement taught southern blacks to perform if they hoped to survive slavery physically and psychologically. The smart ones learned to address their masters—in the words of Solomon Northup—with "down-cast eyes," to keep their masters at ease in their presence, and accept Christmas payouts that at least temporarily eased their deprivations. Slaves who refused to participate in such rituals invited physical or mental abuse, or even seeing their families broken up by sale. Slave Christmas behaviors, in many cases, amounted to performance art calibrated to the oppressive circumstances of bondage itself. Undoubtedly, many bondpeople greatly appreciated being feasted and given gifts at Christmas.

But this hardly comports with acceptance of their day-to-day situation. Receiving gifts and feasts grumpily would have done them no good at all, though sometimes slaves indeed allowed their unhappiness to show, even at Christmas. A low-country Georgia plantation manager admitted in a holiday letter to his employer that even though he had given the slaves large amounts of sugar or molasses, rum, and beef, they danced "but very little." In fact, he noted, throughout the area the "Negroes made merry but very little" over the Christmas season. Similarly, John Thomas noted one Christmas how "quite sober & quiet" his "Negroes" had been over the holiday. Unfortunately though understandably, masters like Thomas never probed why downcast slaves were moody; it was not in their interest to do so.[54]

Of course, these same abject behaviors helped sustain slavery as a labor system, since slaveholders craved feedback that their management methods, though ultimately based on the whip, were nonetheless humane and appreciated by their black workers. During the late antebellum period, slavery was under constant attack as cruel and immoral from abolitionists at home and abroad; antislavery northern congressmen, judges, and newspapers; and even scattered white critics in the South itself. Southerners were ultrasensitive to this criticism. Watching slaves humbly show gratitude for their holiday gifts and cavort and laugh at Christmas banquets, dances, and weddings seemed to give the lie to all the complaints by "outsiders" against their society's norms.

Southern slaveholders took great comfort when their laborers seemed appreciative of their Christmas privileges since, from their perspective, the slaves' behavior confirmed their labor system as humane, regardless of what abolitionists charged. Roxana Gerdine, who infantilized her laborers by telling her sister that "negroes" were "like children" at holiday time and cared only about having a big Christmas dinner and Christmas tree, found it easy to discount slave individuality or any possibility that they resented bondage. Other slaveholders similarly projected their own self-righteousness onto descriptions of their slaves' apparent Christmas joy. After watching her slaves one Christmas Day, an Alabama slaveholding mistress exuded, "How happy they looked, how busting & important! Each had his snug christmas dinner, clean swept cabin & bran[d] new suit, the *christmas finery*." Cane planter Charles Slack remarked on his slaves' "merriment" on Christmas morning, and when a slaveholder long absent in California heard by mail from his mother that on Christmas morning all the slaves had been "playing under your window," he confessed it made him melancholy for home. And a southern social commentator claimed just before the Civil War that throughout his region slaves so loved Christmas that they began preparing for it six weeks early, and when the holiday actually arrived they began "running hither and thither in a fever of excitement, laughing and jumping about" deliriously, and put on their Sunday best to mark the occasion.[55]

Indeed, southern Christmas traditions and slave responses became heavy fodder for the "proslavery defense," propaganda that southern polemicists authored to counter northern assaults on the peculiar institution. As a pro-southern newspaper in Washington, D.C., put it, "misguided Abolitionists" would be disabused of their misconceptions if they would only "glance" at happy slaves enjoying their Christmas dinners and parties: "The humble cabin will blaze with light, and resound with merry voices. The banjo will give out its enlivening notes, and the flat foot of the happy negro will keep time to the simple but inspiring music." William Grayson, as we have seen in this book's introduction, used Christmas as a teaching tool in his epic proslavery poem *Hireling and the Slave*. More briefly, Virginian George Fitzhugh, in arguably the most famous tract written in slavery's defense, *Cannibals All! or Slaves without Masters,* simply claimed that holidays and Sundays off were among the reasons that the South's slaves spent much of their time "in perfect abandon" and deserved acknowledgment as the "happiest, and, in some sense, the freest people in the world." A Carolinian, along similar lines, published a poem with phrasing about how antislavery northerners should focus on improving their own workers rather than freeing southern slaves. The latter had ample clothing and food, nice whitewashed cottages to live in, and the right to raise poultry that they could sell at Christmas to buy silk gowns. But it was not simply native southerners who took Christmas practices as justification for slavery. The Connecticut native Solon Robinson, a widely traveled agricultural reformer and writer, defended the South's labor conditions in a public letter dated Charleston, Christmas Day 1850, in which he condoned slavery partly on the logic that the South's enslaved people received "more money every year in Christmas presents than the total amount of wages" that poor northern laborers took in from their employers.[56]

South Carolina author William Gilmore Simms's story "Maize-in-Milk: A Christmas Story of the South" all but averred that slaves' joy over master gifting legitimized bondage itself, though Simms refrained from couching his tale as a rebuke to northern abolitionists.

Rather, he embedded his paean to master gift-giving practices within a plot about an aristocrat's unflinching holiday hospitality to friends and neighbors (regardless of class differences) and the pursuit of his very eligible daughter by a sleazy suitor/villain cornily named "Skinflint." Still, Simms—who worked slaves on his own upcountry South Carolina estate called "Woodlands" and in an 1837 review vigorously defended southern slaveholders as "the great moral conservators" of the world given the animal irresponsibility and immorality of black laborers—placed his plantation gifting story in a Philadelphia magazine, not a southern one. Moreover, he published it in 1847, the very time sectional controversies about slavery were heating up over a Pennsylvania congressman's proposal (the Wilmot Proviso) to ban slavery from any territory that might be acquired in the U.S. war with Mexico then in progress. It is reasonable to wonder whether Simms might have intentionally penned his story to get the slaveholders' message out to the northern public, especially since Simms was then advocating the conflict with Mexico as a means of expanding slavery's boundaries, though it has also been suggested that Simms's propagandistic tone related to his psychological need to solidify his stature within South Carolina society since he had acquired his plantation through marriage rather than by his own inheritance or efforts.[57]

Simms's amiable main character, Colonel Edward Openheart, beloved by house servants and field hands alike, consistently lives up to his surname. Their laborers, his wife, Emily, reassures him during a moment of self-doubt over the condition of his crops, perform their tasks "cheerfully" because they love him and appreciate all he does for them. Indeed, they are so improved under his genial managerial style that they are becoming ever more "human," sober, and happy. Part of their gratitude derives from how considerately they are treated each Christmas. Then the colonel not only slaughters livestock for their Christmas feasting and visits their quarters to watch their big dance but also, adhering to rituals established by his own grandfather and father, meticulously distributes carefully individualized gifts to his enslaved people in ceremonies lasting an hour or more. In the first of the two plantation Christmases treated in the story, slaves—including seventy-one whom Openheart has humanely just purchased to ward off their families being broken up in an estate sale even though they lack work potential (many are "gray-headed" and "unserviceable")—herald his appearance on the porch prior to the ritual by lovingly saying, "God bless you, maussa" and "Hoping you live tousand merry Christmas more."

When all the presents have been dispensed, the slaves' "greasy, grinning faces" testify to their master's generosity.[58]

The fourth and final installment of "Maize-in-Milk," set three years
later during a second Christmas, affirms Openheart's holiday commitment to his slaves. Once again, the fiscally imprudent but consistently self-sacrificing master distributes gifts to his plantation's
slaves. This time he gives them their presents on December 24, *a day
prematurely,* since a sheriff appears to seize those bondpeople purchased
three years earlier; they had been acquired on credit, and Openheart—
because of crop mishaps and excessive generosity to family, friends,
and neighbors—must immediately forfeit them because he missed the
deadline to cover his debt. The colonel unselfishly insists that he nonetheless must distribute gifts to all his workers, even though within minutes he will no longer possess many of those receiving them. That the
story's final plot twist allows a contrived and predictable merry Christmas ending for slaves and master alike, including the ones the sheriff
has just seized, is immaterial. Simms has grafted master gifting onto a
tale loaded with pathos that he probably assumed would soften negative images northern readers might have harbored of the instincts and
integrity of southern slaveholders.[59]

Nothing makes the case better for Christmas gifting practices as an
element in southern masters' self-indoctrination than the diary of one
southern woman in the wake of John Brown's raid in 1859. Obviously
feeling insecure in the aftermath of a Yankee invasion of southern
terrain that from subsequent revelations appeared intended to ignite
slave rebellions throughout the South, she took great solace in what
might be called Christmas normality on her place over the holiday.
The day after Christmas, she reflected,

> We had a very happy Christmas; just as good as if John Brown
> had never stirred up so much that was terrible. The scene on the
> back porch was just as merry [as usual]; the presents were joy-
> fully received, the drinks as eagerly quaffed and the good wishes,
> which, with the negroes, correspond to toasts, were as heartily
> spoken. I do not believe it will be easy to turn our black folks
> against us though no doubt the abolitionists will keep trying.

But this champion of slavery was hardly the only antebellum southerner to read abolitionist misspeak into slave appreciativeness over
Christmas. On the eve of the Civil War, Sally Strong Baxter Hampton, a northern young woman who had married into the prominent

Hampton family of South Carolina, informed her father how at Christmas the Hamptons had not only helped market their slaves' corn in Columbia as a way of earning their laborers some $500 but also gave them a hogshead of molasses; a barrel of whiskey; supplies of staples like sugar, coffee, rice, and flour; and oxen for a barbecue. "Alas! Alas! they know not what they do not say," she added, sarcastically mocking what she dismissed as abolitionist ignorance. "How do they dare overturn a mighty nation—this fanatical sect, for the propagation of a doctrine . . . founded on ignorance not in knowledge." Rationales about white southerners' Christmas mores, in other words, provided more ammunition for the entire proslavery defense of the late antebellum period than historians have appreciated.[60]

In the end, of course, trying to deconstruct master Christmas paternalism borders on absurdity, since slaveholders lacked any ethical right to own other human beings in the first place. Once human freedom becomes our controlling perspective, even acts of the most extreme Christmas paternalism become irrelevant, as antislavery publications at the time duly noted. Explaining a Louisiana slave "Christmas frolic" to northern readers, one traveling correspondent remarked facetiously that obviously "millions of free-born Englishmen . . . would jump as high as they are capable of jumping, for the privilege of changing places with them." Similarly arguing the error of taking evidence of slaves' Christmas joy as proof of slavery's beneficence, the *Albany (New York) Evening Journal* labeled slave holiday mirth an "unnatural" and excessive reaction "against the constraint and wretchedness" of yearlong bondage, a fleeting moment of time when slaves triumphed over rather than adapted to their own debasement.[61]

Considered from that perspective, the recollection of ex-slave Louis Cain is most illuminating. Cain related the story of a slave on his place who had been tracked by dogs after running away from their master and who had been caught. After his apprehension, the unfortunate slave had been compelled to wear a contraption that held a bell over the upper part of his body (obviously for the purpose of alerting his owner to his whereabouts in the future). Cain recalled that his master finally relieved the runaway of the cumbersome apparatus as a "present to him" on Christmas. Probably, Cain's owner considered this relief a gesture of Christmas charity and kindness to his slave, but he was liberating his slave from a burden that no free man would have suffered in the first place. It is telling that at the end of Natalie Delage Sumter's diary passage about the slave Venus's wedding, she reminds herself to "have the horn blown" for her slaves, meaning that she intended to have the plantation horn sound the next morning in order to summon her slaves to their normal labor duties for the day, regardless of how late they stayed up partying. Christmas might give momentary pleasure, but it also pointed to the year's hard labor just ahead.[62]

Christmas gifting by masters claimed legitimacy in historical memory, we must always remember, within the Old South's unethical, manipulative, and often egregiously brutal labor system. From today's perspective, it matters little whether masters bestowed extra food, drink, clothing and some trinkets, marriage rights, or reprieves on slaves at Christmas or visited the slave quarters. The gift slaves most craved—the freedom to make their own decisions all year long—was always withheld. Masters conveniently repressed the overlying deceptions of Christmas gifting because it was in their collective self-interest. All that mattered to the South's ruling whites and post–Civil War southern apologists was that most slaves *seemed* happy as they reveled over the holidays. As one agent wrote to the owner of a plantation he was helping to provide for, "Your people are now enjoying the holydays, as I put them in a way to do it."[63] Indeed, from the perspective of the South's master class, that was good enough.

3

Human Trafficking on Jesus's Birthday

In an editorial describing how white townsfolk observed the Christmas season, the *Macon (Georgia) Telegraph* mused also about the holiday's meaning for slaves, telling its readers that to "know what pleasure is" they should observe the South's black laborers during the holiday when they dressed up in Christmas suits and could be seen sweating "under a load of finery, their plump cheeks and laughing eyes speaking the joy and satisfaction of their hearts." As repulsive as this racial caricature strikes us today for its ridiculous stereotyping, it arguably was less offensive to the historical record than the *Telegraph*'s assertion, in the same paragraph, that at Christmas slaves became free people and lived in a state of "perfect equality" with the "proud [white] republicans" around them. The latter, the *Telegraph* contended, so willingly acknowledged black equality at that time of the year that they laid aside their ordinary "airs" of supremacy.[1]

Slaves in Georgia, of course, were so "free" that they were denied the right to read and write according to Georgia law, and had been since colonial Georgia's legislature in 1770 had provided that any whites teaching them either skill could get a fine or stint in the county jail, or both, for doing it. However, had Georgian slaves been capable of composing and mailing public letters like the ones white southern politicians released in local newspapers, they might well have protested the *Telegraph*'s rosy picture of their lives over the holiday and reminded readers that at all times, even Christmas, they remained their masters' property to be disposed of as their masters wished. No matter the strong personal feelings slaveholders sometimes developed for their black field hands and house servants, they regarded their slaves as property subject to their whims and financial requirements, a tendency borne out by the Maryland farmer whose account book entry for his "Capital" as of New Year's Day 1854 listed twenty-one slaves worth $9,925, immediately followed by four horses and two mules worth $500 combined and then cattle, hogs, and sheep.[2]

Unfortunately, with all the attention given by memoirists and popular writers to elaborate Christmas partying on antebellum southern plantations, it has been easy to overlook how much southern business activity persisted over Christmas, and the implications of this activity for slaves. Throughout the holiday season, many white southerners, instead of dropping everything for Christmas celebrations, spent at least some of their hours negotiating land deals, making decisions about their crops, and conducting other commercial transactions. On December 24, 1831, for example, Mississippi planter John Nevitt visited Natchez, Mississippi, where, according to his diary, he "did nothing but paid my taxes." The minutes of the board of directors of the Citizens Bank of Louisiana in New Orleans reveal that they held regularly scheduled meetings on December 24 or 26, though meetings that would normally have fallen on Christmas Day were changed to other dates. John McDonough, who resided on a plantation near New Orleans, received letters dated December 24 and 25 from associates writing him about the marketing of hogsheads of sugar and various legal executions. When Louisianan Bennet Barrow mentioned in his December 25, 1842, diary entry that he was "making application to get a Loan out of the Union Bank" because of a decline in cotton prices, one gets the impression that he might have been doing legal paperwork that day. Finances occupied his mind.[3]

The Louisiana Supreme Court ruled in an 1844 decision that it was legal to serve judicial process on Christmas, and throughout the season courts were open in much of the South, undoubtedly to the consternation of some officials who would have rather spent the holiday celebrating the season with loved ones and friends. As Christmas approached in 1811, future U.S. president John Tyler, then a U.S. district court judge in his home state of Virginia, lamented to President James Madison that it would be better if the court in Norfolk held its sessions in May and November instead of June and December, allowing its judge to remain at home over Christmas, "a time which most old-fashioned people prefer to be with their families." On Christmas Day in 1837, John Cocke went off "early to court," according to the diary of his wife, Louisa. In Texas, an Austin newspaper observed bemusedly how lawyers there only got a "one day's respite from the Courts" for the Christmas holiday season.[4]

Importantly, many southern Christmas transactions in one way or another concerned slave property. When a reporter for a Chicago newspaper arrived in the Mississippi River port of Memphis, Tennessee, over the holiday in 1852, he observed the connection, without fully articulating it:

> We landed at this place Christmas morning. The first thing that met my eye, standing on a high bank, facing the river, was the following inscription in large letters upon a fine building, with piazza and pillars in front, "Bolton, Dickens & Co., slave dealers." This was the first thing of the kind which had ever met my eye, and it quick found way to my heart.

Unfortunately, the reporter failed to note whether any activity was occurring at the building that Christmas, since far more inheriting, buying, renting, and simply moving slaves about transpired during holiday seasons in the antebellum South than the common narrative suggests.[5]

Evidence of Christmastime commerce in slaves appears in diverse documents, including the court records of the Old South. In Amite County, Mississippi, in 1856, for example, a committee assigned by a probate court to determine the value of a couple's hired-out slaves submitted its accounting on the day following Christmas, determining that the thirteen slaves at issue rented out for a total of $1,370 for the year. And the 1844 Louisiana Supreme Court case mentioned above involved a shipmaster's appeal of a lower court decision that fined him $13,330 for taking slaves on a voyage from Mississippi to Galveston, Texas, to avoid their being seized from their owner for an overdue debt. Significantly, the case partially hinged on the shipmaster's assertion that the slaves had been immune from any legal process because he had boarded them on Christmas, which in Louisiana was "not a judicial day." In Maryland, where, under 1858 state legislation, free blacks could be themselves forced into bondage as punishment for helping bondpeople escape, several such abettors were auctioned into unfree labor on Christmas Day 1860 at the Frederick city jail.[6]

Similarly attesting to slave conveyances at Christmas are the papers of slaveholders and southern businesses. One Martha A. M. Lide, for example, provided a receipt dated December 28, 1851, acknowledging that she had received from the executors of John Blount Miller's estate the "negro boy named Elias" bequeathed to her in Miller's will. Even more revealing are the minutes for the December 23, 1851, meeting of the board of the Citizens Bank of Louisiana. Much of the day's business revolved around the status of a sixteen-year-old slave named Auguste, who had been pledged to the bank as security on an $1,100 mortgage loan. The borrower wanted the bank to substitute a twenty-year-old slave—who also went by the name of Auguste—as security on the loan, a request approved by the bank's directors.[7]

Transactions in slaves need factoring into any rendering of Christmas in the Old South, given that domestic sales and transfers of human property, especially those disrupting African American families, were arguably the most insidious aspect of the peculiar institution other than the deprivation of freedom itself. Such was the case especially in the Upper South, where in Appalachian southwestern Virginia Christmas-week sales were so commonplace that slaves there sang a hymn called "Mass's Gwyne Sell Us Termorrer." Ex–Maryland slave John Thompson, in his autobiographical narrative published in 1856, still had clear remembrances of a Christmas week over thirty years earlier, because that was when his family passed through a miserable period bereft of the "usual gladness and joy" of the season; their mistress had just died, her estate had been divided up, and they had learned that their new master drove his slaves brutally and frequently sold them off. Instead of reveling in the season, the unhappy slaves convened secret prayer meetings, taking advantage that Christmas week was a time when slave patrols refrained from molesting such assemblies, and implored God for aid in persisting in their new situations.[8]

Memories of moments such as these remained profoundly disturbing for African American survivors of slavery after the peculiar institution itself was no more. When just after the Civil War a northern woman wrote about her experiences teaching former slaves in Richmond, Virginia, the first specific thing she said about her pupils, after a general nod to their dignity, was that they waxed "pathetically" about "the anxiety and terror that they used to suffer at Christmastime, which was the season of hiring and selling servants." Echoing her remark, ex–North Carolina slave Samuel Hall, in recollections published just before World War I, remembered that people who concluded slaves were happy at Christmas "didn't realize what the burdens of the race were" at the time. Hall remembered the interval between Christmas and New Year's as the time when many slaves "would be sold and going with their blankets and bundles on their backs and heads," inwardly anxious about their new situations and possibly incurring heavier labor tasks than previously. Rather than remembering holiday seasons fondly, in other words, some onetime slaves recalled them as occasions for separation from spouses and children alike, without their masters even providing the courtesy of informing them of the destinations of sold-off family members.[9]

Unsurprisingly, some slaves ran away at Christmas for the precise reason that such sales were pending. Harriet Tubman initiated one of her most famous "Underground Railroad" raids from the North at Christmastime in 1854 because she had learned that her three brothers still enslaved in Maryland would be sold off to the Deep South in a sale initially scheduled for Christmas Day and then deferred to the 26th because Christmas fell on a Sunday. She quickly arranged to travel there and for her brothers to rendezvous with her at their parents' cabin north of Dorchester, Maryland, on Christmas Eve. On Christmas night, she guided them in a party numbering six escapees in all out of bondage to the home of a Quaker accomplice in Wilmington, Delaware, and from there (after her party had grown to nine fugitives) to the Anti-Slavery Office of the African American activist William Still in Philadelphia, where, following name changes, they were sent to points even farther away from owners and the slave catchers they employed to recover escapees.[10]

Unfortunately, the mythology of southern plantation Christmases, by highlighting an orgy of slave gluttony and master partying, obscures alternative and highly materialistic white holiday activity that often had horrific implications. To compose a truly comprehensive portrait of antebellum southern Christmases, we need to consider slave traders' auctions and bills of sale, because the holiday brought no surcease for human transactions in the region. And we need to recognize that the Christmastime sales not only doomed the South's current slave population but also its black people for generations to come. Since enslavement became the default condition of virtually all children born of slave mothers in the antebellum South barring special arrangements in masters' wills or other legal documents, purchasers of human property had an unwritten automatic right to the offspring of women they acquired. Occasionally, though, slave bills of sale spelled out the point. Consider the sale document, for instance, that included not only the three females Ann, Ellen, and Marthy but also "their increase forever hereafter" (along with two males) all for the apparent bargain price of $1,800. The document left nothing to chance. Any babies born to Ann, Ellen, and Marthy would be en-slaved for their lifetimes.[11]

Many slave owners' Christmas season letters and diaries expose the continuance of the slave body trade over the holiday, sometimes on Christmas Day itself, or sometimes simply their temptation to engage in it. On Christmas Day 1810, Louisianan William Wikoff sent a let-ter to his son Daniel, then at a boarding school, suggesting the latter. William had just returned from an acquaintance's plantation where the year's crop yield had been so poor that all his "Negroes" had been sold, some of them at very high prices. One "wench" had been priced at $950, and her four children had themselves brought in $1,700. Giv-ing his son a tutorial in commercial transactions, Wikoff explained that the slaves had been purchased on credit, with the balance due in three installments, and also noted the due dates and explained that the seller had been given a mortgage and security for the interim. Reporting matter-of-factly that he himself refrained from purchasing any of the available slaves, Wikoff urged his son to apply himself to his schoolwork.[12]

Perhaps no documents more de-romanticize Old South Christ-mases than slaveholder correspondence and ruminations discussing slave sales around the holiday, as much for their mundane detail as for their monetization of slave property. Thus South Carolina attorney and public official James Louis Petigru sent Christmas season letters in 1858 to South Carolina governor Robert F. W. Allston and Allston's wife, Adele, about the handling of James's widowed sister Mary Ann's slaves and her plantation to the Allstons, correspondence showing that even when owners' motives were benign, they were still making de-cisions about the disposition of slave bodies without the consent of the beings involved. Petigru alerted the governor that his sister was expressing concern that the slaves seemed earmarked for Allston's son Ben rather than the governor himself, since she had promised them she would find them a "good Master" on giving them up. Petigru refrained from any criticism of Ben per se. The important thing is that his letter indirectly shows how dependent slaves were on their masters' goodwill when transacting in their bodies. In a similarly revealing case during Christmas season 1846, the husband of U.S. president James K. Polk's sister Jane, on behalf of the president's mother, overpaid to buy a slave named Dolly and her children, in order to prevent the breaking up of a slave family (Dolly's mother was owned by the president's mother). The point here is less that the president's brother-in-law humanely intervened to keep a slave family intact, than that these purchased slaves would have been marketed to persons "out of the family" over Christmas had he *not* intervened.[13]

The sheer volume of such correspondence exposes the commercialization of antebellum southern Christmases in ways that are not generally understood. "A few days after Christmas, I by a letter informed you of a Sale I had made to your mother, of all my Negroes in Louisiana," wrote one slaveholder to another. "At present I am making an effort to sell out everything, namely mill, land, Negroes and patent right," the low-country Georgia planter James Hamilton Couper confided to his wife while he was on a visit to an unprofitable cottonseed crushing mill that he owned in Natchez, Mississippi, noting later in the same letter how the noise of guns firing reminded him "that it is Christmas Eve." A Georgia plantation mistress wrote her absent husband one December 27 that it was unfortunate that the sale of "70 negroes" would not fully cover the debts he had rung up, so that they could give up planting and slave owning entirely. Revealingly, she reflected that plantations were no place to raise young white boys, who became "*teranical*" as a result, surely suggesting either that her own teen-age sons became bossy from telling slaves what to do or that they learned to be authoritarian from observing masters and overseers control slaves. Not long before the Civil War, another Georgia slave owner penned a holiday season letter inquiring how much money his slave Preston might bring if sold rather than rented out; and on December 25, 1860—months before the Civil War—a southern woman spelled out for her son the financial deal she had sealed in selling her slave woman with her two children ($1,000 down; the $1,000 balance in notes bearing 10 percent interest and due in a year) but chided him for deciding to put up for purchase a slave woman who still had a lot of child-bearing potential.[14]

Other slave owners were in the buying rather than the selling mood at holiday time, as the South Carolinian planter–state legislator Robert J. Gage revealed by cynically exclaiming on Christmas Day 1836, when cotton prices were showing signs of recovery from a recent depression, that people would sell almost anything, even their wives, if the sale price would "bring enough to buy a negro." Mississippi cotton planter William Ethelbert Ervin bought slaves during the holiday, noting laconically in a poorly spelled diary entry for December 23, 1846, "Went to Greelie's Sale. Bough a Negroe Girle & child." Three days after Christmas in 1856, the prominent South Carolina planter-politician James Henry Hammond informed his eldest son, Harry, that he had been involved as an agent in bidding "the other day" for a cash purchase of three slaves ranging from twenty-one to twenty-five years in age, at prices, respectively, of $1,275, $1,165, and $1,060.[15]

Christmas transactions in slave bodies could even entail returns of flawed merchandise. The Tippah County, Mississippi, planter Francis Terry Leak received a letter from the recent purchaser of his slave woman Livy that Livy was suffering from an "old disease," that she might never be "sound again," and that the buyer submitted the problem for Leak's "consideration," meaning that he expected some compensation for not getting the quality of slave he thought he had purchased. Leak offered, in response, either to take Livy back or reduce the price for her. On New Year's Day, Leak noted in his diary that the buyer preferred returning Livy since she seemed to have cancer of the mouth, though she was worth $400 to another potential buyer if she recovered.[16]

To be fair, the Christmas season dispositions of slave bodies were not always tragic for slaves or detrimental to their well-being. Many hired slaves had permission from masters to strike their next yearly rental agreements over the holiday season, and comparative shopping for temporary masters, as we might term it today, certainly was preferable to being at the mercy of their masters' preferences. From Lexington, Kentucky, in 1852, a correspondent of the *Philadelphia Presbyterian* took note of a virtual "negro migration" into town at Christmas, as "hirelings," carrying bundles of clothing, filled the city streets and gave mirthful Christmas greetings to each other during their week of "immunity" from labor. In Richmond, Virginia, it was customary for country slaves to flock to the city in their best clothes, hoping to entice the most promising employer they could identify into taking them on. Furthermore, southern masters occasionally conducted Christmas slave sale transactions for nonmercenary ends. For instance, on Christmas Eve day in 1847, the Virginian Thomas W. McCue hoped to buy the slave Tom from his owner at a "fair price" to unite Tom with his family, claiming that his sole purpose was to do a good deed since he lacked any desire to "increase my family of negroes." It is certainly possible that McCue was trying to drive down Tom's purchase price by claiming financial disinterest in his purchase offer. Still, the overwhelming number of Christmas slave sale documents lacked even the pretension of humanitarian intent. None of the four slaves South Carolina's future secession governor Francis W. Pickens bought at Christmas in 1846, for example, were related. The profit motive drove the typical Christmas slave sale.[17]

Reading the Christmastime papers of slave traders like A. J. McElveen dispels all illusions that Christmas slave transactions were anything but mercenary. Two days before Christmas in 1854, McElveen, acting as the agent of the Charleston and Sumterville, South Carolina, slave trader Ziba B. Oakes, told Oakes it was difficult to do slave trading at Christmas, but he hoped the business climate would improve around New Year's Day. Still he mentioned purchasing two boys of about eleven or twelve years of age for $1,000 (with payment due New Year's Day) and added that he expected to make a profit on them since they were "prime fellows" (meaning they would be "prime" hands able to do a man's daily work in the fields and were thus valuable). He anticipated buying others over the next week and selling several on January 1. In the interim, he needed Oakes to advance $1,000 to him for the boys and another $500 for a girl he had purchased, to carry him over until he could sell them. Six days later, McElveen again wrote, informing Oakes he had "bought 5 negros all Single" and needed an advance from the bank to complete the transactions. On December 30, McElveen alerted Oakes that he had looked at "3 fellows" in their twenties whose asking price was $1,050 apiece that day and had offered $950 each for them, mentioning that they were "pretty likely" active types with good teeth, though one of them was "rather low." His correspondence not only demonstrates the mercenary intent driving slave sales but also makes one wonder whether such men observed Christmas at all. McElveen was hardly unique in conducting business over Christmas week. At the holiday season in 1834, a slave trader who had just taken forty-nine slaves purchased from Virginia farms on a two-month trek to the Natchez District in Mississippi suddenly gave them shirts, hats, sewing materials, and whiskey not out of a Christmas spirit but in order to improve the slaves' spirits and appearance so they would seem more appealing to potential buyers. On Christmas Eve in 1859, a Savannah, Georgia, trader revealed that he had been "full of Business," spending "all day until late at night" in his office.[18]

Southern newspaper publishers felt no scruples about alluding to Christmas slave sales. As the Civil War erupted in the spring of 1861, a Richmond newspaper posted an advertisement for a diffident, "gingerbread"-colored slave named Nancy who had escaped in March, implying that her running away might be related to her being "sold last Christmas" during an estate sale. Nor did southern newspapers pause in running ads for slave sales during Christmas week itself. On a single page of the December 22, 1836, *Vicksburg (Mississippi) Register,* readers discovered six different advertisements that included allusions to slaves for sale. One could buy, for instance, a plantation with "Eighty-nine negroes, most of them workers," along with oxen, hogs, horses, tools, and fodder, from a landowner in Yazoo County. A different notice had William B. Cook offering up his whole plantation on the Mississippi River at Deer Creek, announcing his willingness, if required to seal the deal, to include his "valuable negroes" and livestock along with the place itself. One could even purchase slaves from far away. A landholder in the process of breaking up his plantation in Virginia advertised his holdings of "about eighty" slaves for sale. Letting hyperbole run amok, this seller trumpeted that the "two blacksmiths, two good carpenters, and several valuable house servants" included in the offer made his "negroes" as valuable as those of "any one plantation" anywhere.[19]

At the diagonally opposite end of the Old South to Vicksburg, one could read similar invitations to purchase slaves if one were so inclined. The *Richmond Enquirer*'s interior and back pages for Christmas Day 1854 held plenty of newsprint about opportunities for slave buys. Page three contained announcements of five upcoming sales of slaves by auctioneers and court commissioners, including an executor's sale. Two additional advertisements took up much of a column of the paper's fourth and final page, one of them a strangely worded notice of an executor's sale of "Men, Women, Boys and Girls, besides House and Field Hands," leading one to wonder whether house servants and field hands lacked gender! The same ad, though, was explicit about the skills of those listed, noting that two boys who had been apprenticing respectively to a carpenter and a brick mason for over three years were included.[20]

Of course, not all the Christmas transactions in slave bodies were sales. Although some masters, as noted above, allowed their surplus slaves to hire themselves out around Christmas for the coming years, other masters entirely controlled the rental process, often to the dismay of their laborers. As noted earlier, the antebellum South developed networks of slave hiring, by which masters with extra laborers rented to persons or companies, like factories and railroads short of workers, one or more of their slaves for stipulated periods, often a year. Some hiring contracts bore the date December 25; more commonly, slave hires commenced on January 1. Ironically, even slave-owning churches in the South hired out slaves on Christmas, sometimes separating parents from their children in the process. In 1843, the trustees of the Briery Presbyterian Church of Prince Edward County, Virginia, separated the married slave couple of Vilet and Frank from their nine-year-old son, Spencer, on Christmas Day, hiring the latter out for a year at $4 to its minister, the Reverend Samuel D. Stuart.[21]

In some southern communities, such transactions were consummated at New Year's Day hiring auctions, with horrific implications for the slaves' self-esteem. One former Kentucky slave, though never hired out himself, long after the Civil War could still recall how gangs of slaves chained together had passed his master's house to the hiring grounds, and how on one occasion a chained slave angry over being separated from his wife took his revenge by unlocking his handcuffs and those of some of the other slaves in his coffle, allowing them to kill several of the slave traders conveying them, before he and his comrades were subdued and eventually hanged. On such hiring days, slaves had little if any say about whom they would work for over the next year. Their new employer might have a reputation for cruelty or be of unknown and potentially nasty temperament. A hired-out Tennessee slave named Kelly later recalled Christmas as an "awful" time because on hiring day "red headed yaps would bid us off to the highest bidder and we couldn't do nothin' but pray." Former slave Harriet Jacobs conveyed the terror of New Year's for many hired slaves with a particularly chilling passage in her remembrance. She recalled that slaves hired out on southern farms generally got a four- or five-day Christmas break from labor, but they particularly dreaded dawn on New Year's Day when, at an appointed hour, slave men, women, and children alike gathered on the grounds to "hear their doom pronounced" for the coming year. "The slave is sure to know who is the most humane, or cruel master, within forty miles of him," Jacobs elaborated.[22]

The peculiar juxtaposition of conveyances of human property amid celebrations of Jesus's birth appalled an antislavery-inclined Hampden-Sydney College (Virginia) student, who later complained in a New York abolitionist publication about the incongruity of his college church being in the Christmas "jobbing-slavery" business. Each year, on the very day slaves celebrated "the birth of our blessed Saviour," he recalled, his church had hired out the slaves it owned to raise funds to support its pastor's annual salary. Nor did the jarring relationship of Christmas and slave sales escape the attention of Ohioan Joseph Brady, who moved to Lexington, Kentucky, in the mid-1850s.

Brady sent a letter highlighting the incongruity of slave transactions on Christmas to the *Cincinnati Gazette* and so infuriated local whites he was run out of Kentucky for fear of his life. In his Christmas 1855 letter, Brady explained how the "great day" had arrived in town with schoolchildren getting the day off from studies and local slaves enjoying their time off from labor. However, he had just attended Christmas services at the local Episcopal church and had a very disturbing experience. Although the minister had sermonized about the "holy life and victorious death" of "our Saviour," emphasizing prophecies about Jesus, Brady's satisfaction from the services was immediately marred by what happened afterward. Churchgoers had barely walked two blocks upon exiting the building when they saw a mob of men on the sidewalk obstructing women from continuing on their way and forcing pedestrians to cross the street if they wished to keep going. Curious about the throng, Brady drew near; he soon heard "the hoarse notes" of a slave auctioneer offering his wares to the highest bidder. Expressing his surprise at the bizarre confluence of slave sales on Christmas Day, Brady vented his outrage:

> Never were my feelings so much shocked, though I had before witnessed the horrid spectacle of the sale of a human being, yet upon this day, commemorative of such an event as can never be known again on earth—the birth of the immaculate and only Son of God—and after such a discourse . . . to witness a deed, so revolting . . . and so contradictory to every precept of Him for whom the day has been named, it was really shocking beyond description; and to hear the auctioneer crying, with stentorian voice, "only 1,285 is bid for this boy" "a fine, likely *'nigger'* going for $1,285," "must be sold to the *highest bidder*." It disgusted and shocked me beyond measure.

Brady reiterated his horror of a cruel scene transpiring "almost at the door" of a church and mused about the minister's implied complicity in the scene. He felt the event occurred so close to the house of worship that the minister must have known what was happening even as he sermonized about Lexington as a fine community.[23]

Slaves left their own accounts further illuminating, sometimes inadvertently, Christmastime transactions in their bodies. The Virginia native Louis Hughes related how he had been purchased in Richmond by a Pontotoc, Mississippi, cotton planter in November 1844 and then marched on foot with scores of other purchased slaves on a long journey, first to Atlanta, where some were sold, and then to the Pontotoc place, arriving Christmas Eve. "Boss took me into the house and into the sitting room, where all the family were assembled, and presented me as a Christmas gift to the madam, his wife," Hughes recalled, making a more opaque allusion to the symbiotic connection between southern Christmases and the domestic slave trade than Brady's.[24]

Hughes's experience of being given as a human Christmas present was not unique when it came to the holiday practices within slaveholding family circles in the Old South. Other African American survivors of the peculiar institution alluded to this custom, which reinforced the message to slaves that, even when no monetary exchanges were involved, they remained investment property to be disposed of at the will of their owners. Indeed, one ex-slave who happened to have been born on Christmas Day noted years later that his owner had marked his December 25 birth in a family Bible as having "increased my personal property one thousand dollars." Well after the Civil War, a ninety-year-old former slave known as "Aunt Marthy," laboring as a house servant in eastern Texas, told a Christmastime visitor that she had once been owned by the family she now lived with and had *twice* been exchanged as an in-the-family Christmas present:

> "Ise b'longed to dis fam'ly a long time," said she. "I nussed Master Jim here when he was a baby. . . . His gran'paw owned me in South Carliny when I wuz a chile. When Marster Jim's paw growed up and got married ole marster gin me to him for a christmus gif. . . . After Marse Tom was married he went to his paw one christmus and tole him dat he wanted to gin me to him, and old marster did it."

And decades after this story appeared, another onetime Kentucky slave told an interviewer that when she was only five years old, her newly married master had separated her from her mother "on Christmas" so that she could serve the newlyweds as a maid.[25]

Similar recollections lingered in the family oral traditions of Robert Russa Moton, a leading black educator in the early twentieth century and Booker T. Washington's successor as head of the Tuskegee Institute. In the autobiography he published a few years after becoming Tuskegee's principal, Moton mentioned that his father spoke often of his experiences as an enslaved child in Prince Edward County, Virginia, and that he recollected his father being conferred "as a Christmas present" after his master died, causing the division of his estate. Once in possession of Moton's father, the new owner had handed him over as a holiday gift to his wife.[26]

Slave trafficking at Christmas, of course, gave the lie to absurdities like the *Macon Telegraph*'s quip that the advent of Christmas made slaves as free as whites, but that hardly stopped one of Dixie's stalwarts from teasingly and absurdly suggesting that transactions in slaves made masters *less* free than their human chattels when the holiday rolled around. In a speech in January 1861 that he gave to Alabama's secession convention two weeks after its vote for disunion, delegate William R. Smith of Tuscaloosa contrasted slaves enjoying their leisure over the holiday with their unfortunate masters mired in Christmas monetary dealings. While slaves were "free from debt" and looked ahead to truly enjoying Christmas as a time for leisure activity, their owners sadly experienced the end of the year "as the maturity time" for bills due.[27]

Smith did not specifically cite slave sales, purchases, and rentals among such master holiday obligations, but his audience almost certainly would have made that connection since many of them were slaveholders who presumably engaged in such holiday activities. It was virtually impossible, after all, for any white southern slaveholder, even at Christmas, to entirely forget that his or her slaves were, indeed, slaves, regardless of what he or she might say publicly about how enslaved people enjoyed virtual freedom during the holiday. It is instructive, in this regard, that Robert E. Lee justified the very principle of slave ownership on December 27, 1856, right in the middle of the Christmas season, despite being obviously conflicted about the institution. From his army post at Brownsville, Texas, Lee shared his feelings by letter with his wife back at Arlington in Virginia about rising sectionalism in his country. Lee admitted, in this letter, that slavery amounted to a "moral & political evil" anywhere it existed, but he further reasoned that abolitionists were making things worse by attacking an institution that had taken black people from Africa and benefited them "morally, socially & physically." As a race, blacks required the "painful discipline" of slavery in preparation for freedom, he believed. What abolitionists needed to do, with this in mind, was simply to let slavery die its own natural death, instead of enraging southern masters and increasing sectional tensions in their country. Unfortunately for his historical reputation, Lee elaborated on just how long he expected that process to take, saying that "Merciful Providence" knew best about such things and implying it might require multiple millennia before slavery disappeared. God's "influence," he explained, was "slow" but "sure," and Christianity itself had "required nearly two thousand years, to Convert but a small part of the human race." Abolitionists, therefore, should passively accept that, for God, "two thousand years are but as a Single day." Patience was the order of the day, in Lee's mind that Christmas, not only for abolitionists but also for many future generations of slaves.[28]

No single source better makes the point about the Christmastime commercialization of slave bodies than a revelatory diary entry by a very young north Florida girl, whose early home education included the lesson that she already *owned* slave bodies. Susan Bradford Eppes grew up at her physician father's Pine Hill plantation in Leon County, a place she described as set among green forests and rolling hills, where Guernsey cows chewed their cuds, Kentucky horses grazed the pastures, and benevolent white people referred to their slaves as "my people" and "Quarter folks" from sensitivity that their "dusky people" disliked being called "niggers." Eppes began keeping a diary in March 1854 when she was eight years old, and on December 22 that year she recorded a holiday incident that should give pause to anyone believing mythologies about the joys of slave Christmases. According to Eppes, just that day her family servant "Aunt Dinah" had given her a baby named Lavinia as a "Christmas present," and had offered to take care of the baby for her. Initially on reading this, one might wonder if Dinah has gifted this white southern girl with some kind of a handmade doll that she was willing to store for her, especially since Dinah claimed to have gotten the baby from rabbits and because Eppes's mother said her daughter could keep the baby's outfits in a trunk in her dollhouse and take them out whenever she wanted to play with the baby or—with her mother—bathe it.

Yet why would Eppes need her mother's help with bathing a doll, and why does Eppes casually mention how "of course" Dinah "wanted" the baby "for herself"? Did this adult slave play with dolls? Our chilling answer comes immediately. Noting that Lavinia was "too little and soft to play with," Eppes queries her mother whether the baby is truly hers, like Frances already was. Eppes mother responds by saying, "She is yours, and so are Dinah and Henry and all their children except Nellie and Bethiah, that is, they will be yours some day, they are left to you, in your father's will"! Eppes confesses that she does not exactly know what her mother meant and that she had no chance to get an explanation because their company arrived at that moment and interrupted their conversation. But inadvertently, this girl shatters southern paternalism's veneer. Even for the children of southern slaveholders, Christmas evoked the ownership of African American bodies.[29]

In fact, one daughter of a Virginia slaveholding family, LaSalle Corbell Pickett, learned the same exact lesson from a Christmas tree, if we can trust her later memoir. Her present one holiday was a six-week-old black baby boy, tucked away in a cotton nest lodged in the tree for her, accompanied by "a deed which made him mine." As the baby, Kriss, was extracted from the nest, she was informed by her mammy that the boy one day would be her coachman, and she was allowed to hold him a while on her lap as she sat safely on the floor. Then the boy was scooped up and taken off to the quarters to grow up.[30] Even if Pickett made up the story, it is a telling reminder of what slave Christmases were really about.

4

Gaming the System

In his account of growing up on an antebellum North Carolina plantation, the memoirist James Battle Avirett couched his Christmas morning recollections in the present tense, introducing his readers to the first moments of Christmas Day as dawn broke. By describing a commotion in his mansion house during the early morning hours, Avirett sets his scene aurally more than visually. Daybreak brings loud banging, the sound of merry slave voices from the plantation quarter where the field hands live, and a ruckus in the mansion itself. His siblings are yelling out "Merry Christmas, father!" "Merry Christmas, mother!" Soon, the family's domestics exuberantly join in the noisemaking. "Handy, Buck, Eliza and all the other house servants" shout out to their owners, "Christmas gift, ole Marster; Christmas gift, Ole Mistiss."[1]

Avirett's benign vignette about house slaves soliciting masters for gifts on Christmas morning echoed a recurrent leitmotif in many of the memoirs churned out by southern whites during the late nineteenth century and into the next one, part of an effort playing out at both conscious and subconscious levels to rationalize southerners having held slaves before the Civil War. It is striking how many southern memoirists played on such scenes, not only in full-length books but also in shorter accounts of slave times.

Louise-Clark Pyrnelle was such a memoirist. She grew up on an Alabama plantation and authored a quasi-autobiographical but fictional plantation memoir published in 1882 that was set on a Mississippi cotton plantation. Wistfully recalling when "dear old 'Mammies' and 'Aunties'" governed plantation nurseries and "good old 'Uncles'" supervised plantation workshops, Pyrnelle described a rainy and cold Yuletide morning in 1853 as a prototypical antebellum southern Christmas. In the second paragraph of an entire chapter devoted to the plantation Christmas, she explained how on Christmas morning just after the white children in the house tiptoed into every room calling out "Chris-mus gif'," the slave children Chris and Riar likewise "called out, 'Chris'mus gif'!' and laughed and danced to think they had 'cotch de white chil'en.'" Another memoirist following similar themes was the author of a *Galveston (Texas) Daily News* column entitled "Marse Tom's Chrismus Gif'." He recounted visiting an old friend in eastern Texas several years previously and encountering identical black verbal demands when at the sound of a breakfast bell he stepped out from his room on Christmas morning. Immediately he confronted "Old Aunt Marthy" who, lying in wait, importuned "chrismus gif', Marster Gawge [George]." Likewise, Felix G. de Fontaine, a former *New York Herald* journalist who turned Rebel at the beginning of the Civil War and covered the fighting in Virginia for the *Charleston Courier,* in "A Plantation Xmas" recalled how before "the faintest streak of dawn" appeared on Christmas morning on southern plantations before the war, slaves purposely made noise to arouse the white folk in the "big house" so that they could "catch them with . . . 'Chrismus gif', massa; Chrismus gif', missus.'"[2]

Other accounts in this vein include those of Susan Dabney Smedes and Joel Chandler Harris. Smedes, in her testimonial to life on the Burleigh plantation in Mississippi, recalled slaves bolting from behind doors and springing from "unexpected corners" on Christmas morning with their "Christmas giff! Christmas giff!" refrain. Harris's recollections about the Georgia plantation where he resided during the Civil War depicted its "dusky crowd" of "negroes" addressing "marster" twice with "Chris'mas gif'" and then hailing their mistress an additional time with their call.[3]

But no memoir more comprehensively spelled out how Christmas Gif' was enacted on southern plantations from the master class perspective than Elizabeth Pringle's *Chronicles of Chicora Wood,* about life on her father Robert F. W. Allston's South Carolina place on the Pee Dee River. Pringle served up an especially appealing Christmas morning scene:

> Christmas morning very early, "Merry Christmas!" echoing all over the house; all the house-servants stealing in softly to "ketch yu," that is, say the magic words "Merry Christmas!" before you did. Then joyful sounds, "I ketch yu!" and you must produce

your gift, whereupon they bring from the ample bosom or pocket, as the case may be, eggs tied in a handkerchief—two, three, six, perhaps a dozen, according to the worldly position of the donor. Such jolly, gay, laughing visitors, a stream coming all the time. As fast as one party left another came, always making great plans to walk softly so as to catch you, so that dressing was a prolonged and difficult matter, for you must respond and open the door when "Merry Christmas, I ketch yu!" sounded.

Pringle's account is intriguing in part because she gives a reciprocal dimension to Christmas Gif' rituals that is missing from most other memoirs of slave times. That is, slaves in her household apparently gifted whites with modest edibles despite beating them in the game. Pringle also allows her former slaves the proper English pronunciation of "Merry Christmas," rather than claim that they couched the holiday's name in dialect, as in "Chrismus gif'," raising the possibility that when her peer post–Civil War memoirists used dialect forms, they were either consciously or subconsciously trying to portray former slaves as more simple and childlike than they really were as part of their rationale for enslaving them.[4]

Given all this emphasis on Christmas Gif' in southern white memoirs of slave time, it would be wise to scrutinize this antebellum holiday custom more closely, even if there were no black accounts verifying its commonality. But in fact many African American remembrances of slave times confirm the commonality of Christmas Gif' games on the morning of Christmas Day throughout the South. The prominent early twentieth-century black librarian and writer Charlemae Rollins, a native of Yazoo City, Mississippi, remembered the "custom of 'Christmas Gif'" as "part of the holiday celebration" for her family as far back as she could recall, noting that she had learned about it during conversations with her grandmother, who had been a slave. According to her grandmother, Christmas Gif' "was a surprise game played by the slaves on Christmas Day" in which any two persons "meeting for the first time that day, would compete to be the first to call out, 'Christmas Gif'!!," with the loser being compelled to graciously pay the forfeit of a simple gift that might be as trivial as some nuts or a teacake. Similarly, a 103-year-old former slave told a Federal Writer's Project (FWP) interviewer in the 1930s, "Us had a good time Christmas; every slave ketch white folks wid a holler, 'Christmus gift, Marsta' and they holler it to each other." Booker T. Washington's autobiography *Up from*

Slavery, initially published in serialized form in 1900, reported the ubiquity of the practice among southern blacks, even when there were no white people around to hustle. Noting that scores of children begging "Chris'mus gifts" rapped on his doors the very first Christmas he spent as principal of the Tuskegee Institute in Alabama in the 1880s, he indicated that the custom still prevailed throughout that part of the South at the turn of the twentieth century. Other twentieth-century accounts, such as Julia Peterkin's *A Plantation Christmas* (1929), indicate that the custom persisted among African Americans long after Washington published his memoir. Peterkin, married to the owner of the large South Carolina cotton plantation known as Lang Syne and the first Pulitzer Prize–winning southern novelist, explained how servants on the place still stole into the kitchen before the fire was even up on Christmas morning to play this "old game" and "catch" their employers.[5]

Although variants of the Christmas Gif' game involving house servants were not unknown in northern households before the Civil War,[6] the competition came to be associated with Christmas morning servant behavior in the mansions of wealthy southern slaveholders, and it was by any reading of contemporary documents commonplace across the South in antebellum times. In a diary entry for Christmas 1851, for instance, a privileged teenage Georgia girl explained how she had literally been awakened in the morning by the voice of a family servant "calling upon Sister Anna for a 'Christmas Gift.'"[7] The issue, then, is not whether Christmas Gif' was a construction of southern mythology, but rather what we should make out of multiple accounts of supposedly powerless slaves accosting their masters and mistresses early on Christmas morning and beseeching them for presents. Were they begging for gifts or were they demanding them? Whose scripts were they acting out—their own or their masters'?

In an earlier chapter, we saw masters regularly dispensing Christmas presents to field hands and household servants alike. Those distributions were at the discretion of masters and mistresses. Slaves had no role in what was dispensed beyond holding out their hands and accepting the distributions as gracefully as possible, regardless of whether they privately considered their owners generous or stingy. Still, to leave the impression of slave powerlessness over Christmas distorts the reality of the holiday in the Old South. By playing out Christmas Gif', slaves insistently awakened slaveholders from their slumbers and made pressing demands on their owners' families and sometimes other whites on the

"'I COME TO COTCH YOU CHRISTMAS GIF', OLE MARSE'"

Slave besting his master in "Christmas Gif'." *Century Magazine,* December 1911, p. 307. (Purdue University Library)

scene. The difference between begging and demanding is, of course, profound. It matters whether slaves spent their December 25 morning's servilely imploring their owners for handouts or whether they felt empowered at Christmastime and aggressively asserted themselves. The former implies dependency. The latter implies agency.

Most post–Civil War white memoirists gave every indication that Christmas Gif' was tension free and reaffirmed black-white harmony within slaveholding households. Southern sympathizer Felix de Fontaine, for instance, claimed that even after a succession of servants barged into white bed chambers, slaveholders "good naturedly" resigned "themselves to the fusillade of Christmas greetings" from "woolly heads . . . grown gray in faithful service." But postwar memoirists had every motive to conceptualize Christmas Gif' in the softest shadings imaginable, since they clearly intended to mitigate stains of disloyalty attached to the South because of secession and the Civil War. Throughout the late nineteenth century, white southerners struggled to reestablish their legitimacy as patriotic Americans, even as they romanticized the soldiers who had fought a losing battle for Confederate independence. If slaves before the war had been humanely cared for and loved by their masters, and if slaves had reciprocally adored their masters and engaged in playful repartee on Christmas morning, then who could blame white southerners for believing so strongly in their labor system that they would go to war to preserve it? All that happened when slaves and masters lurked in the halls of the big house hurling Christmas Gif' zingers at each other was an endearing display of mutual adoration, "an affectionate throwing off of the reserve and decorum of every-day life" (as Susan Dabney Smedes put it) that posed no threat to slave ownership. Slaves had fully understood, Smedes implied, that because of their master's beneficence, they were being granted temporary license to transgress fixed racial boundaries.[8] They would know their proper place when Christmas ended.

Louise-Clark Pyrnelle gave the game away, so to speak, in the preface to *Diddie, Dumps, and Tot, or Plantation Child-Life* (1882) by saying that although her tale made no pretense of defending slavery and that she was personally unsure whether it was wrong or right ("there are many pros and cons on that subject"), she had grown up "in the heart of the cotton section, surrounded by negroes" from her days of infancy and purposed her book to revealing the "pleasant and happy relations" binding slaves and masters to each other. Besides, she asserted defensively, northern statesmen had helped make slavery "the law of the land" in the first place, suggesting that since Yankees helped draft the U.S. Constitution with clauses (like a provision regarding fugitives) indirectly benefiting slaveholders, they bore as much responsibility for slavery's presence on American soil and whatever wrongs it produced as did southerners. More startling in its deflection of guilt for bondage is the quip on the dedication page in James Battle Avirett's memoir that his parents had been the "real slaves" on the plantation where they had nominally been master and mistress, implying that slave ownership brought heavy burdens far overshadowing whatever monetary gains accompanied it. In a similar spirit, the Confederate "Surgeon-in-Chief to General Stonewall Jackson," one Hunter McGuire, who authored this book's introduction, explained that Avirett intended the "vindication of his people" from the negative impressions people had gotten from reading *Uncle Tom's Cabin.* Southern whites had suffered for years, McGuire contended, because of the emancipation and enfranchisement of "a race inferior both from heredity and servility." Southerners waited understandably, therefore, for a transformation of public opinion "to our side." McGuire ended his introduction with the obligatory nod to the "happy life" of the old plantation where slaves knew that their masters and their children were their best friends and where the hearts of whites and blacks were bonded together in tender affection.[9]

Given the clearly propagandistic tone of post–Civil War white memorials to slave times, we should be skeptical that Christmas Gif' merely reduces to evidence of playful friendships binding slaveholders and the servants who involuntarily nursed their babies, cooked their meals, made their beds, emptied their chamber pots, cleaned their homes, and, in the case of the domestics' children, often played with their own boys and girls. More rationally, Christmas Gif' suggests a ritual reaffirmation of master power within the context of a competitive game stacked to give slaves a superficial victory, a kind of temporary role reversal acceptable within bounds that was not without parallels in class-stratified European rural society.[10] Although theoretically master and slave had an equal opportunity to triumph in their "game-day matchup" of mental alertness and verbal aggressiveness, Christmas Gif's "rules" prescribed slave victory in advance as part of a purposeful inversion of ordinary household routines. With rare exceptions, almost always on Christmas morning before the Civil War, southern household servants accosted and outwitted masters, becoming the undisputed winners of Christmas Gif'. Gifting in such cases passed in one direction only—from master to slave. And this was by design.

Clever masters realized that by giving slaves the illusion of temporary mastery in game-day victory, they defused tensions in the master-slave relationship detrimental to their own households. Slaves, who worked without wages and had no legal right to property, could offer their owners very little in the way of Christmas gifts that masters could not get for themselves, though there are scattered accounts of slaves gifting masters anyway with items like jars of preserves, eggs, and nonperishables. One ex-slave later remembered that male slaves made walking sticks for her master and elderly white men and women on her place at Christmas, and John Quitman's daughter Rose mentioned in her diary one Christmas that a family servant had given her younger sister a pair of dolls' pillows for her doll collection. Elizabeth Pringle's memoir, we might recall, mentioned Christmas gift exchanges with slaves kindheartedly giving their owners eggs after Pringle's family members paid off slaves for winning the Gif' competition, and her account hardly seems fabricated in this regard. Many southern slaves at their owners' sufferance tended small plots of land for gardens and to raise swine, poultry, and crops like corn that they were allowed to market—a practice especially common along the South Atlantic coastline. These number-literate and consumer-savvy slaves often earned hard cash from what they produced, which they generally expended to buy items for themselves and their families at stores on their own plantations or at nearby shops. Such slaves certainly were positioned to acquire gifts for their masters, if so inclined.[11]

Few masters, though, expected or wanted gifts from their slaves. Such gifting would have implied dependency on slaves, the last thing proud slave owners wished to project in a society defined by concepts of white personal honor and black inferiority. Why not let the slaves win big on Christmas morning, giving them the psychological and fleeting triumph of besting their masters, as a kind of safety valve for slave tensions that simmered all year? Why not bestow on these slave victors token prizes worth little or nothing? This was a small price for free household labor from the same servants all year long. As Joseph B. Cobb, a Mississippi planter/politician/editor/author, reflected in his 1851 local color sketches called *Mississippi Scenes,* it was commonly known that few southerners resisted granting "appropriate indulgence to these creatures of our will" upon losing at *"Christmas gift,"* meaning, presumably, that since slaveholders could boss their human property around 364 days a year, they could easily afford concessions the 365th. Samuel Tillman, who it might be remembered spent his days before the Civil War on a Tennessee plantation, recalled later how the game had been designed to allow slave children "to get the call on one of the white children who would be able to be more liberal" in dispensing gifts. William Faulkner, as obsessed with southern tradition, perhaps, as anyone, weighed in too. In *The Sound and the Fury* (1929), his early twentieth-century white character Quentin Compson engages in Christmas Gif' repartee while traveling through Virginia. With his train temporarily stopped, Quentin wakes up from napping to spy a blanket-wrapped "nigger" astride a mule in a rutted road outside his window, waiting for cars to move. Raising the window shade, Quentin hollers "Christmas Gift!" at the figure, and the African American responds, "Sho comin, boss. You done caught me, ain't you?" But though victorious, Quentin pays anyway. Making no effort at all to dun his victim, Quentin digs a quarter from his pocket and flings it toward the man, telling him to buy "some Santy Claus." Even more revealing is the latter's response of "Thanky, young marster," signifying the master-slave power dynamics of this game's uneven playing field.[12]

Still, Christmas Gif' in antebellum times amounted to extortion by slaves since they usually won, and extortion by enslaved people could not have been a universally comfortable experience for slaveholders accustomed to displaying their complete power over their human property. In fact, for that reason playing Christmas Gif' was potentially risky for slaves if they happened to spring the game on a slaveholder in a foul mood. A slave who worked in an Irvine, Kentucky, tanyard learned the danger. He later recalled the Christmas morning when he tried the Christmas Gif' gambit with the usually good-natured brother of his whip-addicted master. Instead of gaining a present, he wound up being thrown in the tan vat of the operation that the brothers co-owned for his brazenness and almost drowned; repeatedly the brother forced him back into the vat when he tried to extricate himself. He only lived to tell about it because he made it to the other side and jumped over the rim before his master got there.[13]

A mildly aggressive element pervaded Christmas Gif' incidents, after all, even if most white southerners laughed it off as good fun. Slaveholders never succeeded totally in masking their unease about blacks making demands on them. "The servants all came in for some little present & pushed in at the door exclaiming Christmas gift," reacted one Gainesville, Alabama, diarist. "They all expect something at this time from every one whom they catch as they term it." The chronicler of southern mores Daniel R. Hundley covered Christmas Gif' thoroughly in *Social Relations in Our Southern States,* reporting in the same spirit that regardless of how tired or disgruntled the visitor to the southern "Great House" might be on Christmas morning, however much the visitor might swear like soldiers, he or she had better cough up some silver coins for entreating youthful blacks shouting "Chrismus Giff, Mas'r!" "Chrismus Giff, Mistis!" or suffer more unrelenting entreating and having their "grinning ivory" teeth "thurst in your face" until the visitor "conformed" to expectations. Certainly the eighteen-year-old Annie Rosalie Quitman does not seem to have been overly pleased when "one of Ethiopia's fairest daughters" not only woke her up on Christmas morning in 1858 but to arouse her from bed did so waving a snake effigy over her head while yelling out "Christmas gift Miss Rose."[14]

None of this is to deny that considerable affection bonded some, perhaps many, slaves, especially household servants, to their masters and their masters' families. Even Abraham Lincoln conceded that there was much truth in southern claims that slaves and masters shared genuine feelings for each other. The problem is assuming that slaves' playful performing of Christmas Gif' merely evidenced appreciation of being owned property.[15]

Even more problematic for mythologies about southern Christmases in slave times is the custom known as John Canoe (spelled variously as "Jonkonnu," "John Kunering," "John Cooner," "John Kuners," and so forth), which the historian Stephen Nissenbaum dubbed "the single most intriguing and aggressive Christmas ritual practiced by American slaves." This moving performance routine took hold especially among blacks living in coastal North Carolina by the early 1820s, though it surfaced in a few other places on the South Atlantic coast. Harriet Jacobs, who was born into slavery in North Carolina and escaped to the North in 1842, recalled in her pseudonymously authored narrative *Incidents in the Life of a Slave Girl,* that participants considered their John Canoe performances so significant that they began practicing songs for the occasion a month beforehand and that slave children always arose early on Christmas morning to see the "Johnkannaus," whom she dubbed the "greatest attraction" of the whole Christmas holiday. John Canoe involved male performers who donned exotic-looking garments and accessories made out of animal skins and rags and marched from place to place as they shouted, played music, clattered bones, hit triangles, and danced and gyrated, sometimes parodying white authority figures like African Coast slave traders, public officials, and slaveholding aristocrats by adding accessories like periwigs, tricorn hats, frock coats, and black top hats to their motley attire. Often, nonperforming slaves, drawn to the processions' commotion, trailed behind.[16]

John Canoe apparently originated in the masks and other costumes and customs of ancestor-worshipping secret societies among the Ibo or Yoruban peoples of West Africa, and probably came to tidewater North Carolina and to a lesser extent southeastern coastal Virginia in the late 1700s via Jamaica and the Bahamas, though slaves imported into North Carolina directly from Africa may have initially brought the custom there. Along North Carolina's coastline and inlets, and particularly in the ports of Wilmington and Camden, slaves working in fishing, loading and unloading ships, and various maritime trades had frequent contact with sailors from oceangoing vessels, providing ample opportunities for cultural transmissions from abroad. Moreover, the North Carolina ports of Wilmington and Edenton especially

"De John Coonahs comin'!" And there they come,
sure enough!

Costumed slaves performing "John Cooner." *Ladies Home Journal,* December 1891, p. 5. (Dartmouth College Library)

had strong trading ties with the Bahamas and Bermuda, where John Canoe traditions flourished.[17]

An early description of John Canoe as practiced in Jamaica came in a published account of a temporary white resident there, one Matthew Lewis. When he arrived at Black River Bay, Jamaica, at the end of a sea voyage on January 1, 1816, he heard on land "the sudden sounds of the drum and banjee," which caused him to gaze on "a procession of the *John-Canoe,*" a band of marchers with a "train of attendants" that he described as being in the act of celebrating the arrival of the New Year. The John Canoe personage of this particular procession carried on his head what Lewis described as a miniature houseboat made from pasteboard that held puppets of sailors, soldiers, and other figures, including plantation slaves at work. As the paraders moved along to the tunes of "negro music" and beneath scarlet-colored banners flapping in the breeze, Lewis judged it a festive success.[18]

Although Lewis described Jamaica's John Canoe as a New Year's event, it was generally timed there to correlate with holiday work stoppages, and in North Carolina it usually occurred in tandem with Christmas. An eyewitness account by a woman living in North Carolina published in William Lloyd Garrison's antislavery *Liberator* helps illuminate what one might experience in encountering John Canooers on parade. According to this woman, she was on her way to church when she heard bells, the banging of tin plates, and horn blowing heralding the approach of a John Cooner procession, headed by a figure who announced: "We bees Jonny Cooner; good master . . . and we drink to Jonny Cooner, Cooner." The *Liberator*'s observer explained that as the procession's leader presented himself, he passed around a hat "for the collection of pence," and then she provided a wonderfully vivid description of John Cooner—who apparently walked on stilts—and his supporting cast:

> John Cooner was represented by a slave in a mask, with a tall, hideous figure, twice the length of a natural man, with patches of every shade and color hanging from him, and bells attached to him to gingle at all his grotesque motions. By some tradition of their own, this represents the Devil. So many variegated rags, covered with mud, and wet with falling rain, I never saw shaken in mid air before.

Then she added that the paraders danced, shrieked, made "uncouth gestures," and even fought as they passed, all marching along shoeless.[19]

Postwar reminiscences by white North Carolinians confirmed the gist of this woman's account, while varying in details depending on time and place. Dr. Edward Warren, who left a post–Civil War account of John Canoe in slave times on the Somerset Place plantation in North Carolina, rendered the happening in even more comprehensive and memorable language than the *Liberator*'s informant. Warren recalled the procession as a Christmas Day affair led by a "ragman" whose costume was so arranged that each rag hung loose and dangled over others. Other elements of the garment were even more startling, including "two great ox horns, attached to the skin of a raccoon, which is drawn over the head and face, leaving apertures only for the eyes and mouth; sandals of the skin of some wild 'varmint'; several cow or sheep bells or strings of dried goats' horns hanging about their shoulders, and so arranged as to jingle at every movement." Warren recalled the leader as carrying a piece of seasoned wood, while the second performer held "a small bowl or tin cup, while . . . half a dozen fellows, each arrayed fantastically in ribbons, rags, and feathers, and bearing between them several so-called musical instruments or 'gumba boxes,'" which were sheepskin-covered drums. Warren's description was similar in many ways to Harriet Jacobs's. She claimed the John-kannaus consisted of plantation slaves mostly of the lower class (almost certainly meaning they were field hands), led by two well-built men dressed in "calico wrappers" with a net with bright stripes on it covering them. The tails of cows, she noted, were attached to the two men's backs, and horns "decorated" their heads. Additionally, she said, other participants beat jawbones, triangles, and a sheepskin-covered object called a "gumbo box."[20]

Yet another postwar memoirist, Rebecca Cameron, the granddaughter of a Cape Fear River rice planter, remembered how the arrival of the "John Coonahs" was always announced at her family's mansion by the sudden arrival mid-morning two days after Christmas of an "ebony herald," just before a "grotesque procession" of exclusively black males arrived from the quarters, all dressed in tattered outfits resembling men, beasts, and birds, though one of the dancers in the group impersonated a skirted female. Following a leader with deer horns on his head and bare arms dangling with bracelets holding metallic rings and bells that jingled, the rest bore crude replications of "animals' heads, with and without horns" or masks from pasteboard, though some just painted themselves or disguised themselves with beards made with Spanish moss or horse hair.[21]

All this sounds harmless and inoffensive enough—on first glance, a colorful regional curiosity. One minister observing frenzied "John Cooners" in Wilmington in 1830 claimed to be near bursting with laughter at their outfits, dances, singing, and begging. But John Canoe resists reduction to exotic street theater. When the distinctively clad dancers of John Canoe purposely inserted African behaviors and cultural survivals into their passing programs, they asserted their own "collective identity" in contrast to that of their onlookers and confronted viewers with the unfamiliar, a transitory cultural process some scholars call "indigenization." Surely white bystanders must have found such unaccustomed appearances and behaviors unnerving, especially since horned headwear symbolized cuckolded husbands in European culture and because marchers had the effrontery to mock onlookers who refused to contribute to their coffers. Canoers, of course, had to resist any temptation to physically assault onlookers who denied their monetary demands; they hardly had the armed power to attack whites in public spaces in North Carolina and get away with it, given that whites

were in the numerical majority there and fully controlled the local police power. But mocking white bystanders as poor or stingy must have
been humiliating, highly irritating, or possibly threatening to onlookers in a culture based on the honor of society's ruling elites.[22]

In this sense, Dr. Warren's remembrance that nonparticipating
blacks, dressed in common "working clothes," followed the procession "as a guard of honor" is instructive, as is his recollection that the
mob had the effrontery to march right up to Somerset Place's front
door, where the performers beat their drums "violently" while the two
lead Canoers put on a dance performance of gyrations, contortions,
flings, and kicks as the mob of followers clapped their hands gleefully
and wildly. Cameron's account similarly hinted at the intimidating and
extortionist elements in John Canoe. In her telling, the parade pulled
up to the door to the hall in her house, with its leader snapping a whip,
causing everything to "stand still for an instant," with herself and the
other white children so quiet they "could hear the tumultuous beating
of our hearts as we pressed close to mammy or grandpa." Then the
leader's second crack of the whip sprung his followers into sudden action, as they danced increasingly frenetically to "barbaric" melodies,
including the leader's rendition of "the Coonah song," accompanied
by a wide assortment of "plantation musical instruments" such as triangles, bones, drums, fifes, and banjo.[23]

Cameron suggested an extortionate element to these rituals, without explicitly saying that whites were frightened into paying. While
the dancers were in the midst of their performance, a participant costumed as a "hideous travesty of a bear" grabbed a hat off the "head of
the nearest pickanniny" and made the rounds of all the whites present
to accept all the pennies that whites were provided with in advance to
turn over to them, knowing they would be expected to pay up for the
dancing. Harriet Jacobs claimed that the John Canoers commonly extracted $20–$30 plus jugs of rum for their efforts, and that it was rare
for any white children, or even men, to refuse the beggars completely.
Those who did, she remembered, suffered ridicule as cheapskates who
were mocked for being "Down in de heel, so dey say." The sarcasm
was obvious.[24]

Certainly the *Liberator*'s informant found the performance unsettling,
though she did not admit fearing the paraders. Explaining that she and
her companions were "filled with pity and disgust" at observing the
revelers, she reported that the scene caused her to question whether
slaves were as happy at Christmas as they were supposed to be, since

the John Canoers seemed to be singing dismal tunes rather than joyous ones. So disturbed by the incident that it haunted her imagination for days afterward, she added that all the women accompanying her now regretted that "Cooner" had crossed their paths. To her, however, the incident mostly confirmed that "negroes" were more stupid and foolish than whites, since they enjoyed dancing and singing in the rain.[25]

Clearly, John Canoe was such an "in-your-face" performance that there is some basis for claims that participation allowed slaves "to transcend their deracinating everydayness" and to achieve a sense of temporary freedom that contrasted sharply with their degradation all year long. But slaves ultimately needed liberty, not momentary triumphs, and, as the historian Anthony E. Kaye argues, we deceive ourselves if we think slaves achieved anything like genuine autonomy within their oppressive situations. Slavery and autonomy are antagonistic propositions. There was good reason why an observer of a John Canoe procession, like the woman quoted in the *Liberator*, might conclude from songs she was hearing that slaves were unhappy.[26]

Still, John Canoe was disturbing enough to white southerners. Whether white onlookers anticipated black rebellions from the assertive behaviors of John Canoers remains a mystery. But it seems to have had that effect in Jamaica following emancipation in the British Caribbean colonies. Calling John Canoe an expression of "African barbarism," the mayor of Kingston tried to stop paraders during the 1840 Christmas holidays by having police confiscate their drums. His effort failed, as black men apprehended the police making the confiscations and seized the drums back. The next year, when the mayor tried again during a march of John Canoers two days after Christmas, he ignited a riot, with people throwing stones and beating police trying to seize their instruments, eventuating in deaths in the street and the calling out of military force. Much later and many decades after the emancipation of U.S. slaves, white North Carolina public officers in places like Wilmington, where John Canoe persisted into the early twentieth century, took pains to repress it because they considered it destabilizing for the post-Reconstruction southern racial order.[27] Indeed, John Canoe most expressed the tensions, not the reconciliations, undergirding Old South Christmas celebrations.

5

Winters of Their Discontent

In retrospect, it was only wishful thinking. As the Civil War's first Christmas season approached, the *New York Herald* reported that an unnamed "distinguished military officer" had predicted the fighting would end soon. His logic? By mid-January 1862 at the latest, the South's slaves would rise up "in a general insurrection" that would cripple the Confederacy. This Union officer, hindsight tells us, could hardly have been more deluded. Over the course of the war, Dixie's slaves would commit countless individual acts of defiance to their masters and mistresses and run away by the many thousands to Union lines, incrementally increasing the Union's military strength while depriving the Confederacy of a key asset. But no general slave uprising occurred that Christmas season, nor did it happen during any of the subsequent ones during the war. Instead, the fighting dragged on for another three-and-a-half years of horrific butchery. Still, the logic behind the officer's prediction merits attention, since it represented more than idle fantasy. According to the *Herald,* the officer's prediction was based on his personal examination of the "history of slave insurrections" during an earlier tour of military duty in the South.[1]

Assuming the *Herald* reported the officer's thoughts accurately, it is more likely he was musing about the long history of slave insurrection *panics* in the South that occurred regularly at the Christmas holiday season than that he was remembering actual Yuletide uprisings. There were no widespread southern slave rebellions at Christmas before the Civil War. However, white southerners had fallen into repeated panics about *phantom* Christmas revolts year after year. Most likely the report's unnamed officer had been stationed in the South during at least one of these unmaterialized scares and gained the impression that slaves were in a revolutionary state at the time.

Christmas insurrection panics plagued white southerners in the decades before the Civil War for several reasons, especially nervousness about slaves being relatively unsupervised at Christmas as compared to normal working weeks when they were under closer scrutiny by masters and overseers. Not only were masters and overseers frequently preoccupied by family holiday activities, but they also gave slaves opportunities to take to the roads to see and party with family and friends enslaved or living elsewhere, or, as noted earlier, to seek employment for the coming year if they were to be hired out. A Union soldier encamped near Bardstown, Kentucky, during the Civil War's first Christmas gave an account of this phenomenon in a letter to his future wife. Explaining that he and a sergeant had drawn a pass to go to town for Christmas, this Michigan volunteer described how they encountered "a Negro" every few yards they traveled:

> Some were riding mules, others mounted on ponies, some were on foot, all as happy as could be, for this is the negroes' holiday. They are all dressed in their best, many of them splendidly. They have nice shirt bosoms, starched collars. Their boots are blacked, and a white handkerchief is almost sure to be seen protruding from some one of their pockets. They go from one plantation to another thus, gathering and feasting and dancing the time away.[2]

There was nothing uniform about slave leaves of absence, or whether they were unrestricted or subject to rules, though male slaves received these privileges more regularly than did enslaved women. South Carolina planter James Henry Hammond seems to have dispensed carte blanche permissions for slaves to travel. One Christmas he reported he had told his slaves they could "go where they pleased during the holidays." Louisiana planter Bennet Barrow, in contrast, regularly sent his slaves off to "town" with money in their pockets at some point in the post-Christmas week so that they could seek their own pleasures. A New Englander who taught school in Georgia and spent six years in prison there for abetting a slave escape emphasized that slaves traveled to different destinations and for different purposes: "Some go to see their relations; some to parties; some to dances; some to one place, and some to another," he later recalled. The important thing is that southerners had to ponder and sometimes fret about all this frenetic activity. Slaves, as a correspondent for a northern religious journal noted, seemed in "motion" at Christmas as they traveled about from place to place carrying their bundles of clothing.[3]

Slave accounts provide additional perspectives on these holiday privileges, often spelling out that travel permissions included requirements that they carry written passes in case slave patrols or local authorities questioned their moving about, necessary documents to avert possible whippings or imprisonment if they were intercepted on the road by vigilant whites. Thus, in contrast to the former slave who remembered that on Christmas Day slaves were "free to go anywhere they wanted" without restriction, another ex-slave recalled that many slave dances were held around Christmas each year and that he had received "passes to different plantations" so that he could attend them. Solomon Northup recalled that it was the custom each year for one planter on a rotating basis to throw a Christmas supper for not only his own slaves but for all the slaves on other plantations in the neighborhood, and that between 300 and 500 slaves would attend the event, "coming together on foot, in carts, on horseback, on mules, riding double and triple" while fitted out in their best clothing; he also noted that on the days following this event slaves were given passes "and permitted to go where they please within a limited distance." Yet another slave recalled getting passes to "visit 'bout" on Christmas Day under the stipulation that he had to report back in by 9 p.m.[4]

Of course, not all slaves went traveling. Many stayed put in their cabins, where they partied, rested, and devoted themselves to activities and crafts designed to make their own lives and those of their families more comfortable. Our New Englander who spent time in Georgia described how some slaves spent their extra holiday hours making brooms, chairs, mats, horse collars, and other items. Still, the point is that probably a majority of slaves moved around relatively freely over the holidays at the sufferance of their masters, not that some stayed put the entire time. Northup remembered, apropos of this point, that in the part of Louisiana where he had been enslaved, masters customarily paid slaves who remained on their plantations Christmas season (presumably for holiday labor, though Northup did not specify this) instead of traveling about, but that very few slaves took their owners up on the offer.[5]

And paradoxically, white southerners apprehended the very freedom of movement their own liberality provided. At one level, their unease simply reflected the inconvenience of being deprived of the unpaid manual labor their slaves, especially house servants, provided all year long, at a time when white homes had many more visitors than usual and there was much cooking and many domestic chores that needed doing. Without servants on hand, white family members had to take up the slack. When *New York Times* correspondent Frederick Law Olmsted traveled in Virginia at Christmas in 1853, the landlady of a hotel where he stayed in Petersburg vented her frustration that all her servants, including the cook, "thought they must go for at least, one day, to have a frolic" and that when they returned they would likely be inebriated and in poor shape to labor. "She did not think this custom, of letting servants go so, at Christmas, was a good one," Olmsted noted, before adding that the woman wistfully mused that it would be better if Christmas only came every tenth year![6]

Southerners, however, worried about far more than just the inconveniences they incurred by giving slaves holiday time off. More so at Christmas than at other times, slaves congregated together and shared experiences and thoughts with other African Americans of different occupations, residences, and even legal status. Although the historical record is richest about the mixing of enslaved people from different plantations and farms over the holiday, similar intermingling occurred in urban locales, many of which had relatively high concentrations of free blacks. Between 1830 and 1860, the South's free African American community grew from 182,070 to 261,918, and it was especially concentrated in urban centers.[7]

Many contemporary accounts document sudden influxes of blacks into southern urban centers at Christmas before the Civil War, usually failing to differentiate between slaves and free African Americans in the telling. Describing the scene in Savannah, Georgia, a Yankee traveler did note that slaves turned up in the city in the early hours of Christmas Day, arriving in throngs from nearby rice plantations and carrying shillings for their expenses, laughing and talking excitedly; but when Mississippian Benjamin L. C. Wailes, a prominent slaveholding agriculturalist, witnessed similar scenes in Natchez, he merely recorded that an immense "throng of negroes" had turned up in town and were making purchases. Along similar lines, South Carolina writer William Gilmore Simms explained in a magazine piece that so many blacks in their best apparel arrived in Charleston just before one Christmas to buy hats and handkerchiefs as holiday gifts for their loved ones, that he had difficulty purchasing a railroad ticket out to the country for the holidays given the mobbing of both races at the ticket booth.[8]

More to the point, in Franklin, Tennessee, a newspaper rendered a condescending and racist take on a gathering at the Franklin market house at Christmas in 1857 that is extremely suggestive of the spontaneous dynamics of black urban gatherings during the holiday season:

> The "niggers" had a grand time of it Tuesday afternoon in our market house. It was raining hard, and about one hundred of them, in the full enjoyment of all the Christmas holiday, assembled in that public place, and such a shooting of squibs, such yells of delight, such hearty guffaus, and such uproarious jolity has rarely been witnessed upon our public square. The holidays are not past and they will have no opportunity—so many of them—to show their handsome ivories for another twelve months.

Today we might dub such a gathering a flash mob.[9]

Although such interpersonal holiday activity functioned on one level as a safety valve for slave and free black discontent, allowing African Americans to divert their thoughts from daily frustrations and resentments to new acquaintances and experiences, in addition to reunions with family members they normally did not see, it also was a cause of considerable concern for southern whites given the potentially subversive nature of such assemblages. However much white southerners proclaimed slaves were happy in their speeches, writings, and even personal correspondence, many suspected otherwise and worried that during the holiday slaves were permitted for days to drift beyond the radius of the whip, allowing their normal inhibitions to be compromised by alcohol. Drawing the attention of the Mississippi legislature to how local shopkeepers allowed blacks to frequent and hang about their premises over "Christmas Holidays," when they made a racket drinking, fiddling, dancing, cursing, singing, and "whooping," a group of sixty-three white Wilkinson County petitioners asked for a new law making it a penal offence if merchants allowed any "clamorous assembly of negroes" in their shops. In Florida, a Tallahassee editor announced that allowing slaves long Christmas holidays was "productive of no good on earth." Asking rhetorically "Where are they?" when addressing how slaves passed their time, he answered his own question disgruntledly: "Look at the places of dissipation, the street corners, the free negro settlements along the highways, &c., and you will find them." Paradoxically, though, even slaves remaining sober during their holiday peregrinations caused whites to worry, for the very reason that their behavior controverted stereotypes of prescribed black incapacity in the absence of white supervision. When a slave seeking his own employment in Richmond one Christmas approached a local judge who was in the market to hire an attendant for his dining room and then insisted on inquiring into the judge's reputation before contracting for the job, a Richmond newspaper complained about the frequency of such outrages during the Christmas season. Clearly this slave and others of his ilk behaved too self-confidently for the paper to be comfortable with their sobriety.[10]

Above all, nervous whites fretted that blacks might capitalize on their expanded holiday liberties and circle of contacts by plotting a rebellion. As a Mississippi paper carefully worded it, slaves had been taught, even as children, "if any thing is ever going to happen in this country, for their (supposed) advantage, it will occur at Christmas," and seemed to succumb to "hallucination" every year while the holiday approached. What the paper seems to have meant but did not want to explicitly articulate was that blacks should know they were better off as slaves than being free, but since they did not, they might make a bid for liberty at Christmas. In 1841, a reporter informed William Lloyd Garrison's *Liberator* from Alabama that whites there believed blacks thought their freedom would be gained either right after Christmas or after the date, March 4, of the next U.S. presidential inauguration. Alabama slaves supposedly were convinced that the outgoing president Martin Van Buren was already at Montgomery, Alabama, with 200,000 men to free them. The patent absurdity of the report hardly matters (the New Yorker Van Buren's policies as president had leaned proslavery more than antislavery). What counts is the linking in white southern minds of Christmas with a coming race war.[11]

One gets an added sense of prevailing white unease about the revolutionary potential of Christmas gatherings of blacks in towns and cities from punishments meted out by urban courts to slaves accused of holiday misbehaviors and from town ordinances quashing slave Christmas partying. In Mobile, for example, the Mayor's Court doled out ten strikes with the whip for slaves "keeping Christmas by getting drunk." In Milledgeville, Georgia, town authorities passed an ordinance disallowing slaves the right to hold balls over Christmas unless their owners or guardians applied in advance consenting to the events.[12]

But masters whose slaves remained at home for part or all of the holidays had their own concerns that the very celebrating they funded might get out of hand and lead to trouble, and sometimes serious misbehavior indeed erupted on their places during Christmas, though of course not all of it can be traced directly to the holiday per se. On Christmas night in 1837, for instance, male laborers on one of the All-ston family plantations in South Carolina murdered the Allston's slave driver Cudjo by chasing him through a pond by boat, killing him, and depositing his body on the pond's bank. Since drivers were specially selected and often privileged slaves who helped masters and overseers enforce discipline and labor rhythms in the fields (sometimes whip-ping fellow slaves to get their obedience), it is likely that simmering resentment of workers against Cudjo simply erupted on Christmas, though holiday conditions may have fed the unrest.[13]

Natchez, Mississippi, planter John Nevitt harbored apprehensions of undesired holiday behaviors by his enslaved people, writing after the Christmas "Negro Ball" on his place in 1831 that he stayed up all night at the slave quarters to make sure that "order" was maintained. More revealing is the remarkable confession by a Georgia rice planter's son three days after Christmas (as his slaves returned to their labors) that it always seemed a "God-Send . . . when that Holyday is over, and we all resume our quiet plantation work." Accordingly, he thought of Christmas as a "bad time" when it came to one's black workers. It is difficult to ascertain how many slave owners felt similarly, since they may have sometimes coded or guardedly phrased their language in speaking of the season. Thus a slaveholder wrote her sister that "Christmas has passed" and that while there had been "causes for *excite-ment*" there had been no "real danger," though her "negroes" had been "much alarmed." What was she driving at? When another slaveholder expressed delight at being "happily through . . . the holydays" before reporting his slaves once again preparing timber for the sawmills, was he thinking of the revenue he would again reap from their labor or re-lief that he had survived one more Christmas without slave resistance? Perhaps both matters were on his mind. It is impossible to be sure.[14]

Southerners, in short, had cause to worry more about rebellions at Christmas than at other times, and the fact that the only major southern slave rebellion in the four decades before the Civil War—Nat Turner's revolt in Virginia in 1831—was a summertime affair hardly reassured them. Over and over again, large numbers of southerners surrendered to a contagion of slave revolt fears as Christmas approached, respond-ing with repressive measures to tighten control and ensure such insur-rections never began, sometimes denying slaves the very Christmas privileges that supposedly helped keep them happy. These fears, of course, exposed more than anything else a paradox of southern slavery: southern whites worried that slaves might slit their throats even as proslavery polemicists insisted publicly that slaves were considerately cared for and loved their masters for being treated so well.

Such worries had plagued southerners since colonial times, as evidenced by the observation of a foreign-born Anglican missionary in South Carolina in early 1714 that over the recent Christmas a rumor had been spreading there of a planned slave insurrection at Goose Creek resembling what had occurred a couple of years earlier in New York City—an allusion to an outbreak of murders and acts of incendiarism by blacks in that port.[15] Certainly the colonial South Carolina and Virginia slave codes (1712 and 1726, respectively), mentioned in an earlier chapter, addressed such fears. Their provisions for a heightened guard against black misbehavior at Christmas had an obvious subtext of warding off potential slave insurrections arising from black socializing and drinking together over the holidays beyond the purview of their owners.

Southern colonial paranoia over Christmas slave revolts understandably heightened when the holiday coincided with crises involving foreign powers since foreign powers might try to spark slave uprisings as tools of war. This danger presented itself especially in the wake of the September 1739 Stono slave rebellion in South Carolina, the only major slave rebellion before the American Revolution in England's southern colonies. The Stono uprising occurred on the eve of an Anglo-Spanish war sometimes called the War of Jenkins' Ear. The related Christmas crisis occurred after the Stono rising collapsed and followed Britain's actual declaration of war on Spain that October. Though the slaves' rebellion had been suppressed brutally, South Carolinians remained tense partly because Spain controlled nearby Florida and might use that colony to launch attacks on Britain's colonies in North America, perhaps intending to free South Carolina's slaves and make them allies in their cause. In late November, with some of the rebels still on the loose, the colony's assembly exposed white fears by specially petitioning the colony's English-appointed lieutenant governor, William Bull, to detach men on special detail for patrols over "the Christmas Holy Days" so they might nip in the bud any "further wicked Designs" slaves might "have in Agitation" at a "Time of general Liberty to the Slaves throughout the Province."[16]

No slave rebellion actually occurred at Christmas in 1739, but similar fears arose in Charleston a generation later during the Stamp Act

Crisis of 1765, one of the earliest in the chain of events that would lead the American colonies to rebel for independence from Great Britain a decade later. At that time, violent colonial protests erupted against British attempts to raise revenues by taxing newspapers, wills, and other documents, and these demonstrations inspired blacks in South Carolina during the Christmas season to echo white resistance to Britain with their own calls for liberty. Two black males there supposedly had been overheard conversing about plans for a general uprising scheduled for Christmas Eve, in which whites would be massacred, and a couple of black informers reportedly had independently confirmed the rumor. These reports were enough to induce governing officials in the colony to call up militia, mobilize sailors on hand in Charleston port, recruit Catawba Indians to track suspects who had abandoned their plantations, and round up suspected insurgents. As was the case with many supposed southern slave rebellion plots, there may have been little or no substance to the rumors triggering the reaction.[17]

Although neither of the feared Christmas rebellions in 1739 and 1765 came to pass, the latter produced a striking if offhanded admission by colonial South Carolina authorities that slaves hated bondage. In defending South Carolina's pending boundary claims before the British government at the expense of neighboring North Carolina, a committee appointed by South Carolina's council emphasized that South Carolina depended on slave labor far more than North Carolina (due to its much heavier production of staples—especially indigo, rice, naval stores, and hemp) and therefore required continued access to the white western settlers and allied Catawba Indians who had put down the resistance in 1765. In the context of noting that South Carolina's black population now outnumbered the colony's whites, the committeemen conceded that the very "condition of Slavery" of these laborers was "apt to raise in them Ideas of an interest opposite to their master," endangering public safety. Southern leaders afterward would rarely concede liberty as a motivation for slave Yuletide resistance. Indeed, when just a few years after the South Carolina panic of 1765 an *actual* Christmastime fracas erupted with some forty-plus slaves fighting whites in Hanover County, Virginia, a newspaper in that colony, rather than see anything problematic in slavery itself, attributed the affair to slaves being accorded "too much lenity and indulgence." Well-managed slaves, in other words, would lack any cause to contest the system.[18]

Southern nervousness over the potential for Christmastime revolts persisted into the early years of national independence, matching nervousness about the holiday elsewhere in the Americas like Denmark's colony of St. Croix, where in 1759 a suspected slave revolt plot revolved around supposed intentions to kill whites distracted by Christmas partying. Tory exiles from the American War for Independence brought insurrection apprehensions to the British Bahamas colonies in the 1790s, leading to the beginning of slave patrols in Nassau by legislative enactment in 1795, with the patrols timed for the period of December 23 to January 8 and their purpose specified as the stopping of fires, murders, meetings of people of color, and other "outrages and disorders." In 1801, in Britain's Tobago colony, after several slaves were reportedly overhead discussing plans for a possible Christmas night uprising, island authorities conducted a preemptive arrest and jailing of suspected insurgents, declared martial law, deferred the Christmas holiday, and even sought the aid of foreign naval officers. In 1805, British authorities in Trinidad took similar actions, including the hanging of three reported ringleaders to forestall a rumored slave rebellion involving hundreds of enslaved women and men supposedly scheduled for Christmas Day. In Portuguese Brazil during the early nineteenth century, where authorities regarded Christmas as one of the three times during the year that slaves were most likely to take advantage of religious "distractions" and rebel, an uprising actually did occur at Christmas 1808 amid the sugar plantations in Bahia, with slaves setting cane fields on fire before marching on the town of Nazaré, where a pitched but losing battle resulted involving several hundred rebels. Moreover, Portuguese authorities apprehended that escaped slaves living in "maroon" outposts on the borderlands with French Guyana might capitalize on customary Christmas feasts to, in the words of one historian, "cause mayhem." On France's sugar-producing colony in Martinique in 1823, slave plotters chose Christmas Eve for an intended rebellion, one that authorities preemptively suppressed.[19]

Not only were a statistically astounding one-third of all known slave conspiracies and rebellions in Britain's sugar-producing West Indies colonies either attempted or planned in December, the greatest slave rebellion in all these colonies—Jamaica's sometimes labeled "Baptist War" of 1831 involving around 20,000 slaves and damaging over 200 estates—originated in a slave work stoppage scheduled for Christmas and ignited the day after Christmas. News of that uprising and the brutal methods used to repress it propelled public opinion in the mother country toward abolitionism and became a turning point against slavery's continuance in the British Empire. Parliament began initiating legislation to eradicate colonial slavery a week after authorities executed the rebellion's leader in May 1832.[20]

Certainly Christmas insurrection rumors intermittently roiled the southern states of the new American Union during the nineteenth century's first three decades, the same period when northerners completed the process of ending slavery in their region that had begun during the American Revolution. In late 1808, when President Thomas Jefferson's home county of Albemarle in Virginia (as well as several other Virginia counties) became consumed by an insurrection panic, the wife of a congressman from the area wrote her absent husband about how relieved she was that God's mercy had spared her the "horrors of massacre" and expressed her hope that the family could move westward where there were fewer blacks. On Christmas Eve 1811—nearly a year after the Louisiana Territory experienced what historians now consider the largest (but not most murderous) slave rebellion in American history— the territory's governor reacted to rumors of a continuing black threat northwest of New Orleans, where the uprising had occurred, by remobilizing the militia forces that had suppressed the original revolt. North Carolina, at Christmas 1825, fell into a state of emergency; supposedly slave preachers were stirring up a plot to be triggered on Christmas Eve. Meanwhile, statehood for Louisiana in 1812 failed to insulate whites there from persisting Christmas rebellion fears. In 1829, plantation slaves from various estates on Thompson's Creek in West Feliciana Parish hatched plans over Christmas for an uprising that was thwarted by a slave woman who overheard their plotting and informed her master. Several executions of accused rebels followed.[21]

Even non-Christmas southern slave insurrection panics sometimes had Christmas elements, including the murky, hot-weather Denmark Vesey insurrection panic that shook Charleston, South Carolina, between May and July 1822. The trial transcript of the free black artisan Vesey and fellow conspirators alluded repeatedly to Vesey hatching the plot around Christmas 1821. The slave harness maker Monday Gill, for example, confessed first learning of "the intended insurrection" around the prior "Christmas from Denmark Vesey, who called at my shop and informed me of it." In all, thirty-five blacks were hanged in punishment for the plot, though Gill, who gave authorities testimony that implicated forty-two others, got his death sentence commuted to being transported beyond the United States. Undoubtedly, all the testimony cemented the connection between Christmas and slave insurrections in the minds of white South Carolinians, if not southerners in other places as they learned about the affair.[22]

So intense were southern insecurities at Christmas that the mere shout of "fire" in the night might make urban whites assume a general slave insurrection was under way. In fact, Christmas, arson, and black rebelliousness all merged in Charleston at holiday time just three years following the Vesey plot. After a Christmas Eve fire ravaged King Street's vulnerable wooden structures that night in 1825 leaving $80,000 in damages, six months of arson events followed, which locals attributed to slave incendiaries.[23]

Christmas insurrection fears among white southerners deepened as the abolition movement swept through the northern states beginning in the 1830s, exacerbated by the efforts of abolition activists to appropriate Christmas for their own purposes. Abolitionists saw little reason to concede the holiday to the slave states, even if many Christmas traditions had more long-standing tenures in the southern United States than elsewhere in the country. Just the opposite, as the Underground Railroad activist (and son of a once-enslaved mother) Henry O. Wagoner declared to his good friend Frederick Douglass in a letter proposing that all colored people of the United States, whether slave or free, make Christmas or New Year's *their* annual day of prayer and humiliation instead of Thanksgiving. Wagoner believed that during the Christmas season alone, black "brethren" in the South could spiritually connect themselves with northern blacks in simultaneous "devotional services." They could not do so at Thanksgiving, which never became a general slave holiday in the South.[24]

Many northern abolitionists utilized Yuletide allusions as an antislavery reference point in their poetry and polemics, and believed the holiday season itself the perfect time to raise public awareness for their cause. In "Christmas," written for the early abolitionist newspaper *Genius of Universal Emancipation,* a contributor foreswore sugarplums and holiday cakes so long as the "wretched slave" toiled from "cradle to the grave." Releasing a book of verse as a means of raising funds for the cause, another antislavery poet entitled his work *Christmas and Poems on Slavery, For Christmas, 1843.* In 1855, John Sullivan Dwight, a onetime Unitarian minister with links to many New England reformers, translated the French Christmas carol "Cantique de Nöel" as "O Holy

Night," adding a third verse giving Jesus's story a powerful antislavery and antiracialist subtext:

> Truly He taught us to love one another;
> His law is love and His gospel is peace.
> Chains shall He break for the slave is our brother;
> And in His name all oppression shall cease.[25]

Right up to the eve of Civil War, Yankee abolitionists repeatedly hammered at incongruities between the Christmas spirit and enslavement. When announcements circulated in 1854 that Georgia's prominent U.S. senator Robert Toombs, in the capacity of estate administrator, ran a July 4 sale in the town of Columbus including 90–100 slaves, William Lloyd Garrison's *Liberator* highlighted the irony that the marketing of slaves occurred on Independence Day and that the terms of sale called for full payment on Christmas Day. Similarly, the prominent Massachusetts writer Lydia Maria Child employed Christmas allusions in her remarkable late 1859 correspondence in the aftermath of John Brown's raid on Harpers Ferry, Virginia, with Virginia governor Henry Wise and Margaretta Mason (wife of Virginia senator James M. Mason), which was quickly published in a slight volume that sold some 300,000 copies and drew much public attention. In her note to Wise, Child emphasized how British slaves in the West Indies had demonstrated perfect deportment at Christmas following their emancipation and contrasted how southern slaves depended on charitable hand-outs from masters at Christmas after laboring for them all year while domestic wage servants in the North earned the funds to buy "as many Christmas gowns" as they desired. On Christmas Eve 1860 in Boston, the Unitarian minister and reformer James Freeman Clarke delivered a sermon at the Indiana-Place Chapel that contrasted Christmas in the just-seceded South Carolina with Christmas in his own Massachusetts and told the congregants that they had a "duty" to help slaves trying to escape their bondage. Abolitionists like Clarke obviously saw Christmas as holding special meaning for their crusade.[26]

Most important, northern abolitionists held yearly antislavery fairs over Christmas, and these happenings apparently provided more funding for the abolition cause than any other single source, though exactly how much remains in dispute. White and black female antislavery activists, including Child, initiated the movement in Boston in the mid-1830s (authorities debate whether we should date them from 1834 or 1835), and eventually the fairs spread into the New England countryside and the mid-Atlantic states, lengthening in Massachusetts from one-day events to two-day happenings and for a while an entire week. Starting in 1845, what had previously been called the Massachusetts Anti-Slavery Fair transitioned into the American Anti-Slavery Society's national bazaar, a recurring event held at Boston's Faneuil Hall until 1859. The fairs, remembered in part for introducing German Christmas trees into American public life, served as recruiting tools for the movement as well as fund-raisers since women participated in year-long sewing groups and knitting circles churning out gift items so that enough goods would be available for sale when Christmas arrived. Further, the fairs attracted donations of items for sale from Great Britain, linking the events to the international movement against slavery.[27]

Abolitionists implored their fellow citizens to attend and buy items on sale at these annual gatherings for the good of the cause. One women's antislavery committee in Boston in 1838 invited readers of the *Liberator* who wished to "contribute to the cause of the slave" to turn out for the "Ladies Anti-Slavery Fair" on December 19 and 20 where they could buy pink satin, bonnets, gloves, and other presents for Christmas and New Year's while enjoying music, original poetry, and hot coffee and candy. Three days before Christmas in 1841, a Philadelphia paper published a story entitled "Attention, Friends of Humanity. Who will bestow a Christmas Gift on the Slave?" That appeal suggested readers forego buying their customary Christmas presents at fashionable stores and instead purchase gifts at the Philadelphia Female Anti-Slavery Society's fair, where they could support the cause as they bought clothing, ornaments, poultry for a Christmas dinner, and other items. The author urged northerners, as they enjoyed their own holiday comforts, to remember the slave parents in Virginia who had no way of preventing their children being sold separately to different buyers.[28]

Another important way northern abolitionists tweaked the holiday season to their own ends was framing the story of Christmas in the British Caribbean to make the case that if southern slaveholders would only free their slaves, they could cease worrying about black insurgencies during the season. Britain's Parliament, by its Emancipation Act of August 28, 1833, ended slavery in Britain's West Indies colonial holdings as of August 1, 1834. The legislation liberated all slaves under the age of six immediately as of that date and provided (except in Antigua, where freedom became immediate for all on August 1, 1834) that the balance of the slave population would have to serve terms of apprenticeship of either four or six years, depending on their occupation. When Christmas in the colonies in the mid-1830s passed relatively quietly despite predictions by cynics that Caribbean blacks could not handle liberty and would be dangerously disorderly at Christmas without the constraints of slavery to rein them in, northern abolitionists in the United States hailed the news and drew lessons from it. An antislavery almanac published in 1835 trumpeted that instead of facing worse holiday dangers than before emancipation, Antigua's planters were so relaxed they did not even bother with the usual Christmas proclamation of martial law and exempted their militia from holiday duty entirely. Similarly, the *Liberator* reported that Jamaica witnessed none of the disorder of Christmas that had been customary before emancipation and experienced so calm a post-emancipation holiday that not a single complaint was lodged against slaves. Rather, the latter turned out for the holiday well dressed, orderly, and respectful. An American traveler in the West Indies at Christmas in 1836 came to similar conclusions, remarking that "Christmas in America" had never been as quiet as it had become in Antigua after emancipation, with holiday carousing and riots vanishing now that slavery was over there.[29]

Given the publicity generated by Yankee antislavery Christmas campaigns, it should be unsurprising that white southerners came to fear that white northerners might subversively capitalize on the special circumstances of the holiday season to instigate black uprisings. Although southern Christmas panics undoubtedly would have occurred occasionally in the absence of a vibrant antislavery movement in the North, agitation against slavery in the free states exacerbated the tension, perhaps the clearest example being the Christmas insurrection fear of 1856, which affected virtually every slave state. When a Raymond, Mississippi, newspaper in January 1857 reflected on the previous month's agitation, it largely blamed the November 1856 presidential election, when the new antislavery Republican Party ran its first presidential candidate, John C. Frémont. Anyone familiar with election campaigns in the slave states, the paper elaborated, knew that tolerant masters customarily allowed slaves to "hang around the outskirts of public meetings." In recent weeks, therefore, slaves might have gotten the misleading impression from the speechmaking that a political party was trying to end slavery. A Richmond, Virginia, newspaper similarly blamed northern antislavery for the Christmastime nervousness, announcing that the reason slaves had become "eager for revolt" was attributable to the "incendiary operations of the Black Republican Party." Southerners should learn from revelations of "extensive preparations" for slave resistance all the dangers averted by Frémont's defeat in November.[30]

Most pre–Civil War southern Christmas insurrection panics, in fact, occurred in tandem with antislavery happenings of one sort or another, though the link was not always as obvious as in 1856. North Carolina's fear of 1830, for example, was triggered by the publication of a remarkable antislavery pamphlet the year before that historians usually call David Walker's *Appeal,* though it had a much longer title. Walker, a North Carolina free black, had moved to the North, gaining literacy; after settling in Boston, he had maintained a store selling used clothing. His pamphlet not only claimed the United States belonged more to blacks than whites because they had enriched the country with their labor, it also warned white Americans that blacks might commit violence if slavery continued, declared that God sided with slaves, forecast the destruction of the nation in war if slavery continued, and told blacks to be ruthless if it turned out rebellion was the only way to end slavery: "they want us for their slaves, and think nothing of murdering us in order to subject us to that wretched condition—therefore, if there is an *attempt* made by us, kill or be killed." More alarming to white southerners, Walker mustered agents to distribute his pamphlet in southern urban centers, including Wilmington, North Carolina. When police magistrate James McRea found out about the *Appeal,* he tipped off North Carolina governor John Owen, indicating that slaves and free blacks were designing a conspiracy to overthrow slavery and that the rebellion would probably occur at Christmas. Owen then informed the state legislature. Fears persisted into the Christmas season. On December 20, slaveholder Charles Pettigrew informed his father from Hillsboro that "the negroes" supposedly had already revolted in New Bern and that authorities effectively quelled the uprising, killing sixty blacks and taking no casualties themselves, a report later confirmed in a Roanoke, Virginia, paper, which added that the sixty armed slaves had been surrounded in a swamp. People in Hillsboro remained on guard, however, about the "intended insurrection of the slaves about christmas in this place," according to Pettigrew. Local whites, he confided, had made contingency plans, mobilizing precautionary patrols of twelve military companies of about ten men each. No rebellion occurred, but the panic reinforced the Christmas-insurrection connection in white southern minds while evidencing white dissonance about slave happiness. According to a man who dropped out of the Christmas patrols after two days, his company had orders to search blacks' houses for any kind of printed matter, including Bibles and hymnals, and to whip slaves found in possession of such materials. North Carolina authorities obviously lacked genuine trust that slaves were contented and especially worried that education and outside ideas would corrupt their loyalty.[31]

In the summer of 1835, as northern abolition societies initiated an ill-fated campaign to flood slave states with mailings of hundreds of thousands of cheaply printed antislavery tracts to turn southern public opinion against slavery, the cotton-producing counties of west-central Mississippi erupted in a bizarre revolt panic revolving around the rumored doings of a shady white figure named John A. Murrell, then serving a ten-year term of hard labor in the Tennessee penitentiary in Nashville (after being convicted in 1834, possibly wrongly, on two counts of stealing slaves). According to a pamphlet authored by a con artist and published in March 1835 under a nearly eighty-word title dubbing Murrell "the Great Western Land Pirate," the convict masterminded a network of conspirators called the "Mystic Clan of the Confederacy" organized to recruit blacks on large plantations to rebel for freedom and kill whites on Christmas Day. Clan members would incite the insurgents with arms and liquor, while using the disorder to fire towns and rob banks and the homes of rich merchants. Despite lacking proof that an actual plot was afoot, white Mississippians overreacted over the summer in what a historian dubs "one of the deadliest incidents of extralegal violence and mass hysteria" ever occurring in the slave South. In vigilante-type committees of safety, panicked whites whipped slaves and apparently some whites also—highly unusual in the Old South—into forced confessions, and hanged approximately thirty white suspects and fifty blacks. Additional victims were confined in prison, tarred and feathered, or banished from the state.[32]

Making matters worse, Mississippi's panic festered until Christmas. A resident of Vicksburg confessed to a relation of being "almost frightened to death at the ap[p]roach of Christmas" since Murrell's "negroes" would be making their move; and as late as Christmas Day, a newspaper in the state capital editorialized that "for all we know" the rebellion might erupt momentarily, and urged nearby planters to deny their own slaves any customary permissions to visit the city for the holiday. Moreover, the panic spread to at least seven other states, causing new persecutions. In northern Louisiana's East Feliciana

Parish, a slave girl–turned–informant told her master on December 24 that his slave "Sam" and other plotters, abetted by two white men, intended a murderous Christmas uprising. They would kill white inhabitants (sparing only attractive white females to make into wives), take the town of St. Francisville, and proceed toward Texas, where they would acquire free papers and disperse. Authorities broke up whatever plot, if any, was actually in the works by hanging Sam and one of the white suspects, and severely whipping suspected slave accomplices. As in many incidents of this kind, the vigilantes meting out these punishments legitimized them on the basis of suspect confessions, which in turn brings into question whether a plot had existed at all. One report claimed that the vigilantes separated Sam from the other suspects and induced the latter to confess by telling them Sam had done so.[33]

Nothing remotely comparable to the Murrell 1835 insurrection panic occurred at Christmastime in the South during the 1840s, though scattered outbreaks of rumor and repression surfaced over the course of the decade, potentially to the bemusement of antislavery northern commentators sensitive to the paradox of slaveholders quaking in fear of supposedly contented slaves. In early December 1842, press reports announced that three Louisiana parishes were succumbing to fevered excitement over indications that 300 armed runaways hiding in the swamps intended a Christmas Day assault, and that authorities had arrested and interrogated suspected insurrectionists. Reviewing a southern magazine's biblical defense of slavery in the aftermath of the panic, a (Boston) *Christian Examiner* critic noted that the article being reviewed had been coincidentally authored by a writer residing in one of the very parishes under recent insurrection watch. Obviously, slaves were seriously discontented and capable of significant resistance, despite the article's contrary pretensions.[34]

In 1844, two Christmases later, a Norfolk, Virginia, paper expressed relief that area slaves had been as "orderly and free from all suspicion of insubordination," despite reports that a "diabolical" plot had been hatched in New York City for a "Christmas-tide" uprising in Norfolk's vicinity. That same 1844 pre-Christmas also saw residents of Holly Springs in northern Mississippi summoned to an urgent courthouse meeting because two slaveholders had "finally succeeded" in inducing a "negro girl [to] confess" an insurrection was intended "about Christmas." Not only had a keg of gunpowder reportedly been found in the possession of one group of slave plotters; accomplices had broken into a gunsmith's place near Memphis and stolen arms. Diarist Ellen Kenton McGauley Wallace of Christian County, Kentucky, married to a slaveholder, ominously observed at holiday time 1846: "Christmas Eve. The night the negroes intended to have risen and murdered the whites had the plot not been discovered." Earlier diary entries for the month clarified her meaning, indicating that some seven or eight blacks had been hanged and that neighboring jails were filled with others who had supposedly confessed their intention to rebel, kill whites, and flee to the North. Wallace expressed doubt that she would ever feel safe again, given what had been discovered.[35]

As the sectional crisis over slavery increasingly roiled the nation between the mid and late 1850s, southern Christmas panics gained renewed frequency, occurring in 1856 during that fall's presidential canvass, in 1859 in the aftermath of John Brown's raid on Harpers Ferry, and in 1860 following Abraham Lincoln's election as president. The 1856 scare infected more of the South geographically than even the 1835 Murrell terror. The *Richmond Enquirer* noted a week before Christmas that fears had erupted virtually simultaneously in Texas, Arkansas, Kentucky, Missouri, Tennessee, and Louisiana that "the slaves are meditating schemes of insurrection." Additional sources show that the scare infected all nine of the other slave states. On the day before Christmas, for example, five county justices of the peace in North Carolina alerted their state's governor that insurrectionists intended to initiate a rebellion at a plantation in Orange County.[36]

Most of what we know about the 1856 panic derives from newspaper accounts, which were often sketchier than historians would prefer. An eastern Texas newspaper, for instance, claimed that authorities had averted a Christmas "rising" in San Augustine County without providing any proof that an insurrection was actually planned or any details about the steps taken to preclude its success. As was the case with all reports of black resistance, southern journalists had to balance their responsibility of reporting the news against the possibility that blacks might learn what was transpiring from press commentary and join plots that they otherwise might not even know about if they overheard whites talking about press reports or read the news themselves. Scattered slaves knew how to read and write despite laws prohibiting whites from educating them. A paper in Georgia's capital of Milledgeville two days before Christmas gingerly mentioned that because slave rebellion was "a delicate subject to touch" it had not previously printed anything about current reports of insurrections in other states, including neighboring South Carolina. The editor explained he had decided all men deserved to know about present dangers so that they could take preventive measures, so his newspaper was coming forth with its information in the hope that all gatherings of blacks anywhere in Georgia until New Year's Day would be dispersed by patrols. The *New Orleans Picayune* made the same editorial decision at the same time.[37]

White authorities throughout the South took precautionary measures, though the panic was by no means universal and the holiday passed normally in many places. In Savannah, residents experienced an unusually quiet Christmas because authorities banned the explosion of firecrackers, though police did take into custody a couple of men accused of expressing antislavery sentiments in public, one of them a Yankee who reportedly did so "to a few little niggers." After "discoveries" that slave workers intended insurrections at rolling mills and ironworks in Stewart and Montgomery Counties, Tennessee (both had pockets where blacks outnumbered whites), the city council in Clarksville (Montgomery County) notified ironmasters and other slaveholders in the area that slaves would not be welcome in town over Christmas and any slaves entering its limits would be subjected to a twenty-lash whipping, unless accompanying a "respectable white person" or visiting with their wives and carrying a pass from their master. Up in the northern reaches of neighboring Kentucky, Louisville's mayor ruled that all black slaves had to clear themselves from city streets after 8 p.m. throughout the Christmas season, in reaction to the rumors of revolt. In Missouri, where there were fears of a coordinated December 25 uprising involving slaves living in two east Missouri counties and Obion County, Tennessee (located across the Mississippi River from Missouri), a public meeting requested that slaves be barred from attending "public preaching" without their masters' presence and that blacks be prevented from preaching themselves.[38]

Worried whites hardly contented themselves with tweaking municipal regulations; much as had occurred during the Murrell panic of 1835, they dispatched extra slave patrols and vigilance committees with the intention of nipping in the bud acts of slave resistance. "The police in Augusta were very vigilant," noted Ella Gertrude Clanton Thomas, a young plantation mistress in the Georgia town over the holiday. In Southampton County, Virginia, patrols went out four or five nights in a row after reports arrived around December 27 of what one small slaveholder called a pending "stur in the County." Whites in Tennessee's iron district conducted raids that reportedly resulted in the arrests of several hundred blacks, brutal whip-induced confessions, and the hanging of at least seven suspects, including several slaves of the influential U.S. senator John Bell; while in Sumter County, Alabama, the "confession" of a "negro girl" to a patrol unit about a planned insurrection during "the Christmas holidays" prompted the arrest of twenty-five to thirty "negroes." According to a newspaper report, a local public meeting then chose a committee to interrogate the suspects, leading to additional confessions of a planned "general outbreak about Christmas." Two suspects were more precise, saying that 500 to 600 blacks planned to meet in the town of Livingston on Christmas night and rob stores and kill whites on the signal of a bugle blaring. One confessor added that a white man had promised them ammunition and arms for their uprising. However, despite apparently thorough and persistent searches, only one loaded pistol in working order was found in the possession of any blacks supposedly connected to the presumed plot there. Around the same time in southwestern Kentucky, near both the border with Tennessee and the reportedly infected ironworks, all sorts of white vigilante action erupted. Arrests and whippings of suspected collaborators in the town of Hopkinsville produced coerced confessions and preemptive reprisals, including the hanging of a free black suspect at Cadiz, Kentucky; the beating to death of a slave ironworker; and additional arrests and jailings. Unsatisfied that the danger was over, one local judge even scheduled a court meeting for Christmas Day. In Louisiana, a jury found a slave named John guilty of planning a rebellion in Assumption Parish and gave him a punishment of two months confinement in the parish jail, 350 stripes with a whip, and two years of being bound in irons.[39]

According to the count of the historian Douglas Egerton, more slaves were strung up and hanged throughout the South for complicity in the 1856 scare than had been executed for complicity with Nat Turner's bloody 1831 affair. Further, once the emergency seemed abated, southern authorities considered adopting further preventive measures to ward off similar crises in the future. A Georgia newspaper advised the state legislature to make a start by limiting contact between free blacks and slaves.[40]

Two documents not only help convey the scope of the 1856 panic but suggest what it was like to live in the South during insurrection angst. The first is a paragraph by a Mississippi woman tucked into a letter explaining her family's delight in the parties and dining of the season:

> There has been an excitement in Carrollton about the negro rising. Several were taken up and I believe some are in jail. Daniel was taken up, he says for selling whiskey to negroes but it could not be proven on him. He has been here all through Christmas. Negroes are kept very close at home, none permitted to go off without a pass. Mrs. Phillip's Deb and one of Thomas' negroes was accused of burning Mr. Henry's cotton. They were taken to Carrollton. It could not be proven on them. It is said Henry's own negroes burnt it.[41]

The second document illuminates from a black perspective the steep price slaves and free African Americans paid for white Christmas panics. About five weeks before Christmas 1856, the once hired-out Kentucky ex-slave George Knox recalled in his later autobiography, some rumors "got out that the slaves were going to rise and kill all the white people." Reacting to what he was hearing, Knox's master began interrogating Knox as to when the "Negroes" planned to launch their revolt, leading Knox to ask what he was talking about. Knox's master, in reply, expressed suspicion that a bugle a slave acquaintance of Knox's had just acquired in trade was intended to sound the signal for "all the colored people to rise up." Knox left unsaid whether he was personally punished over his master's suspicions. However, he did mention that local whites called a public meeting in response to the rumors and dispatched patrols that whipped any slaves encountered on the roads who were not carrying passes from their masters. Noting that whites grew more anxious by the day as Christmas itself approached, Knox recollected how authorities issued notice that slaves had to remain in their cabins over Christmas unless they were going to fetch a doctor for their master. Patrols grew increasingly severe, searching slave residences at night and returning in the daytime to give any slave who had been missing during their previous evening's search thirty-nine lashes. Some slaves who reportedly had hid pistols and knives in haystacks received an astounding 500 lashes in punishment. Eventually, when the holidays ended without incident, masters returned normal travel privileges to their slaves and the patrols limited themselves to Saturday night outings.[42]

As was the case with all antebellum Christmas insurrection rumors, no significant uprising occurred anywhere, though it is impossible to discount entirely the possibility that slave insurrectionary activity occurred, especially since there appear to have been an unusual number of acts of individual violence by slaves over the 1856 holiday season. A Prince William, Virginia, court in early January 1857, for example, judged a mother, her three sons, and her own mother as guilty of the killing and burning of their master on Christmas night. Still, it is likely that most and conceivably all the thwarted schemes listed in news accounts were imagined, the products of the paranoiac minds of whites never fully secure in their own slave ownership, who felt especially challenged in the fall of 1856 because for the first time in American history a major U.S. antislavery party was fielding a presidential candidate.[43]

Some southern commentators gave voice to all possibilities at the same time, exposing the conflicted minds of slaveholders who wanted desperately to believe in the benignity of their rule over black laborers yet probably were troubled at the subconscious if not conscious level by fleeting thoughts that perhaps something was amiss in their system, that enslaving people was immoral and exploitative, and that persons in bondage might retaliate violently against their oppressors. Consider, in this light, Georgia plantation mistress Gertrude Thomas's summation of the panic. Reporting in her diary that Tennessee authorities had taken their revenge on accused blacks by whipping them, hanging them, or cutting off their heads, she confided *both* that she "never at any time experienced the slightest fear" during the crisis *and* that she was greatly gratified that the plotters were "stopped before Christmas" since so much "intercourse" occurred at holiday time that it "might have enabled them to organise [*sic*] some extensive plan." Translation: black rebels hardly endangered white planters like herself, but maybe they could if they timed things just right. Later on, though, Thomas allowed herself more honesty. Recalling the events of 1856 on Christmas Day 1858, she remembered that one of her aunts had visited her place the earlier holiday for fear of remaining at her own home and confessed that she had probably been naive in dismissing the danger in 1856. Now she admitted that she sometimes considered southerners as endangered as people living near Mount Vesuvius, alluding to the Italian volcano whose eruption in A.D. 79 destroyed the ancient city of Pompeii.[44]

Equally arresting for similar reasons are Edmund Ruffin's thoughts about the panic. Ruffin's diary on Christmas Day affirmed that rumors of "negro plots" had induced "proper methods of vigilance" in the form of patrols by "respectable men" scouring his neighborhood for signs of trouble night after night. Nothing had been uncovered indicative of slave misbehavior, Ruffin admitted. Yet he remained unwilling to entirely dismiss the danger of a Christmas rebellion. Northern "incendiaries" had occasionally attempted conspiracies in the South in the past. For that reason it would be helpful if southerners could hang a dozen of them. This would dissuade "abolition agents" from future such attempts. Had Ruffin been absolutely convinced of slaves' steadfastness, abolition infiltration would have little worried him.[45]

What Ruffin and many similarly minded other southerners never considered, or tried to ignore for their own equanimity, was the possibility that slaves might not require outside prompting to resent their bondage at the very time of the year when they were reputedly most happy. Reflecting on the 1856 excitement in a kind of head-in-the-sand piece, a Nashville newspaper concluded that only "political and social causes" (meaning northern antislavery agitation) would cause the "happiest" and "most contented serf population in the world" to become insubordinate. A Georgia newspaper echoed its Tennessee counterpart. Once the "fright" ended, it professed to have never really worried about the danger of revolt since "the great mass of the negroes" were so well treated and had a higher standard of living than local whites. They lacked motive to revolt. Similarly, in a piece disputing Yankee reports that southern slaves had been significantly stripped of their usual Christmas privileges the previous month over rumors they would revolt, the *New Orleans Daily Crescent* in January 1857 claimed a mood of normality for the holiday, with southern masters and their families casually observing the "cutting up" of their slaves. Repeating the common southern trope that the South's enslaved blacks had far better lives than northern factory workers, the *Crescent* asserted they only misbehaved when masters were excessively indulgent of their workers, since blacks were too weak-minded to enjoy such freedoms appropriately. Over and over again, southern polemicists drove home their contention that Christmas's happy slaves verified their way of life. Self-delusion, the big lie, allowed southerners to rationalize their repressive, often cruel, and always immoral labor system in pursuit of profit and convenience.[46]

During the last two years before the Civil War, white southern anxieties about slave uprisings at Christmas became subsumed within broader panics that started, respectively, in the fall of 1859, during the aftermath of John Brown's raid on Harpers Ferry in October, and the following year as Abraham Lincoln campaigned for the presidency over the summer and fall. Both Brown's attack and the Republican campaign evoked regional fears about impending slave insurrections that began long before Christmas week arrived and were hardly restricted to holiday concerns.

Still, fears that Christmas presented special danger remained part of the mix, an integral part of a regionwide insurrection psychosis. Even in normal times, southerners at Christmas felt gnawing insecurities about slave loyalties, and their fears worsened at times like these, making it hard to separate uprising worries from the holiday. Thus, when a youthful Florida diarist on December 26, 1859, remarked that her family had enjoyed its Christmas "just as good as if John Brown had never stirred up so much that was terrible," she all but confessed that her family was having trouble dismissing the radical abolitionist from their collective consciousness as they celebrated the holiday.[47]

Certainly southern whites took more precautions than usual, that second-to-last antebellum Christmas. Shortly following the holiday season, Charleston, South Carolina's postmaster felt obliged to explain his absence from town during the U.S. postmaster-general's recent arrival there, noting that he had thought it necessary to be among his slaves "during the Holy days when excitement was most likely to be manifested." During the same period, Georgia whites curtailed normal slave holiday freedoms, and Vicksburg's denizens passed through days of worries that an attack there had actually been scheduled for Christmas night. In Bolivar, Missouri, a riot occurred on the night of December 26 after a grocery store owner denied a slave as much whiskey as he wanted for holiday celebrating. According to a local newspaper, the slave had permission from his owner to get as much whiskey as he wanted until New Year's Day, but the grocer was suspicious and refused the slave's continuing requests, causing a number of slaves to concoct a plot to burn the store and slit the owner's throat as well as the throats of other grocers. When whites learned what was afoot, they began arresting slaves; eventually a brawl occurred that lasted several minutes and eventuated in the citizenry conducting a "vigilant watch" until the following morning.[48]

Though neither Abraham Lincoln nor his Republican Party endorsed John Brown or called for slave rebellions at any time before the Civil War, many southerners instinctively connected Republicans with insurrections and became hypersensitive about the potential for slave uprisings over Christmas following Lincoln's election in November

1860, which arrived just five days after South Carolina, on December 20, began a parade of slave states withdrawing from the Union. Indeed, in some parts of Dixie, holiday activities became virtually intertwined with the politics of secession. South Carolina's secession convention conducted important business on the days before and after Christmas, and in places like Harrison County, Texas, and the entire state of Alabama, Christmas Eve day was scheduled for the election of delegates to state secession conventions. Public figures everywhere had disunion on their mind, even as holiday activities unfolded around them. On Christmas night, an editor in Montgomery, Alabama, vented hatred of "fanatical" northerners in a letter to his brother. And some secession celebrants even deemed it auspicious that South Carolina had birthed its experiment at Christmastime. Thus a southern newspaper correspondent in Charleston envisioned people during future Christmases commemorating the holiday as "the natal day of new independence."[49]

Uncertainty reigned, though, with no one really knowing what lay ahead. How many slave states in all would secede? Which ones would they be? Would a viable new nation emerge from the turmoil, and what kind of a government would it have? Would war with the North follow? Nerves were taut, especially in South Carolina where already a clash was brewing over the status of federal forts in Charleston harbor. From his Chicora Wood rice plantation, former governor Robert F. W. Allston offered the state as many of his male slaves as it needed to help in military preparations, and began readying ten of them with a supervisor to go off and labor for his state's cause, furnished at his own expense with provisions for their first week of state service. Visiting a South Carolina coastal plantation for the holiday on the invitation of a local planter, an English traveler learned from his host that elite women in Charleston were donning plain holiday clothes, foregoing their usual satins and silks, skipping concerts and balls, and even foregoing marriages for the emergency. The "Colonel's" own daughters had requested money instead of the usual jewelry they received as Christmas presents, so that they could donate funds to the state of South Carolina as a means of helping to equip military companies for the crisis; his son Phillip was absent for the holidays "doing military duty" at Sullivan's Island, undoubtedly in preparation for an assault on Fort Moultrie, the federal fortress there dating from American Revolutionary days.[50]

Would slaves stay loyal if war erupted with the North? Reading between the lines of slaveholders' letters and diaries over Christmas, southerners may not have been certain they would, despite their self-congratulations that slaves remained content with their bondage. In Texas, a planter in Wharton County, for instance, sent a letter to a Houston paper reporting that slaves in his vicinity so hated abolitionists that during the holidays they put an effigy of Abraham Lincoln on mock trial and then burned it. But why would the Florida panhandle physician and small slaveholder Charles Hentz even mention in his diary that "the negroes" (his? all blacks locally?) seemed to enjoy themselves during the holiday, "unconscious and unconcerned about our great national troubles," unless he held concerns that they might be restless? When Brazoria County, Texas, plantation diarist Sallie McNeill described her "Negroes" as dancing "strangely in earnest" that Christmas, she perhaps was leaving coded language for later readers to decipher. What was she *not* saying? Did she sense unrest within her slave community and fear that her workers were considering playing the political turbulence to their own advantage? Was South Carolinian Mary Petigru coping with signs of slave restlessness when she wrote Adele Allston on December 27 that her family had given the Christmastime to their servants and asked of them "as little as possible," and that the slaves, even with a wedding scheduled for that very night, seemed "very quiet, more so than usual"? Long afterward, Louisiana plantation memoirist Eliza Ripley claimed that during the holiday in 1860 her "negroes" were already showing signs of being "restless and discontented," foreshadowing what came later.[51]

At any rate, southerners took few chances that secession Christmas of slave discontentment morphing into rebelliousness, though some masters, like John Selden, carried on over the holiday as if nothing had changed. At his Westover estate on Virginia's James River, Selden recorded on Christmas Day that the weather had been fine, that his church had been nicely decorated with evergreens for its service, and that he had given his slaves "350 lbs. of bacon and beef, 2 lbs. of superfine flour, 1 pint of molasses each, lard, etc., for their Xmas," adding that he had also thrown a big dinner for his neighbors. No signs of nervousness about slavery here.[52]

But elsewhere, worries about Christmas slave revolts had white folk on edge. As early as September, slaveholders in South Carolina's upcountry Spartanburg District feared the worst, partly because escaped slaves who had been apprehended in a cave hideaway spoke of a coming insurrection "around Christmas" in Spartanburg and another Piedmont district. Closer to Christmas, the correspondent of the *New York*

Tribune in Charleston informed his paper that local landowners, aware their slaves knew the national election results, were taking preemptive measures against the possibility that Lincoln's success would inspire black resistance. Local city authorities had tightened up enforcement of nighttime curfews on blacks traversing city streets, and nearby plantation owners were considering a curtailment of Christmastime passes for slaves to travel about. Motivated by concerns local blacks were "playing thunder" in his area that holiday, north Mississippi slaveholding minister Samuel Agnew stayed up Christmas Eve until Christmas Day dawn with other nearby slaveholders so they would be ready for action in case trouble erupted.[53]

In Tennessee, a diarist noted on Christmas Day that many local slaveholders had kept their "negroes" at home rather than allowing them to roam through the nearby town of Jackson as they usually did during the season, and that the holiday seemed uncharacteristically quiet. In Georgia, a woman noted that three slave rebellion plots had already been uncovered within a six-mile radius of her plantation, that reportedly a slave rebellion was being timed for Christmas on the Sea Islands off the coast, that people in her vicinity were sleeping each night "with loaded firearms at hand," and that some of her neighbors were "much frightened." Visiting Richmond, Virginia, a British traveler detected "anxieties and foreboding" overcoming people in the city, and found herself in a peculiar situation on Christmas Eve during what began as an "oyster supper" at her boardinghouse. Suddenly, two men burst into the room, began whispering to people there, and left with one or two young men following them. Later, she learned that "rumours of a negro insurrection in one of the suburbs" had compelled the calling out of the "Home Guard" as a precaution, explaining the sudden exodus from the party. During that night, she was awakened from her slumbers by false alarms of "negro" riots and that the city was on fire.[54]

Similar hypersensitivity in Alabama led to a more serious insurrection panic, with talk in the press of slave intentions to kill all whites, including children, on Christmas Eve, excepting "marriageable girls" they would take as wives. One conspirator had supposedly even admitted intentions to drink his master's blood before aiming a gun at him and missing with two shots. According to a report dated December 11 in the *Montgomery Mail,* a "deep-laid plan among the negroes of our neighborhood" and apparently "all over the country" had been hatched for a "general rise during the Christmas holidays." Whippings had caused some blacks to admit that a plan was in progress: insurgents would kill the white families they lived among on the night of December 26, and then drive off mules, carry off furniture, and head into the country until support could arrive from Lincoln and the northern people. Although vigilantes hanged six or seven blacks and two whites in response to such reports, the climate of fear persisted in central Alabama. Supposedly, insurgents planned to use homemade pikes to butcher whites and strychnine to poison them. Additional executions, including two of white suspects, reportedly followed, but the *Montgomery Mail* still wanted slave Christmas celebrations cancelled, with the blame falling on Lincoln, as a way of warding off potential trouble.[55]

In an ironically worded post-Christmas editorial reflecting on the 1856 pre-Christmas insurrection scare, the antislavery *New York Times,* a Republican paper, expressed its "pity" for southern masters who in recent days had been so "fearful of the poor darkies" that they been forced to spend their holidays closely monitoring them. This, the *Times* reflected, must have taken the joy out of the holiday season for the slaveholders. Musing sarcastically that given this plight, southern masters were perhaps more deserving of northern sympathy than the slaves themselves, the column pointed out that slave owners had three worries over the holidays: being murdered by their slaves; seeing their entire labor system challenged by a "general rising"; and being plagued by a "general stampede," meaning, as the *Times* clarified, a plague of slave runaways.[56]

In retrospect, it seems clear that though antebellum white southerners had cause to worry about acts of slave confrontation, they put disproportionate effort into eradicating the phantom of rebellion. The southern states in the thirty years after Nat Turner's uprising in 1831 never experienced a significant slave rebellion attempt at Christmas or, for that matter, at any other time of the year. Nor did many slaves murder white southerners over the holiday, though it happened occasionally, as did occasional acts of arson by enslaved persons against their masters' property. In 1824, for example, a jury in Perquimans County, North Carolina, sentenced a slave named George to death for assaulting a tavern keeper while en route to a "John Canno" celebration the previous Christmas Eve, though it is unclear whether the sentence was carried out. William Lloyd Garrison's *Liberator* reported in January 1857 that a family of slaves in Prince William County, Virginia, had murdered their owner on Christmas Eve and were then sentenced to hang after a two-day trial. Slaves on Hugh Fraser Grant's place in Georgia chose Christmas Day 1858 to set Grant's storage houses and barns on fire, causing him the loss of his sawmill, machinery, and 7,000 bushels of rice. Such incidents, however, were rare.[57]

Actually, the most serious and frequent black resistance slaveholders faced over the holiday was the third method mentioned by the *Times,* one usually much less communal than insurrection. Rather, slaves repeatedly took advantage of their Christmas privileges by attempting to escape bondage entirely, either individually or as couples or small groups, often fleeing for some of the same causes impelling slave rebelliousness. When escaped slave Charles Thompson was questioned as to why he had left his master, he not only mentioned never getting Christmas gifts but also said he had been mistreated for twelve years and often whipped, most recently when he had been put in jail pending an intended sale. As an early history of the Underground Railroad in Pennsylvania put it, the days following the Christmas holidays commonly witnessed an "influx of fugitives" arriving in the state, generally slaves who had taken advantage of their Christmas travel passes from their masters to flee. And free black William Still's nearly 800-page post–Civil War compendium of his work with the Underground Railroad in Philadelphia, with its many case history synopses, is full of allusions to Christmas runaways. "For the commencement of their journey they availed themselves of the Christmas holidays," reads the summary for the flight from a mistress "accustomed to rule with severity" of Anna Scott and her husband. In a manuscript journal for "station no. 2" that Still maintained, an entry dated January 16, 1856, marked the arrival of five Loudoun County, Virginia, escapees who had all "left home" on Christmas Eve.[58]

Enough slaves chose Christmas for their bolts for freedom that one northern abolitionist suggested, probably naively, that northern antislavery could deal a telling blow against slavery by intentionally channeling this energy. In his 1859 book, *The Roving Editor,* the journalist James Redpath urged the movement to capitalize on the vulnerabilities of southern masters over Christmas by facilitating slave escapes, particularly in coastal North Carolina, a place where the holiday season left slaveholders especially vulnerable. Redpath proposed a multiyear Christmas campaign, reasoning that merchant sea captains visiting the state's ports over the holiday season could annually conceal on their vessels and spirit away hundreds of slaves, since North Carolina's coastal communities at Christmas were full of slaves who had been

A BOLD STROKE FOR FREEDOM.

Armed slave fugitives fending off apprehension by whites following a Christmas Eve escape. William Still, *The Underground Rail Road: A Record of Facts, Authentic Narratives, Letters, &c....* (Philadelphia: Porte & Coates, 1872), 124. (Purdue University Library)

hired out for the year to Deep South renters and were in transit back to visit their families for the holiday. This travel pattern at Christmas brought these slaves closer to freedom in the North in a geographical sense than at other times of the year. Sea captains could erode slavery's hold on North Carolina, Redpath implied, by mounting unrelenting campaigns of seaborne Christmas exits from the peculiar institution.[59]

We would greatly err by minimizing the threat that Christmas slave escapes, as compared to servile insurrection, posed to the very structures and logic of southern slavery, even though statistical analysis does *not* suggest slaves disproportionately attempted their flights at holiday time. A published compilation of 2,145 North Carolina newspaper advertisements for fugitive slaves printed between 1791 and 1840 includes just 44 ads for slaves who ran away between the period December 20–31 in any year. This suggests, if North Carolina was representative of slave states as a whole, that only a little over 2 percent of all slave runaways picked the Christmas season to make their bids for freedom. Since there are about thirty 12-day periods in a 365-day year, this volume's statistics indicate that slaves ran away at a *below*-average rate at Christmas (70.519 runaways rather than 44 would have been average for the 12-day Christmas period).[60]

Still, it is highly significant that as many as 2 percent of all escaped slaves chose Christmas, when their lives were generally most pleasant, to schedule their flights from bondage, especially given the sometimes severe weather of the season and the difficulties of subsisting in the wild. As Still's compendium noted in Anna Scott's case, she and her husband suffered "from the cold weather they encountered" on their way to Philadelphia. Similarly, the abolitionist Charles Parsons, during his stay in Savannah over Christmas 1852, learned that a light-skinned slave boy named Joe had run away from his hotel's steward during Christmas to escape a threatened whipping for a "misdemeanor," but returned after five days in a famished state, being unable to hold out in the woods. Even more important, as a scholar of Jamaican slavery recognizes, it is all too easy to appropriate the thinking of slaveholders in addressing slave escapes by regarding such incidents as a kind of transgression of masters' legal rights to own human property, without considering how much the actors in such escapades saw their seizures of liberty as expressions of freedoms that they already possessed in their own minds. These southern Christmas escapees were challenging the peculiar institution's legitimacy in a profound way, perhaps more so than when they fled at other times during the year.[61]

A surprising number of fugitive slave narratives tell tales of Christmas escapes, including John Andrew Jackson's harrowing account of how he fled cruel owners in South Carolina by making his way to Charleston during a three-day Christmas work break in 1846, melding in with hired slaves working in gangs on the docks, and then stowing away on a ship bound for Boston. Facing an overdue whipping for trading some of his own chickens for a pony owned by a neighboring slave, Jackson, who knew the 150-mile route to Charleston from prior trips there driving his master's cattle to market, slipped away from his plantation while other slaves were dancing and rode the pony to the port city, capitalizing on the fact that it was Christmas throughout his journey. When interrogators questioned his right to be traveling the road, he simply said he was going to a neighboring plantation, a seemingly reasonable proposition given how many slaves passed their Christmases partying around their neighborhoods; then, at the Santee River, he was conveyed across by a slave ferryman, who earned extra pay for working on Christmas Day and had no wish to blow Jackson's cover after collecting his fare. Arriving at a hotel, the keeper's suspicions were disarmed by Jackson's claim that he was heading to Charleston for his "Christmas holiday," another falsehood that seemed reasonable in light of common customs throughout the South of country slaves passing their holidays in nearby towns and cities. South Carolina slave William Craft described in his famous autobiography how accompanied by wife, Ellen—the human property of a different master—he escaped bondage in 1848 (making it to Philadelphia and then Boston) by taking advantage, as William put it, of the custom of slaveholders giving favored slaves "a few days' holiday at Christmas time." That Christmas season, both Crafts talked their masters into giving them travel passes and then fled to the North by using a ruse to avoid detection and apprehension: the light-skinned Ellen impersonated an invalid master traveling with "his" servant (William). After the U.S. Congress passed the strict Fugitive Slave Act of 1850, the Crafts sought greater safety abroad from the danger of recapture and became famous lecturers in Great Britain.[62]

Another Christmas escapee who told the story in a published narrative was Henry Bibb, who sought his freedom after his master stripped and whipped his wife for not sorting out grass from some cabbages she had dug up. Afterward, in a speech at Faneuil Hall in Boston, Bibb explained he chose Christmas for his escape from bondage in Kentucky because masters often gave their laborers "the privilege of working for themselves for a few days" over the holiday. Bibb accumulated $2.50 in cash toward his venture and got his master's permission to go several miles away to assist in hog killings on the Ohio River over Christmas, promising to give his master a dollar for each day he worked; instead, Bibb arrived at the river at night, commandeered a small vessel he found on the shore, paddled across the Ohio, and caught a steamboat for Cincinnati.[63]

Other Christmastime escapees or thwarted escapees leaving published accounts of their schemes include James L. Smith, John Thompson, and Isaac Mason. In 1837, the first of these, a skilled slave shoemaker in eastern Virginia hired out to a man who threatened to whip him, made an arrangement with a slave sailor he knew to jointly seek freedom on Christmas Eve; unfortunately, their gambit fell through because of a frozen waterway preventing their escape by river craft, and they postponed their bid for freedom until the next spring. In Thompson's case, his former owner's granddaughter did not want to see the family's slaves sold to pay off debts, so she went to the slave quarters, alerted them that the estate was being contested, and drew their attention to the coming "Christmas holidays" as a time when they could get passes to visit friends and relations and then escape. Thompson recalled that most of the slaves followed this advice and headed for the free states. As for Mason, he escaped to the North, taking advantage of Christmas week "when slaves are generally allowed to visit their friends for one or two days," in reaction to threatened corporal abuse for supposed impudence because he had refused to eat spoiled beef offered him and fed it instead to his owner's dogs.[64]

Perhaps more than any other account by an escaped slave, the narrative of Jermain Wesley Loguen shows how Christmas circumstances loomed for slaves scheming their escapes. Writing in the third person, Loguen explains how, while known as the slave Jarm on a southern Tennessee plantation, he and a fellow slave named John fled an abusive master in 1834 on stolen horses, with the assistance of a poor but sympathetic neighboring white man. This fellow, one Ross, provided them with forged travel passes and advised them on how to react if whites challenged them during their flight. Loguen and his companion escaped all the way to Canada, after planning initially on stopping in Illinois; yet several years afterward, Loguen risked arrest by returning to U.S. soil. He became a key figure in Underground Railroad and black political activism and self-improvement efforts as a minister in Syracuse in upstate New York. Loguen's narrative gives us slaves resolving that they could not "pass the holidays" without action, deciding that "freedom begins with the holidays!," planning to take their leave on "the first holiday night," hoping to acquire pistols because "Christmas is at hand," and then actually setting out on a cold, clear, and beautiful "evening before Christmas."[65]

One hardly has to depend on escaped slave autobiographies, however, to grasp Christmas's salience in fugitives' calendars. Southern newspapers published a miscellany of items touching slave flight at Christmas—like a tantalizing piece about an apparently deluded Boone County, Kentucky, master who let nine of his servants visit their freed "Ohio branch" of their family for a Christmas break in the mid-1840s, giving them horses, his wagon, and a pass to cross the Ohio River. Upon arrival at their destination, they unsurprisingly decided to stay, though the now-ex-slaves reportedly sent word they would return the horse team on demand. On January 10, 1855, a Winchester, Virginia, paper boasted that the four slaves who had run away from

"Apple-Pie Ridge" ten days earlier and who had been caught after losing their way in the woods would have fared better "at their homes" for Christmas.[66]

Most especially, southern sheets printed advertisements promising monetary rewards for the recovery of slaves by masters whose human property ran away on Christmas Day or "about Christmas." Subscribers to the Charleston, South Carolina, *City Gazette* learned in January 1790, for instance, that if they handed over Dick—who spoke "very thick," had "lost" his right hand's forefinger, and disappeared "ABOUT Christmas"—to either his master or the warden administering Charleston's workhouse, they could earn a $4 reward. North Carolina newspaper subscribers could make $20 for the return to the plantation of James Battle "two Negro Men named Sam and Isaac," who ran off December 22, 1820; the former described as dark complexioned with gray hair and talking with a lisp, the latter likewise dark complexioned with a scar from a knife wound on an ear and another scar below the jaw. Three years prior, another North Carolina holiday advertiser sought the return of the "Negro Man" Cupid, "common yellow" in complexion with an "unpleasant countenance" and a missing finger, who had "DESERTED from the service of his employer in the 25th of December last." Cupid had left with a "tall yellow wench" named Eliza Toole, a free woman he had married, taking with him tools, leather, and shoes that he used in his shoemaking trade. Closer to the Civil War, a couple of Virginia slaveholders published a Christmas Day advertisement promising $50 apiece for the return of the yellow-colored, twenty-five-year-old slave Barney Grigsby; his delicate and "very black" wife, Elizabeth; and her heavier sister Emily, if they were apprehended within the state. Slave catchers would get $100 for each if the retrievers had to travel beyond state borders to catch them. The trio had run away on Christmas Eve.[67]

Sometimes, Christmas escapes became the focus of northern fugitive cases. A hearing in New York City not long after the Fugitive Slave Act of 1850 passed Congress, for example, concerned alleged fugitive Henry Long, hauled before a U.S. commissioner's court and claimed under a power of attorney from a Virginia slave owner. A witness testified he had known Long while he was working as a waiter in Richmond, Virginia, and that "two years ago this Christmas, he ran away." In 1859, a U.S. commissioner in Columbus, Ohio, remanded to a Virginia claimant an alleged escaped slave apprehended by a federal marshal; the accused runaway named "TOBE, *alias* John Tyler, *alias* Price," reportedly left his owner "about Christmas, 1854." Further evidence of Yuletide escapes comes serendipitously in state and local histories of the Old South. Such works sometimes allude casually to Christmas fugitives, without particular attention to the holiday connection. A book about Baltimore, for instance, mentions a 1790 advertisement for a fugitive who left his Georgetown owner, noting that he claimed to be a Methodist and could easily quote Scripture. A study of central Georgia tells of two brothers who ran off over the holiday season "without any provocation," according, that is, to their master (as if enslavement itself was no provocation!). A book about slave resisters in Florida mentions a bondman named Primus who made the first of three escape attempts on the day before Christmas 1839.[68]

Real Christmas fugitives, in short, threatened antebellum southern slaveholders more than did phantoms of Yuletide rebels, and would continue to do so after war with the North broke out in the spring of 1861, though few if any southern secessionists spent their last Christmas in the Union worrying that the presence of northern armies in Dixie would ignite virtual slave stampedes to freedom. They might have seen the danger ahead of time, though, if they had paid closer attention to their slaves' attitudes. Instead, slaveholders were typically oblivious to their slaves' innermost feelings, taking for granted that their black laborers accepted their condition.

Nothing better illustrates this point than the observances of the English visitor mentioned above once he reached his "Colonel" host's plantation. Arriving at the 700-acre, 200-slave coastal South Carolina cotton estate for Christmas, our traveler initially got the impression that despite his own reservations about slavery, workers there seemed happily engrossed in the season, encouraged by their master's paternal oversight. He was pleasantly greeted upon his arrival by "decently clad house-servants" and was served a holiday meal by "decorous and attentive negroes." During a ride with the Colonel over the grounds, he observed giggly, diffident field hands bantered with their master over six weddings of field workers planned for the holiday and burst into "negro laughter, hearty, infectious, irresistible." When the Colonel held out the possibility that he might bring in an outside preacher to marry them, the laborers seemed delighted since that privilege usually was accorded exclusively to house servants. True, they seemed a bit tawdrily dressed, but the Colonel reassured his guest with an explanation that the slaves would all get new sets of clothing as Christmas gifts. On Christmas morning, a house servant brought our Englishman a tumbler of peach brandy and honey for a "Southern 'eye-opener'" and all but begged for a tip by saying "Merry Christmas, sa!" more than once.[69]

Still, intimations of slavery's instability are detectible, even on this estate. Our traveler encounters signs of possible slave discontent even over Christmas upon being introduced by the Colonel to a favorite house servant named "Pomp" (short for "Pompey," a slave name bestowed cynically by some southern masters since Pompey the Great was one of the most powerful figures in ancient Rome). The Colonel informs his visitor that during a trip he had once taken with Pomp into the free states, this "first-rate boy" had been offered his freedom by New York abolitionists but turned them down. Seeking absolute confirmation of his own paternalistic relations with Pomp in front of the Englishman, the Colonel then makes the mistake of querying his servant: "You don't want to be free, do you Pomp?" Rather than confirm his master's leading suggestion, Pomp parries it by remarking only that free blacks living in the "Norf" lived miserable lives of their own, a pointed evasion leaving open the possibility that he just might prefer taking his chances in the free states despite black poverty there. Later, Pomp also confides that he fears the day his master will die since his own family would be divided up among their master's descendants and separated.

Also worth noting is this Englishman's observation that laborers in the Colonel's fields worked under the gaze of a horse-mounted overseer, who conspicuously and proudly carried a cowhide whip with him. Rather than being embarrassed by being caught with his whip by a potential critic, the overseer quipped that his instrument was the very thing that Yankees made such a fuss about in attacking slavery. When the Englishman tried to turn the point to the overseer's advantage by suggesting that surely he used that whip infrequently, the overseer instead blurted that sometimes "the devil" seemed to get control of his workers, that a "nigger will be a nigger, you know," and that he had to "lay on all round"—implying that he whipped quite a few if not all of his laborers. Although the precise date of this encounter is somewhat unclear from the Englishman's text, it seems to have occurred on Christmas Eve day.[70]

6

Ransacking the Garret

Two-and-a-half years into the Civil War, a newspaper in the Confederate capital insinuated that the very way southerners commemorated the annual holiday of Christ's birth—so warmly as compared to how descendants of cold-hearted Puritans in the northern states observed it—was cause to keep fighting for independence. In its lead editorial on December 28, 1863, the *Richmond Examiner* mused that northern enemies as well as anyone "gloating over the prospect of our impending starvation" might be shocked that southerners would celebrate Christmas. Yet despite their dire circumstances, Confederates had just observed the Yuletide in their customary fashion, the *Richmond Examiner* took pleasure in noting. As a time of camaraderie and family affection, Christmas united Dixie's diverse regions and provided markers of southern identity in contrast to the northern states, where people either "from the old puritanical leaven which rendered them averse to every exertion of human happiness" or from adopting foreign customs gave "an inferior rank to Christmas." Southerners acted smartly by disregarding their wartime cares and throwing fine holiday meals, embracing the season in "the time-honored Virginia fashion." Just by doing so, Confederates affirmed that southern independence and the English roots of Dixie society remained intact.[1]

Curiously, the editorial ignored how slaves spent *their* holiday season, missing an obvious propaganda opportunity. It would have been simple enough for the editor to say something about how masters still went about pleasing their field hands and household servants with their accustomed presents, feasts, and dances despite the hardships of wartime. Such a storyline might have helped rally readers behind the flagging Confederate cause, projecting normality when slavery's future, a year after Abraham Lincoln's Emancipation Proclamation, was in serious jeopardy.

Given the paper's silence, one wonders just how well long-standing southern holiday customs involving slaves were holding up by Christmas 1863 under the stress of war. Had masters stopped lavishing their slaves with holiday presents because of wartime shortages? Were servants' Christmas Gif' cries rebuffed? Were slave holiday feasts and dances suspended for the emergency? Meanwhile, how were slaves behaving at Christmas as war raged around them? Surely the presence of Union army and navy forces, combined with the necessity that high numbers of southern white males serve in the Confederate military, offered the greatest opportunity for black resistance to bondage since British forces had flooded the region during the American Revolution offering freedom to slaves who escaped to their lines. Logic suggests that the Civil War Christmastimes would have been perfect occasions for slave flights to freedom, or even for the staging of the mass holiday uprising that southern whites had feared since colonial times.

Although Confederates won their only major battle against Union forces in 1861 (First Bull Run, or First Manassas, in July), Union naval forces were beginning to impose a blockade on the southern coastline by the time Christmas came around, and Confederate ground forces had absorbed some early setbacks. Yankee troops drove Confederate defenders out of most of western Virginia in July, and in early November Union naval vessels carrying thousands of marines and infantry had blasted their way into Port Royal Sound below Charleston on South Carolina's Atlantic coast. The Port Royal affair, recalled afterward by some slaves as "the day of the big gun-shoot," not only gave the Union an excellent deep water harbor for blockading purposes; it also provided the Yankees with control of one of the most valuable planting regions in Dixie, the coastal islands north of Savannah where about 83 percent of the population was enslaved. There, Sea Island or long-staple cotton—a lint used in fine clothing—reigned, and landowners reaped enormous profits from immense gangs of slave labor. As Union troops arrived, many slaves, suddenly freed from their fleeing masters' constraints, looted abandoned property and destroyed cotton gins. Within months, waves of mostly antislavery northern reformers, educators, and missionaries began flocking to these islands, initiating the "Port Royal Experiment"—an effort to Christianize, educate, and succor abandoned slaves, while teaching African Americans the virtues of laboring for wages and providing opportunities to acquire land so they could provide for their own welfare. Meanwhile, many coastal South Carolina planters shuttled their families and slaves to secondary homes and landholdings in the interior to remove them from continuing Union operations in the area.[2]

Despite such reversals, Confederate holiday spirits in 1861 were bolstered by awareness that the Union and the government of neutral Great Britain were embroiled in a diplomatic impasse over the "Trent Affair" (an incident at sea involving a Union naval officer's seizure of two Confederate diplomats from a British mail packet) that might draw the English into the war on the Confederate side, possibly sealing Confederate independence. Given this development, combined with a relatively stable military situation, many Confederate slaveholders felt justified in passing Christmas in their accustomed style. Gertrude Thomas, a wealthy Georgian plantation mistress living near Augusta, provided a wood tea set, china set, and some parlor furniture (presumably for a doll house) to her daughter Mary Bell, then three years of age. At Mulberry, the plantation residence near Camden, South Carolina, of diarist Mary Chesnut (the wife of a former U.S. senator), feasting included mince pies and plum puddings and drew on "everything . . . that a hundred years or more of unlimited wealth could accumulate as to silver, china, glass, damask," as she put it.[3]

Throughout the metropolitan South, white shoppers spent freely on gifts despite the blockade and a rise in consumer prices. Because the Union navy initially lacked sufficient ships to interdict all shipping along two lengthy southern coastlines, its blockade remained porous in 1861 (and to a lesser degree throughout almost the entire war), and southern merchants managed to procure enough Christmas items for sale at less than extortionate prices. In Richmond, toy and candy stores reportedly had articles available equivalent to Christmas stocks before the war, and a confectioner on King Street in Charleston not only had trinkets, fancy candies, and toys for sale, but even some items apparently of French manufacture that had slipped by Union ships outside the harbor on blockade-runners. The *Macon (Georgia) Telegraph* claimed that a grocer near its office sold sixty boxes of merchandise on Christmas morning alone, and a San Antonio, Texas, newspaper told readers on December 24 to expect a "*Good old Christmas*" with Santa Claus making his expected visits that night, since a "superabundance of good things" was available for the holiday celebration. With similar gusto, a Waco correspondent claimed his village experienced "Egg noggs, entertainments, celebrations, etc." for over a full week of Christmas rejoicing.[4]

Some exposed Confederate locales witnessed their Christmas observances self-consciously with an eye on the unfolding war, but not at the expense of their celebrations. As one South Carolina newspaper put it defiantly in a Christmas Day editorial entitled "Happy Greeting," it was appropriate to wish "Merry Christmas" to its readers, even with Union naval vessels accumulating off the coast and Yankee soldiers making "a temporary lodgment" on the state's shore. Up in the national capital of Richmond, an observer recorded that a local company of troops, the Richmond Blues, marched off to a fine Christmas dinner behind a band of musicians; children's Christmas gifts, he reasoned, had been militarized by the war, as exemplified by all the young boys strutting the city's streets "with drums swung from their necks" just after getting their presents on Christmas morning.[5]

Already, some nationalistic commentators gleaned patriotic meanings in the very ability of the Confederacy's populace to transcend the war's misfortunes with Christmas celebrating. In western Louisiana, Shreveport's *Semi-Weekly News* called on its readers to properly observe the "first Christmas in the Southern Confederacy," and it was by no means the only paper mirroring Richmond's *Examiner* in linking the holiday directly to southern nationhood. Charleston's *Mercury* exulted that Confederates, finally freed "from the incubus of Puritan bigotry," could learn to observe the holiday with the "zest" accorded by southerners' English ancestors, and a correspondent of *Charleston Daily Courier* highlighted how city stores in Nashville, Tennessee, had sold out their stocks of Christmas toys with northern labels during the holiday, evidence that secession had been economically astute. Having been dependent on Yankees for everything from toys to complicated machinery, southerners now could abandon northern merchants, leaving them stewing over the "valuable customer" they had "lost in the South."[6]

Certainly, few Confederates imagined this first Civil War Christmas that the conflict would entirely uproot their slave labor system. Had there been much doubt on this point, the bottom would have fallen out of the slave labor market. Instead, commercial transactions in slaves continued unabated, and they would do so even after the Lincoln administration began seriously implementing emancipation policies in 1862. As if slavery would continue indefinitely, the Virginia and Tennessee Railroad Company at Lynchburg, Virginia, at holiday time in 1862 advertised "500 Negroes Wanted," noting that persons who had previously hired out slaves to the firm had the option of calling their hands home for Christmas or leaving them with the company. "FOUR NEGRO MEN AND ONE WOMAN to hire," announced an advertiser in the Christmas Day 1862 issue of the Griffin, Georgia, *Confederate States*. On the same page, the paper carried a notice of an estate administrator's sale of a plantation as well as a twenty-year-old "negro man by the name of Martin" to satisfy claims against the deceased. In Atlanta, store merchant Sam Richards decided to invest in his very first slave, a servant girl named Ellen, whom he had previously hired out, during the Christmas season in 1862. He meticulously recorded in his diary his negotiations at his residence with her Macon, Georgia, owner, one Asa Sherwood:

> [H]e and I tried to outgeneral each other in making a bargain, he demanding $1300 for her and declining to *hire* her, and I offering to give him but $1200 and proposing to hire if he would not take the sum I offered. . . . I finally bought her for $1225 being $275 less than he priced her three months ago. So now I had committed the unpardonable sin of the abolitionists in buying a negro. I am tired of the trouble of getting a servant every Christmas. . . . As near as we can tell she is 13 years old, healthy, and ugly. The children are delighted at the thought that Ellen belongs to us now.[7]

Even at Christmas in 1863, a full year after Lincoln's Emancipation Proclamation (also less than half a year after disastrous setbacks at Gettysburg and Vicksburg and a month after bloody Confederate losses at Lookout Mountain and Missionary Ridge opened up Georgia's heartland to invasion), slavery persisted intact in many Confederate locales. In the South Carolina low country, Stephen Boineau, managing the Combahee River rice plantations of Charles Heyward, reported to Heyward on Christmas Eve day that their rice yield was over 5,500 bushels, and four days later he reassured Heyward that their hands were threshing corn and "again at work." The first page of the *Mobile Daily Register*'s Christmas Day issue announced the availability of a Marengo County plantation with "Negro Cabins for a hundred Negroes" and an offer to hire "200 ABLE-BODIED NEGRO MEN" for the coming year with payment going to their owner in either money (presumably highly depreciated Confederate paper) or salt (then a scarce commodity in the South). It also held one C. F. H. Hatcher's offer to sell a black woman with sewing, washing, and cooking skills, along with her daughter and son.[8]

Yet the real story of Christmas in the Confederacy for most southern whites, even before the fighting became truly destructive, was declension rather than normality, stress rather than celebration. According to Richmond resident Sally Putnam's recollections, the war's first Christmas was the saddest one that residents had ever experienced, with few locals having any inclination to celebrate when everyone was making "anxious inquiries for dear boys in the field." Plenty of contemporary documents confirm her memories. "It is a useless gesture to wish me a 'happy Christmas,'" diarist Sallie McNeill declared, thinking not only about absent family members but also about possibilities of Yankee attacks on the Texas coast and being "abandoned to the depredations of the vandals." Mary Eliza "Ida" Powell Dulany, left by soldier husband Henry to comanage with an overseer an 850-acre Fauquier County, Virginia, farm, mused that candy, cakes, toys, and nuts might keep her children happy "as if there was no cruel war to make a day of festivity a mere mockery," but that for herself Christmas seemed unhappier than any she had experienced in a long time. At Brokenburn, a sizable Louisiana cotton plantation northwest of Vicksburg, Mississippi, where some 150 slaves labored, Kate Stone, a young unmarried woman in her early twenties, recorded a quiet family holiday with no gift exchanges. True, the customary prebreakfast eggnog was served, but she thought it tasted like turpentine, adding this was the first Christmas she could remember lacking "fun and feasting." At Pooshee plantation in South Carolina, Henry Ravenel reflected how the "war cloud" cast a "somber" shadow over the holiday, and that his whole family sensed that gaiety was inappropriate. So the Ravenels dispensed with exchanging Christmas gifts or putting up their traditional Christmas tree, and they seem to have adhered to this practice throughout the rest of the war.[9]

Already, casualties of war caused an Augusta, Georgia, newspaper to suggest that readers buy copies of a special Christmas issue as a way of supporting its carriers, some of them already the primary supporters of widows of deceased soldiers. Already, calls rang out for charitable efforts to boost the cause. A Georgian's Christmas Day 1861 letter to his son reported that friends and family of a local military unit were assembling a "contribution dinner" for soldiers who could not join their families for the holiday. Sojourning in New Orleans for the holiday, members of the Quitman family and their spouses attended a concert at the Opera House dedicated to "the benefit of the soldiers." Everywhere, it seemed, women were organizing musical events to help the cause. A Jackson, Mississippi, newspaper alerted its readers that local women had organized a Christmas Eve entertainment at the city's concert hall, with proceeds for the entertainment and raffle benefiting "our brave volunteers." Girls attending the Petersburg Female College staged a musical benefit two days before Christmas in support of wounded and sick soldiers at local hospitals, as well as to help troops from town stationed near Norfolk and even soldiers from other states. Southern free blacks, too, demonstrated their constancy, undoubtedly in many instances from fears that if they did not, they might be suspected, given the unprecedented situation, of disloyalty or abolitionism. Free African Americans in Petersburg scheduled a concert to benefit soldiers from their city then stationed at Norfolk.[10]

Many of these Confederate Christmas benefits took the form of contemporary performance art known as the *tableaux vivant,* when costumed performers would strike a sequence of motionless poses of scenes telling a story or projecting a particular idea. Each human picture was arranged behind a curtain or screen before being revealed to the audience. "Had Tableaux on Christmas," reported one Mississippi planter at Christmas 1861, adding that a "pretty large crowd" had turned out and he had played the violin during the *tableaux vivant,* supper, and dance. Such happenings unfolded across Dixie. At the Mansfield Female College near Shreveport, Louisiana, students scheduled a Christmas Eve benefit of *tableaux vivants* with instrumental and vocal accompaniment to support wounded and sick Louisianans stationed at Columbus, Kentucky. Augusta, Georgia's Confederate Philharmonic Association announced Christmas week *tableaux vivants* to help the city's poor.[11]

The longer the war persisted, the more Confederates felt conflicted about celebrating Christmas at all. Keeping up the holiday as usual, for all the patriotic appeals, was more easily said than done. By the end of Christmas week in 1861, over 200,000 volunteers were on duty in Confederate army units; others belonged to Rebel naval crews or had been taken prisoner by the enemy. Ultimately, somewhere between 750,000 and 850,000 men would serve in Confederate forces, representing a shockingly high percentage of the southern military-age white male population—some 75 to 85 percent. Of these, nearly 40 percent would either die in battle or suffer a wound in the fighting. About 20 percent would die from a disease contracted during their service. Given such probabilities of mortality, as well as the greater average size of families in antebellum America as compared to today, few southern white families could insulate themselves from the war's destructiveness, even if their residences escaped unscathed and they were fortunate enough to avoid joining the Confederacy's ever-growing refugee population.[12]

As a result of the "vacant chairs" at holiday tables (to use a common idiom of the day), many Confederate civilians expressed compunctions and even guilt about celebrating Christmas, sometimes in profoundly despairing language suggestive of clinical depression. Things had been bad enough in 1861, but by holiday time in 1862, with shortages and inflation staking a presence in many locales, the national holiday mood had turned far more somber, even though the holiday arrived in the wake of one of the Confederacy's most lopsided battle victories of the whole war at Fredericksburg, Virginia. Earlier in the year, the Confederacy had suffered many setbacks in its western regions, including the first surrender of a state capital (Nashville, Tennessee, in February), the loss of New Orleans in April and Memphis in June, Union consolidation in Missouri, and the repulse of Confederate offensives in New Mexico and Kentucky. As Christmas approached, Union forces were threatening Jackson and Vicksburg, Mississippi. So in this light, it is hardly surprising that impeded celebration was Christmas's calling card in most Confederate locales in 1862, despite the Fredericksburg victory.

No wonder that a Confederate private from Pendleton, South Carolina, stationed in Virginia mused wistfully in his Christmas Day letter home to his sister about a holiday whose meaning had been virtually transformed by the second wartime Yuletide:

> This day, one year ago, how many thousand families, gay and joyous, celebrating Merry Christmas . . . but today are clad in the deepest mourning in memory to some lost and loved member of their circle. If all the dead (those killed since the war began) could be heaped in one pile and all the wounded be gathered together in one group, the pale faces of the dead and the groans of the wounded would send such a thrill of horror through the hearts of the originators of this war that their very souls would rack with such pain that they would prefer being dead and in torment than to stand before God with such terrible crimes

blackening their characters. Add to this the cries and wailings of the mourners . . . [and] how deep would be the convictions of their consciences.

A Virginia woman told her brother that it was Christmas "only in name," though she had enjoyed cake and pies ("great rarities in these times"), since there were "few, indeed if any, merry hearts" with so many loved ones far away in the military service.[13]

Some poetically inclined Rebels vented their Christmas melancholy in holiday verse. These poems sometimes declared continuing defiance toward the enemy. More commonly, they highlighted the inappropriateness of celebrating Jesus's birth when so many were hurting. Margaret Preston, a northerner who had morphed into a proslavery southerner after her father became president of Washington College in Lexington, Virginia, composed "A Christmas Carol for 1862," which feistily cautioned her countrymen to resist "Talk of failure, subjection, surrender, despair!" over the holidays. "Christmas," a poem by Henry Timrod—the Confederacy's "poet laureate"—offered more distraught thoughts concerning the difficulties southerners experienced emotionally in maintaining a holiday in the midst of horrific fighting and deprivation:

> How grace this hallowed day?
>   Shall happy bells, from yonder ancient spire,
> Send their glad greetings to each Christmas fire
>   Round which the children play?
>   . . . .
>   Is there indeed a door
> Where the old pastimes, with their lawful noise,
> And all the merry round of Christmas joys,
> Could enter as of yore?
>
>   Would not some pallid face
> Look in upon the banquet, calling up
> Dread shapes of battle in the wassail cup,
>   And trouble all the place?
>
>   How could we bear the mirth,
> While some loved reveler of a year ago
> Keeps his mute Christmas now beneath the snow,
>   In cold Virginia earth?[14]

And Confederate poets continued writing depressing Christmas verse right up to the surrender. A verse in the Christmas Day issue of the *Charleston Mercury* in 1863 began, "No more, with glad and happy cheers / And smiling face, doth Christmas come." A Georgia paper's "What We Sing on Christmas Day, 1864" suggested it would be improper to "sing to day" about "glory to God, With peace and good will to man," when the southern land was so "weary" and "war-worn." Better, the poem's author suggested, to sing of revenge and hatred.[15]

Meanwhile, Confederate Christmas charity events bore continuing testimony to the war's toll. A theater in relatively war-untouched Mobile scheduled a Christmas benefit in 1862 to support the "Wives and Children of our Brave Soldiers IN THE FIELD." At the Virginia Military Institute, a cadet mentioned in a letter to his mother on December 20 that "several Tableaus and a gymnasium performance" were scheduled "for the benefit of the soldiers," adding he hoped she would send him money by Christmas so that he could attend them. The next Christmas, in the north Alabama town of Florence, a group of young local women staged "*parlor theatricals*" to benefit impoverished families of Rebel soldiers.[16]

Paradoxically, though, some Confederates parsed positive meanings for their country in the growing Christmas shortages, sometimes couching them as signs of God's favor for their cause. Before Christmas in 1862, the *Southern Illustrated News* imagined Confederates someday telling their grandchildren how they persevered despite having Christmas "without mince-pies or egg-nogg," rather than succumbing to the "yoke" of Yankee rule. Blaming the "fanaticism of the Puritan North" for a widespread dearth of Christmas pies and roast turkey, a Mobile, Alabama, paper argued that the "Christmas sun of 1863" brought cause for celebration because the Confederacy had already surmounted the "heaviest thunderbolts" the "Abolition North" could send its way and independence would be secured by the next Christmas. During Christmas 1864, long after the Union began enlisting black troops, a Richmond, Virginia, newspaper asked its readers to imagine what Christmas would be like under Yankee rule: residents would be forced to get permits even to shop from a German northern officer and display them to a "negro-guard" at the market. Far better, the paper urged, for Confederates to observe the holiday with hope and joy and anticipate Christmas 1865 when as an unconquered and independent people they could "please God" and pass a genuinely merry holiday.[17]

Were southerners destined to lose, the thinking seems to have been, they would have lacked all capacity to celebrate Jesus's birth. Rather, as a North Carolinian put it, Christmas tidings about goodwill toward men and peace on earth comingled in the Confederacy "with those which declare the triumph of *liberty, independence,* and *country.*" The *Augusta (Georgia) Constitutionalist* urged that readers, instead of mourning the difficulties of freeing themselves from a people "deaf to the teachings of peace and good will," should accept Providence's tribulations while ensuring that their children enjoyed the holiday and that naked Rebel soldiers in the field were properly clothed. Even during the holiday season in 1864, just months before Appomattox, Augusta's *Constitutionalist* prayed that God would cause the Yankees to cease their "wicked war" and allow the "beloved Confederacy" to enjoy *both* independence and peace. In neighboring South Carolina, the transplanted Bostonian turned defiant Confederate Caroline Gilman put what she described as "belligerent" (if makeshift) Christmas gifts in her children's stockings, like fighting cocks made from pumpkin seeds, and improvised "Confederate blacking" (likely shoe polish) from some poison berries.[18]

Compounding holiday miseries for Confederates, Yankee military operations and foraging raids occurred on Christmas throughout the war, including a horrific incident in Missouri in 1863 when Unionist Missouri militiamen broke up a Christmas dinner at a Confederate camp meeting, in the process killing and wounding some sixty civilians there, including children and women. Occasionally, Christmas Day forays by the Confederacy's own soldiers compounded the misery. A South Carolina planter on Christmas Day 1864 apprised Confederate president Jefferson Davis that Confederate cavalry had been "robbing—plundering—whites, negroes & free negroes . . . of money—horses & goods." Yankee troops, though, were far more likely to break up Christmas celebrations than were Confederates, and sometimes their raids included liberating slaves. Writing from Portsmouth, Virginia, on Christmas Day 1863, a Union soldier in the Fifteenth Connecticut Infantry informed his homefolk how two pickets with his unit had just liberated from their master three sisters of a female slave who had already gained her own freedom earlier in the war.[19]

Southern civilians in contested areas never knew when Yankees might disrupt Christmas, as happened in 1862 to a small slaveholder named Cornelia Peake McDonald while her husband was away in Confederate service. McDonald lived in Winchester in Virginia's fertile and ceaselessly fought-over Shenandoah Valley. Two days before Christmas, she reported that the mere rumor Yankee soldiers were nearby had caused local storeowners to shut down their shops, and she noted that 500 Union cavalry had appeared at her place and posted guards at her gate. A day later, she described how two cavalrymen had entered her yard and seized the dressed turkey that she had hanging from a tree branch intended for her next day's Christmas meal. Although her protests persuaded the soldier, who had said that being a "secesh" she lacked all right to keep the turkey, to return it, her victory proved short-lived. A band of infantry soon afterward confiscated her cut wood and dismantled and seized wood from her fence, carriage house, and other buildings (apparently for their campfires). Even more insulting, the soldiers took her Christmas cakes, and she literally had to wrestle seized biscuits out of one soldier's hands. And making matters worse yet, she felt she had little choice but to feed and temporarily take in a Union surgeon who was under the weather. No wonder, on Christmas Day, she felt "too restless to enjoy, or even realize that it was Christmas."[20]

McDonald's humiliations paralleled what was going on at Christmastime in 1862 throughout occupied and contested parts of Dixie, though later in the war the pickings sometimes seemed scant to foraging soldiers. ("At breakfast," noted one Georgia plantation woman on Christmas Day 1864, "two Yankees rode around the lot, but seeing nothing to take went away.") On Christmas Eve in 1862, some blacks crossed from the Union-controlled north bank of Virginia's James River and stole $1,000 worth of meat and other property on the south bank, according to an official Confederate military dispatch, although the dispatch attributed the thefts to independent action by vagrant "negroes" living in vacated farmhouses rather than a collaboration with Union army operations. In northern Louisiana on Christmas Day, a Confederate woman discovered on arriving home that Federal troops, assisted by some blacks, were in the process of searching for her money and jewelry and that they had already forced open her trunks; stolen Christmas cake, milk, and butter from her storeroom; overturned furniture; and confiscated forty recently slaughtered hogs. In Mississippi, Sarah E. Watkins of Forest Place plantation wrote her daughter that she was passing a "lonesome Christmas morning" worrying about the imminent arrival of Federals. As one precaution, since Yankee troops were confiscating slaves on nearby holdings, her husband had set off for Alabama with several male and two female slaves, hiring them for railroad work there. A few days after the holiday, another Mississippi civilian registered her disgust not only that Union troops pursuing Confederate raiders had just taken her family's food and quilts but also that the Yankees had the gall to make her family serve them by cooking up the confiscated food, even though it was Christmas Day.[21]

Charleston, perhaps the most hated city in the Confederacy in Union eyes for starting the rebellion, came under a horrific bombardment just after midnight on Christmas Eve 1863 that burned some houses, outbuildings, and a cotton press. Early on Christmas morning, Yankee batteries on Morris Island and Folly Island in the harbor set the "cradle of Rebellion in flames," with smoke and fire bellowing out from the city's south side and burning for eight hours and the sky turning red. Rubbing salt in the wound, Yankees celebrated the insult of committing their aggression on the South's vaunted regional holiday. "Charleston on Fire—'A Merry Christmas'" headlined a Milwaukee paper, adding that the decision to open up on Charleston at the very time that "dance and wassail were at their height" was motivated by a Union general's resentment of how "arrogant and opinionated Charlestonians always 'kept Christmas.'" A New Hampshire newspaper playfully quipped that the Yankees had "entertained" Charlestonians for Christmas, and that the shelling probably had town denizens worried that Santa Claus had been distributing "suspicious gifts" to private residences. Horrified local Confederates, in turn, made special mention that Yankee "fiends" had chosen to proclaim the day of "Peace on earth, good will towards men" by cannon.[22]

Meanwhile, in fully occupied parts of the Confederacy, white southerners endured what they considered outrageously repugnant holiday humiliations by enemy forces, though sometimes Yankees proved surprisingly compassionate. After reaching Savannah in December 1864, for example, some Federal soldiers took up a Christmas Day collection to support orphans there. Because the occupiers could have acted far more oppressively than they did, many slaveholders found it in their best interest to quickly adjust to their control and regulations. Sarah Morgan, the daughter of a deceased slaveholding district court judge in Baton Rouge, Louisiana, enjoyed what she called "almost a Merry Christmas" in 1863, despite spending it with her family in occupied New Orleans. Delighted at meeting acquaintances on busy streets, she also liked "smiling at the bright, eager faces in the stores" and described eating bonbons, as well as liberal Christmas gift exchanges between her family members, including "magnificent diamond earrings" that her brother gave her sister. General Walter Q. Gresham,

Union occupation commander of Natchez, Mississippi, in December 1863, cheerily wrote his wife the day after Christmas about how he had just enjoyed the "finest [Christmas holiday] dinner" he had ever experienced at the home of a local aristocrat, and been very warmly treated by all the members of the local elite in attendance. His experience was similar to that in Louisiana of an assistant surgeon with the 160th New York Volunteers, who was welcomed into the home of a family with different attitudes than his own "on vital questions to the Country" for a Christmas dinner of turkey, mutton, tongue, wine, and trimmings. Not only did they treat him as if he were a relation, but they took obvious pleasure in looking at pictures of his own family.[23]

More typically, though, civilians recoiled at being forced to deal with Yankees at holiday time. On Christmas Eve in 1863, a woman living in unoccupied Petersburg, Virginia, penned a letter alluding to news from occupied Norfolk that residents there had to swear obedience to the Emancipation Proclamation and that a "negro" had "kissed a white lady" on Norfolk's streets, exacerbating her fears that racial miscegenation would follow Union rule. Emilie McKinley, a native Pennsylvanian who tutored Mississippi plantation children and fervently embraced the southern cause, not only resented the "contemptible" Yankee abolitionist soldier from New York who barged into the house where she resided that Christmas Day but also his ranting about southern mistreatment of northerners before the war. She was disgusted, too, that he threatened to audibly torture his captive audience by making them listen to him sing the abolitionist song "John Brown's Body." "He talked and talked," the exasperated McKinley complained, adding, "We thought he would never go."[24]

Fanny Yates Cohen, a young Jewish daughter of a Savannah, Georgia, cotton exporter and commission merchant, experienced "the saddest Christmas that I have ever spent" after Union general William Tecumseh Sherman's forces peacefully entered Savannah shortly before Christmas in 1864 following their march from Atlanta (with Sherman famously gloating in a dispatch to Lincoln that he was giving him "as a Christmas gift the City of Savannah"). Cohen's distress was primarily a reaction to what happened leading up to Christmas, with "the Goths" entering her family home, nearly confiscating it for officers' quarters, threatening her father ("you know you Rebs *will* fight and when you are Conquered you must submit to what ever will contribute to our Comfort"), stealing the family's wood, and eventually compelling them to lodge one of Sherman's subordinate generals.

Christmas itself was not so disagreeable, as Cohen consoled herself by huddling with acquaintances in what she called a "rebel *meeting*," where they "abused the Yankees" to their "hearts content" and laughed together about a newspaper that had just appeared in the city professing to represent Georgians who wanted to restore the Union.[25]

Many Confederates subjected to what they considered holiday indignities by Yankee occupiers could barely stifle their feelings, risking retribution for their seething resentment. The fiery Fanny Cohen, who quipped that having enemy soldiers within her residence would render her whole family "prematurely old," almost allowed her contempt to go too far, finding it so difficult to feign politeness toward one Union officer appearing in her house that she was rendered virtually speechless, since she could not risk giving expression to her actual thoughts. A Yankee soldier encamped on a wealthy Confederate's estate near Nashville noted the day before Christmas in 1862, unsympathetically, that its landowner had complained it was a "shocking cruelty" that Union authorities assessed him $2,500 to support the destitute wives and children of Confederate soldiers left behind in Nashville.[26]

Some Confederate civilians went farther in their verbal resistance to Yankee demands during the Christmas season, and they sometimes paid a severe price for their obstinacy. In occupied New Orleans during Christmas 1862, where a new Union occupation commander as of Christmas Day reopened churches closed by his predecessor with the caveat that clergymen refrain from any prayers, exhortations, or sermons designed to incite resistance to the U.S. government, eight persons reportedly suffered arrest by Union authorities by cheering for Confederate president Jefferson Davis. A more infamous wartime holiday incident involving the Union's repression of pro-Confederate speech occurred Christmas Day 1863 in Vicksburg. There, during morning holiday service at Christ Episcopal Church, five female congregants (two of them daughters of a local judge) earned the wrath of Yankee soldiers present by standing up at the point of the service where their minister, under compulsion himself, asked all worshippers to pray for Union president Abraham Lincoln. Horrified at that thought, the five women left their pews and then the church itself, purposely swishing their skirts as they exited to emphasize their spite. Informed about their peevish display, the Union general in command in Vicksburg issued an order banishing them from the city under the threat of imprisonment for insulting the U.S. government, and imposed penalties for similar offenders in the future.[27]

Among Fanny Cohen's complaints about Union occupiers of Savannah in late 1864 was mention of a Union general on Christmas Eve trying to convince a relation's servant girl that she was now free and an allusion to Henry, one of the Cohens' servants, leaving the family "to enlist in the Federal service." Henry's departure may have had nothing to do with the Christmas season beyond the coincidence of timing; Yankee troops simply had not been in the city previously.[28] Still, wartime transformations of customary southern Christmas practices seem implicated in slavery's weakening throughout Dixie over the course of the conflict, exacerbated by increasingly radical emancipation policies emanating from Washington.

Although Abraham Lincoln and the Union's Congress initially waged war on the Confederacy to reunite the nation, in order to win victory their objectives soon broadened to include undermining and possibly ending slavery in the Confederacy and weakening it in those slave states—Delaware, Missouri, Kentucky, and Maryland—remaining in the Union. A succession of legislative enactments and executive decisions in Washington and policies adopted by Union officers in the field, abetted by actions by slaves themselves, put Dixie on a virtually inexorable path to general emancipation.

Congress's First Confiscation Act (August 1861) allowed federal authorities to confiscate slaves being used by Confederates for military purposes, leaving those slaves' legal status in limbo for the time being. In March 1862, Congress banned military personnel from returning escaped slaves to their masters under fugitive slave statutes; and that July, federal lawmakers freed all slaves doing military labor for the Union army (as well as their dependents) and authorized the president to accept blacks into the military and pay them for their labor. Four months after that, in July, the Union Congress's Second Confiscation Act emancipated outright slaves held by Rebels in places the Union army occupied, further limited applications of the Fugitive Slave Act of 1850, and allowed the president to use blacks to help the government suppress the rebellion. Most famously, Lincoln's Emancipation Proclamation of January 1, 1863, declared as free all persons held as slaves in the Confederacy, except those in Tennessee, specified Louisiana parishes, the entirety of what a few months later became the new state of West Virginia, and several specified eastern Virginia counties (areas considered either loyal from the war's start or already wholly or mostly pacified by Union forces). The proclamation also emphasized Lincoln's intention of accepting former slaves into the military. Combined, these measures seriously threatened slavery throughout the South.[29]

Not only were Yankee troops operating under increasingly punitive statutes stripping disloyal southerners of federal legal protection for their slaveholdings; the mere presence of Yankee soldiers in the Confederacy encouraged slaves to attempt Christmas work slowdowns or escapes to Union lines, especially as standards of supervision on southern farms and plantations declined because of the war's manpower demands on southern white males. Though much is made of how Confederate conscription laws caused class friction and even disloyalty within the Confederacy because they exempted slaveholders and sometimes their sons and overseers from Confederate military service, an enormous number of southern slaveholders and their immediate male relations and overseers volunteered for military service. Further, a very high percentage of slaveholders were either unwilling to claim exemptions in Confederate conscription legislation or unable to comply with particular requirements for exemptions. According to one recent study, up to 95 percent of Confederate plantation owners failed to capitalize on conscription provisions exempting overseers and sons.[30] Their commitment to Confederate service, in turn, greatly diminished the number of white authorities on the home front available to discipline slaves.

Even in the war's early months when the Fugitive Slave Act remained technically in force, many slaves welcomed Yankee troops and installations in their vicinity as a "counter-state" to the sway of their masters, locales where the "police powers of southern slave society" became inoperable. Though most Union commanders enforced their nation's fugitive legislation during this period, General Benjamin F. Butler set a very important precedent otherwise a little over a month after the war started that was soon followed by other Yankee army and naval officers. As commander of Fortress Monroe at Hampton Roads, Virginia, he decided in late May 1861 to retain three escaped slaves as seized enemy property (or "contraband of war") rather than return them to their Virginian master for labor assignments on Confederate fortifications. Gradually, Union liberation policies combined with other wartime changes to trigger an enormous exodus of enslaved people to Yankee lines.

Some 400,000 slaves from all the southern states combined reached Union lines by 1864, including thousands from states like Missouri, Maryland, and Kentucky that had remained in the Union and were therefore technically immune from the Emancipation Proclamation, some of the latter apparently forced to Union lines by angry masters. Just after Christmas 1864, the adjutant general of the Union army reported from Lexington, Kentucky, that a "large number" of black women and children had arrived on Christmas Day at a Union contraband camp in Kentucky, having been made to vacate their cabins by masters who were upset that the Union army had recruited the women's husbands and were unwilling to support black dependents once deprived of their spouses' labor. By the war's end, some 146,000 blacks from the slave states, and thousands more from the North, served in the Union army, making in all about 10 percent of Union ranks. Additionally, somewhere between 20,000 and 30,000 African Americans served in the Union navy, accounting for about one-fourth of all Union naval personnel.[31]

Wartime Christmas shortages played a role in encouraging slaves to capitalize on evolving northern emancipation policies. Christmas parties and gifting had long been a crucial element in slavery's glue, one of the things that allowed the South's peculiar institution to function as smoothly as it did. As Eugene D. Genovese suggested in his classic study *Roll, Jordan, Roll,* slaves and masters established an "organic relationship based on reciprocal obligations" within households and on plantations. Under such conditions, a "good master" decently clothed, housed, and fed his slaves; whipped with restraint; and conceded to his workers "holidays and good times." Slaves, in return, responded by providing labor on demand and figuring out ways to cope with and triumph over their own adversity. During the war, a Confederate soldier obliquely made this point by remarking that his comrades anticipated winter quarters and getting a respite from fighting as much as "Cuffy"—a generic term, like "Sambo," that many southerners used for slaves—awaited Christmas.[32] Breakdowns in Dixie's Christmas-giving mores in wartime, on the other hand, naturally had an opposite effect.

Wartime cutbacks in masters' Christmas gifts for slaves amounted to announcements that slaveholder paternalism was in a downward spiral, dovetailing with other transformations damaging to slave retention rates, which were particularly noticeable over the holiday. House servants, for example, could not help but overhear whites talking about wartime setbacks or Union troop movements over Christmas, witness the dwindling number of white people around to control them, or observe sadness in their masters' households over the holiday because male family members normally around the hearth were absent in the war or among its casualties. Additionally, disruptions of normal post-Christmas work routines for field hands may well have told slaves that the war was changing the rules of the game and that that their masters' power over them had new limits. General Robert E. Lee, who in the winter before he took command in Virginia (in 1862) had the responsibility of organizing Confederate defenses along the South Atlantic shoreline, wrote about the possibility of impressing slave laborers to finish constructing the fortifications defending Charleston immediately after the slaves' holiday ended. Slaves impressed to work on Augusta, Georgia's defenses did get Christmas 1864 off to return to their families for the holiday, but were immediately summoned back once the holiday ended. It likely occurred to them that their masters were no longer calling the shots regarding their labor.[33]

Given changing perceptions of masters' power, white southerners tried to keep up pretenses of holiday normality in master-slave relations, grasping for signs that their slaves remained subservient. Certainly this was the case in the household of C. C. Jones, a onetime Presbyterian minister in coastal Liberty County, Georgia, who before the war had been one of the most zealous advocates in the entire region of Christian ministries to the South's slave population. Dr. Jones and his wife owned 129 slaves according to the U.S. census of 1860, dispersed around several plantations. Spending Christmas 1861 at their Montevideo sea-island cotton and rice coastal plantation south of Savannah, they seem to have observed the holiday fairly normally, even though they had two sons in the Confederate military. Reverend Jones's Christmas Day letter to his son Charles Jr. reported the sounds of cannonading in the distance and the outbreak of measles among some of the local troops, while hinting at some doubt on his own part that God favored the southern cause. Still, Jones described Christmas morning as brilliantly sunlit, recounted that the servants showed up early "with their Merry Christmas," and told his son that his own grandchildren were enjoying "all manner of things pleasing to their eyes and their ears and their tastes" that they had discovered in their stockings. That same Christmas, a Florida teenage diarist who lived on a plantation near Tallahassee noted in a similar spirit in her Christmas Day entry that even though the "flavor of Christmas" seemed lacking among the adults in her household, her father had gifts for all the household servants and field hands as was customary and provided them with "Sweetened Dram," saying (as she paraphrased it) that the slaves were "just children and must have their pleasure the same as ever."[34]

Throughout the war, many masters and mistresses continued providing Christmas holiday gifts and parties for their laborers as best they could. This was one of the most effective signals they could convey that no matter what their slaves were observing around them or hearing through their own channels about the war, all remained normal so far as their own status was concerned. Joel Chandler Harris (later the famed author of the "Uncle Remus" tales), who in 1862 apprenticed himself to a small newspaper published on a Georgia plantation, later described Christmas there during the war as a "happy time" immune to the ongoing struggle. Similar scenes played out elsewhere. "Gave the negroes to day instead of next Monday," Samuel Porcher Gaillard of Orange Grove cotton plantation in the Sumter District of South Carolina remarked the day before Christmas 1863, "as I give 3 days not including Sunday." In Texas around the same time, Lucy Stevens's cousins whipped up eggnog to make Christmas Day a special occasion for their enslaved people and threw them a special dinner a day later. Even when wartime hardships precluded normal holiday distributions, many made an effort to do the best they could. The manager of Charles Heyward's rice plantations informed his employer the day before Christmas in 1863 that despite the "trying circumstances" of the time he would "distribute to the negroes such rations as you have always allowed on Christmas." As late as Christmas 1864, the Confederate First Lady, with difficulty, managed to come up with modest gifts for all the Davis family servants.[35]

In an attempt to encourage continued loyalty among their slaves with their gifts, many masters additionally continued to grant their enslaved people expected holiday time off and travel privileges, further fostering the impression that little had changed or was likely to change regarding their bondage, despite the war. This was especially true in 1861 and 1862. During the war's first Christmas, for instance, the Prestons of Lexington, Virginia, gave presents from their Christmas tree to all their servants, and then granted them a work holiday through New Year's Eve. Kate Stone's mother that Christmas granted her elderly slave "Uncle Hoccles" a holiday pass so that he could visit his children across the Mississippi River—perhaps the last time he would ever be able to travel to see them given his age. Louisa Quitman informed her husband that she had given all her household "darkies" several days of holiday immediately after Christmas, and another southern woman told a friend that family members were waiting on themselves since "the holidays are given up entirely to the negroes."[36]

Such patterns continued the next year. In a letter that had possibly been written for her, a slave woman on a Harrison County, Texas, plantation informed her absent husband (who had gone away to the war as a personal servant of the son of their owner) that their master had given all the slaves a three-day Christmas break. At the Buffalo Forge ironworks near Lexington, Virginia, manager Daniel Brady let eleven slaves off for the holidays to visit their families elsewhere and gave those slaves remaining there the full Christmas Day–January 1 work vacation that they had received before the war. Former U.S. treasury secretary Howell Cobb's son John informed his father that he had instructed their plantation overseers to give slaves an abbreviated three-day Christmas break, but terminated their Christmas visiting privileges in hopes of containing an outbreak of measles contracted by some of the slaves who had recently been to Savannah.[37]

Still, once the war started, it was more difficult than in past years for slaveholders to provide the customary Christmas gifts to servants and field hands, given shortages of goods and wartime inflation for items that were available. Candy, for example, shot up 50 percent in price at the stores in Petersburg, Virginia, directly south of Richmond, by Christmas 1861, making it already unaffordable for the city's lower and even middle classes. Realizing how difficult it was for his wife to get his Louisiana plantation's cotton to market that year, a Confederate officer advised her to allow their slaves to raise money for their normal "Christmas frolics" by selling some of the plantation's excess cottonseed. Many slave owners responded to wartime financial pressures by cutting back on gifts. In Natchez, Mississippi, Louisa Quitman exposed the difficulty of reconciling slaves' persisting holiday expectations with wartime shortages in a letter to her husband explaining the challenges of identifying suitable presents given the times. Saying she had "ransacked the garret to meet the ever recurring greeting of 'Christmas gift miss!',", she admitted she "dared not brave them empty handed." Adding that "ancient garments" had been "brought to light . . . amid the dust and moth, to bedeck our sable damsels and matrons," she identified the "greatest prize" as a "gaily colored dressing gown, resembling much an astrologer's mantle." Left implied was the obvious: that masters failing to satisfy the expectations of dependable servants might find them less dependable in the future. One senses such concerns from the December 26, 1861, diary entry of Alabama cotton farmer and state legislator Augustus Benners, who owned dozens of slaves. Although able to give his children "more from Santa Claus than they expected," he apparently had trouble mustering appropriate gifts for his house servants: "Windsor, Milly, Edward, Dred came up—Presents were very scarce as times are very hard." He then added that only God knew how his family would provide itself with meat.[38]

Naturally, such pressures on masters escalated as the war progressed, leaving many of them with few options other than to curtail Christmas spending. Booker T. Washington later recalled how the slaves on the farm where he was enslaved had felt the "pinch of hard times," when instead of getting a normal holiday gift of shoes he had been given a pair of inferior soles made from hickory wood. South Carolinian James Henry Hammond kept up the pretense of holiday normality for his slaves in 1861 and 1862. In the former year, he "sent a dozen bottles of my wine to each plantation to add to the enjoyment of the people"; the next year he threw his slaves holiday barbecues and claimed that his slaves were dancing and "enjoying themselves backwards & forwards." By 1863, though, plagued by the absence of sons in the Confederate military service and the unavailability of competent overseers, he remarked that although Christmas once brought "smiling faces & merry hearts," he was now simply providing his laborers with an extra week of provisions instead of their traditional barbecue, leaving his "people to enjoy themselves as they liked." In 1864, a Georgia slaveholding mistress observed that she lacked any pies, cakes, or candy for the holiday, and that a holiday that had been always celebrated with "mirth & gayety" had become an occasion of "sadness & gloom." When on Christmas morning her servants came into her room beseeching "Christmas gift, mistress; Christmas gift, mistress!," all she could manage was to cry and pull her cover up over her head.[39]

The inability of slaveholders to match in wartime what they had provided before the war weakened their ability to manipulate their laborers' behavior, encouraging slaves to slow down their work pace or attempt to escape from bondage. Some slaves simply abused their Christmas leave privileges, like the workers on the Harris farm in the Spartanburg district in South Carolina. Managing her North Carolina husband Charles's Cherry Hill plantation in South Carolina in 1863, Caroline Pettigrew pleased her slaves with a special holiday dispensation of molasses, pork sausages, and beef. However, due to inflation, she was unable to provide the normal Christmastime distribution of shoes. Three of the slaves, as a result, refused an assignment to clear flooded land just after the holiday in 1863. Rather, all they did was "sit round the fire & warm their feet," as Pettigrew explained to her husband. Similarly, during the Christmas season in 1864, Allston family overseer Jesse Belflowers reported to Adele Allston that slaves on the Allston's Nightingale Hall place were "grumbling" about their shoe and clothing situation, likely an indication that they had not received their expected Christmas distributions. During that same last Civil War Christmas, Emily Harris was plagued, at a time when her husband was absent in the war, by slaves who took lengthy Christmas holidays without her permission as well as by slaves who did have permission to leave but failed to return on schedule.[40]

The proximity of Yankee forces increased the odds that slaves would prove troublesome at Christmas. Georgia planter Louis Manigault recognized the challenge as early as the war's first Christmas. Upset by considerable running away and other forms of resistance at his Gowrie island place near Savannah, he reflected how such acts had become of greater concern over the holiday, since "Christmas is always a very bad time for Negroes . . . any year but far more so this." Compensating for the altered state of affairs, Manigault shifted potentially rebellious low-country slaves to an inland property more removed from Union coastal operations. On a Louisiana sugar plantation, slaves stopped work on Christmas in 1862 even though they were expected to work until January when their grinding season ended, undoubtedly encouraged in their obstinacy by the Union takeover of many of the state's sugar parishes.[41]

Often, slaves remained in place despite wartime shortages, as proved the case during the shoe crisis on the Pettigrew place in South Carolina. Eventually getting high prices for her plantation's corn in the Augusta, Georgia, market, Caroline Pettigrew bought the shoes and other clothing that she had been unable to provide her slaves as Christmas gifts, and the recalcitrant slaves then undertook spring plowing. One Alabama slaveholding mistress observed during the Christmas season 1862 that not only had her house domestics remained cheerfully obedient despite Lincoln's "infamous" emancipation edict but also that they voluntarily helped with the extra cooking required to help give Confederate soldiers passing through her neighborhood a Christmas meal, declining reimbursement for working the holiday. Her slaves further earned her gratitude by saying they wished to help the soldiers in whatever way they could. Still, it seems safe to suggest that household and plantation holiday cutbacks under wartime duress fostered attitudinal changes among slaves. Deprivations naturally made slaves more resentful of their bondage and thus more open to the allure of

Union lines, despite the continuing risks of punishment for unsuccessful bids for freedom.[42]

Evidence suggests that numbers of slaves timed their freedom bids during the war for the Christmas holidays, such as the slave Gordon mentioned in the first chapter. In her memoir about Christmases on her family's place in eastern Virginia, LaSalle Corbell Pickett mentioned that the household servants chose Christmas Eve 1862, just before the Emancipation Proclamation went into effect, to flee as a group to Union-held Newport News. In fact, she claimed that her father, discerning their intentions in advance, gave them their Christmas gifts and a little extra money the night before rather than await Christmas Gif' rituals the next morning. Down the coast around the same time, on the Eldorado rice plantation in South Carolina of the prominent Pinckney family, a "prime field hand" named Renty chose Christmas to flee to the Union fleet, which he subsequently joined. That holiday too, Louis Hughes ran away from his master's plantation in Pontotoc County, Mississippi, for Union lines at Holly Springs in the northern part of the state, but became the victim of a Rebel patrol. The patrollers lashed him and then returned him to his master's place, whipping him a second time in front of his master's wife to drum home their point.[43]

Some slaves sought permanent relief from bondage by spontaneously taking advantage of fortuitous circumstances that placed them behind Union lines. A slave named Becky, for example, was sent by her master on a Christmas errand in 1864 to Union-occupied Nashville, and then simply stayed on, protected in her right to do so by Union authorities after her owner turned up in town and tried to forcefully retrieve her back into bondage. Mississippi slaveholder Everard Baker not only mentioned in his day-after-Christmas diary entry in 1863 that his place had been plagued both by Federal cavalry stealing his finest horses and Confederate soldiers burning his cotton (to keep it out of enemy hands); he also wrote that a "good many negroes" had "left through the community," though his own "so far" had "shown their good sense & stood true to mind their interests," and he was giving them a lengthy post-Christmas holiday. In one case, a group of forty-three North Carolina slaves absconded on Christmas Eve in 1863 and successfully made their way to Union-held Roanoke Island.[44]

As in peacetime, southern newspapers held fugitive wanted ads that specifically cited Christmas escapes. One Virginia slaveholder advertised in a Richmond newspaper after the holidays in 1862 that his "negro man" Jim had chosen Christmas Day for his escape and that he would pay $50 for Jim's delivery to the Hanover County jail. A slaveholder in Mobile advertised for an escaped slave in a newspaper published in Jackson, Mississippi, noting that his slave boy Henry had chosen Christmas for his escape and was reportedly somewhere in Jackson. Another master offered as much as $100 in a Georgia paper for his boy Isaiah, who "at Christmas" had forged a pass and escaped under the pretense of traveling to visit his wife.[45]

Although, as we saw earlier, Mary Chesnut feasted well at Christmas in 1861, she did not enjoy a completely carefree Yuletide that year, and her disquietude merits our attention too, because it highlights another dimension of how masters and slaves experienced the holiday amid the turmoil of war. Rather than entirely immersing herself in the celebration, Chesnut found herself ruminating about slaves who had murdered one of her South Carolina relations months earlier, and what the killing might portend for the future. Back in September, Chesnut and her husband, James, had learned that Betsey Witherspoon's slaves had smothered her to death while she was lying in bed. Then in October they gleaned additional specifics; apparently the slaves committed their murderous act to avert a whipping for using their mistress's linen and silver at a party without her permission.

The initial news of this murder had been enough to send Mary Chesnut reeling, not only because of its intrinsically shocking nature but also because she had considered the Witherspoon slaves particularly pampered. If her cousin could be murdered despite her benevolence, then any slaveholder was at risk of similar reprisals; "the ground is knocked up from under me," she wrote shortly after the incident. "I sleep & wake with the horrid vision before my eyes of those vile black hands—smothering her." Now, on Christmas Day, Chesnut found herself mulling over the incident again despite the passage of time, because she had just heard that the murderers had been hanged. It infuriated her, she reported, that a lawyer "with a John Brown spirit" had served as "Devil's counsel" throughout the case and given the slaves a vigorous defense. In fact, she was so disturbed that when her servants entered her room that day with their expected "Christmas Gift" entreaties, all she could do was cover her face and weep.[46]

Chesnut's angst suggests that the specter of Christmas slave insurrections, so worrisome to southerners in antebellum times, continued after secession, just as coping with holiday fugitives persisted, despite the promises of southern disunionists that a separate nationhood would help alleviate both concerns. And things only worsened as the war lengthened. By Christmas of 1862, with large numbers of the slave states' white males in military service, state authority over slaves eroding, Union troops penetrating many locales, and knowledge of Union emancipation measures circulating, many southern whites agonized about how precarious their control over laborers had become. "What do you think of Lincoln's proclamation?" a Virginia woman inquired of her soldier husband in late 1862 some six weeks before the Emancipation Proclamation was scheduled to take effect. "Do you think there will be a general massacre of whites before Christmas? I do have the thought." Driven by similar fears, a group of Confederate soldiers in Columbus, Mississippi, petitioned Governor John J. Pettus that they be granted fifteen to twenty days leave from Christmas to travel home to protect their families. They reasoned, in support of their request, that "the negroes" were "making their brays" of expecting freedom by January 1, and that a "general outbreak" was likely when their expectations were disappointed. Around the same time, a woman whose husband was serving in the First Battalion of Alabama Artillery wrote Confederate president Davis explaining that her husband had only volunteered for the military under the impression that he would be swept up in the Confederate conscription act if he did not. She urged that he be detached or exempted (under the draft law's exceptions for slaveholders) so that he could supervise his slaves and farm, because many people believed "we will have trouble here about Christmas holidays, with our slaves, growing out of the Emancipation Proclamation."[47]

Insecurity about the war's potential for bringing a slave revolution infected Union-occupied parts of the South, like New Orleans and its vicinity, as well as areas remaining under Rebel control. One Crescent City–area planter was especially expressive in his communications with Union authorities. Appalled that the Union officer commanding the Department of the Gulf, General Nathaniel P. Banks, was deploying two regiments of locally raised free blacks and slaves, he implored Banks to reverse what he deemed a very dangerous policy. Explaining that there had always existed a tradition among the local "negro population" of expecting freedom for Christmas that had "caused us many a sleepless night," this slaveholder predicted that "negro regiments" would use their weapons to compel the U.S. government to free slaves. Along similar lines, on December 21 two residents of St. John the Baptist Parish petitioned that the First and Second Louisiana Native Guards should be withdrawn from their parish on the basis that three carts of slaves had just turned up there "Shrieking threats, singing and exciting to insurrection, and mentioning Christmas as being the time Set for the emancipation of Slaves." Such apprehensions were pervasive enough that the general on Christmas Eve day issued a proclamation reassuring Louisiana's white populace that the army had no intention of fomenting slave insurrection.[48]

Such frights persisted through the war. On December 23, 1863, a farmer in western North Carolina's mountains called for a meeting in the town of Flat Rock due to reports that "negroes" in nearby Transylvania County intended an uprising "to demolish the white," at which gathering a special patrol was organized to keep blacks under surveillance. One local woman considered these rumors merely a pretext to get local militiamen recalled from Confederate service; but Harriott Kinloch Middleton, a refugee of aristocratic lineage from Charleston who had been living there since the previous year to escape the war, took them seriously enough. On Christmas Day, Middleton wrote a cousin that three members of the Boykin Rangers—a cavalry unit also called Boykin's Light Mounted Rangers—had arrived from Greenville, South Carolina, to warn residents that "15 able bodied negroes" were involved with Unionists in a conspiracy scheduled to begin "in this part of the country" on Christmas Eve. In a sentence concluding with three exclamation points, she said the black insurrectionists had sworn to die for the cause. "I suppose there must be some foundation for the story," she intimated, "or the Rangers would not have been sent here so suddenly." In December 1864, a correspondent of North Carolina's governor claimed eastern North Carolina was imperiled by an insurrection scheduled for "about Christmas" in which each white inhabitant in an area stretching into South Carolina, regardless of age or sex, would be massacred by about 100 insurgents and several white accomplices—excepting women the rebels desired for concubines or wives. Although the citizenry preferred sending suspects to prison, local authorities lacked the jails to hold them or even men to make apprehensions and deliver them, because army manpower needs had siphoned off white males over the age of thirteen. So vigilante justice was handling the exigency: one suspect had already been hanged, and four or five additional hangings were scheduled that very day. That same last Confederate Yuletide, apparently without evidence, a Texan slaveholder told a newspaper correspondent that blacks were increasingly attempting to "violate" white women and urged that Texan newspapers spread the alarm.[49]

Occasionally intimations of major rebellions panicked Confederates so much as to jeopardize their government's logistics and manpower allocations. Over the Christmas holiday in 1862, Confederate secretary of war James A. Seddon diverted 10,000 pounds of gunpowder to Georgia because the legislature and Governor Joseph E. Brown feared a Christmas insurrection, and because the gunpowder had originally been loaned to the Confederacy by Georgia's government. Seddon told Brown that he was not immediately supplying the requested 25,000 pounds because he believed that "anticipations of trouble with the slaves during the Christmas holidays will not be realized." The historian Stephanie McCurry not only notes that rumors of black uprisings disturbed all Confederate Christmases, but that these apprehensions caused civilians to pressure authorities to arm home guards and local militias, with the potential to undermine Confederate strategic needs. In December 1864, Wilmington, North Carolina—the Confederacy's last major port open to blockade-runners—came under attack by a powerful U.S. naval force; and Fort Fisher at the mouth of the Cape Fear River, the port's primary defense, came under bombardment on Christmas Day itself. As they reacted to these unfolding events, civilians in North Carolina counties far from the coast urged the retention of troops in their home locales for fear that the anticipated arrival of Union forces in their midst would spark a holiday uprising by slaves in their path.[50]

As we have seen, Civil War Christmases were fraught with discouragements for southern slaveholders that went far beyond the absence or loss of family members in the war and severe shortages of customary holiday edibles and presents. Yankee soldiers pillaged or appropriated their property, refusing to respect the holiday. Slaves resisted work assignments and ran away. Intimations of slave Christmas insurrections roiled the landscape. But slaveholders at least were spared bearing witness to one final aspect of Christmas's Civil War meaning, the experiences and sentiments of their escaped African Americans passing wartime Yuletides within Union lines. When the liberated slave at Portsmouth, Virginia, mentioned earlier in this chapter was reunited with her sisters after Union troops took them into custody and freed them, for instance, she ecstatically praised the Yankee soldiers with no hint that she had ever internally accepted the logic of her own enslavement. Not only did she consider the Yankees "de bravers' fellers dere ever was" for freeing her siblings from their mean-spirited master and mistress, but she also promised to throw a party with dancing and music to celebrate her family's liberators.[51] Her reactions were indicative of many reactions among her peers when reaching what their masters' had told them were *enemy* lines, even though the treatment that formerly enslaved people received in Union encampments was uneven and often abusive.

Yankee soldiers harbored widely variant attitudes about slaves, ranging from what might be called egalitarian abolitionist to hatefully racist. As a result, some Union soldiers treated slave arrivals at their lines with contempt or cruelty, even at Christmas. A Michigan officer in the Union army, for example, exposed very unenlightened attitudes when he was stationed in Kentucky, noting that "all the niggers" considered Christmas simply a time "to dance, make love, race horses and raise the devil." So far as he was concerned, they were better suited for serfdom or servitude than freedom.[52] Encampments at Union positions where escaped slaves congregated, often for the duration of the war, were notoriously overcrowded, disease-ridden, and plagued by shortages of shelter and supplies. Many male ex-slaves who wound up in Yankee ranks were either impressed into the service or voluntarily signed up in desperation to keep themselves and their families from starving. Life for former slaves behind Union lines, in other words, was no romance.

Still, even in 1861, when escaped blacks within Union lines remained in legal limbo as contraband of war rather than freed, Christmas held transformative political meanings for them, because the holiday already implied liberation. Take the case, for example, of the literate ex-slave William Roscoe Davis from the town of Hampton, Virginia, who before the war had hired out his time to operate a pleasure boat. Taken north in December 1861 to raise money for relief efforts for blacks in the Hampton area by an agent of the antislavery American Missionary Association, he gave a speech at a New York City church the next month in which he poignantly compared the "glorious time" of the Hampton blacks' first Christmas under Yankee auspices with preceding Christmas seasons. Formerly, he noted, slave sales were common in town on New Year's Day, and the cries of slaves being separated from family members careened through Hampton's streets.[53]

Some of the most poignant surviving accounts of escaped slaves' Christmas experiences in 1861 come from Yankee reporters and soldiers in occupied parts of the South. In a piece entitled "Christmas Among the Contrabands," a correspondent for a Boston newspaper described Christmas at Fortress Monroe in Virginia, the very place near Hampton where General Butler had inaugurated his contraband policy, saying that on Christmas Eve, Union soldiers decorated tents with evergreens, put a wreath on their chaplain's tent, and lit a large bonfire. But what the reporter especially emphasized was the inspiring display of learning that slave children (likely students in the Chesapeake Female Seminary, a school established by a free black resident of nearby Hampton named Mary Peake) put on during Christmas Eve to show their appreciation of being given the first education in their lives:

> I doubt, Mr. Editor, if you had anything in your city so unique as the exhibition of the colored children at the Seminary, on Christmas Eve. One could laugh or weep according as the mood struck him or the aspect which he viewed things. It was touching to see two hundred children just rescued from slavery, coming before their white friends, the soldiers, whom they regard as deliverers, and exhibiting what they have been able to learn of reading, and of God's word, and of singing during the last four months. Each child seemed to look pleadingly at the soldierly group present as if asking, "Am I not worthy to be free."
>
> And it was astonishing how much they had learned in so short a time.

On South Carolina's Sea Islands, down the southern coastline from Fortress Monroe and Hampton, according to another press report, blacks on the Union-occupied and owner-abandoned plantation of Confederate general Thomas Drayton on Hilton Head also ecstatically celebrated Christmas 1861. Weeks before, Drayton had been commanding Confederate troops on nearby Port Royal Island, just to the northeast. Now, on Christmas Eve, his plantation's "colored people" held a festival they called "serenade to Jesus," with much singing of hymns and spirituals, followed by a prayer meeting at which they gave a loud shout when mention was made of the Yankee soldiers who had arrived to "'help save the poor slave, and like Jesus, bring dem good tidings of great joy."[54] These 1861 Christmas celebrations pale in significance, though, compared to the way escaped slaves and even southern blacks remaining in bondage rejoiced over the holiday in 1862. By Christmas, with Lincoln's Emancipation Proclamation one week from taking effect and preannounced months earlier, slaves within Union lines were psychologically prepped for a holiday of jubilee. Tellingly, this was true whether or not their vicinity was exempted from the proclamation's scope, though many southern whites misinterpreted what was going on, having long since persuaded themselves through processes of self-delusion, or self-indoctrination, that slaves were content with their situations. "They are having a merry time, thoughtless creatures, they think not of the morrow," mused one Louisiana plantation mistress cluelessly about her celebrating slaves that Christmas. She obviously missed the possibility entirely that the "morrow"—when Lincoln's Emancipation Proclamation was scheduled to take effect—may have been the very thing in her supposedly mindless slaves' thinking that made them so joyous, especially since Union troops had entered their part of the state. Having just read news reports that the North's Congress now intended to recruit 100 black regiments for Union armies, Confederate war clerk John Jones naively predicted on Christmas Day that southern blacks so preferred their former situations to being with the Yankees that once armed, they would "cut their way back to their masters," bringing their Union-issued guns with them![55]

The reality, of course, was otherwise. At New Castle, Kentucky, slaves held a Christmas Eve parade when they "shouted for Lincoln" even though the Bluegrass State was technically unaffected by the proclamation since Kentucky had remained in the Union. Reporting from occupied Gallatin, Tennessee, a soldier correspondent of a Rock Island, Illinois, newspaper claimed that slaves there had been dressing up and dancing, seeming to be the only happy persons in town. One of them had been overheard declaring Yankee troops would give them three or four Christmases a year instead of the one that Confederates provided. A white Ohio soldier stationed at Holly Springs, Mississippi, observed in racialist tones how the town's "Niggers" had held a "jollification dance" on Christmas "in honor, I suppose, of Massa Lincum'z Prolimation." And in the occupied Sea Islands off South Carolina's coast, where contrabands were designated for freedom under the Emancipation Proclamation, some particularly emotional Christmas moments occurred within the black community, though one northern teacher on the scene got the impression that the contrabands pined for the days when their masters gifted them with entirely free suits of clothes at Christmas.[56]

Thomas Wentworth Higginson, a fervent abolitionist and formerly one of John Brown's most active supporters, was there to witness what happened within the local black community during Christmas 1862 in the Sea Islands. So did Laura M. Towne—an abolitionist member of what was known as the Philadelphia Port Royal Relief Committee who traveled to the Sea Islands in April 1862 to help coordinate aid efforts for former slaves there but quickly transitioned into education work— and fellow Philadelphian Charlotte L. Forten, a very light-skinned free black educator active in abolitionism who traveled to the islands that summer and then schooled black children on St. Helena Island.[57]

Higginson had arrived at Beaufort in November to take command as colonel of the First South Carolina Volunteers, an all-black regiment of ex-slaves in the area that had been authorized by the Union's War Department in August 1862 and organized over the fall, the very first black troops officially recruited during the war by the U.S. government rather than by a Union military officer acting on his own authority. In his "Camp Diary," Higginson explained that although the men were mostly subdued in their holiday observances, deferring their real celebrating for New Year's Day when they would gain their freedom, they did hold prayer meetings and that he had overheard one of the regiment's captains making a rather moving Christmas prayer comparing the bounties of the holiday under Union auspices as compared to when their masters governed their behavior: "O Lord! when I tink ob dis Kismas and las' year de Kismas. Las' Kismasd he in de Secesh, and notin' to eat but grits, and no salt in 'em. Dis year in de camp, and too much victual!" Higginson added that the phrase "too much" was common within his command, indicating the slaves' gratitude to their Union benefactors rather than a judgment that they were being overfed by Union authorities.[58]

Forten spent the days leading up to Christmas teaching slave children attending what was called the Philadelphia School (on St. Helena Island) how to sing a Christmas hymn composed at her request by the antislavery poet John Greenleaf Whittier, which they had mastered easily and loved singing. On Christmas morning, by her account, the "people" awakened their teachers by knocking at their windows and doors and shouting "Merry Christmas!" The teachers then distributed presents among their pupils before attending a church decorated with mistletoe, pine, holly, Spanish moss, and a sign facing the pulpit bearing the phrase "His People Are Free." On this "wonderful Christmas" of a sort that the children had never before experienced, the 150 or so youths gathered at the church gave their rendition of Whittier's song, with its celebratory "We're free on Carolina's shore / We're all at home and free," and its lines about God's holy day being a time that they no longer had to fear the whip or hear the horn of the slave driver summoning them to work.[59]

The symbiosis of Christmas with freedom persisted among African Americans on the occupied Sea Islands as the holiday arrived in December 1863, at a time when thousands of recent slaves from the Sea Islands and elsewhere were already fighting in the Union military. Up the coast that very Christmas morning, in an engagement with Rebel artillery on the Stono River near Charleston, a liberated slave named Robert Blake, who was serving as a steward on a Union vessel, demonstrated so much courage that he would be recognized with the first Congressional Medal of Honor ever accorded an African American. In a harrowing situation and entirely on his own initiative, he serviced powder to his undermanned ship's artillery when the vessel came under Confederate bombardment. That same morning, other former slaves back down the coast on St. Helena Island gave rather dramatic evidence of how deeply appreciative they were for their wartime birth of freedom. According to the journal of William Francis Allen, a New England schoolteacher who arrived at St. Helena in November 1863 as part of the Yankee educational outreach to former slaves, after the teachers distributed presents and candy to some 485 gathered black recipients, the gathered crowd burst into a spontaneous rendition of the patriotic song "America," or "My Country, 'Tis of Thee" as it is generally known today. Allen's account is suggestive of the liberation meanings Christmas assumed during the Civil War for African Americans in the South.[60]

7

Sanitizing the Past

It must have seemed a Christmas miracle to panicked white southerners. In the wake of the Confederacy's defeat in the spring of 1865, many of Dixie's citizenry feared their first Yuletide under Yankee subjection would ignite the black holiday revolt they had been dreading for two centuries. Now, for the first time since the 1600s, there were no legally enslaved blacks anywhere in the region; the Thirteenth Amendment to the U.S. Constitution, ratified on December 6, had guaranteed irreversible freedom for all southern blacks, including enslaved peoples in locales exempted from Lincoln's Emancipation Proclamation. Preconditioned by decades of Christmas slave revolt rumors, white communities throughout the Southland instinctively assumed blacks would capitalize on their new status and the absence of slave patrols to unleash the Yuletide mayhem of murder, rape, and pillage so long anticipated. Yet, as had been the case so often before, nothing of the sort came to pass.

Exacerbating Dixie's tempest was an illusion, especially among blacks in rural areas, that Christmas would bring a significant redistribution of land in the South (along with farm implements and animals) under the auspices of Union occupiers, allowing onetime slaves to become landowners in their own right. As early as August, an agent of an association of Massachusetts textile manufacturers reported from Quitman, Georgia, that plantation blacks there expected "that next Christmas the lands are to be divided among them," saying they had been told so by Union army soldiers. Such expectations persisted, spreading throughout the region. Ten days before Christmas, South Carolina rice country plantation mistress Adele Allston complained that in her vicinity all "nigs" anticipated a "great thing" and were refusing to sign labor contracts with whites for the coming year. Similarly, a Boston paper's New Orleans correspondent reported the case of a deluded black woman who announced she was going to select a vacant lot for herself and her husband, adding it was impossible to convince her that no Christmas land redistribution was in the works. And it was largely because of these rumored land giveaways that many whites and some federal officials surmised blacks would angrily revolt over Christmas when their dreams were shattered.[1]

There was, in fact, a basis for the rumors. During the war, Union occupation forces had initiated limited experiments in black land ownership of abandoned white properties in scattered locales like the South Carolina Sea Islands, and there was talk among Radical Republicans in the Union Congress about expanding such programs once peace arrived. Indeed, as the historian Eric Foner points out, Congress's establishment of the Freedmen's Bureau in March 1865 nodded to the idea that former slaves should get some kind of "access" to the lands of southern whites. Ultimately, though, the land hopes of the South's formerly enslaved people were mostly doomed to disappointment. Few Yankee politicians had the will or interest to push such policies through Congress, and the assassinated Abraham Lincoln's successor, Andrew Johnson, favored returning land to former Confederates swearing renewed allegiance to the federal government. Attempting to implement the president's directives to restore landholdings to southern whites, Freedmen's Bureau head Oliver Otis Howard and bureau officials throughout the South gave speeches and issued proclamations over the fall of 1865 to disabuse blacks of their Christmas landholding dreams and encourage them to avoid vagrancy by signing labor contracts to work for whites the coming year. However, many southern blacks resisted this messaging, hoping right up to Christmas that their land bonanza was still on its way. Indeed, as the historian Steven Hahn notes, some southern blacks saw the political utility of gossip and astutely spread rumors of land redistributions to rally their communities and stake claims to estates where they had labored for free for generations, hardly an irrational expectation at a time of turmoil.[2]

Intimations of a rising began roiling the South over the summer of 1865 and, in conjunction with the redistribution rumors, continued up to Christmas. In Texas, Union army major Elijah P. Curtis expected major problems at Christmas among blacks living on the Colorado River's left bank when their current labor contracts expired, and, while traveling in September from Charleston to the interior state capital of Columbia, the northern journalist Sidney Andrews encountered a white man "of much apparent intelligence" convinced "the negroes have an organized military force in all sections of the State, and are almost certain to rise and massacre the whites about Christmas time." In Vicksburg, Mississippi, a newspaper announced that people living in outlying areas were fleeing into the city in reaction to news that local blacks, with the connivance of black Union army occupation forces, were arming themselves as prelude to appropriating the lands of whites unless they were ceded to them by Christmas. A newspaper in Memphis, Tennessee, detected a "general uneasiness, among both whites and blacks, of trouble to come about the Christmas holidays," while in Milledgeville, Georgia, a reporter discovered that whites were in virtual panic about rumored black insurrectionary speechmaking and threats to rape and murder them "at Christmas." Down in New Orleans, one report forecast a Christmas Eve revolt, claiming that houses and businesses were already premarked with chalk for destruction. Ten days before Christmas, a telegraphic report announced that southern white women and children, to escape "the dreaded Christmas times," were waiting out events up North.[3]

Particularly dire and false reports emanated from Augusta, Georgia, a key center of Confederate military production during the war, that local blacks had forced their way into the arsenal. According to one account, a regiment of black Union army troops currently stationed there would have been disbanded before the holiday had it not been feared that once they were no longer under Union army orders, the men would combine with "bad town negroes" in a "holiday saturnalia" and "rising." Reportedly, "hair-brained fanatics" had been distributing inflammatory propaganda to potential insurgents, and their efforts were bearing results. The county jail already held seventeen African Americans under suspicion of planning to kill white males and old women, divide white landholdings among the black population, and force the remaining white women into marriage. On December 15, an editorial in an Augusta paper attacked those whites with "leprous souls" who were inducing blacks to cling to their land hopes despite official disavowals of such programs; so many rumors of Christmas land redistributions were circulating that every local child knew about them. The piece added menacingly that local blacks lacked the "intellectual resources" to realize their absurdity and predicted a thousand whites might die battling back the coming insurrection, warning that the eventual result of such a race war would be the extermination of African Americans.[4]

Throughout the South, authorities acted to lessen the odds of insurrections, though Florida's provisional governor, William Marvin, suggested to his state's constitutional convention it would be best simply to allow blacks to test their own freedoms over Christmas. Mississippi's newly elected governor, Benjamin G. Humphreys (a former Confederate general), thought otherwise. He issued a proclamation calling on citizens to form voluntary military units, which immediately earned the endorsement of a correspondent for a Natchez paper. The next day he reaffirmed his decree, given all the "reputable" reports "that something is contemplated by the negroes at the coming Christmas." "ORGANIZE! ORGANIZE!!" demanded a Jackson, Mississippi, paper. Alluding to fears of black insurrections "about the Christmas Holidays" sweeping every corner of the state, it recommended that people organize companies of minuteman-type volunteers who could accept ammunition and muster "at a moment's warning." In Spotsylvania County, Virginia, the county court solicited the local Union army occupation commander, General Thomas M. Harris, to take precautionary measures against the coming "negro insurrection during Christmas." Such steps apparently occurred in South Carolina's Sumter District; planter Samuel Gaillard noted in his journal five days before Christmas that a squad of men had just gone out under orders "to visit all the plantations around & seize all guns in possession of negroes." In southwest Georgia's cotton country, police and white militias carrying guns and ropes barged into blacks' cabins, assaulted strangers, and seized weapons.[5]

Yet nothing resembling a revolt occurred, though accounts of holiday rowdiness percolated through the press. In Natchez, Mississippi, the *Courier* claimed there had been "several fights among the negroes" at Christmas, adding they were inconsequential, not even interrupting brisk holiday shopping at local businesses. Scattered interracial friction occurred elsewhere, but nothing like race war. In Wilmington, North Carolina, and Alexandria, Virginia, where fighting broke out, U.S. occupation troops wound up intervening and making arrests, though accounts differed in attributing blame for the friction. Alexandria's melee, reportedly involving inebriated participants of both races, resulted in a number of whites injured by gunfire and the deaths of two African Americans, with many rioters afterward confined in the city's former slave pen. Although just what happened remains murky, it would seem that the fracas resulted from attempts by resentful local whites—some of them cheering Jefferson Davis, brandishing revolvers, and dressed in Confederate uniforms—to break up black religious meetings and attack black Union soldiers and strolling black couples encountered on the streets. Additionally, as the historian William Blair indicates, Alexandria whites, already uneasy about signs of black unruliness now that the constraints of slavery were absent, took especial alarm at the sight of black paraders in the streets banging drums (an instrument associated in the past with servile insurrection) to celebrate the holiday.[6]

Most places reported unusually tranquil Christmases. On December 28, a Washington, D.C., paper reported that Petersburg, Virginia, had never seen so *few* blacks on the streets over Christmas, an observation that was echoed in Edgefield, South Carolina, where a newspaper claimed hatefully that despite the panic, never in its "Southern nigger-blessed life" had there been "so few colored people roving about at the season." Raleigh, North Carolina, passed its most "orderly" Christmas week ever, and a local paper in Jacksonville, Florida, judged Christmas the quietist that city had experienced. Throughout the South, it appears, black laborers had gradually if reluctantly come to believe the Freedmen's Bureau's handbills and circulars cautioning them to disregard reports of federal land confiscations from southern whites and signed labor contracts either over the holiday period or soon afterward. Ironically, some of these contracts embedded slavery's Christmas traditions in freedom by stipulating that employees could not be forced to work on the holiday or deprived of wages for not working, and that workers must be reimbursed if circumstances created a "necessity" for their labors over Christmas and other holidays.[7]

Indeed, many southern blacks passed the holiday in 1865 not so differently than when they were enslaved, with employers still providing their workers gifts and extra time off to party and travel. A Yankee journalist traveling by rail toward Memphis through western Tennessee during the preholiday in 1865 reported that large numbers of "well-dressed blacks" boarded his train at points en route, going to the city to make Christmas purchases for relations and friends. Botanist and onetime South Carolina slaveholder Henry William Ravenel recorded in his diary on Christmas Day that he was at his upcountry home place Hampton Hill at Aiken where an hour after breakfast his "negroes" had "come up" to his house as they had in slave times to get "a trifling present" and to give the Ravenels their Christmas greeting. Along similar lines, Georgia landholding widow Dolly Lunt Burge wrote in her diary on Christmas Day—a day after mentioning that her "freedmen have been with me" working "for one-sixth of the crop"—that early in the morning her daughter had shared with "eight little [household] negroes" all the gifts she could from her stocking, though Burge also expected that 1865 would be the last Yuletide they would spend together since her black workers would wish their "own vine & fig tree" in the future. Further evidence of such continuities in landholder gifting practices comes from a later pension deposition of a onetime slave and widow of a black Union infantryman, who recalled that she had remained on the place of her master for a year after being emancipated and that he had given monetary Christmas presents that year to workers staying on.[8]

It took time for traditional scripts of Christmas behaviors to thoroughly break down, partly because many once-enslaved people remained in the employ of their own former masters well after that first postwar Yuletide. Customs forged over generations accrue inertia of their own. In rural areas in particular, a high percentage of ex-slaves emerged from the Civil War as an impoverished peasantry, still laboring for and dependent upon white landholders under a variety of formal and informal remuneration arrangements, including sharecropping. In fact, in parts of the South where there had been relatively little fighting during the war, many slaves did not even learn they were legally free until months after the surrender of Confederate armies. Some Texan slaves apparently still were uninformed of their new status a year after Appomattox. Given these circumstances, it would have been surprising if all traces of antebellum southern slave-master Christmas practices vanished by the first postwar Christmas or if they did not exert some pull afterward. With such considerations in mind, there is no cause to disbelieve a report appearing in the *New York Times* in August 1866 from a correspondent visiting a planter friend in Oglethorpe, Georgia, noting not only that almost all of his friend's black workers had stayed on after emancipation but also that the few who had struck off on their own had returned there for a barbecue and asked their former owner if it would be all right for them again "to come home at Christmas."[9]

In Georgia's Cotton Belt, a majority of ex-slaveholders followed antebellum precedents after the war and released their workers from labor on Christmas Eve night. At the Buffalo Forge ironworks in Virginia, according to the historian Charles B. Dew, the main change in Christmas practices following the war was that workers were now allowed to start their Christmas holiday earlier than in the past, indicating that the length of Christmas breaks remained contested after the war as in antebellum times. This indeed seems to have been the case in the postwar South, with black laborers having more leverage than when they had been enslaved. Noting on December 19, 1865, that his black laborers already "had their heads full of Xmas," the manager of several Mississippi estates concluded that they would likely "knock off" from work on December 22 and stay away until after January 1. In the Louisiana cane fields that year, workers negotiated the expansion of their usual post-Christmas holidays from one week to up to two weeks.[10]

As in slave times, some landholders manipulated holiday gifting as a means of pressuring their workers to better perform their tasks at other times of the year. Just after Christmas in 1866, South Carolina rice planter Robert F. W. Allston's widow, Adele, decided that the stealing of fifteen chickens out of her yard on Christmas night, as well as poor crop yields, gave her cause to deny almost all her "people" their usual Christmas beef, excepting workers on one of her places. Her attitude echoed the kinds of weighted holiday determinations the Old South's master class had made regularly about slaves' work efficiency, loyalty, and honesty before the war. In November 1868, a Freedmen's Bureau official in Georgia claimed a majority of employers there hoped to "allure" workers with "liberal potations of whiskey about Christmas times" into signing highly exploitative labor contracts for the coming year.[11]

Already, though, one can detect signs that black-white social interactions in the southern states over the holiday season were dwindling, with one Texan white plantation woman reflecting in early January 1867, "Christmas was dull—duller than usual. Not even a darkey claimed 'Christmas Gift.'" The next Christmas season, the *Southern Home Journal* posted a letter from Betsey Bittersweet, supposedly a woman in North Carolina but likely a made-up name, lamenting how there had been no house servants to assist in holiday preparations and comparing that year's celebration to the "very good thing in the old time when we had servants and money." It is telling that the famed antebellum southern author William Gilmore Simms, who had so glorified master Christmas gifting of slaves in his prewar writings, unburdened himself of Christmas bitterness in a pseudonymously signed letter to a Charleston paper. After downing tumblers of eggnog at his South Carolina estate on a sunny, nearly "scorching" Christmas Day 1867, Simms wished that inebriation would induce dreams of "what Christmas *used to was*' in Carolina," while reflecting on the impoverishment of his state's cotton planters—blaming their ruination on "capricious"

attitudes about "the negro" regarding work, at a time when landholders remained "stewards" for their onetime slaves. Simms's suggestion,
that Yuletide, was that South Carolinians should henceforth forswear
planting, separate themselves from their black wards, and take up sub-
sistence farming.[12]

As segregation norms gradually claimed the former slave states after
Reconstruction ended in the mid-1870s, holiday social interactions between the races further lessened, though residuals of antebellum Christmas master-slave customs persisted in some family circles. On a sleety
Christmas Day in 1872, Henry William Ravenel gave testimony to the
persistence of such mores at his Hampton Hill farm, appreciating in his
diary how his family had just been "exchanging pleasant greetings with
the negroes, reminding us of old times." Elaborating, he explained that
"Pompey, Jimmy & Thomas have been to the house" and that "we have
sent a big cake & bottle of wine around for all," possibly meaning that
his own family reciprocated for the visit by sending their former slaves
back to their own households with holiday treats. Several years later
the press carried a letter from Confederate general Joseph Johnston to
an "old slave" named Jim. In the letter Johnston called himself and his
wife Jim's true friends, and mentioned that he had sent a $50 check to
Jim and his family as a belated Christmas present in reciprocation for
Jim's recent visit to Johnston's wife in Richmond.[13]

Still, no less an expert on the Old South than Jefferson Davis was
ready, by the early 1880s, to declare a coda for antebellum Yuletide
traditions. "This season is no longer the festival we remember it to
have been before society was overturned," he confided in a letter to
an old friend in 1882, without elaborating just what he meant by his
pronouncement that "corruption" rather than "virtue" now ruled the
holiday.[14] A sense of malaise and nostalgia for slave times, though, is
unmistakable in his words.

What are we to make of southern fears of a black insurrection at Christmas in 1865? Undoubtedly, in one sense, it marked a residue from
slavery's sudden destruction, as southern whites experienced natural
anxieties about their own future in a revolutionized society under military occupation. Just a few years earlier in Russia there had been a
striking uptick in "peasant disturbances" after Tsar Alexander II's edict
of February 19, 1861, with its qualified freeing of some 2.3 million serfs,
leaving them with residual monetary and labor responsibilities to landowners that persisted into the twentieth century. It was not entirely

irrational for southern whites to fear disorder over the holidays, given the huge transformation in human and labor relations that their society was compelled to absorb in a compressed period of time following Appomattox. It is telling that the *Edgefield (South Carolina) Advertiser*'s explanation for the revolt fizzling out was that southern blacks, if belatedly, had finally looked "at things in their right light" and recognized that instead of "streaming about the country, idle and gaping," they should buckle down to "the requirements of the situation." Implied was an expectation that blacks should resign themselves to being cheap and highly controlled peasant labor for white employers in the postwar order, the closest thing to continued slavery that southern whites could hope for given their vulnerable situation after losing a war.[15]

Contemporary northern observers recognized the panic's race control elements, though some Yankee commentators had far different perspectives than Edgefield's *Advertiser* about just what had been going on. One northern publication attributed the ferment to southern whites' guilt about depriving "colored people" of their rights even after emancipation, a view similar to the charge in an Ogdensburg, New York, paper that white southerners hoped to use insurrection rumors as a means of justifying restrictive laws (known as "Black Codes") imposed on African Americans by state legislatures in the months since the war. Contrarily, another northern publication suggested counterintuitively that white southerners actually *wanted* the projected insurrection to begin; black violence would have serviced their contentions that slavery—with its "patriarchal restraints" of bloodhounds and thumbscrews—was right for blacks *and* justified the South's "chivalry" taking up arms to begin "the extinction of the colored people."[16] Although the implication that southern whites as a whole subconsciously wished a purging race war was undoubtedly an overreach, it held an element of truth, given the growing hatred of African Americans in some white southern circles after the war.

Yet the phantom 1865 Christmas revolt also marked a kind of grim finale to a long-running scenario that had been playing out over generations, since white southerners never again experienced a regionwide Christmas insurrection panic. Indeed, some of its victims apparently considered the white vigilantism of that December a slaveholders' persecution, even though the peculiar institution had been legally eradicated. Ponder the panicked reaction of a seized Georgia black, who, about to be abducted by five whites, reportedly screamed out, "Oh Lord, Master don't kill me."[17] But as time passed without new

Christmas insurrection panics, southern whites found it convenient to forget, or subconsciously repress, that they or their ancestors had feared slave holiday revolts in the first place. Recalling such panics would have been inconvenient in constructing the legend of the Lost Cause.

Between Reconstruction's end in the mid-1870s and the Roaring Twenties, a veritable legion of southern white memoirists, essayists, novelists, folklorists, children's writers, and editorialists defied the axiom that the writing of history belongs to war's victors. As the decades rolled by, Dixie's defenders forged a genre of stereotypical slave Christmas idylls glorifying the coercive labor system that lay at the root of their antebellum society and the recent Civil War. These vignettes had profound consequences for American race relations. Appearing in works aimed at children readers and listeners as well as in adult magazines and books, they had a cradle-to-grave impact. When they were young, literate Americans encountered positive southern white stereotypes of how Christmas was celebrated by masters and slaves in antebellum times, and they likely encountered these softened images again in readings later on in their lives.

Although this wave of publications dates from the 1870s and 1880s, its authors echoed pre–Civil War southern proslavery propaganda and may have drawn for tropes on earlier books, like a British woman's retrospective glance at Christmas on an estate in Trinidad in the 1820s. A. C. Carmichael's *Domestic Manners and Social Condition of the White, Coloured, and Negro Population of the West Indies* (1833), which was advertised and sold in Charleston and other U.S. locales, contained many of the elements of Yuletide master generosity and slave appreciativeness common to later southern literary recollections about plantation experiences. On Christmas morning, slaves at the Carmichael family's estate not only entertained their masters with fiddle music but also wished them a happy Christmas and good health, some of them doing so in excessive speechmaking. Giddily absorbed in holiday bliss, slaves surrendered themselves to light-hearted partying and foolishness, such as throwing flour all over each other. "Massa" and "missus" are so instinctively benevolent, she explains, that they gladly give up hot food for the day so their household servants can cook for themselves and fully enjoy the occasion. Seeing "dependent" "fellow creatures" so happy justified sacrificing plum pudding.[18]

Similarly, Caroline Gilman's book *Recollections of a Southern Matron*, purportedly the memoir of Roseland plantation mistress Cornelia Wilton but really a fictional work, foreshadowed later representations of antebellum Christmases by southern authors. A Bostonian by birth, Caroline Gilman in her twenties moved with her husband, Samuel, to Charleston in 1819, where they pursued professional careers and established a household with domestic slaves. He assumed a ministry in a Unitarian church, and she edited children's periodicals and authored domestic novels. *Recollections* gained a reading audience in serialized form in Gilman's magazine, before the New York publisher Harper & Brothers released it as a book in 1838. Significantly, Gilman, who professed strongly proslavery attitudes despite her northern roots, announced in her preface that the novel was "founded in events of actual occurrences," and we know she had familiarity with plantation life despite her urban residence, if only because she had stayed at her brother's Georgia plantation for a while during her adolescent years. Regardless of whether we take her guarantee of veracity at face value, her description of slave plantation Christmas experiences provided a prototype for the professedly authentic reminiscences southern writers produced decades later, and one has to wonder whether some later memoirists read Gilman's text before committing their own thoughts to paper.[19]

In explaining "Country Christmas" customs in South Carolina, Gilman noted how slaves on Wilton's place and a neighboring holding had the privilege of inaugurating the holiday by, respectively, firing a small fieldpiece of artillery or making a clamor with brass and tin; and she emphasized how well they were provided for over the holidays. Not only did slaves get eggnog, beef, gingerbread, and gifts from their master and his family but also the gifts were conveyed in formalized rituals revealing masters' attentiveness and slaves' appreciativeness:

> After breakfast the people withdrew from the piazza, and we took possession while they came up in *gangs* to receive their gifts. As we had each several hundred to supply, the Barnwells and ourselves stood on opposite sides. The women almost universally twined their handkerchiefs about their heads as soon as they received them, with an air of grace that would have surprised a stranger. The men flung up their new woollen caps, and stopped to make two or three flourishing bows, while the women dropped a courtesy [curtsy] with a pleased look, turning up one eye, and showing their beautiful teeth.

Gilman reported that slaveholding women spent long hours cutting fabric for handkerchiefs to be distributed as presents to female slaves, that slaves visited other plantations over the holiday, and that the holiday brought a five-hour slave Christmas dance to music by fiddle, triangle, and drum (with whites watching). Virtually all the elements in Gilman's vignette resurfaced in later writings.[20]

Southern postwar writings about slave Christmases, therefore, elaborated on prior literary themes. Living in Port Gibson, Mississippi, immediately after the Civil War, Mississippi native Irwin Russell penned "Christmas-Night in the Quarters" after observing a black Christmas evening dance during a holiday plantation outing. Though this young lawyer's poem, eventually published in *Scribner's Monthly* in 1878, lacked the paternalistic masters of Gilman's novel, it contained black dialect and other elements common to subsequent southern white accounts of antebellum slave Christmases. Russell's "darkeys" hold "high carnival" in the quarters on Christmas night following a "merry" day, as they come together riding four to a mule, from "all the countryside," to laugh, sing, shout, and party.

Russell gives us quite the party. "Old Fiddling Josey" uses his bow to "Rap out the signal dancers know" and instructs the "niggers" to "whoop up," keep their rhythm, stop looking at their feet, and swap lady partners. After a supper, dancing resumes. Then "Aunt Cassy" tells ghost stories about devils holding gatherings in the smokehouse and why possums' tails lack hair. The latter draws loosely on biblical allusions and has Noah building an ark to beat the Mississippi River steamer *Natchez* in a race and Ham using free time on the "packet" during the great flood to shave the tail hair of a possum on board as string for his banjo—an instrument Ham had just invented! As daybreak dawns on the 26th, Russell's partyers head homeward, passing "through the field beyond the gin" and seeing Santa Claus departing "His own dear Land of Cotton." One "colored youth" whimsically wishes that Santa Claus had been born as twins so that there would be two Christmases each year.[21]

If Russell's mellow verse said virtually nothing about the role of slaveholders in facilitating such Christmas celebrations, his southern literary contemporaries during Reconstruction and their successors compensated for the omission many times over. In a novel published in 1867 and set on a Georgia plantation, Natchez, Mississippi, native Catherine Ann Ware Warfield had her central character, a nineteen-year-old northern girl working as a plantation "instructress," reflect that the owners of "Beauseincourt" had "never appeared to such advantage" as when distributing Christmas presents to their slaves from their mansion's back gallery, and that in observing the process, she had understood "for the first time, how patriarchal was this Southern institution [slavery] when governed by humanity." Not only were the presents generous but also the workers clearly were thrilled about their gifts. Besides, they got an entire week off from labor at Christmas, with younger slaves holding nights of "carnival" in a large kitchen in the slave quarters.[22]

Virginia native Mary Tucker Magill similarly championed Old South slave Christmas experiences in her novel *The Holcombes,* published in 1871 in the middle of Reconstruction and set on a slaveholding estate in the Blue Ridge Mountains called "Rose Hill." Magill's regional defensiveness could hardly have been more transparent: her dedication admitted an intent to rescue Virginia's "honored" "palmiest days" from "oblivion"; her preface confessed a desire to rebut misleading impressions of "pictures of life in our Southern States" conveyed by Harriet Beecher Stowe's *Uncle Tom's Cabin,* a motive coursing openly through many postwar southern white publications recounting antebellum Christmases. Indeed, Warfield's *Romance of Beauseincourt* suggested white southerners in the postwar period still seethed over the abolitionist attacks on slavery that had helped incite secession, war, regional defeat, and emancipation, and were having great difficulty laying the past to rest. When Warfield's narrator recounts Christmas gift disseminations at her fictional plantation, she wryly sneers that the very sight of "beaming" slave women displaying their "ivory" (teeth) when exchanging hearty Christmas greetings with their mistress would have made any abolitionist "gnash his teeth and tear his hair," it was so contrary to their warped stereotypes of plantation life.[23]

In *The Holcombes,* a novel revolving around a planter's teenage girl and her reactions to her father's remarriage that Magill insisted was based on true events, whites care more about their slaves' happiness at holiday time than their own; a member of the master's family dons a St. Nicholas costume and shoulder pack and leads his family in a procession to the slave quarters, throwing sugar plums into the snow for delighted "woolly-heads" crying out "Christmas-gift" to recover. High points of the slaves' holiday include a feast featuring the same venison, duck, and turkey that whites dined on and a washhouse dance to their own fiddle, banjo, and bones that, because of its exceptional rhythms and freedom of movement, impresses the place's new mistress as superior to the white elite dance steps that she was accustomed to. On December 27, the white family's brood of children distribute gifts to "the people" from the branches of a special Christmas tree loaded with handkerchiefs, small doll babies, colored marbles, bags of candy, pin cushions, and other items, many of them lovingly handmade by the white children. There are no hints that slaves wanted anything more: "Thank ye, marster. I knowd you wouldn't forget me, marster." There is playful bantering between blacks and whites on this Old Dominion estate over Christmas, as well as occasion for the white children to tromp into the mammy's hut to warm up by her fire, reminisce about earlier days, and enjoy servings of her coffee.[24]

The true postwar wave of southern white literary romances about antebellum slave Christmases, though, began *after* Reconstruction ended, as Dixie Lost Cause romanticism gained momentum in American popular culture. In the 1880s and for long afterward, at a time when the voting and office-holding rights of southern African Americans secured during Reconstruction were eroding, a procession of southern white writers rehashed antebellum Christmases as interludes of excessive master paternalism and exuberant releases of slave joy and gratitude, with nary an inkling of the insidious aspects of slaves' Christmas experiences or allusion to the monetary impulses driving slave ownership in the first place. Although these writers refrained from outright claims that enslavement was so wonderful it never should have been abolished, they sometimes implied as much, in ways calculated to evoke empathy for the South's onetime masters. And the sheer volume and repetitiveness of these accounts drummed home white southern messaging about Dixie's racial mores, with lasting repercussions.

In 1878, a year after federal troops stopped propping up Reconstruction governments and black political participation in the southern states, Celina E. Means of Spartanburg, South Carolina (writing under a pen name), helped launch this apparently uncoordinated literary movement with a novel unabashedly admitted as an effort to convert people in the "North, South, East, and West" to her take on the "*real condition*" of affairs in the South Carolina upcountry, the locale of the story. In recounting an antebellum Christmas at "Cedar Gove" plantation (which takes up a whole chapter), *Thirty-Four Years: An American Story of Southern Life* portrayed a master so sensitive to his slaves' feelings that he ponders "the peculiar fancies" of each before allocating gifts during Christmas distribution time on his back piazza. Means waxes about the "child-like, affectionate natures" of slaves gratified with tobacco, pipes, "cast-off garments," peppermints, harmonicas, and the like, and she relates how excited, dressed-up slaves man plantation gates and call out "Christmas gift" as relations of the master arrive in carriages. Naturally, the slaves revel in their holiday party. Until late at night, "the sound of the fiddle and the shouts of laughter mingling with the dancing feet down at the negroes' quarters" evidenced what a wonderful Christmas every slave experienced.[25]

Soon after this book appeared, Louise-Clarke Pyrnelle exposed America's children to southern Christmas mythologies with her semi-fictional *Diddie, Dumps, and Tot, or Plantation Child-Life* (1882). This Harper & Brothers' book vigorously defended slavery, despite professing neutrality on the institution's morality; its chapter "Christmas on the Old Plantation" could hardly have rendered a more misleadingly pleasant or condescendingly racist take on interracial plantation holiday traditions. Pyrnelle's Christmas morning begins with "Chris'mus gif," before getting to gift distributions. Happily, she tells us, the "little nigs," the household's mammy, and another servant discover fruit, nuts, raisins, and candy in their stockings. Following breakfast, a ringing of the plantation's large bell summons black field hands. They approach the house in a procession, where a great store box of items purchased weeks earlier is opened, and its contents—hats, dresses, coats, vests, bonnets, and the like—are distributed to the slaves' unveiled delight. Through "thick lips," slaves exclaim, "Thankee, mistis! thankee, honey; an' God bless yer!," while "little bits of black babies" simply look "all around in their queer kind of way," not understanding what is transpiring. As the white girls of the household give toys, oranges, apples, and candies to the hands, all the "darkies" joyously break out in laughter before bowing down and making curtsies on the prompting of their elders. Afterward, the master and his wife benevolently stride off to deliver Christmas gifts to those slaves too infirm or sick to walk up to their house—like "Aunt Sally," who is nearly blind, and the elderly Daddy Jake, who avoided leaving the quarters in bad weather.

Pyrnelle emphasizes the extreme efforts of masters and mistresses to maximize their slaves' happiness over Christmas, recalling how that same night a favorite slave named Jim is to marry a housemaid whose veil and white dress would be on loan from her master family's wardrobe. The master has already built a cabin for the newly married couple's life together, and the wedding would never have occurred in the first place had it not been for the benevolent intervention of the mistress into the slaves' courtship. Toward the end of Pyrnelle's Christmas idyll, the kindly mistress gives her pleading daughters special permission to break convention and bring up several black children from the

PLAYING "INJUNS."

Picture showing adult servants protecting slaveholders' children during Christmas playtime in a southern mansion, in Louise-Clarke Pyrnelle, *Diddie, Dumps, and Tot, or Plantation Child-Life* (New York: Harper & Brothers, 1882), 39. (Scan by Neal A. Harmeyer, Digital Archivist, Purdue University Library)

quarters to "play Injuns" prior to the Christmas dinner, a meal that no slave would miss "for all the scalps that ever were taken" since it was served on tables laden with fine food topped off by pudding and cake. But there is more! The chapter relates a molasses pulling in the quarters to the tunes of Uncle Sambo's fiddling and explains how the slave marriage ceremony—with its attendant pleasures of dancing and drinking eggnog—kept the older slaves up until dawn.[26]

In contrast to Pyrnelle, who aimed her white plantation Christmas lore at youthful readers, Georgia folklorist and journalist Joel Chandler Harris sought adult readers for his treatments of slave-time Christmas, which greatly surpassed *Diddie, Dumps, and Tot* in long-term cultural clout and commercial success. A bastard by birth who experienced an underprivileged youth, Harris gained his insights for his "Uncle Remus" tales while he was a teenage printing compositor working for a Georgia plantation newspaper called *The Countryman* during the Civil War. Hired in 1862 by Joseph Addison Turner, whose thousand-acre place was located some nine miles northeast of Harris's birthplace of Eatonton, Harris became accustomed to visiting his employer's slave quarters, where he relished the animal tales related by the people he encountered there. Following the collapse of Turner's paper a year after the war ended, Harris bounced around from place to place in various newspaper jobs until he settled in at the prominent *Atlanta Constitution* in 1876. There he rose quickly to the position of associate editor and began honing his Uncle Remus storytelling character in writings for the paper. Initially, Harris presented "Remus" as an elderly urban African American who dropped in at the *Constitution*'s offices espousing opinions on matters of current concern; but later on Harris introduced a senior rural slave named Uncle Remus, who in a thick dialect related a virtual lode of engaging plantation stories about anthropomorphic animal characters to a white plantation boy. Ultimately, Harris published 185 Uncle Remus tales in a succession of volumes, beginning with the internationally acclaimed *Uncle Remus, His Songs and Sayings: The Folklore of the Old Plantation* (1880). His books sold briskly, going through multiple reprintings. Given how beloved these stories became for generations of readers, it is hardly surprising that Walt Disney adapted Harris's tales for the screen in his 1946 film *Song of the South,* exposing them to multitudes of additional Americans.[27]

Although scholars have long held that Harris's Uncle Remus stories contained undertones of black resistance to enslavement,[28] the folklorist stated outright that Remus only remembered his plantation experiences in pleasant tones, virtually insulating white readers from potential antislavery readings of his stories. In fact, Harris's popular plantation tales, autobiography, and other writings further embedded Old South stereotypes about master Christmas paternalism within late nineteenth-century U.S. popular culture.

This was the case with the last two chapters of *Nights with Uncle Remus,* published by Houghton Mifflin in 1883. Using the device of a story within a story, chapter 70 ("Brother Rabbit Rescues Brother Terrapin") covers the pre-Christmas ambience on Uncle Remus's plantation before turning to its animal tale, explaining how "the air filled with laughter day and night" as blacks arrived from the white family's outlying "River place" to share in the boisterous annual Christmas festivities to come. Remus explains to the little white boy that these River place folk traditionally turned "de whole place upside down" every Christmas Eve, singing, dancing, hollering, and "whoopin'," even starting the ruckus before darkness fell. In the final story of the collection, titled "The Night Before Christmas," Harris fully recaptures long-standing southern white mythologies about Christmas Eve day and Christmas Eve being joyous experiences alike for "negroes" in their cabins and whites in the big house.

Here, Remus accompanies the white boy to a slave wedding on Christmas Eve, which the participants intend to light up for a grand dance with piles of lightwood (a form of resin-laden and highly inflammatory pine). Even before the white boy arrives, blacks are singing, laughing, and dancing. And when the wedding scene occurs, the groom is decked out in a coat with tails so long they nearly brush the floor while his bride wears a white dress and artificial flowers in her hair. Harris vividly particularizes the celebration, with servings of cake and persimmon beer and a climatic dance scene with Remus himself calling off the fiddle playing and taking over pacing the steps, which he does by rhythmically slapping his leg and breast with his left hand. Harris further embellishes his scene's nostalgic power by turning to the white folk at the big house. Despite being sophisticated veterans of European tours, all are tearful and entirely absorbed with the simple "tempest of melody" and "heart-breaking strain" of Remus's voice wafting to them from the quarters.

Nothing in Harris's story evokes the disappointment and abuses some slaves experienced over Christmas. In fact, the only tension he offers is that the servant bride becomes upset that the "nigger" taking over her responsibilities in the big house will not be as capable as she was in waiting on the white folk. Harris's story implies that anyone visiting southern plantations over Christmas could not have helped but be impressed by the fondness that slaves and masters shared for each other nor avoided concluding that slaves were well provided for and treated with loving respect.[29]

Harris addressed slave Christmases less directly in "The Baby's Christmas" in his 1898 anthology *Tales of the Home Folks in Peace and War,* since it was set after the Civil War. Still, the action indirectly endorses antebellum slavery by having a loyal ex-slave emotionally laugh and cry in joy upon being reunited with her white folk from antebellum times. More important, Harris's autobiographical *On the Plantation* (1892), defined by its dedication page as a fusion of "Fact and Fiction" written in memory of his plantation mentor Joseph Addison Turner, reinforced southern plantation Christmas mythology with a chapter about a "happy" Christmas during the Civil War. In this case, Harris has onetime slaves he knew at the Turner quarters anticipate the arrival of Santa Claus, chat about farm animals instinctively sensing when Christmas is arriving, and hang stockings. The exception, "Aunt Crissy," eschews that practice since she is confident she will get her Christmas gift the next morning regardless—once playing Christmas Gif' with her mistress and master is over. One can almost guess what comes next. On Christmas morning, the slaves gather in Turner's yard, and while they wait for their master's appearance, the "dusky crowd" sings a plantation song "freighted with a quality indescribably touching and tender." Soon they are exclaiming "Chris'mas gif'" on sight of Turner, who, after they assemble at his storeroom's doors, distributes "substantial" gifts to all, an extra "dram" for elderly slaves, and payments for whatever extra crops of cotton and corn they had cultivated on their private plots.[30]

Throughout the late nineteenth and early twentieth centuries, additional southern paeans to antebellum slave Christmases rolled off America's presses. In 1887, for example, Cushings & Bailey of Baltimore released the first printings of Susan Dabney Smedes's influential *Memorials of a Southern Planter,* which earned three more U.S. editions over the following three years, a London release in 1889, and many reprintings under three separate titles by a smorgasbord of publishers, including Knopf in 1965 and the University Press of Mississippi in 1981. With picturesque descriptions of "Holiday Times on the Plantation," Smedes likely sold many readers on master paternalism. In her pastoral, Smedes meticulously summoned up loving memories of her kindly father—the plantation's master—beating eggs for the holiday eggnog; field "Negroes" decked out in their holiday clothing for doings at their quarters, at the "'great house,'" and in town; and house slaves launching "affectionate" Christmas Gif' surprise attacks on their owners' children on Christmas morning.[31]

The same year *Memorials* went to press, local colorist James Lane Allen, in recounting Christmas slave-merrymaking and "Christmas gif'" games in his home state of Kentucky for the *Century Illustrated Magazine,* told a possibly imagined tale of an unspecified elderly slave couple who asked for freedom and got it when their mistress queried them as to what they wanted for Christmas. Since their mistress had always treated them benevolently anyway, all freedom meant was moving to "the neighboring farm of their mistress's aunt and being freely supported there as they had been freely supported at home"! Allen insisted not only that Kentucky's antebellum slaves lacked any "burning desire for freedom" but also that they resented abolitionist "agitators" who encouraged them to run away. In a similar vein, in a piece about Jefferson Davis's onetime body servant and coachman James H. Jones, a Galveston newspaper reminded readers of the genuine attachments ex-slaves had to "their old plantation homes" and their lingering "affection" for onetime masters like Davis deriving from recollections of things like the Christmas presents they had received as slaves.[32]

Two significant southern white distillations of slave Christmas experiences achieved national readerships in 1891. That was the year Ruth McEnery Stuart's ecstatic celebration of slave Christmas morning joy, "Christmas Gifts," appeared in *Lippincott's Monthly Magazine*'s January issue. Stuart's tale got added exposure when it was republished in her 1893 anthology *Golden Wedding*, which itself was reprinted in the 1890s and as late as 1969. Attesting to its circulation, a theatrical company of black and Native American students in New York City staged an adaptation under the title "Christmas on the Old Plantation," for a $2 admission fee, at the Carnegie Lyceum (which met at what today is Zankel Hall at Carnegie Hall) in 1901. At the end of 1891, *Ladies Home Journal*'s Christmas issue published Rebecca Cameron's piece about Christmas at her family's Buchoi rice plantation in North Carolina.[33]

Few recollections excelled Cameron's idealizations of slaveholders and the glories of being enslaved at Christmas. She recalled how the family's mammy vigorously "scrubbed" the household's white children each Christmas Eve, knowing they would be too agitated to wash themselves the next morning amid all the holiday ferment, and how mammy's stocking, "by universal consent," got the best spot on Christmas Eve—on a chair in front of the fireplace. Early Christmas morning, Cameron's family had a mahogany table carried to the wide veranda. Once the sconces there were lit and a bowl of eggnog placed on the table, slaves were summoned by loud beats on a drum, so that, carrying torches, they could come up and "wish 'Ole master' a happy Christmas." Cameron's grandfather gave each hand a glass of eggnog, and, knowing all his slaves by name, even the small children, engaged in scripted banter of this sort: "'Sarvant Master; merry Christmas to you, an' all de fambly, sir!' Thank you Jack; merry Christmas to you and yours!" Cameron added that once the drinking was over and the slaves breakfasted back in their quarters, they returned to the veranda, which awaited them with hampers full of their Christmas gifts. According to Cameron, her grandfather gave money to all the slaves, including fifty cents in silver to each full-grown male, and the white women dispensed aprons, cravats, handkerchiefs, toys, knives, pipes, and all the things that her family had learned "the negroes most delighted in," including gingerbread and apples. Then the enslaved women marched in a line to draw their allowances of staples like meat, molasses, coffee, and flour, so they would be adequately provided for Christmas feasting. At the whites' dance Christmas night, a slave called "Uncle Robin," dressed in Cameron's great-grandfather's regimental uniform, took up tunes as head fiddler, "bowing with great ceremoniousness" to the assembled gentry, hoping to get silver and gold coins as tips for his playing. Meanwhile, the quarters' slaves returned to the big house so they could observe the goings on. Cameron suggests that the slaves may have enjoyed their onlooker experiences more than the whites enjoyed their own partying, and further reports that her grandfather provided his slaves with a grand ball of their own before their holiday ended. That affair occurred in a servants' hall connected to the main kitchen, with the room festooned in myrtle and holly.[34]

Christmastime 1891 additionally brought the *New Orleans Daily Picayune's* publications of Albert H. Shepard's poem "Christmas Eve on the Old Plantation" and a short story titled "Henriette's Christmas: An Episode of the Olden Days," the latter by a New Orleans's chronicler of Creole local color lore, Marie L. Points. After describing how the quarters "niggahs" built up a big fire and held a fiddle-driven dance (with fiddler "old Sam" needing "anudder dram" to keep the music going), Shepard's poem concludes:

Twelve o'clock! A merry Christmus!
   Stop de musick till we dine.
Sam'l, play "Ole Folks at Home"
   While de couples form in line.
Fo'ward, Hannah, lead the comp'ny,
   Take de arm ob Uncle Pete.
Lawd-a-mussy, did yer ebber?
   Tell yer what, wo's hard ter beat!

While Shepard's poem embraced Christmas joy in the slave community, Points's sentimental, tear-worthy story about the "Ste. Marie plantation"—a fictional Louisiana place of expansive orange groves and fields of sugarcane and rice along nine miles of the Mississippi River—revolved around a master's generosity toward all his slaves and his sensitive compassion for his most troubled one. In this tale, the far-flung St. Alexandre family traditionally reunites for Christmas on the home place (a great mansion with wide galleries, gabled turrets, and fluted columns), where Henri St. Alexandre, plantation heir and family head, dispenses hospitality worthy of the aristocratic denizens of New Orleans's salons and courtyards. The story colorfully recounts slave labor being happily performed in the days leading up to Christmas, with the "darkies" singing in the fields as they cut down "ripe, juicy cane" stalks and haul them by wagon to the sugarhouse, where they are ground into sugar and syrup that glitters "like streams of molten gold." For the holiday, workers don their best attire, having earned their reward of a week of rest and a big feast and dance for their conscientious, uncomplaining labors. Unsurprisingly, nostalgia permeates the narrative, with passages about "mirth and revelry in the picturesque row of negro cabins" and the immature character of simple-minded African Americans who, implicitly, were well-suited for paternalistically regulated enslavement:

> Till far into the night the thrum of the darkies' banjos echoed, and the measured strokes of old Jean Baptiste beating the time with sticks upon an empty barrel, the refrain of plantation songs, and the glimpses of the negroes dancing with infantile glee in the flickering firelight, marked a phase in the life of antebellum days on the Mississippi that has for us in latter days the soft and lingering glow of an autumnal's twilight adieu.

"Henriette's Christmas," uncharacteristically for the genre, does notice slave sales during the holiday season, but within a plot twist that redounds to the credit of the Old South's master class. The master's slave Henriette, elderly nurse to his children, after singing a lullaby filled with pathos on December 23, is persuaded by one of the children in the nursery to repeat, as she customarily did each Yuletide, her own sad Christmas story. This she does while her master eavesdrops from the hall. Her story reverts to an earlier Christmas in her life, when she and her family had been owned by a different Louisiana master and labored at a place on Bayou Teche. Unfortunately, that master had died one Christmas Eve, a night when she had sung the very same lullaby to her own boy, Balthazar, and her father, Pierre. By the time the next day, Christmas Day, ended, all the slaves on the place had been sold "far and wide," with Henriette going to a different owner than the one who bought her son and father. In a plot device grossly violating statistical probabilities, author Points locates her main character, the master Henri St. Alexandre, in New Orleans on Christmas Eve day, Christmas shopping one day after overhearing this sad story. There, he stumbles on a slave auction at the grand rotunda of the St. Louis Hotel, with chained "darkies" of both sexes awaiting sale. When St. Alexandre realizes that the last two slaves awaiting sale are Henriette's very Balthazar and the now "decrepit" Pierre, he doubles the bid of an expectant purchaser, relieves the slaves of their shackles, and takes them back to Ste. Marie plantation to surprise Henriette with a Christmas morning reunion. This he stages with great drama in the grand hall of his mansion.

This horribly hokey story reinforces postwar rationalizations of slavery. In fact, in its closing sentences, Points's story tells us that the "fortunes of war" had cost the St. Alexandres their plantation, leaving Henri and his wife to live modestly in the French Quarter in New Orleans. Still, they keep up old customs of Christmas hospitality and family gatherings each holiday season, with the help of Henriette's son, Balthazar, who had never wanted the freedom that emancipation brought him and had remained with his former owners.[35]

Additional white southern takes on antebellum slave Christmases followed throughout the decade, further embedding proslavery holiday stereotypes in the national imagination. In 1892, William P. Trent, a Virginian son of a Confederate physician teaching history at the University of the South in Sewanee, Tennessee, published his biography of the antebellum South Carolina writer William Gilmore Simms. Discussing Simms's Woodlands plantation, acquired by marriage, Trent claimed without documentation that when northern guests happened to visit Simms during the Christmas season, they "likely" were roused early from their sleep by sounds of "sweet singing, blended with tones from numerous banjos"; if they stirred from their quarters in time, they would have seen the author "standing in the porch distributing all sorts of presents to all sorts and conditions of grinning and grateful darkies"—scenes so pleasant the viewers might possibly have returned to bed convinced that "slavery was after all not such a bad institution."[36] On Christmas Day 1892, the *Galveston Daily News* published "Marse Tom's Christmus Gif'," in which an obviously white narrator recounted a visit several years earlier over Christmas to his friend Jim's place in eastern Texas.

What is notable about the *News* piece is not so much that black household servants are still engaging playfully in Christmas Gif' begging, but rather that a "superannuated" servant there named "Aunt

Marthy" explains her own personal history. She had been owned during her childhood by the host's grandfather back in South Carolina, given to the host's father (Tom) as a Christmas present, and had nursed the host himself when he was a baby. At the end of the Civil War, upon being informed that the Yankees were allowing her liberty to go where she wished, she had chosen to remain with the family in South Carolina and then move to Texas when host Jim had married and relocated there. Rather than hate the people who had owned her, Aunt Marthy resents Yankees for destroying southern property during the war. Now nearing death, she looks ahead anxiously to rejoining her deceased master and mistress in heaven, where they will all wait upon the arrival of Jim, his wife, and their children. There, she can once again share a Christmas dinner with the white people who had once claimed ownership of her![37]

During the mid and late 1890s, the *New Orleans Daily Picayune* continued churning out pieces about how antebellum Christmases had been glorious for masters and slaves alike. On Christmas Eve day 1893, the paper printed an apparently fictional tale of a visitor going "some years ago" to a Mississippi River plantation that had the "largest pack of fox hounds in the country" and a "great number of slaves." In those glorious antebellum days before "blue-coated" invaders "sacked" the mansion, "thrusting swords and bayonets through picture and mirrors," Oakhurst plantation's excessively hospitable owner was "kind to his slaves, and the negro quarters resounded at the December festival with revelry and singing." Just one day later, the *Picayune* marked the holiday with naval secretary Hillary Herbert's recollections of childhood Christmas experiences at his father's Alabama plantation, with its joyous slave merrymakers. December 1894 brought the paper's reprinting from *Century Magazine* of Baltimorean John Williamson Palmer's memoir "Old Maryland Homes and Ways," highlighting slave Christmas reunions and quarters visitations, reciprocal master–family servant gift exchanges, slaves downing gin and jugs of rum provided by their masters, and frenetically rhythmic slave dancing ("Round the corn, Saly!"). Then, the day before Christmas in 1895, the *Picayune* published "Christmas and New Years Days," insisting that during antebellum times black plantation slaves of all ages found "unalloyed enjoyment" at holiday time. Prior to Christmas, slaves killed the hogs, oxen, and sheep on which they would feast days later, when they were given copious amounts of meat to take back to their cabins. Four years farther on, the *Picayune* ran Elizabeth M. Gilmer's "Uncle Isom as Santa Claus," a plot with a Civil War twist that had an African American explain in dialect that postwar Christmastimes hardly stacked up compared to slave Yuletides, a judgment that undoubtedly had an element of truth in a materialistic sense for many impoverished former slaves still alive at the turn of the century. Isom highlights antebellum Yule log traditions, freedom from labor other than for feeding stock and carrying wood to the big house, dancing and feasting, and all "de carryin' on" the slaves did. On Christmas Eve, Isom recalled, "ole master" sent "a bowl of eggnog as big as a washtub" down to the quarters. Maybe the most significant element in this tale is author Gilmer's subtitle, "A Characteristic Southern Story of Christmas Time," which implied Uncle Isom's Christmas experiences paralleled those of most other southern slaves.[38]

Other 1890s works in this vein included Sallie May Dooley's 1896 fictional reminiscences in heavy dialect of an elderly ex-slave to his granddaughter, with about half a chapter devoted to slave Christmastimes, and Ruth McEnery Stuart's short story "Duke's Christmas" that same year. Dooley, the wife of a wealthy Richmond, Virginia, businessman and Confederate veteran, described Old Dominion slave house servants drinking unthinkably good eggnog from an heirloom silver bowl, with the plantation mistress regulating their servings since slaves lacked the discipline to moderate imbibing of "sperits" from "Satun." Naturally, slaves got more food, presents, and partying in one Yuletide than postwar blacks would enjoy in a hundred years, and they even witnessed the Christmas Eve fireworks initiating the celebration—"de firy sarpent shoot un wriggle in de air"—alongside their white owners on the Big House porch. Stuart's "Duke's Christmas" concerned a nine-year-old boy (Little Duke) and his elderly grandfather "Uncle" Mose, who suffer hardship because of the latter's crippling rheumatism and incapacity for work. In this postwar tale, Mose apprises his grandson "'bout Christmas on de ole plantation" during slavery, when "all de darkies had to march up ter de great house fur dey Christmasgifts." Once "olde marster axed a blessin', an' de string-ban' play, an' we all sing a song . . . boss, he'd call out de names, an' we'd step up, one by one, ter git our presents," with the master telling good-natured jokes about particular slaves that set everyone laughing. One Christmas, Mose's master had given him a ring made out of silver, which Mose offered immediately to his love interest, Zephyr, and they had been married that very Christmas night. The plot hook is that during the postwar Christmas when this reminiscing occurs, Little Duke goes out to procure Christmas scraps promised by a wealthy white woman to whom he had sold some bricks. The bundle of tea, coffee, and buckwheat flour she provides includes a ten-cent piece, alerting Mose that their benefactor was none other than his former mistress, who had made a tradition of giving her slaves that very present. Mose and Little Duke hunt the woman down for a reunion of hugs and tears. But as if one Christmas miracle is not enough, Stuart's plot includes the artifice that the black servant appearing in the room carrying a tray is Mose's son and Little Duke's father. Tragically, Mose and Little Duke had been permanently separated from him seven years earlier when a levee broke during a flood that killed Little Duke's mother. The emphasis here is not just the generosity of southern whites toward dependent blacks at Christmas before and after the Civil War but also their persisting concern afterward for formerly enslaved people. Near the story's end, we learn that Mose's ex-mistress has been sending out bundles of buckwheat flour with money inside to "needy colored people" for years, hoping that one of them would identify her lost former slave.[39]

Unsurprisingly, Jefferson Davis's widow, Varina, weighed in too on slave Christmases, publishing "Christmas in the Confederate White House" in the *New York World*'s December 13, 1896, number while she was living in New York. Her piece represents the Davises' "man servant" Robert Brown as very enthusiastic during Christmas 1864 about making a miniature house toy to be given as a prize at the Christmas festivities at the St. Paul's Church Episcopalian home for orphan children in the Confederate capital of Richmond—a charity the Davises were deeply involved in facilitating. When Brown's house toy was revealed for advance viewing at the Confederate White House at a Christmas Eve party, the servant (as Mrs. Davis recounted the moment) "bowed his thanks for our approval" while youths in the room applauded. Naturally, the following morning the household's "negro women" consecutively caught all the Davis family in Christmas Gif' parries, apparently without losing an encounter. "Of course, there was a present for every one," the ex-Confederate First Lady recalled, "small though it might be, and one who had been born and brought up at our plantation was vocal in her admiration of a gay handkerchief," extolling her benevolent mistress for knowing just what she wanted.[40]

In 1897, not only did Thomas Nelson Page publish *Unc' Edinburg,* but he also reinforced its message with his retrospective *Social Life in Old Virginia Before the War,* a republication of an article he had placed in the *Christian Union* years earlier. What is perhaps most significant is less Page's repetition of the usual details common in such accounts than Page's professing to get into slaves' thinking. Thus, all year long, slaves are so obsessed with Christmas's magic that they measure time by a given day's distance from either Christmas's arrival or departure. Thus a black wagon driver's feigned indifference as he brings boxes of Christmas gifts for slaves from the depot to the plantation storehouse masks his true feelings. Thus fellow slaves purposely talk just loudly enough as they unload the packages about what they wish is in them to ensure their mistress or master overhears them.[41]

Also in 1897, the ever-prolific Ruth McEnery Stuart published "An Old-Time Christmas Gift" for *Saint Nicholas* and "A Christmas Gift That Went . . . A-Begging" for the *Milwaukee Journal.* The former, set "in old slavery days, on a Louisiana plantation," concerns a plantation mistress's girl and a black slave girl born on the same Christmas Day, with the latter immediately designated (in a ceremony on the mistress's birthing bed) as eventual maid to the former. The girls grow up together, spending their early teens in each other's company during the Civil War. When the war ends with news that the slaves are free, the black youth claims that emancipation only applied to slaves who had been bought and sold and exempted slaves like herself who had been given out as "a Christmas gif'." She wishes to remain her companion's "little nigger," and Mimi, the white youth, pledges to be "a better little mistress than I've been" for the future. At story's end, we learn that thirty years after the war, they reside in the same southern city, and always visit together on special occasions of sadness and joy. Stuart's tale in the *Milwaukee Journal,* later a book, presents a very sad and poor ten-year-old black youth named George Washington Jones who resists arising on a post–Civil War Christmas morning, taking no interest in Christmas stockings filled with toys; his grandfather, his last living relation, has just died, and he is temporarily staying with a non-related black woman he calls "Aunt Caroline" while his future is being determined. Significantly, George starts ruminating about things his grandfather had told him about his own life, which also had its disappointments. While still a boy of ten, his grandfather had been the one privileged slave of 500 field hands to be selected by his master "as a Christmas gift" to be the personal servant of "the loveliest and sweetest mistress in all the world." His life had been glorious attending this "princess" until the Civil War, when things fell apart ("Like most of the old plantation stories, it ended with '—an den de war come.'"). George decides to resolve his Christmas blues by strolling down Prytania

Street—a wealthy part of his community where people had lawns and stables—and offer himself as a Christmas gift to one of the elite women living there. The story evolves into a warmhearted, whimsical tale, with George coincidentally winding up in the service of his grandfather's onetime mistress and the former slaveholder identifying her family as George's "folks . . . your people, in truth" in an emotional reunion moment of discovery.[42]

As should be apparent by now, a high percentage of defensive proslavery southern white publications using Christmas themes were authored by females, reinforcing findings by many historians that women spearheaded the Lost Cause movement of the period, some of them as much to extend the influence of women in southern society as out of nostalgia for the old times.[43] In 1898, Georgian Eugenia J. Bacon, herself the product of a Liberty County cotton plantation upbringing and still seething about Harriet Beecher Stowe's *Uncle Tom's Cabin,* authored a novel of rebuttal with so many autobiographical elements and thinly disguised historical figures that it is truly difficult to discern where fiction lets off and history begins, or was it vice versa? Its main character even bears the name of a slave whom Bacon inherited from her father's Green Forest estate. Bacon's account of slave holiday celebrating and Christmas Gif' playfulness in *Lyddy: A Tale of the Old South* is unremarkable, except for implying that in her household slaves gifted whites as much as vice versa: losing slaves gave white family members eggs; defeated whites offered slaves cakes from a hamper. More notable is the quoted blessing that one slave "reverentially" pronounced before the assembled plantation community of blacks and whites before a shared annual Christmas feast (with whites, of course, getting first dibs)—an offering to God instructing his black peers to appreciate the bounty their owner provided and reminding them they owed willing fealty in return: "De Lord help we niggars ter be true an' faithful ter we [to the] w'ite folks who has spread dis here bounty fer we spacious [our special] 'joyment.'" Drumming home her slave character's point, Bacon concluded her Christmas passages with the moral that black workers in antebellum times needed no pay, since their masters served them as surrogate bankers, letting them draw on them whenever bad health or advancing age prevented their labor. Indeed, Christmas provided "cords to bind even tighter the owned and the owner," a kind of icing on slavery's cake, so to speak.[44]

A year after *Lyddy* appeared, a Presbyterian publication in Louisville offered Mrs. A. M. Paynter's "Christmas in the Old Southern Home," which opens with a turbaned and aproned "dear old mammy" crying "Chris'mas gif'" as she appears in the doorway of "old Marster and Missis" on Christmas morning with "her retinue of little woolly heads." Not only are the black children delighted with large red apples and gingerbread figures from their mistress, but mammy is satisfied with the silver dollar, apron, and colorful handkerchief she is allotted (and the candy, nuts, and raisins given her for "the younger fry"). In fact, she is so pleased that she happily returns to her kitchen "domain" to prepare the grand Christmas breakfast so common in "old Southern" homes in slave times. After all, mammy is the real "queen" of this "realm"—self-satisfied that everyone in her owners' household truly loves and respects her and that her mistress defers to her judgment. Attempting to evoke sympathy for the Old South and its labor system, Paynter reminds her readers sadly that such occasions, with their many slave marriages, "have passed," giving way to modern selfish children with tastes for expensive holiday toys.[45] Gullible readers, of course, would have projected Paynter's story upon all southern slaves, assuming the author's rose-tinted take on forced labor in the Old South.

White southern remembrances of benevolent Christmas customs uniting masters and slaves persisted into the new century, an antiquarian counterpoint to the racial segregation and black disenfranchisement sweeping the region, validated by the U.S. Supreme Court's *Plessy v. Ferguson* decision (1896). In 1900, the well-traveled public lecturer Belle Kearney, the daughter of a Confederate officer who, because of her birth midway through the Civil War could not possibly have harbored memories of slavery on her father's plantation in Madison County, Mississippi, nonetheless assured readers of *A Slaveholder's Daughter* that every slave received generous gifts at Christmas. Also that year, LaSalle Corbell Pickett's published reminiscences of antebellum Yuletides at her family's place in Chuckatuck, Virginia, suspicious if merely for its lengthy quotations of conversation in thick black dialect despite the passage of over forty years, recalled fondly "the merry-making of the simple-hearted colored people to whom the Christmas holidays were the great festival of the year, the gratitude which lit up their dusky faces as they received their presents, the joy of the pickaninnies in the possession of their new toys." Slaves, in Pickett's unlikely telling, not only revel in Christmas fireworks, eating hog meat, and getting gifts; they incredibly consider their master—LaSalle's father—*a slave to them* because he does so much on their behalf. And additionally in 1900,

Georgia Bryan Conrad—the daughter of a Macintosh County, Georgia, rice planter and the granddaughter of onetime Georgia governor George Troup—anecdotally confirmed master/slave holiday goodwill in *Reminiscences of a Southern Woman.* In recalling Christmas 1859 at her uncle's place in Gloucester County, Virginia, she recounted the time when the dining room slave accidentally spilled the entire Christmas dinner because of failing to pull out the table's supporting leg. Instead of being infuriated, Conrad's kindly uncle benignly laughed, exclaiming "I never!" and had the table refilled with what was left in the kitchen.[46]

A year after these memoirs appeared, James Battle Avirett's *Old Plantation,* a work flawed by flagrant lies about time and place, rendered meticulous delineations of Christmas gifting, feasting, and partying practices on Avirett's parents' North Carolina turpentine estate. And in 1903, Floridian Comer L. Peek came out with the novel *Lorna Carswell.* In Peek's story, a male teacher from New England at the Carswell family plantation Rural Shades in Georgia discovers he cannot in good conscience fulfill his paid assignment from the Yankee "abolition press" to report on the South's "horrid 'slave oligarchy'" and slaves pining for liberty, partly because slaves at Christmas got a full week off for visiting, dancing, hosting visitors, and frolicking. Unsurprisingly, *Lorna Carswell* attracted praise in Dixie publications. In the *Confederate Veteran,* a former Florida governor embraced the way Peek, having "really lived through such experiences," convincingly reversed the common wisdom in the "nonslaveholding section" about slave-master relations.[47]

Southern Methodist minister Howard Melancthon Hamill, a Confederate veteran who had served with Lee, recalled "grinning rows" of "dusky" "negros" awaiting present distributions on antebellum plantation back porches early on Christmas mornings in his 1906 work, *The Old South;* that same year, North Carolinian Margaret Devereux employed similar wording in her own *Plantation Sketches,* a volume "based on actual events." After alluding to the shoes and Kilmarnock (Scottish-style) caps that slaves on her grandfather's plantation Runiroi received each Yuletide, Devereux passed to the "happy, grinning black faces" of male laborers there on being paid off by their master on Christmas Day for crops raised in their spare time. Revealing in an aside how badly the South's master class wanted reassurance from their black victims about their own good intentions, Devereux described laborers on the piazza humbly demonstrating "deep obeisance" to their master on getting their payoff with a noticeable "scrape of the foot." Later on, in a special chapter about Runiroi's mammy, Devereux recollected how she "laughed and showed her dimples" on getting her own "gorgeous" holiday gift. [48]

Just before World War I, Eliza Ripley, Cornelia Branch Stone, and Esther S. Reynolds added to plantation Christmas lore their reminiscences discussed earlier, with glowing accounts of master gifting, bowls of eggnog for the "darkies," holiday slave weddings, and laughing slaves. Hardly coincidentally, their accounts found receptive readers in formal organizations dedicated to the Lost Cause and southern white racial mores like the United Daughters of the Confederacy (UDC) and the Confederate Memorial Association. Ripley's *Social Life in Old New Orleans* was donated to the UDC's book collection when the organization around this time was establishing a Confederate library. And Stone, who published her account in the *Confederate Veteran,* had previously served as president general of the UDC, the organization's highest rank, presiding over its 1909 convention.[49]

Indeed, UDC and Confederate Memorial Association activists deserve attribution for many of the literary productions that on the eve of the Great War enshrined antebellum southern Christmases, underscoring the propagandistic underpinnings of the whole project. In 1909, Eugenia Dunlap Potts of Lexington, Kentucky's UDC chapter read a paper about slavery, later published, with mention of "negroes in grinning rows" awaiting their Christmas presents on slaveholders' back porches and how slaves had a week to enjoy not only their gifts but also their "grand eatables" and eggnog. Two years later, the *Century Illustrated Monthly Magazine* carried "'Christmas Gif'!': A Memory of the Old South" by Tennessean Virginia Frazer Boyle, a life member of the Confederate Memorial Association and the daughter of a Confederate officer who spent part of the Civil War in a Yankee prison. Her tale had much in common with Potts's, portraying a Yuletide slave quarters community on a cotton plantation where a mammy cooks for Christmas two weeks in advance, where "piccaninnies" dance in holiday excitement, and where Christmas morning sees universally smiling slaves proceeding to the big house for cider and distributions of "warm flannels" and "goodies for everybody" on the mansion's back veranda. Additionally, its plot's climax reinforced tropes about master paternalism and slave gratitude, revolving around a slave carpenter named Jerry, who for forty consecutive years had triumphantly mastered his owner in Christmas Gif'. When, one Christmas, "Ole Marse" tells a triumphant Jerry to expect nothing more than cider that year for winning because his cotton remained unsold and he could not afford extra gifts, Jerry sulks over the disgrace of being snubbed and how the insult would hurt his status in the slave quarters, foregoing the annual Christmas slave feast in his hurt pride. Still, when Jerry later on Christmas Day discovers that the gin-house is on fire, threatening all his master's stored cotton, he bravely risks his life to roll the stored bales out of the burning building. Overcome by gratitude at this supreme act of loyalty, a grieving Ole Marse pleads with his blistered, bloody, and prostrate slave to cling to life and grants him freedom as an encouragement. Predictably, though, Jerry declines liberty, saying he "ain't know" what freedom is. Rather, the slave whispers, he merely wants his customary Christmas gift, and he wishes it bestowed in front of the other slaves to restore his prestige in the quarters. And that is where the story ends![50]

Then, in 1912, Virginian and UDC activist Edna Turpin's fictional "Abram's Freedom" for the *Atlantic Monthly*, reprinted as a small book a year later, told of a young male plantation slave who so enjoyed his Christmas eggnog and other holiday benefits, including a bag of candy and a red silk bandana, that he lorded it condescendingly over nearby free blacks who only had sweet potatoes and turnips for Christmas. Although Abram eventually convinces his master to allow him to earn his own freedom so he can marry one of those free blacks, it is only because she refuses to wed a slave, not because he resents enslavement himself. Perhaps the most telling line is when Abram's master, watching his slave's delight in getting a bonus serving of holiday eggnog, says, "Umph! Wish Mrs. Harriet Beecher Stowe could see you now." In fact, Abram's master is so caring that he presents Abraham and his wife with a gift of thirty acres of land and a mule as northern emancipation policies take hold in the Civil War. Turpin's tale was succeeded, in 1914, by Mrs. F. C. Roberts's reminiscence "Christmas in the Confederacy," appearing in a magazine published by the North Carolina Division of the UDC (*Carolina and the Southern Cross*). It depicted slave Christmas loyalty amid the whirlwind of war. Without identifying the specific Civil War Christmas being related, Roberts described how slave children helped decorate her family's parlor and claimed slaves accepted the war's reduced gifting without complaint. On Christmas Day, a visiting pastor even baptized thirty slave children, with the Roberts's mammy playing an important role in the procession. Most tellingly, Roberts explains that during the service, she and her brother assumed the role of sponsors for these children, resolving always to "do our duty by them"—a sincere obligation that "Fate" (an oblique allusion to emancipation) prevented them from carrying out. Drumming home the propagandistic value of Roberts's piece for Lost Causers, the magazine's editor added an explanatory note calling the southern slaveholding class "true missionaries" bent on uplifting slaves as compared to teachers arriving later on from the North who corrupted and degraded their pupils.[51]

Two years after Roberts published her reminiscence, the "Historian General" of the UDC weighed in. On November 9, 1916, in a speech at a public hall in Dallas titled "The Civilization of the Old South," which was immediately published, Mildred Lewis Rutherford suggested that veterans in her audience take pity on youths who had never experienced antebellum southern Yuletides. Back in "old plantation" days, Christmas Gif' shouting began "early in the morning at the Big House," spreading joy down to the slave cabins, and not only did every "negro" woman and man receive "a complete outfit from hat to shoes," but even "old negroes too feeble to work" snagged "special gifts," cozy shawls, and comfortable shoes, all purchased to make their lives more comfortable. Wistfully musing that "Christmas can never be the same again," Rutherford implied that slaves were the primary beneficiaries of holiday delicacies like gumdrops, boxes of almonds, and coconuts. Perhaps her confidently glowing remarks about slave times drew extra inspiration from the reelection of Woodrow Wilson just two days previous to her talk, the South's first president in half a century and an ardent supporter of segregation. Several times in her remarks Rutherford alluded positively to Wilson and his advocacy of states' rights.[52]

Into the 1920s, southern whites continued elaborating tropes about antebellum Christmas customs to legitimize their region's coercive labor system. In 1921, the prolific South Carolina nature writer Archibald Rutledge—a descendent of one of his state's most distinguished Revolutionary-era families and later the Palmetto State's first poet laureate—finished his book on hunting in the South with a chapter entitled "A Plantation Christmas." Although Rutledge highlighted twentieth-century southern holiday customs, he noted that older black family servants on large southern plantations sprang Christmas Gif' moments on their victims, all but suggesting that this tradition derived from slave times. Indirectly, by insisting that modern plantation owners purposely allowed their servants to win these games and that they cared deeply for their black employees, Rutledge reinforced decades of southern claims that masters had been paternalistic and generous in slave times too: "After the children have gone to bed in the great rambling plantation house, we begin arranging the Christmas presents; and these include not only the number for the family, but those for the servants, and the servants' families, friends, and visitors. . . . There must always be a reserve store of gifts for cases of emergency in the form of negroes who come unexpectedly." The year after Rutledge's book appeared, moreover, Elizabeth W. Allston Pringle published *Chronicles of Chicora Wood,* with its romanticized rendering of slave Christmas mornings on a South Carolina plantation and considerable staying power. Pringle's remembrances of antebellum plantation Christmases in *Chronicles,* themselves previewed in a work she had already published under a pseudonym in 1913 entitled *A Woman Rice Planter,* were not only immediately reprinted in 1923 by its initial publisher Charles Scribner's Sons but also between 1940 and 2017 by four other publishers, including Harvard University Press.[53]

Just as proslavery argumentation before the Civil War—the ideological defense of the South's peculiar institution in books, journals, newspapers, and speeches—was never exclusively the work of southern whites, so too post–Civil War and twentieth-century idealizations of the antebellum slave Christmas experience had Yankee collaborators. Surprisingly, *Uncle Tom's Cabin* author Harriet Beecher Stowe was one. In a piece for the weekly magazine *Christian Union* published during Reconstruction after she and her family had begun wintering in Florida and invested in land there, Stowe described how antebellum mistresses and masters liberally dispensed presents to their slaves and how the latter capitalized on their holiday privileges: "Dressed in their best, visiting from plantation to plantation, and dancing all night to the sound of the corn-fiddle and the banjo, the light-hearted race gave themselves freely up to enjoyment."[54]

Stowe's account, with its unfortunate racial coding, foreshadowed what ensued in many northern publications, even the muckraking socialist author Upton Sinclair's early novel *Manassas* (1904).[55] At Christmas on the "Montague" cotton and corn plantation in Mississippi, slaves get a ten-day holiday, and the mistress and her children give them "endless presents" from a brick storehouse. An early twentieth-century history of Arkansas, supervised by the director of that state's Department of Archives and History but written by a northerner and published in Chicago, struck similar themes. In this supposedly "authentic" and "reliable" *undocumented* account (as compared to prior state histories by "conscientious" but uninformed writers), all Arkansas cotton plantation slaves enjoyed three months off from labor—other than undemanding "chores"—once the crop was picked and harvested in the fall. Christmas brought "feasting and merry-making, in which the negroes were not neglected." At holiday time, masters collaborated with their planter neighbors in setting up a single Christmas tree where "pickaninnies" and older slaves assembled and received their gifts. Over the Yuletide, blacks and whites were alike happy, with the former partying well into Christmas night.[56]

Between 1882 and 1893, the *Youth's Companion,* a weekly published in Boston, carried four Christmas plantation tales set in antebellum times and drenched in black dialect, virtually indistinguishable from what southern white authors were saying about antebellum holiday traditions. In "A Christmas of the Past," the obscure writer M. B. Williams related holiday times among the hundred or so enslaved people belonging to one Colonel Falkner, the "kind master" of "Westlea" plantation. The colonel provides his joyous, dancing, and exuberantly singing slaves with feasting, lots of eggnog, and generous gifts (ceremoniously doled out) for the holiday. In service of a plot about the prior banishment of the master's daughter for marrying the wrong suitor and her return and reunion with her parents on a particular Christmas, author Williams suggests the slaves care about their owners more than themselves, and that masters tolerate virtually anything on Christmas. The colonel not only accepts the annoyance of Christmas Gif', but he even cooperates with a long-standing and uncomfortable tradition of "walkin' roun'"—being carried to and from the quarters on his slave men's shoulders—hoping to please his enslaved people at the price of his own comfort. In another *Youth's Companion* tale, a slave body servant who has run away to escape what he wrongly thinks will be his first whipping earns his freedom papers by saving the life of his master's son. Yet he stays voluntarily "on the old plantation" and remains there at age thirty as the story closes. The story condescendingly stereotypes blacks as "quaint" and reminds readers of the generosity of master holiday gifting, with every slave getting a half-dollar piece and each child getting an extra picayune.[57]

Northern adult periodicals and newspapers, meanwhile, published Christmas stories and essays with identical themes. In 1880, a Philadelphia journal carried an unattributed essay recounting slaves playing Christmas Gif' and lauding the quality of presents enslaved people received: bright head kerchiefs for the "negro women" and "a pair of shoes for 'Uncle Tom,' a warm coat for 'Old Uncle Elijah,' a smart suit for Tony the waiter." On Christmas morning, white and black children ignited fireworks together in biracial camaraderie. Meanwhile, "ladies" of the white family had to make the eggnog and keep the huge bowl of it constantly replenished because it was so difficult to persuade servants to work during Christmas. Similarly, in 1891 the New York–based *Catholic World* published "Mammy's C'ris'mus"—a post–Civil War story revolving around the near-death Christmas baptisms of both a onetime Georgia cotton plantation mammy and her former mistress. Still living on the old place, now in horrific decay with rotting fences and wild razorbacks trampling its gardens, the mammy nostalgically recalls its antebellum heyday as "lak de promus' lan." At the holiday, she wistfully recalls, slaves processioned to the big house screaming, "C'ris'mus-gif," earning for their earnestness "head han'k'chers en blankets en Sunday coats en all sich." "I dunno whar C'ris'mus gwine cum f'um now," the mammy sadly laments. "Dey ain' no marster en dey ain' no niggers."[58]

A year later, northern newspapers carried Felix Gregory de Fontaine's Associated Press piece, "A Plantation Xmas." A Bostonian by birth, de Fontaine had spent virtually his entire career in newspaper work in New York and Boston, with one glaring exception. At the beginning of the Civil War, his employer, *New York Herald* editor James Gordon Bennett, sent him to Charleston harbor to cover the Fort Sumter situation, and he had stayed on in wartime Dixie, covering some of the fighting and working for newspapers in Charleston and Columbia in South Carolina and in Savannah, Georgia. By the time de Fontaine returned northward in the late 1860s, he held southern partisan attitudes, which shaded his later writings. In his very nostalgic plantation retrospective, de Fontaine lamented that despite some carryovers, "the genuine plantation Christmas" of antebellum times had faded "into the realm of legend and tradition." Amid drawings of slaves saying "Chrismus Gif', Massa" and a slave fiddler sitting in a chair overlooking energetically dancing slaves ("The Fun Began"), his narrative told about the lengthy lapse from work slaves enjoyed at Christmas. Before the holiday even arrived, "the mouth o[f] every hand on the place" had been "watering for a month" in anticipation of the goodies, including a "fatted calf" the master always provided on the holiday. During the celebration, "Old Aunt Riah" testifies "dar'll be chicken pie an tater pudd'n an 'simmon [persimmon] beer fur dem niggers ter eat an drink," when she goes to the main house to report on the goings on to her mistress.[59]

The *Milwaukee Daily Sentinel* reinforced southern Christmas tropes more than once in its columns. In a sarcastic piece during Reconstruction, the *Sentinel* imagined ex-Confederate president Davis getting a reprieve from the too-forgiving President Andrew Johnson just before his scheduled hanging on Christmas Day, giving a positive twist on slaves' Christmas experiences. Before the war, over Christmas "old massas" gave their slaves a week for "visiting and idleness and frolics" and "dusky" slave folk in the quarters laughed joyously and danced to banjoes, fiddles, and tambourines. In 1887, the *Sentinel* published James C. Plummer's "In the Quarter" about "The Holiday of the Year on the Plantation." Plummer described "Christmas morning 'befoh the wah,'" when slaves awakened masters with 'Chris'mas gif, massa' cries," and Christmas Eve, which carefree slaves in the quarter passed fatiguing themselves while dancing to fiddle and banjo tunes and gorging themselves on hog meat ("the negro loves pork"). According to Plummer, a week of enjoyment followed. Unfortunately, Plummer maintains regretfully, such happy celebrations were "a thing of the past," never to return. His piece's last words?: "I doubt whether Christmas makes any people happier than it did the old plantation negroes when they danced the chinquapin." How could any reader not crave the good old antebellum times southern slaves so enjoyed, or so such writers seemed to be saying.[60]

Even the New York sporting magazine *Forest and Stream* hallowed Old South slave Christmases, carrying Charles Hallock's "Holumdays in Old Dixie" in a Christmas week issue. Hollock, a New York City native and naturalist who had spent part of the Civil War helping to publish a newspaper in Augusta, Georgia, burnished Confederate credentials by publishing a fifty-eight-page biography of Stonewall Jackson while the war was in progress. His "Holumdays" not only proclaimed the usual benefits of slave Christmases—eggnog, masters watching slave "capers," visitation privileges, loads of downtime, and mutual gift exchanges between masters and slaves (delicacies from the "great house" for Aunt Dinah's "best corn cake or chicken fixin's")— but it also misleadingly left the impression that masters were accustomed to giving slaves their freedom as Christmas presents.[61]

Possibly no northern media outlet had greater potential, though, for affirming white southern claims about antebellum slave Christmases than *Harper's Weekly.* Founded in 1857 by the book publishers Harper &

Brothers, the heavily illustrated *Weekly,* grandiosely subtitled "A Journal of Civilization" and more a magazine than newspaper, gained a circulation of about 90,000 by the Civil War and almost 500,000 at the peak of its popularity in the 1870s, when it played a key role in exposing New York City's municipal corruption scandals. Though most of the time its circulation lagged several other publications, like *Ladies Home Journal,* it reigned, in the words of one assessment, as "the most important of American pictorial magazines" for most of six decades.[62]

A week after Christmas in 1871, at the pinnacle of its popularity, *Harper's* published "Christmas in Virginia," invoking some of the sentimental tropes that would dominate later depictions of how enslaved people and their masters had passed the holiday before the war, though the piece actually concerned an incident that supposedly had occurred just a week earlier. In this two-paragraph story, accompanied by a nearly full-page illustration entitled "Christmas in Virginia—A Present from the Great House," the author explains that despite the war, there were still "large estates" where onetime house servants persisted in their "dependent relation" to former masters before relating the particulars of a "humble but comfortable cabin" on one such estate, occupied by an elderly black couple. In this brief vignette, a little white girl from the estate's "great house" arrives at the blacks' cabin on Christmas with a contribution of something "extra nice" for their holiday dinner, and to wish them the best of the season. Musing that perhaps these old people had been born on the estate and lived there their entire lives and shared childhood experiences with the girl's grandparents, the author surmises that the black couple conceived of themselves as still "belonging" to the white family. In the picture, a slightly built and bonneted white girl of about ten appears in the cabin's doorway bearing edibles covered by a small, light-covered cloth towel or napkin for protection and possibly to keep the heat in.

Perhaps the only thing differentiating this piece from southern romanticizations of slave-master Christmas traditions is that instead of lamenting emancipation for threatening such idylls of intimate white-black social relations at Christmas, the essay welcomes their inevitable disappearance as befitting of a nation growing increasingly "practical," almost certainly an allusion to the escalating industrialization of the nation after the Civil War. In such an age, the author concludes, people should have little sympathy for perpetuating anomalies like "a dependent peasantry," but rather look forward to "nobler" conditions of affairs.[63]

Yet some years later, *Harper's Weekly* published another piece about residuals of slave-master Christmas relations that more fully embraced nostalgia for slave times, perhaps an indication that as the federal government abandoned Reconstruction policies of imposing black voting and office-holding on recalcitrant southern whites, northern commentators became increasingly sympathetic to white southern perspectives on slavery and race. Titled "Christmas in the South," the piece, which appeared two weeks before the holiday in 1885, imagined a one-time slave and his family appearing at the house of his "old master" on Christmas morning so as to "Come to pay yo' our 'specs sah, an' wishin' aw yo' happy Chris'mus," using language that differed not at all from what (according to the writer) he would have said in similar circumstances in 1860.

Suggesting that masters had felt genuine affection for their enslaved people before the war and that ex-slaves were entirely sincere in expressing fondness for their onetime owners, the writer relates the "heartiness of the old master's welcome" as he displayed "the tender qualities that slavery allowed and even encouraged in masters that were kind and slaves that were obedient." Given such tendencies and that ex-slaves had warm recollections of antebellum Christmases as times of family reunions, it was no wonder to the author that blacks who had once been treated affectionately by their owners considered themselves "yet a part of their old masters' families" into the present.[64]

Just before Christmas 1904, the once antislavery *New York Times* published in its Sunday magazine the transplanted southerner Lillie Devereux Blake's piece about the unhurried nature of antebellum Christmases on her father's sizable North Carolina plantation on the Roanoke River's banks, long before her family moved to Connecticut. Dressed in their holiday best, slaves held a "merry" "grand ball" in the place's large barn—specially decked out with pine and holly branches—dancing to tunes by a "negro fiddler," with slave men clapping "Juba" to keep the rhythms up (accomplished by clapping in time "or perhaps bringing the palm down sharply on the leg or chest"). Although white family members did not attend the entire ball, they did observe its early stages, and all Christmas Day "groups of our people" visited the "great house" to give "Masser and Missis" their Christmas greetings, sometimes carrying small gifts like flowers, eggs, and small birds they had tamed. Most important was Blake's benevolently racialist celebration of a posited mutual fondness between enslaved and enslaver: "Ah! those dusky friends of long ago! How they dwell in memory! How deep and strong was the affection which existed be-tween these simple people and those in whose hands was the great re-sponsibility of their welfare! Of course, gifts were distributed lavishly. No one was forgotten, and at night there were gay parties for the feasts that were generously provided." In a refrain common among her peers' recollections, Blake all but wishes slavery had never been eradicated, admitting that though it was "no doubt" best the institution ended, nonetheless whenever she returned to the area she became troubled by the "desperate poverty" of former slaves, now stripped of "the protec-tion to which they had been accustomed." Indeed, the obvious depri-vations of former slaves brought her to tears.[65]

All this time, December issues of illustrated northern publications reinforced positive messaging about slave Christmases with imagery, often by Virginia native and ex-Confederate soldier William Ludwell Sheppard, who seems to have been as obsessed with drawing slave Christmases as Ruth McEnery Stuart was with writing about them. If a picture is worth a thousand words, as the common idiom has it, then there is no calculating the potential impact on public opinion of Sheppard's pictures, as he churned out a succession of such repre-sentations. Take, for instance, Sheppard's picture for *Frank Leslie's Illus-trated Weekly* depicting a room festooned in greens, with a bewhiskered black servant, decked out in bow tie and serving jacket, waiting for partying whites to take the cups of eggnog he is holding patiently on a tray. In a picture for the same magazine's later iteration, *Leslie's Weekly,* Sheppard sets his scene in the front yard of what appears to be a sturdy slave cabin. In this appealing illustration, some thirty or so well-attired blacks mill about, while a male-female couple dances in the foreground to the tunes of a black banjo player, with most of the figures, including a white male in top hat and two white females (presumably their owners or plantation guests) paying some attention to their exertions. Though Sheppard's 1885 picture for *Harper's Weekly's* December 12 issue, "Christmas in the South—A Suggestive Visit to the Old Family," concerned a postwar incident, it nonetheless indirectly authenticates the benignity of antebellum southern masters. Why else would what seems to be a three-generation black family call on their onetime owner outside his door? They obviously bear him only good-will. Two years earlier, in *Harper's Weekly's* December 22 number, Shep-pard had even more explicitly pursued such themes, showing a black woman and her girl taking a present to their former owners under the title "A Christmas Gift to 'Ole Marster and Missus.'" This picture,

William Ludwell Sheppard's implicitly proslavery image of ex-slaves taking Christmas presents to their former owners (entitled *A Christmas Gift to "Ole
Marster and Missus"*) in *Harper's Weekly,* December 22, 1883, p. 820. (Purdue University Library)

supposedly within the interior of their onetime master's home, depicts
him as white-bearded and of seemingly gentle visage. Combined,
such images were emblematic of the North's popular media endorsing
southern tropes about slave Christmases, and undoubtedly influenced
public attitudes throughout the country.[66]

Even as memoirists and fiction writers churned out one account after
another of Christmas's rewards for antebellum southern slaves, news
reports about contemporary southern holiday visitations reinforced
their collective implication that slavery had been all right. What else
could one assume when press vignettes, as one commentator put it,
revealed southern "gray-headed negroes," as Christmas approached,
expecting and eagerly anticipating invitations to return to the homes
of "old missus" and "old master," whose dwellings they considered
virtually "their own"? This writer claimed that the ex-slaves, once their
calls were over, returned to their own residences "laden with presents," a theme echoed in many visitation vignettes. Ex-slaveholders,
in other words, held their ex–human property in deepest affection,

caring about their well-being even after losing their personal financial stake in them. Little critical consideration was given in such accounts to the financial inequities impelling ex-slaves' dependence on former masters during the post-Reconstruction decades, especially the low rates of remuneration for their labor that many rural blacks received in the heyday of sharecropping. One historian has discovered in looking at Christmastime annual contract payoffs for Belmont plantation workers in Buckingham County, Virginia, in 1886 that workers there typically garnered less than a dollar when their year of labor expired, and that one worker only cleared five cents.[67]

According to a *New York Times* story that ran on Christmas Day in 1940, since 1917 members of the Ex-Slave Association of Atlanta and Fulton County, Georgia, had convened each Christmas Eve for reunions, with financial support from descendants of the whites who had "owned them long ago." The reunion tradition had survived a funding shortfall in 1920, when local Ku Klux Klansmen had bailed out the event with a $125 donation (apparently seeing their donation as a way to reaffirm white supremacy over dependent blacks). The *Chicago Defender,* arguably the nation's leading black newspaper, noted that the organizers' acceptance of the donation sparked protests within Atlanta's black community. At the reunion in 1940 at the Holmes Institute, a black school in the city that also had served as the site of the 1920 gathering, ex-slaves reminisced about those "Christmas mornings in the long ago" when they had traipsed with their parents from slave quarters to big houses to call out their owners with "Chrismus gif'" and pick up their presents—drams of "'master's' best" for the elderly, bolts of red calico and shoes for adults, and a candy stick and orange for each "pickaninnie." Following the singing of songs "they had heard in the cotton fields during their childhoods in slavery," the swapping of tales, and a reunion sermon preached by a onetime slave who was now a minister, the former slaves, ranging in age from 90 to 107, accepted the holiday sacks of flour, corn, meat, coffee, and other items "prepared for them by the white folks," and then returned to their homes.[68]

Similar traditions held in Athens, Georgia, where local white do-gooders got up Christmas baskets for impoverished former slaves, proving, as a local paper put it, that white people in the city "still" cherished "the memory of some faithful family servant who was of the type typified in those few souls now living." One press appeal urged such assistance on the logic that "old and faithful negroes" had remained "true and loyal" to the Confederacy during the Civil

War, when they had cared for southern white women and children so that the menfolk could fight for "the cause our people believed to be right." It was urgent to donate now, because within a few years "these old servants and ex-slaves will have passed to the great beyond." And in the South Carolina low country, the northern insurance executive Howard S. Hadden and his wife, after gaining control of Springbank plantation on the Cooper River, earned press coverage in 1937 for replicating the Christmas giveaways of slaveholders long before. Reportedly their 115 white guests that year observed from the veranda and lawn as the Haddens gave gifts to a line of African American employees and other neighborhood blacks "260 darkies long." Afterward, the guests watched on as the recipients danced and sang spirituals, as white onlookers would have done at quarters' parties in slave times.[69]

Sometimes southern white writings and press reports highlighted acts of Christmas kindness and affection by onetime slaves toward former owners, reinforcing the idea that slavery could not have been all that bad, since presumably once-enslaved people would not want to have anything to do with their former owners if they had been mistreated. Arguing that abruptly freeing "our slaves" had been "cruel" since it had cast thousands of "old and infirm" blacks "upon the world to starve," Ellen Call Long, the daughter of Florida's onetime territorial governor Richard Long, nonetheless related an incident during the first Christmas "following emancipation" when the former slaves of a now impoverished plantation widow felt so grateful to her for letting them stay on and cultivate the "Old Plantation" that they presented her with flour, syrup, eggs, and chickens as a holiday thank-you. Along similar lines, the *New Orleans Picayune* ran a story about one Robert Dandridge, a family "dining-room servant of ante-bellum days" who unexpectedly turned up smiling on Christmas morning at the residence of "his old mistress," a Mrs. J. W. Warren, to wish her a merry Christmas. When Mrs. Warren misconstrued Robert's gesture as a mercenary bid for a present and tried to hand him a silver dollar, the "faithful servant" declined the gift and gave his onetime owner a fancy Moroccan leather case, holding a couple of pure gold napkin rings inscribed to her. The article explained that although Robert had enlisted in the Union army, he had received his enlistment bounty after the war only because of Mrs. Warren's intervention affirming his claim, and he remembered the "uniform kindly treatment" he had received as a slave. The Christmas present, in other words, represented payback for being treated decently by his former owner. Not only was this heart-warming

vignette about an appreciative onetime slave published in the *Picayune,*
but it was also reprinted in other papers.[70]

Such stories surfaced year after year. In January 1890, an account
appeared in northern newspapers about a traveler in Sand Hill, Georgia, coming upon an elderly black woman carrying a basket with flowers in a cemetery on Christmas morning. The traveler learned that the
woman was laying the flowers "in tender loving memory" on the graves
of her former mistress and master and their deceased children. Two
days after Christmas in 1898, a Georgia paper ran a piece about how
an ex-slave named Ezra Martin ("Old Ezzy") living in south Baltimore had been complaining that "Dar ain't no mo' Christmas days
like do ones we used to hab when I was a boy." Martin, according
to the paper, was prone to reminisce about his Christmas dinner "on
Master Daniel's plantation, on de James river," with its plum pudding,
fat turkeys, and hard cider, and that the "puriest black piccannanies"
kicked up at the plantation holiday dances. Naturally, Martin finished
his commentary saying that he would rather be a slave than a free man
on Christmas.[71]

In the aftermath of World War I, newspapers coast to coast picked
up a story about an aged onetime slave named Bill Yopp. Between
1917 and 1919, Yopp had made it his Christmas practice to turn up at
the local Confederate Soldiers' Home in Atlanta with small gifts, purchased with dimes he had raised in the Macon area where he resided
(and with the help of the editor of the *Macon Telegraph*), to distribute
to Confederate veterans at the facility. These residents included his
own former master, whom he had not only accompanied to war but
also rescued and nursed back to health after his master was wounded
in battle. Recognizing that "Ten Cent Bill" would probably be unable to continue his charity work much longer given his advanced
age, the Georgia legislature had months earlier appropriated funds
for 1920 that would carry on this loyal slave's Christmas tradition. Unsurprisingly, this story resonates with today's Confederate apologists,
especially the "camps" of the Sons of Confederate Veterans (SCV).
A Jacksonville, Florida, SCV camp posts a book excerpt on its web
page retelling the story of this "Southern Sympathizer," emphasizing how Yopp's fund-raising efforts enabled him to give each veteran
at the Atlanta home a $3 Christmas gift each year, and that Yopp
had eventually gained admission to the United Confederate Veterans camp in Atlanta. An SCV blogger seizes on Yopp's identification
with the Confederate cause to put down "PC crowds" and alleged

falsehoods being taught American schoolchildren about the Civil War to justify the retention of Confederate monuments, flags, and street names. If African Americans, even slaves, supported the Confederacy, who could complain? Or so the logic goes. Neo-Confederates reacted delightedly when Georgia governor Sonny Perdue legitimized Yopp's Confederate résumé in 2008 when continuing Georgian gubernatorial traditions of designating April as Confederate history month. Perdue's proclamation said Yopp "served four years in Co. H, 14th Regiment Georgia Infantry," implying misleadingly that he was a regular Confederate soldier rather than body servant.[72]

As should be apparent by now, literate Americans in the post–Civil War decades were bombarded with a staggering number of publications by authors of diverse backgrounds romanticizing slave Christmases. Still, a few works did suggest alternate narratives. Though Harriet Beecher Stowe's *Christian Union* piece looked positively on the slaves' holiday experience, it acknowledged that southern masters feared the "mutual converses" of slaves over their Christmastime breaks might foster holiday servile rebellions and "trembled" at their bondpeople's Christmas privileges. Also during Reconstruction, the Ohio native and Union army lieutenant turned Carpetbagger politician Albion W. Tourgée, who promoted black voting and officeholding while living in North Carolina, began *Toinette* (1874)—his first novel—with a Christmas plot development that cast the peculiar institution unfavorably. A "young and likely" female serving-maid (Toinette) learns to her great distress of her transfer as a holiday present from her master to her master's son, who is setting up a new household on a different family plantation his father is conveying to him. This move will compel Toinette to live apart from her mother, causing her a sorrowful holiday as she anticipates the change. Additionally, Tourgée debunks the Christmas celebrations of her master's other slaves as "a ludicrous mimicry of freedom, with an undertone of sadness, like the refrain of a plantation melody"—a weeklong "saturnalia" that gave slaves "a far-off glimpse of freedom, the one thing that kept alive their faith in the good time coming, the oft-predicted 'Jubilee.'" Tourgée's holiday scenes, however, also have slaves playing Christmas Gif', being ribbed good-naturedly by their master, hunting for coins in their master's bedroom in a treasure hunt, getting stockings loaded with coins, and bowing and scraping respectfully for their holiday bounty. Like Stowe's essay, Tourgee's challenge to southern Christmas mythologies is conflicted, and in retrospect problematic.[73]

More pointedly, Ohio native Henrietta Matson, a white missionary who schooled former slaves in Nashville, Tennessee, in the 1870s,
later wrote a novel set in Mississippi during Reconstruction that less
equivocally rebuked images of slave Christmas contentedness. After
acknowledging that masters used the holiday to distribute clothes to
professedly grateful slaves that they would have anyway had to dis-
pense at other times in the year, Matson insisted paternalism was in-
compatible with enslavement and that many blacks felt the dissonance
but wisely suppressed their true feelings:

> On the part of many [slave recipients] this gratitude was sincere
> and the gifts were received with a child-like dependence befitting
> the patriarchal nature of the institution; but this class was gener-
> ally largely composed of children and aged persons. Among the
> younger and the middle-aged of a slave community there have
> always been those who rejected with secret scorn and contempt
> this dependence which has been so eloquently discoursed upon
> by the defenders of the system. It is not probable that they often
> manifested this feeling, but the thinking black man who wore his
> chains in seeming submission knew and felt how necessary it is to
> be just before one can be truly generous.[74]

Sometimes, even a white southern author might intimate that something was amiss at holiday time in the Old South, but such admissions
were couched in phrasing unlikely to register on readers. In her story
for the *Picayune* about Uncle Isom and slave Christmas traditions, for
example, Elizabeth Gilmer has Isom allude to how, during the Civil
War, with the master and his sons away and no longer able to care
for them, "de cuillud folks dey gun to slip off, one by one," without
suggesting that slaves might have been dissatisfied with their circumstances in the first place. John George Clinkscale's *On the Old Plantation*,
published in 1916, has a similarly suggestive but easily overlooked
passage. In a reminiscence written to reverse the damage to "our young
people" caused by negative images of slavery in *Uncle Tom's Cabin*, Clinkscale mentions how his father overcame the Christmastime shortages
of the Civil War by buying sorghum syrup candy and rag dolls for him
and his little sister, and alludes to his hopes on one of those wartime
holidays of getting a red wagon for Christmas. What is intriguing is
not that he eventually got his wagon, a homemade one by "Unc' Es-
sick," black foreman on the place (though not in time for Christmas);
rather, what is curious is Clinkscale's casual phrasing about what he

intended to do with the wagon once it was in his possession: "I wanted to hitch Jack and Peter, two negro boys to the wagon and have them pull it, while little sister did the riding and I did the driving." Harmless play? Perhaps. But Clinkscale's admission carries a whiff of the nearly unbridled power whites, even children, could exert over slaves. Apparently, at least on Clinkscale's place, a white plantation boy could boss around youthful slaves at will. Clinkscale gives no indication that he ever considered reversing roles and pulling his black play companions around. It is a possibly telling if inadvertent revelation. One doubts, though, that readers mulled over these undertones.[75]

No white writer in the late nineteenth- or early twentieth-century United States, in short, launched a full-blown literary attack on southern stereotypes about slave Christmases, and African Americans likewise proved reticent, hindered by the limited access of minority voices to the nation's mainstream newspapers and magazines and by their own conflicted feelings about slavery. Many black commentators put a premium on what was known as racial uplift, a widespread movement holding (with white racial stereotypes about black laziness in mind) that African Americans needed to achieve self-reliance for lasting racial progress. So instead of bluntly repudiating long-standing white racist presumptions that slavery "civilized" Africans, many black writers conceded the argument or tempered their verdicts about the price slavery extracted from its victims.[76]

It became common, in this context, for African Americans to repress memories of slave times, including Christmas experiences, as a kind of "prehistory," upsetting to recall much less write or speak publicly about, so much so that some black leaders at the time hesitated to condone what had become customary Emancipation Day celebrations in their communities. Significantly, at a Methodist conference in Baltimore in 1884, James Walker Hood, a bishop in the African Methodist Episcopal Zion Church and influential educator, chided an Episcopalian minister for encouraging black communicants in their dancing on the logic that such amusements were a legacy of slaves' "drunken, Christmas frolics" before the war. Given such avoidances, it is unsurprising that a compilation of ten Christmas tales and one poem authored by African Americans during the Gilded Age–Progressive period contains no stories at all set during slave-time Christmases.[77]

At times, African American commentators did more to substantiate southern Christmas mythologies than to undercut them. Consider the obscure northern publisher and newspaper editor James H. W.

Howard. On the one hand, Howard's stridently antislavery novel *Bond and Free* (1886) undercuts southern Christmas tropes with a clueless slaveholder, Abraham Biggers, who cannot understand why some of his slaves try to escape despite his allowing them a Christmas holiday. Yet, on the other hand, the novel credits Virginia slave owners as typically giving enslaved people three to four weeks entirely off from work for Christmas—far more time off than even ardently proslavery southern polemicists had claimed.[78]

More remarkably, in a 1901 historical novel exposing one of the most horrific racial episodes in the entire era of segregation—the Wilmington, North Carolina, massacre of November 10, 1898—black author David Bryant Fulton softened his account with nostalgia about antebellum Yuletides in North Carolina, where he had grown up. In the Wilmington violence, white mobs had not only murdered black locals, but they had also set fire to and destroyed an African American newspaper, extinguished for some time growing black political power in the community, and caused an appalling number of black residents to forfeit their businesses and homes in seeking safety elsewhere. Still, Fulton inserts into this depressing story a black musician wary of provoking local whites, noting that this "Uncle Guy" before the Civil War had sparkled in Wilmington's Christmastime "Cooner" performances. In those days, Fulton informs us, all slaves received a "week of absolute freedom" at Christmas when they "folicked" and danced and got their dram at the "door of the 'Big House'" on Christmas morning.[79]

Even the activist black "race leader" and journalist T. Thomas Fortune, in published reminiscences about his childhood as a slave of a north Florida county seat merchant, cut slaveholders slack when it came to Christmas. Labeling the Yuletide a "gala" time for young and old slaves alike, Fortune remembered how much the former enjoyed holiday candy and visiting relatives in other places and the latter capitalized on their time off to fish and hunt opossums.[80]

But no black commentator did more to buttress southern Christmas legends than did Booker T. Washington, the famed principal of the Tuskegee Institute in Alabama and the most politically influential African American in the turn-of-the-century United States. Washington weighed in with mellow recollections of slave Christmases in Virginia in his widely sold autobiography, *Up from Slavery* (1901), and subsequent writings. In December 1907, Washington published memories of the "fragrance" and "charm" of the holiday in Virginia, where it had been his "privilege to spend the Christmas season" during his boyhood, the "great event" of the entire calendar year for slaves, with all its gifts from masters and opportunities for slave reunions. Just two years later in his book *Story of the Negro,* Washington recalled the joy his family experienced Christmastime when his stepfather, hired out all year to railroad construction in a remote part of Virginia from Roanoke, returned for the holiday. Washington emphasized how throughout their section of Virginia, Christmas brought "great rejoicing" among blacks because of similar reunions involving other hired-out family members.[81]

Two years after Washington published *Story of the Negro,* the South Carolina African American minister Irving F. Lowery, enslaved while a boy as a house servant on John Frierson's place near the town of Mayesville in Sumter County, South Carolina, included a more detailed account of the slave Christmas experience within *Life on the Old Plantation in Ante-bellum Days.* Lowery mentioned the fattening of hogs beforehand so that slaves would have ample servings of fresh meat during the holiday, the custom on some neighborhood plantations for all the slaves to go as a group to the master's residence on Christmas morning for a holiday "dram," the "exquisite joy that thrilled" the slaves upon hearing their names called during present distributions, and how slaves were "as happy as angels" upon returning to their quarters following festivities at the master's residence. Though Frierson, being a Methodist and temperance practitioner, prohibited liquor distributions for the holidays, slaves still found Christmas "on the old plantation" greatly pleasurable.[82]

As late as World War II, the African American academic Merl R. Eppse rendered an uncritical generalization about slaves' Christmas experiences in a revisionary textbook intended to highlight the positive contributions blacks made to the nation's past. Eppse, who taught history at what was then known as Tennessee Agricultural and Industrial State College, pronounced that slaves had "wonderful" Christmases filled with "joy."[83]

It would be unfortunate, however, if we drew the conclusion, given such texts, that late nineteenth- and early twentieth-century black commentators offered no pushback at all against proslavery Christmas mythologies. A human-interest story in the *Syracuse (New York) Sunday Herald* in 1896 carried countermessaging by pulling the domestic slave trade into the customary narrative. The article featured one of the few "COLORED people who were born and raised in slavery" still resident in Syracuse, Joseph B. Terrill, who had been enslaved in Kentucky for twenty-five years. Terrill told his interviewer that blacks on his Kentucky place always enjoyed a lengthy Christmas break from December 26 until January 6, during which "colored people" would set up improvised tables loaded with sweets, oysters, and beer to hawk during local hiring days when slave traders and hirers gathered together in a central location. One year, a coffle of slaves passed his master's house on the way to this hiring market, including one chained victim who had threatened to kill his master if permanently separated from his wife by sale. Somehow getting possession of the key to his handcuffs while en route to the human market, this slave had not only unlocked his shackles but also those of some of his companions, and they had killed several of the white men conveying them. Soon, they were overcome and, eventually, hanged. Though Terrill said many blacks had grown so accustomed to the Christmas season hiring market that they regarded it as "a time of festivity," his story undercut common narratives, as did his allusion to slave whippings and sales by his own owner.[84]

Although not a tale of slave Christmastimes per se, African American activist and New York native Fannie Barrier Williams's short story in the December 1902 issue of the *Colored American Magazine* linked Christmas and antebellum southern slavery together in a very untraditional way. The action of "After Many Days" occurs during a "Christmas festival" time, long after emancipation. But though its setting is a functioning plantation where elderly former slaves like its central character Aunt Linda still reside, its plot revolves around the consequences of sexual exploitation of slave women by the South's antebellum master class. There are no recollections, here, either of exuberant slave Christmas dances or enslaved quarters folk milling around the porch of the big house in nervous expectation of their masters' Christmas gift distributions. Instead, Williams gives us an elderly ex-slave cook named Aunt Linda who is living in a "gloomy cabin" and preparing foods for the Edwardses and their holiday guests, still emotionally scarred from having had to surrender custody of her mixed-race granddaughter many years earlier so that the girl could have a better life. Williams's tale emphasizes the angst suffered by the now very accomplished and beautiful seventeen-year-old girl after learning from Aunt Linda that she was of mixed rather than pure white heritage (does she dare tell her New York lawyer fiancé or others, risking everything?), and tortured confessions by the plantation's mistress to this young woman that the South's peculiar institution had made slave girls into sexual objects by stripping them of their own "moral rectitude" and allowing masters to sell their own offspring. Though Williams does allow that the Edwards family had treated Aunt Linda so kindly that she had never wished to fully realize her own emancipation, she more importantly illuminates how the "shadow of the departed crime of slavery" still haunted blacks in the new era.[85] The story uses plantation Christmastimes for its setting, but this is a work of recrimination and a far cry from the plantation Yuletide stories most Americans were reading.

Then, too, readers of the black paper *New York Age* were greeted on December 24, 1914, with a page one picture entitled "Recollections of a Christmas Morning Long Ago," which included a stark reminder that holiday time for some enslaved people in the Old South entailed the distress of being sold away from their families. The background of this drawing depicts a slave child being sold by a slave auctioneer, with the auctioneer holding the child by the hand and the child's mother imploring the auctioneer not to complete the sale; the foreground shows an elderly man, likely the auctioned slave grown up, recalling the event to a black youth (possibly a grandson). In the drawing's caption, the narrator remembers, pathetically, how it seemed "my Ma's heart would bust" on that Christmas sixty-one years earlier (making the date 1853) and how her pleading had no effect on the transaction. Wrenched from each other, mother and child never saw each other again.[86]

By erasing holiday revolt panics and Christmas slave whippings and sales from the heartwarming postwar narratives they constructed about antebellum holiday times, late nineteenth- and early twentieth-century southern white writers and their Yankee accomplices coronated Christmas in the Old South and forged literary conventions persisting to this day. Without probing the conflicted attitudes slaves harbored about their holiday experiences, they reconstructed Christmas as a time when masters universally driven by paternalistic instincts, and enslaved blacks in appreciative servility, bore witness to slavery's benign sway. Before the Civil War, proslavery propagandists like William J. Grayson had pursued such lines of thought, but hardly to the extremes regional champions did after slavery ended. The Old South, in their telling, emerged from its own destruction an imagined, organically natural society that Confederate gallants had reasonably fought to preserve, with Christmas one of its figurative crown jewels.

Indeed, it is symptomatic that one of the Confederacy's most prominent figures joined these ideological battles. In 1900, former Rebel general John B. Gordon—and onetime leading Georgia Klansman in the battle to overthrow Reconstruction—wrote about his boyhood growing up on an isolated Georgia plantation for *Youth's Companion,* remarking on slaves' joy at Christmas. As Gordon told it, slaves had "no limit" to the liberties they could take on their "marster" and "missus" (and their children) when it came to the "great holiday of the year," including the right "to creep silently" into the great house to spring "Chris'mas gif'" on their startled owners. If Gordon gave any thought, before writing these lines, about all the holiday revolt panics white slaveholders endured during antebellum times, he certainly was not sharing it with his reading audience. Rather, he rammed home the impression that plantation life forged such mutual sympathy between slaves and their white owners that the former instinctively remained remain loyal during the Civil War, rallying to the protection of defenseless white women and children when the menfolk marched off to war.[87] Today, we know better.

Epilogue

BEYOND CANDLELIGHT TOURS

As an arbiter and reflector of cultural norms in the onetime slave states, *Southern Living* seems a promising medium to probe the longevity of stereotypes about antebellum southern Christmases. One might think that given the nation's civil rights revolution in the 1950s and 1960s and modern understandings of slavery, nostalgia for antebellum and Civil War plantation Christmases would have been waning by the end of the twentieth century and certainly unacceptable in a mainstream magazine like *Southern Living*—a publication that, with consistently over two million paid subscribers, has for decades ranked in the top twenty of all U.S. magazines.[1] But through the 1990s, *Southern Living*'s glossy pages rendered approving takes on historic southern Christmas traditions, highlighting traditional holiday recipes and decorations while expunging slaves entirely from the old Yuletide plantation scene.

Southern Living's December 1998 report on how Stately Oaks plantation in Jonesboro, Georgia, designed its holiday commemoration is especially revealing. Quoting the site's coordinator of tours, the piece claimed reenactors did everything possible "to educate the public" on the basis of "historical fact" about plantation life there during the Civil War, with that year's seasonal programming specifically pegged toward Christmas in 1863. Yet one senses the event entirely ignored the pervasiveness of slaves in antebellum southern plantation life. The article, rather, focuses on how fruit pomanders and pine boughs gave Stately Oaks a festive look, how its owner served humbly as a private in the Confederate army of Tennessee, and how outside the mansion Rebel soldier reenactors sought warmth by a crackling fire. Nowhere in this piece will you find the terms "slave," "enslaved," or "slavery." Likewise, no reference to slavery appears in *Southern Living*'s 1993 piece about how "Scarlett" (an obvious allusion to Scarlett O'Hara of *Gone with the Wind*) would have loved visiting an outskirts-of-Natchez, Mississippi, plantation and residence thrown open to friends one Christmas season. This article credited its hostess for properly laying out silver for dinner but ignored the human bondage that virtually all glitzy southern "historic plantations," as the piece called such places, revolved around.[2]

One *could* argue that this historical amnesia was harmless, since such pieces at least avoided traditional commentary stereotyping southern masters as humane to their laborers or southern slavery as a mild system of bondage. How could articles about plantation recipes or freezing Rebel soldiers by campfires offend anyone? Yet, in subtle ways, *Southern Living*'s benign endorsements of plantation holiday traditions perpetuated into the twentieth-first century the misperceptions that this book challenges and which impair racial reconciliation today. *Southern Living*'s luscious photographs of plantation holiday meals conjure nostalgia for the slaveholding world that enabled this feasting, in the process condoning slavery without even alluding to it. They legitimize, in very subtle and I believe insidious ways, the confrontational attitudes of Dixie flag wavers and monument defenders. By exclusively projecting positive imagery about antebellum southern Christmas customs without referencing their coerced labor underpinnings, such writings preserve the flawed stereotypes embedded in post–Civil War memoirs and fiction discussed in the preceding chapter and disseminate them to new generations of Americans.

The question is whether *Southern Living*'s Christmas pieces in the 1990s were a harbinger of today's U.S. popular culture or a kind of last hurrah of sorts for the Old South. What do contemporary commentators say about Christmas in slave times? Is it still common to extract slaves from the plantation scene, as if they never existed? Or, do modern assessments reiterate the Yuletide themes favored by southern memoirists, fiction writers, news reporters, and illustrators in the time of Thomas Nelson Page, which incorporated slave actors but elided

black resentment, agency, and resistance? In the end, our inquiry necessarily probes the contested contexts of modern public history.

Given the cumulative effect of some 100 years of memoirs, fiction, and
news accounts celebrating plantation Christmastimes in the Old South,
it is hardly surprising that *Southern Living* rendered plantation Christmases in loving text and photographs. After all, *Southern Living* is in the
business of selling magazines, not writing objective history, and its
mission is boosting southern lifestyles. Similarly, we might expect that
commentators and interpreters at modern historic plantations and plantation museums (there are hundreds of them) would echo traditional
mythologies, since tourist dollars bring their own imperatives. Administrators within this "industry," as it has been dubbed, some of them
running bed-and-breakfasts or inns, have monetary incentives to perpetuate misleading stereotypes about antebellum southern Christmases.[3]
High costs accompany the restoring and maintaining of air-conditioned
southern historical mansion properties. Without messaging that visitors
find appealing, many such sites would fail financially.

Even a cursory reading of web pages, blogs, and tourist listings
about these sites (many of them historically legitimized as National
Trust Historic Sites, National Historic Landmarks, or listings on the
National Register of Historic Places) suggests not only how important Christmas celebrations and reenactments—especially candlelight
tours—are on many of their annual calendars but also that "heritage
tourism" often depends on Christmas revenues for fiscal viability. According to a 1999 published report, the three-week series of holiday
visitations to "Plantation Row" on Virginia's James River—including
such famed sites as Sherwood Forest (President John Tyler's place),
Berkeley plantation, Shirley plantation, Westover, and Bacon's Castle—
in just a few years had become one of the county's largest "draws,"
"adding thousands of visitors to a gate that now hovers—depending
on the site—at some 50,000 people a year." The organizers of Christmas
tours at the Edenton (North Carolina) Historical Commission's Greek
Revival/Hayes Plantation site (charging $25 in advance; $30 at the
event) announced that they anticipated 800 visitors at both of its two
Christmas season evening events in 2012, and noted that attendance
had been growing each year. In Louisiana, the educational foundation
running the Oak Alley Plantation Restaurant & Inn's annual "Christmas Bonfire Party" (there have been over forty of them) publicly

recognizes the event as one of its "major fundraisers." No wonder. The charge, including an elaborate meal, was $130 per person as of 2015.[4]

Admissions to most southern Christmas plantation tours, though hardly extortionate, are expensive enough. Adults wishing to take the 2017 holiday tour scheduled at the Edmondston-Alston House, "the most seasoned manor along Charleston's high battery," paid $20 in advance or waited to spend $25 for admission on event day. When Belle Grove, the Virginia birthplace of President James Madison, scheduled its "1st Annual Christmas Candlelight" tour in 2013, it posted comparable prices ($15 for daytime adult tickets; $25 at nighttime). On the more pricey side, patrons shelled out $42 for a combined "Candlelight Christmas Progressive Tour" of the Shirley and Edgewood ("ancestral home" of the two presidents Harrison) plantations in Tidewater Virginia in 2016. Middleton Place in Charleston, South Carolina, has charged $55 for its annual Christmas "Grand Illumination," which includes a "Southern Buffet dinner." Such sums help historical sites balance their budgets.[5]

To maximize Christmas revenues, surviving and re-created southern colonial, early Republic, and antebellum historical mansions and plantations, *even those that have made efforts to incorporate black history and culture into their story,* have financial incentives to pamper their (overwhelmingly white) holiday guests with romance and nostalgia, and many disincentives to discomfort them with exposure to the racial and punitive exploitation that made such grandiose properties realities in the first place. Tourists anticipate "feel-good" Christmas season experiences, not glimpses of whips and slave bills of sale, much less narratives about holiday escapees and white paranoia over Christmas revolts. As the late James O. Horton, an expert on public history, once observed, white visitors to the Custis-Lee family home at Arlington, Virginia, "bristle" at the mere allusion that Lee even owned slaves. Such visitors lack tolerance for anything but benign interpretations of antebellum Christmases when they attend seasonal events at the South's historic plantation sites.[6]

As a result, most site owners and managers and local boosters have staged their seasonal events as sensory delights of sight, sound, taste, and ubiquitous "holiday cheer" centered on decorative touches and master-class dining, musical, and gifting customs. At George Washington's Mount Vernon estate, a Martha Washington reenactor hosts "an enchanting evening of candlelight tours, fireside caroling, and hot cider and ginger cookies," during which "characters from Washington's world" guide tourists about as period dancing occurs around them to "merry music." In a news story anticipating the James River Christmas tour of Virginia plantations in 2014, a local reporter emphasized how gardens would be converted into "beautiful wreaths and garlands" and added that tourists would behold mansion doorways and tables "decorated with fruits," with aromas of spices filling the air. Nashville, Tennessee's Belle Meade plantation plugged its Christmas candlelight events in 2016 by telling visitors they would meet Santa Claus and enjoy "wine tasting, holiday shopping, and caroling." The Nottoway plantation restoration's Greco-Italian revival-style mansion, the "Grande Dame of Louisiana plantation homes" and allegedly the largest surviving mansion in the South from the pre–Civil War period, beckons Christmas guests to verandas "draped in fresh green garland" and "gates, doorways and lampposts bedecked with wreaths."[7]

Post-event reports dwell on the sensory nature of visitors' holiday experiences. Thus an account of the candlelight tour in 2015 at the Texas Historical Commission's Varner-Hogg plantation in Brazoria County—a place whose mansion, smokehouse, quarters, and sugar mill were all constructed of slave-made bricks and where forty to sixty enslaved persons labored in the pre–Civil War decades (according to the site's own web page)—emphasized not what tourists learned about slavery from their visits but rather how the place was illuminated for the season by "twinkling lights and glowing candles," and how guests learned about military life in the 1800s and witnessed volunteers in "period costumes" as they toured the house.[8]

Sometimes, southern mansion/plantation sites' Christmas promotions highlight a specific historical context for their events, or what one modern commentator studying the general programming at such places has dubbed a "frozen moment." By focusing entirely on one year's Christmas happenings—or on a single aspect of the holiday—owners, managers, and docents can divert visitors from the disturbing interpretive morass of slavery, if they so choose. Mount Vernon's advance publicity puts considerable weight on visitors' opportunities to "meet" its "Christmas Camel" Aladdin, acquired by the site in recognition that Washington paid eighteen shillings in 1787 (the year of the U.S. Constitutional Convention) to acquire a camel for his estate. Middleton Place in Charleston asks visitors to celebrate Christmas 1782, when British forces were pulled out of the city toward the end of the American Revolution. Rosedale plantation, a small slaveholding site with a Federal-style main building in the North Carolina "backcountry," expects its "costumed docents" to evoke holiday customs "circa

1840" during candlelight Christmas tours. Promotional material for "Christmas 1860 at the Edmonston-Alston House" in Charleston emphasizes that costumed translators will tell visitors about "Charleston's last extravagant Christmas" before the Civil War erupted.[9]

When it comes to less date-specific programming, sites oriented around colonial or Early Republic times often dwell on how early southern Christmas customs originated in Olde England. At Virginia's Bacon Castle in 2013, guides in period dress explained seventeenth-century Christmas practices, emphasizing English Yule log traditions, kissing boughs hung around light fixtures, and wassail bowls filled with spiced punch. Sites dedicated to antebellum times emphasize how southern Christmas observances in white households became transformed as the Civil War neared and how mid-nineteenth-century southern holiday traditions conformed to Victorian standards. "See how festivities changed . . . between the colonial days to the antebellum ways," beckons Historic Latta Plantation, a living history cotton estate in Huntersville, North Carolina. Much is made at John Tyler's Sherwood Forest of the advent of candle-decorated Christmas trees in family observances before the Civil War. Shirley plantation on the James has recently featured a descendant of its creators explaining "the stories behind her family's holiday decorations and traditions." Jonesboro, Georgia's Stately Oaks (a nonprofit-administered site promoted as "truly home of *Gone With the Wind*" given its location in the city where the novel's Scarlett O'Hara supposedly paid her taxes on Tara) serves up a "Victorian Christmas celebration" featuring hung stockings and greenery in an 1860s style.[10]

Commonly, the story of the South's enslaved population over the holidays, if treated at all, has been superficially presented as sideshow, secondary to the festive decorations and seasonal ambience being highlighted. Many southern plantation tour guides find it safer all year long to avoid slavery completely rather than to risk offending anyone in earshot by seriously discussing it, as a popular culture expert taking Oak Alley's tour discovered one December. She encountered tour guides who refused to use the word "slave" and waxed about the labor-intensive nature of the plantation mistress's responsibilities at Christmas rather than the demands on black laborers. A study of southern plantation historic sites and museums from 1996 to 2001, focusing particularly on Louisiana, Georgia, and Virginia, discovered that 55.7 percent of what it called "white-centric sites" (as compared to black-administered sites) engaged in erasing or minimizing "the presence, labor, and contributions of African Americans," terming this "symbolic annihilation." When one group of college students toured North Carolina's Latta plantation in 2015, a docent who had been neglecting slavery, in a remarkably revealing excuse, begged off answering questions about it until an African American family accompanying the group absented themselves. Unsurprisingly, similar silences pervade many southern plantation Christmas events. Although an 1840 slave cabin is among the six structures on the restored Callaway plantation in Washington, Georgia, which is operated by the city, it was the only building not specifically mentioned as designated for special activities during the site's 2012 Christmas events in advance publicity. Pre-event publicity about Nottoway plantation's Christmas guided tours has nothing to say about the people once enslaved there, even though owner John Hampden Randolph and his family put 155 slaves to work in the late 1850s to construct it.[11]

Even places conscientiously incorporating modern research on slavery within their educational mission sometimes fall short of the mark in their Christmas scheduling. In 1999, the National Park Service officials administering Melrose, the preserved mansion in Natchez of John A. Quitman's law partner John McMurran, experimented with how to convey the modest experiences of slave children during the holiday in 1857 in addition to glamorous partying by the southern elite. For Christmas season tours, visitors experienced big house glamour, even arriving at the mansion's front entry by horse-drawn carriages; but they also observed reenactors of slave children making their own dolls from handkerchiefs and their own miniature Christmas tree decorations from string and pine cones in a two-room cabin located behind the McMurran house. Unfortunately, nothing in the publicity for these tours suggests that visitors gained exposure to any of the more disturbing aspects of slave Christmases addressed in this book. Along similar lines, participants in candlelight Christmas tours at Montpelier—President James Madison's Virginia estate—in December 2013 encountered African American reenactors, but apparently only as articulate and polite household servants anxious to field questions. In a light-hearted blog posting about attending Montpelier's Christmas programming, the owners of Belle Grove plantation, the bed-and-breakfast operating at Madison's birthplace, remarked on the pleasantness of being greeted by the "joy and laughter" of servants on arriving at Montpelier. There, "devoted servants" provided visitors with a list of events, guided them to the "grand house," and ushered them to handshakes with Dolley Madison's reenactor, before the head servant took them to meet the fourth president's impersonator. None of this seems couched to prompt serious thinking about Christmas's underside. It might even reinforce stereotypes that blacks are naturally suited for servants' roles.[12]

At their most extreme, southern mansion and plantation Christmas site promotions imagine seasonal events and decorations as wondrous Dixieland takes on Shangri-La, where visitors achieve nirvana by surrendering to sensual delights. The Georgia State Parks system's coastal Hofwyl-Broadfield Plantation Historic Site (a onetime rice plantation with more than 350 slaves) promotes its annual Christmas event as "a magic experience" of candlelit strolls, hot wassail, and Civil War reenactors. "Darshana is a magical place . . . during the holidays," promises a privately owned, onetime 12,000-acre North Carolina plantation that once worked nearly 100 slaves. Nottoway, in time-travel phrasing, assures that its holiday toys, caroling, and fifteen-foot-high tree will transport tourists to a "bygone era." Oak Alley plantation describes its annual Christmas bonfire as "a celebration like none other," given the ambience created by illuminated paths, docents in period dress, and a mansion "adorned" in period decorations. Promotional materials for Madison's residence at Montpelier entice visitors wishing to "celebrate Christmas" there with candlelight tours, "wine and wassail," and a chance to warm up near Yule logs and hear Confederate reenactors talk about an encampment there during the Civil War.[13]

No site excels better at promising nostalgically sublime visitations than Monmouth Historic Inn and Gardens—the Natchez suburban Federal-style mansion (with manicured grounds) of antebellum Mississippi governor, secession leader, hero of the U.S.-Mexican War, and multiple plantation slaveholder of hundreds of enslaved people John A. Quitman. After leaving his descendants' hands in 1924, Monmouth fell into disrepair until purchased in 1977 and then lavishly restored with great attention to historical authenticity by California developer Ron Riches and his wife, Lani. This the Riches accomplished so successfully that their twenty-six-acre site emerged not only as a participating property in Natchez's famed spring and fall grand house tours known as "Pilgrimages" but also as a National Historic Landmark with an inn and restaurant that have gained wide acclaim. Although Monmouth fell briefly into foreclosure in 2012, it was almost immediately acquired by a hotel management company based in New Orleans and continues today as a luxurious inn owned by company president

Warren L. Reuther Jr. and his wife, Nancy. Reuther also manages the property. Monmouth's promotional advertising emphasizes its being "beautifully appointed with period furnishings and antebellum-era antiques" and its listings among the top inns and bed-and-breakfasts in the country, as the best hotel in Mississippi (*U.S. News and World Report*), and as one of America's "most romantic places" (*USA Today* and *Glamour Magazine*).[14]

Unlike some peer historic sites, Monmouth's recent proprietors acknowledge the importance of slave labor for the lifestyle of members of the antebellum southern elite like John Quitman's family. Monmouth's web page and links, as of 2017, acknowledge that the main house became "a stately antebellum, suburban villa built from the labor of human hands both free and enslaved" and that slaves kept working there throughout antebellum times. The site's timeline marks Quitman's purchases of slaves, the role of a personal servant who accompanied him into the Mexican War, and even that one household domestic in 1842 was demoted to field work at one of Quitman's non-contiguous plantations, certainly a hint that some of the family's slaves might have been dissatisfied or resistant to their condition.[15]

Still, Monmouth's website and promotional advertising prioritize the estate's dreamy aura, emphasizing that visitors "looking to savor 'a page from the past'" will discover Monmouth's "mystique" as a "perfect romantic getaway." How could guests be other than enraptured by the estate's "exquisite rooms" with "beautifully appointed . . . period furnishings," authentic crystal gasoliers in parlors, Jacuzzi baths, and landscaped acres with moss-draped oaks, pebble paths, and resident songbirds? Monmouth's Christmas advertising, unsurprisingly, builds on this enticing boosterism. In 2006, while the estate was under the Riches' management, its blog emphasized a two-night "St. Pius X Christmas Gala" at "Romantic Monmouth Plantation in Natchez," which became a "magic place" over the holiday where guests dined on "five course gourmet dinners beneath romantic gaslight chandeliers." Such themes continue under its new management. In 2014, Monmouth's publicity beckoned guests by calling itself the "perfect getaway during the Christmas season" for anyone seeking a "romantic escape." Why? Because the mansion, "draped with wreaths, garland and red bows" appeared "simply magical" at holiday time, so much so that visitors would find themselves in a "Wonderland." None of this promotional hype per se, of course, precludes Monmouth's tour guides from engaging visitors in cogent discourse about slavery on John Quitman's holdings or what Monmouth's enslaved people might have been doing and thinking on a typical Christmas Day. Did the Quitmans worry about Christmas slave revolts? What about their neighbors? But who would wager on the likelihood of anything of the sort?[16]

One gets a whiff of how problematic this stilted public history has been from a 1993 account of the Florida writer J. P. White's visit one Christmas Eve day to the National Park coastal Florida site northeast of Jacksonville known as Kingsley plantation, not far from the Georgia border. Taking the park ranger's tour of a place where a sizable force of enslaved workers had once cultivated sea-island cotton, White noticed how the colonial kitchen house, a separate structure from the main plantation house, had been decorated for the holiday with mistletoe, wreaths with apples, and lemons, supposedly according to "authentic Christmas decorating tips from a Kingsley family diary." But White also mentioned that his guide skirted over the punitive slave labor that had made the celebration possible, ignoring iron leg stocks on the site instead of incorporating them into her presentation. White recorded that as he strolled the grounds, he resented "the colorful Christmas ornaments in a place where slavery was the password." The ranger's bias seemed skewed toward the master class, as she announced her certainty that the place's master would have allowed slave family members on his other plantations to visit their kin there for Christmas.[17]

Similarly, given an account in the Asheville, North Carolina, press in 1999 about how the Vance Birthplace State Historic Site—the two-story log cabin first home of the controversial North Carolina governor and congressman Zebulon Vance—had been "doing up Christmas in the Vance style since 1968," we can guess that tour guides there said little about the underside of antebellum slave Christmas celebrations. According to this story, what the tour guide emphasized was how the Vances' celebration was calibrated to the burning of a Yule log as well as the importance to site managers of making Christmas decorations as "authentic as possible" with galax (an evergreen plant), bittersweet, and mistletoe. The article did mention that the Vance family had owned slaves and that a slave cabin site had been preserved, but the only mention of how slaves spent Christmas that got into the newspaper piece was the curator musing that enslaved people "likely would have been part of the holiday celebrations." It would be surprising if many of the

20,000 reported visitors to the site each year gave any thought at all to slave doings at Christmas, much less to the horrors of enslavement.[18]

Fortunately, complex understandings of slave Christmases are seeping into U.S. popular culture, paralleling more complex and thought-provoking treatments of the enslaved experience at historic sites and museums like the Whitney Plantation Museum near New Orleans (which opened in 2014) and the National Museum of African American History & Culture in Washington, D.C. (which opened in 2016), as well as in print, in film, online, and on television. Certainly, following the civil rights movement of the 1950s and 1960s, black commentators became bolder in tackling the tropes of southern plantation Christmas traditions than they had been earlier.

In the 1970s and 1980s, for instance, *Black News* carried pieces highlighting not only Frederick Douglass's complaints about slaves' forced inebriation at Christmas but also how shrewd ones manipulated holiday opportunities to their own ends. As one of the publication's writers put it, "the Christmas of our slave foreparents reflected a complex intermingling of resistance and compliance, survival and creation." Around Christmas in 1979, the black outlet *Chicago Metro News,* in "Janey in Slave-Land Byrne," slammed city mayor Jane Byrne for thinking that taking Christmas trees and a few cookies to black public housing residents mattered much. Rather, such acts of holiday tokenism evoked "the old tradition of the slave master visiting the slave quarters at Christmas." Black cultural figure Willie Dixon Jr. made similar points writing for the *Chicago Metro News* at Christmastime in 1983, arguing that religiosity allowed slaves to survive bondage's horrors, and that slaves dissembled when professing appreciation for Christmas gifts that masters dispensed during their visits to the quarters. Recently, in his best-selling historical novel *The Underground Railroad,* African American author Colson Whitehead has a female slave stomp and hoot "as if it were the height of the Christmas celebrations" upon being ordered by a slaveholder to dance, wryly explaining that slaves learned to dissemble regarding their feelings to avoid earning their owners' wrath.[19]

Perhaps the most widely known treatment of plantation Christmases in modern children's literature, Patricia C. McKissack and Fredrick L. McKissack's award-winning *Christmas in the Big House, Christmas in the Quarters,* also signals a shift in conventional thinking. The

McKissacks, though recognizing that slaves partied over the holiday, depict savvy ones worrying about being sold or hired away from their families on New Year's Day. Further, the enslaved people in this story crave emancipation and are cognizant both of John Brown's recent raid on Harpers Ferry and the Underground Railroad. And in a 1998 book for grades 5–7 entitled *1853: Daily Life on a Southern Plantation,* Paul Erickson addresses life on an imagined Louisiana cotton plantation with more than 100 slaves in unconventional ways. Set eight years before the Civil War, the story takes the owner's wife to New Orleans on a holiday shopping trip, where she will be able to buy "ready-made shoes, stockings, caps, and shawls" for Christmas distributions to the slaves—whose clothes, always distributed once a year at holiday time, are badly in need of replenishment since they go threadbare by November. There are no frills here. For anyone missing the point, Erickson adds that this plantation mistress will also pick up needles, thread, and colored cloth so that her "slave women can sew extra clothing for their families," a pointed reminder that presents to slaves were often calculations in the master's interest. After all, if slave women did not sew clothing, masters would have to purchase them. Erickson's story is as significant for its omissions as its inclusions. The book lacks the usual commentary on slaves' Christmas feasting, dancing, and fiddling.[20]

Some historical sites have been scrambling to catch up with historical knowledge. As early as 2006, Christmastime visitors to the Savannah Historical Foundation's Davenport House, owned by a small slaveholder in the 1820s, learned that the kinds of presents house slaves got at Christmas were as modest as twists of tobacco or material to make their own clothes; visitors also heard that house servants likely got no time off for Christmas, since they had tasks of preparing and serving food for white holiday parties and cleaning up afterward. At Stratford Hall, Robert E. Lee's Virginia birthplace, site managers' plans for Christmas in 2016 emphasized that visitors would be encouraged, in a four-hour experience, to "ponder" the history, dances, songs, and stories of enslaved peoples as compared to "privileged" classes. Taking a similar approach, Redcliffe Plantation State Historic Site in South Carolina, the Hammond family place where South Carolina governor and U.S. senator James Hammond died, has provided an annual seasonal program since 2002 (with the exception of 2013 and 2014) called "Christmas in the Quarters." It now includes first-person interpretations and handouts with reading suggestions, and it has explored the holiday experience for slaves from different perspectives, including things like vacation rights and religious practices. Redcliffe's staff tell visitors that masters sometimes cancelled Christmas celebrations and that Hammond once bought slave children in December; and they prod guests to ponder the possible self-serving purposes of masters' gifts to slaves at holiday time.[21]

Further evidence of this trend comes from Thomas Jefferson's Monticello, which now has exhibits about enslavement there and no longer conceals the Declaration of Independence author's longtime sexual relationship and children with his slave Sally Hemings, who was his wife's half-sister. Monticello's website includes excerpts from documents under the heading "Christmas in the Enslaved Community," not all of which put the Jefferson slaveholdings in a favorable light. Several show that Jefferson's slaves had to petition him to visit spouses at Poplar Forest, a separate plantation property that he owned in Bedford County, Virginia, over Christmas. Further, the site shows that Jefferson's granddaughter Mary found such requests tiresome. In 1821, she expressed satisfaction when not one slave asked for a Christmas pass and when the only evidence she witnessed of the customary "little disagreeable business" of "Christmas gambols" (a term for cavorting and related behaviors) among slaves was encountering a closed-eyed slave fiddler keeping time with a foot to the approval of onlookers while she was on the way to the smokehouse. The implication seems to be that Jefferson's granddaughter frowned on boisterous partying over the holiday by those she enslaved. By 2015, James Madison's Montpelier was instructing its interpreters to emphasize during their holiday program not only slaves' time off and visitation privileges over Christmas but also that the latter practice unsettled nearby whites. More sites need to deal as Montpelier does with the antebellum South's collective phobia about Christmas slave revolts.[22]

One site does just that—the Ben Lomond plantation site at Manassas, Virginia, in Prince William County, a place used as a Confederate hospital during the First Bull Run and where some slave cabins had been preserved. Just before Christmas 2013, the *Washington Post* reported that county historians had brainstormed how to more organically incorporate the slave population at Ben Lomond into their annual holiday programming, and had come up with a refreshingly—though chillingly—different kind of Christmas candlelight tour from what is normally experienced at many modern tours of surviving southern antebellum mansions. As explained by the manager of the county's historical sites, tour guides would try to interpret the fears as well as the hopes of slaves at holiday time, who, though they might be the beneficiaries of a particularly good meal at Christmas or accorded release from work, also had to pass their holidays worrying whether they might be sold off or rented to a different plantation, or even given away as a gift. One thing that tourists would be told was that Ben Lomond's owner in 1856 had a reputation for being a vindictive, punitive master and that his slaves planned to kill him that Christmas Eve and burn down his house to mask their crime. Although they did kill him, the ringleaders were exposed and soon afterward hanged. This is hardly common fare for southern mansion Christmas tours.[23]

Additionally, the Booker T. Washington National Monument near Roanoke, Virginia, has been running annual Christmas events on the first Saturday in December, emphasizing, as the National Park Service puts it, what Christmas in Virginia was like in different years before and during the Civil War for "enslaved and free" residents alike. Striving for realism, the Living History Guild Re-enactors for the 2013 happening emphasized all the insecurities slaves there likely faced in 1863, while the Civil War was raging: Would they get enough to eat given the demands on their owners to fulfill food quotas for the Confederate army and suffering families of wounded or killed Confederate soldiers? Would male slaves be impressed into Confederate army labor service? Would separated black family members get their accustomed Christmas travel passes to visit family members elsewhere?[24]

Still, it is likely that misconstructions of slave Christmases will persist at many historic sites, with unfortunate consequences for public understandings of our nation's history and modern racial reconciliation. After all, many imperatives beyond mere financial incentives keep southern tourist destinations adhering to traditional narratives and resisting substantive changes in their programming.

It would be surprising, for instance, if the Gamble plantation historic site in Ellenton, Florida, upends its Christmas messaging in the immediate future, even if it is administered by the Florida Parks Service rather than by private interests. This onetime sugar plantation with mansion earns a share of its historical significance as a reported temporary refuge for Confederate secretary of state Judah P. Benjamin after he fled Richmond toward the end of the Civil War. In fact, it is formally known as the Judah P. Benjamin Confederate Memorial at Gamble Plantation Historic State Park. Not only did the United Daughters of the Confederacy (UDC) once own Gamble plantation; UDC has also continued to play a major role in its preservation and programming since turning it over to the state. Promotional materials for Christmas events there emphasize that Florida's UDC chapters have decorated mansion rooms and that they give a "special touch" to the programs with their "gentle grace" and by wearing hoop skirts. One photograph of Christmas programming there shows children taking tea with a General Robert E. Lee impersonator. No wonder, given this ambience, that a 2017 visitor (apparently *not* at Christmas) posted a Facebook review expressing disappointment that Gamble plantation romanticized "slavery and human trafficking." Given the UDC mood there, however, it is a safe bet that site administrators are more likely to heed the posting of a different and later visitor who claimed to be a descendant of both Confederate and Union soldiers. This reviewer affirmed, in response to the earlier comment, that Gamble plantation's programming provided a "good example of history the way it was" and pleaded that nothing should change.[25]

As with other issues connected with race and Confederate preservation, Christmas programming at southern historic sites will likely be contested for the foreseeable future. As recently as December 2015, a backlash erupted when Gunston Hall, the onetime eastern Virginia residence of George Mason—an important figure in the history of the American Revolution and Constitutional Convention and owner of almost 100 slaves—put on a Christmas program urging the public to attend its "celebration of the season!" Critics, including black activists and an essayist for *Mother Jones,* took issue with rejoicing about a household deeply implicated in human bondage, and were hardly mollified by learning that Gunston Hall's reenactor participants included slaves in period dress. Merely acknowledging that slaves were present and participated in Christmas events falls far short of critically examining the South's peculiar institution. Since administrators at the site refused to confirm the input of any black staff members or historians in event planning, it is likely that the program was designed with no or little thought about its potential impact on black attendees. For good reason, one administrator at nearby George Mason University, which lacks a formal affiliation with the site, called the event title "beyond unfortunate" and recommended revised publicity in the future.[26]

Around the same time, African American Vanderbilt University professor Brandon Byrd, a specialist in black intellectual history, apparently reached conclusions similar to Gunston Hall's critics after visiting seasonal events at the Belle Meade plantation in Nashville,

Tennessee. Knowing his southern history infinitely better than the typical tourist, Byrd for good reason anticipated a sustained treatment of slavery and southern racial attitudes during his visit in December 2015, when Belle Meade calibrated its programming to evoke Christmas 1853, eight years before the Civil War. Well over 100 slaves worked the place in the 1850s, and Belle Meade's owner then, one William Giles Harding, was known as an anti-abolitionist who supported expelling Davidson County's free blacks from the state. But though Belle Meade's own website devotes a page to African Americans—not only detailing some of their labor assignments but also mentioning an escaped slave, Harding's fears of slave rebellion, and his support for black expatriation—Byrd's hopes were dashed.

True, at the end of his guided tour of the mansion, Byrd had the opportunity to self-tour Belle Meade's two slave cabins, filled with pictures of black workers before and after emancipation as well as excerpts from black autobiographies. He even found an explanatory poster at the cabins noting that Christmas was not universally a happy time for enslaved people. But the guided tour itself was a letdown; its mentions of slaves reinforced romanticized old stereotypes. Byrd's white guide, taking note in the foyer of a picture of a black figure in the act of leading a horse, explained that the person in question was one Robert Green, Belle Meade's leading horse tender before the war, and emphasized that he remained on the place after the Civil War brought his emancipation. Later, in the kitchen, Byrd's guide explained that he knew little about a biracial man pictured there, but that the black woman's portrait on a wall was of Susanna Carter, who had been the head cook before the Civil War and the third-highest paid employee afterward. As Byrd saw it, this guide reinforced tropes of master-class paternalism in two ways: first, by emphasizing Green's and Carter's successes under enslavement, the guide implied the South's peculiar institution amounted to a "moderate" labor system allowing its subjects to achieve self-fulfillment; second, by noting not only that both remained at Belle Meade when they could have left legally but also that all pallbearers at Green's funeral were white, the guide underscored traditional southern white messaging that masters and enslaved people held each other in mutual affection.

Byrd mused over the irony of such interpretations given the makeup of his particular tour group. Besides himself, the only other members were Asian Americans. If Belle Meade's guides could not probe deeply into slavery's realities with these visitors, one can assume they felt far less compunction to do so with white attendees of the plantation's Christmas season.[27]

Given such considerations, we should hardly profess surprise that still in 2018 *Louisiana Travel* was pumping the opportunity to "Celebrate the Holidays at Louisiana's Grand Plantations," with nary a word about enslaved people. Once again, a commercialized Yuletide in Dixie beckoned visitors to "step back into" wonderful "Christmas traditions of long ago," in this case to grand halls decorated with citrus and other unique Creole holiday touches.[28]

So what do we make, in the end, of roughly a century-and-a-half of post-slavery stereotypes in print and at historic sites about antebellum southern Christmases? Necessarily, we begin with a caveat: we go down the wrong path if we start with outright denials of their factual details. Undoubtedly, the great majority of these accounts were truthful in the *literal* sense. That is, there is simply too much evidence "out there" to deny that a high percentage of slaveholders, at least the wealthier ones, ladled out copious servings of eggnog and distributed gifts to slaves over the holiday. Likewise, the evidence is overwhelming that what might be called the Old South's master culture accorded slaves holiday feasts and balls, and substantial downtime and mobility—certainly much more largesse and laxity than enslaved people were accustomed to getting the rest of the year. We can assume, likewise, that on many slaveholdings during antebellum Christmas seasons, sounds of happy workers dancing and partying wafted up to masters' and mistresses' residences from the quarters, just as all the white southern memoirists later said.

Why should we doubt, even, that the heartwarming incidents of Christmas intermingling between masters and slaves recollected by later memoirists, including the repartee of "Christmas Gif'," actually occurred? We might suspect that Varina Davis misrepresented Robert Brown's emotions during the last Christmas in Confederate Richmond in the incident discussed in the preceding chapter; but such skepticism runs smack into evidence that the Confederate president's servant was capable of such feelings. Brown expressed a willingness to be imprisoned with Jefferson Davis following the president's capture by Union forces at the end of the Civil War, and he remained voluntarily connected to the Davises long after his own emancipation. At times, Brown served in their employ as butler. When the ex-Confederate president died in 1889, Brown turned up for his burial at Metairie Cemetery in New Orleans, standing aside Varina and Davis family members.

Why would he not, then, have bowed his head in gratitude when applauded for the toy he had made that last Confederate Christmas?[29]

Nor are there sound reasons to challenge reports that former slaves and former slaveholders held heartfelt reunions and exchanged gifts at Christmas in postwar times, as if they still belonged to shared household communities and mutually wished to perpetuate slave time holiday traditions. Undoubtedly, many household servants especially still held their former masters, whom they had come to know on very intimate levels, in feelings of affection long after the Civil War. Conversely, many onetime slaveholders genuinely maintained fondness for their favorite former household servants, with Christmas providing them with an ideal occasion to channel their charitable feelings in constructive ways.

Rather, the real problem is that the cumulative effect of the retrospectives recovered in this book rendered *slavery* redeemable—or more accurately, invisible—for generations of readers since they all but erased the forced slave labor underpinning Christmas giveaways in the first place. Many of these accounts and site holiday presentations barely hint that millions of southern slaves toiled year after year in violation of their own wishes, often in brutally punishing, unhealthy, sexually exploitative, and demeaning conditions, for the benefit of their masters' ledgers and lifestyles, and that their enslaved condition was justified by their oppressors on the logic of white supremacy. Nor do they tell us about transactions in slave bodies or corporal punishment of slaves over the Yuletide, Christmas slave escapes, or how many white southerners of all social classes feared that slaves supposedly reveling in holiday bliss might choose their very Yuletide vacations as the time to launch a bloody revolution for freedom. Conventional slave Christmases, as related in memoirs, fiction, and historic tours, make it far too easy, to put it simply, to forget the fundamental reality that even the most outwardly paternalistic masters held slaves to make money and relieve them of daily household chores, and that their seemingly whopping Christmas liberality reduces, retrospectively, to a means in furtherance of those ends. Slaves lacked the option to forfeit their Christmas bounty for freedom.

In fact, by implying that the Old South's enslaved people achieved ecstasy at Christmastime, traditional narratives bring us uncomfortably close to the suggestion that slavery was, in the famous words of antebellum southern leader John C. Calhoun, a "positive good"— a highly admirable form of human relations in its own right. Or to put it another way, such narratives verge on absurdly implying that some four million southern blacks before the Civil War were *lucky* to be slaves. Regarding this very stereotype, the city editor of a Norfolk, Virginia, African American newspaper once exclaimed sarcastically, "Bring back slavery and I'll join up. Regular hours, job security, a cozy hut, and a free drink at Christmas." The editor's particular animus focused on a Virginia social studies textbook authored by the prominent southern white historian Francis Butler Simkins and two others, which his seventh-grade daughter was required to read. In addition to several sins of omission respecting the civil rights movement in Virginia like massive resistance, the book offended with its sins of commission, including its stereotyping Christmas as the slaves' "great holiday of the year" when they received "extra rations and presents" and "a Christmas drink." But the editor's anger could just as easily have been unloaded on the racialist ambience of Christmas observances at southern plantation historic sites.[30]

In this sense, it would further racial progress in this country if all modern historic plantation sites would follow the practices of their most progressive peer institutions by integrating critical deconstructions of Christmas practices into their seasonal programming. Condemning slavery on websites while contradictorily taking visitors on pleasant Christmas candlelight tours glorifying antebellum plantation life is an exercise in cognitive dissonance, unless tour guides are carefully trained in evoking the underside of slaves' Christmas celebrations and compelling visitors to consider the actual perspectives of enslaved people. By following the links on Oak Alley plantation's website, one can fairly easily discern it was a working sugarcane estate with between 100 and 120 slaves at a time depending on the year. Website managers make no bones about sugarcane fieldwork being punitive and even fatal, and they add that house slaves were punished for underperformance in the owners' eyes with banishment to the fields.[31] But how many people read and assimilate Oak Alley's informative web information about enslavement as compared to how many residents at its inn or participants in the annual bonfires there walk away from their experiences with fuzzy impressions that antebellum plantations were unblemished?

Addressing antebellum southern Christmases critically implies far more than having costumed reenactors show how slaves made primitive holiday toys for their children as Christmas approached. But serious engagement with the South's *real* Christmas past is urgent, lest we allow misleading stereotypes to linger in the American public imagination much longer. Misconstructions of antebellum slave Christmases feed into the constellation of historical stereotypes that enslavement in the Old South was tolerable, even rewarding, and we pay a price for the constant repetition of these mythologies in print, in imagery, and at southern historic sites. Modern Americans have already been so exposed to such materials in one way or another that it is too easy for people unthinkingly to concede traditional white southern narratives of the holiday without pondering their implications for modern race relations or whether alternative perspectives are available.

Consider the columnist for the *Atlanta Journal Constitution* who recommended not long ago, almost certainly out of no racial bias, that people attend Christmas programming at four of the South's "most gracious plantations" since such places offer charming ways to celebrate the holidays. "Immerse yourself," the columnist intoned, "in the antebellum spirit of Christmas," and let "a true 19th century Dixie Christmas" recapture for visitors these places' "joy" and "grandeur." One can wager fairly safely that this particular columnist never considered the possibility that slaves were mistreated over Christmas; that antebellum southern whites spent some holiday moments worrying that slaves might slit their throats; that some slaves saw through the labor control purposes of their holiday barbecues and presents; or, most important, whether such programming is harmful to African Americans. In this regard, southern plantation historic sites need to more carefully parse their own discourse. What are descendants of slaves to make, for instance, of Historic Rosedale Plantation's Christmas promotions? Rosedale omits mentioning slavery in its holiday programming (though its website discusses slave blacksmiths) and promises that attendees will experience "antebellum Southern hospitality" for their $12–$15 admission fee. One wonders how the term "antebellum Southern hospitality" resonates with African Americans visiting not just Rosedale but all the southern plantation sites. These places rely on their historical ambience to entice their visitors; yet they often render that history's most significant factor invisible once their guests arrive on site.[32]

Admittedly, more holistic treatments of slave holiday experiences at plantation sites risk offending *both* African American and white visitors. Colonial Williamsburg has discovered the risks of edgy programming. In 1994, it became engulfed in nationwide controversy when critics denounced as racist and exploitative its African American Department's staging of a mock slave auction to sensitize onlookers to the full horrors of bondage. But risking backlash is a small price to

pay for conscientious efforts to convey historical experiences mean-
ingfully instead of superficially. As David W. Blight puts it all too
well, memory represents "one of the most powerful elements in our
human constitution." It holds within it the power to "poison us" when
mishandled.[33] And plantation tourist sites have proven socially irre-
sponsible in mishandling the antebellum southern Christmas story,
poisoning our collective imagination for far too long. Presumably,
neo-Confederates would wave Dixie's flags even in the absence of mythologies about harmonious antebellum southern Christmases binding slaves and masters together in mutual appreciation. But these
narratives offend many contemporary Americans, especially African
Americans, and they reinforce divisive neo-Confederate efforts to preserve Dixie's heritage. They demand drastic rewriting.

NOTES

ABBREVIATIONS

ASCA   *The American Slave: A Composite Autobiography,* ed. George P. Rawick, 19 vols. (Westport, CT: Greenwood Press, 1972)

ASCA-1   *The American Slave: A Composite Autobiography,* Supplement Series, ed. George P. Rawick. 12 vols. (Westport, CT: Greenwood Press, 1977)

ASCA-2   *The American Slave: A Composite Autobiography.* Supplement Series 2, ed. George P. Rawick. 10 vols. (Westport, CT: Greenwood Press, 1979)

GHQ   *Georgia Historical Quarterly*

HT   Howard-Tilton Memorial Library, Tulane University

JNH   *Journal of Negro History*

JSH   *Journal of Southern History*

LSU   Special Collections, Hill Memorial Library, Louisiana State University Library, Baton Rouge

NODP   *New Orleans Daily Picayune*

NYT   *New York Times*

OR   *War of the Rebellion: Official Records of the Union and Confederate Armies.* 128 vols. (Washington, D.C.: Government Printing Office, 1880–1901)

RSP   *Records of Ante-Bellum Southern Plantations from the Revolution through the Civil War,* ed. Kenneth M. Stampp. University Publications of America. Microfilm.

SCL   South Caroliniana Library, University of South Carolina, Columbia

SHC   Southern Historical Collection, University of North Carolina, Chapel Hill

INTRODUCTION

1. Edmund Ruffin, *Anticipations of the Future, to Serve as Lessons for the Present Time. In the Form of Extracts of Letters from an English Resident in the United States to the London Times, from 1864 to 1870* . . . (Richmond, VA: J. W. Randolph, 1860), 85–93.

2. Penne L. Restad, *Christmas in America: A History* (New York: Oxford University Press, 1995), 6, 8–15; William Chauncey Fowler, *Local Law in Massachusetts and Connecticut, Historically Considered* (Albany, NY: Joel Munsell, 1872), 27; Jack Larkin, "Christmas in New England before 1860," Old Sturbridge Village Research Paper, 2002, http://resources.osv.org/explore_learn/document_viewer.php ?DocID=2063; Larry B. Massie, "When Christmas Was Just Another Day," *Michigan History* 80 (Nov.–Dec. 1996): 10–15; William D. Crump, ed., *The Christmas*

Encyclopedia (2001; 3rd ed., Jefferson, NC: McFarland, 2013), 425; (Philadelphia) *Pennsylvania Inquirer and National Gazette,* Jan. 4, 1843; Karal Ann Marling, *Merry Christmas! Celebrating America's Greatest Holiday* (Cambridge, MA: Harvard University Press, 2000), 255; Harnett T. Kane, *The Southern Christmas Book: The Full Story from Earliest Times to Present: People, Customs, Conviviality, Carols, Cooking* (New York: David McKay, 1958), 15; Charles B. Hosmer Jr., *Preservation Comes of Age: From Williamsburg to the National Trust, 1926-1949,* 2 vols. (Charlottesville: University Press of Virginia, 1981), 1:294–96; "Harnett T. Kane, 73, Author of Books About the South," *NYT,* Sept. 14, 1984, p. B5; David Hackett Fischer, *Albion's Seed: Four British Folkways in America* (New York: Oxford University Press 1989), 354.

3. Landon Carter Diary, Dec. 24, 1874, quoted in Rhys Isaac, *Landon Carter's Uneasy Kingdom: Revolution and Rebellion on a Virginia Plantation* (New York: Oxford University Press, 2004), 282.

4. Daniel R. Hundley, *Social Relations in Our Southern States,* ed. William J. Cooper Jr. (1860; rpt. with a new introduction by Cooper, Baton Rouge: Louisiana State University Press, 1979), 359 and introduction, xiv–xix; "Causes of Aristocracy" (unattributed review) in *De Bow's Review* 28 (May 1860): 551–64 (quotation on 564).

5. *Witness to Sorrow: The Antebellum Autobiography of William J. Grayson,* ed. Richard J. Calhoun (Columbia: University of South Carolina Press, 1990), 3–10; William J. Grayson, *The Hireling and the Slave, Chicora, and Other Poems* (1854; Charleston, SC: McCarter, 1856), 21–75 (quotation on 52).

6. White southerners began calling slavery a "peculiar institution" by 1829, and the term caught on during South Carolina's resistance to federal protective tariffs in the 1830s. See (Fayetteville) *Carolina Observer,* Jan. 1, 1829 quoted in *Oxford English Dictionary Online;* (Georgetown, SC) *Winyaw Intelligencer,* Apr. 13, 1833, p. 1; report from Beaufort District, Sept. 8, in *Charleston Courier,* Sept. 11, 1835, p. 2.

7. Restad, *Christmas in America,* 87; William W. Freehling, *The Road to Disunion,* vol. 1, *Secessionists at Bay, 1776-1854* (New York: Oxford University Press, 1990), 66.

8. David W. Blight, *Race and Reunion: The Civil War in American Memory* (Cambridge, MA: Belknap Press of Harvard University Press, 2001), 221–22.

9. Thomas Nelson Page, *Unc' Edinburg: A Plantation Echo* (1889; rpt., Charles Scribner's Sons, 1897), 35–38.

10. Kane, *Southern Christmas Book,* 71–74.

11. Metta Victoria Victor, *Maum Ginea, and Her Plantation "Children"; or, Holiday-Week on a Louisiana Estate: A Slave Romance* (New York: Beadle, 1861), esp. iii, 34–39; Michael K. Simmons, *"Maum Guinea:* A Dime Novelist Looks at Abolition," *Journal of Popular Culture* 10 (June 1976): 81–87; Sarah N. Roth, "The Mind of a Child: Images of African Americans in Early Juvenile Fiction," *Journal of the Early Republic* 25 (Spring 2005): 79–109, esp. 105. *Maum Guinea* was released for the Civil War's first Christmas holiday by the London and New York outlets of the dime-novel publisher Beadle and Company, and was intended to influence opinion against the Confederacy on both sides of the Atlantic. A double dime novel since it cost twenty cents, it sold 100,000 copies at a time when most publishers only issued 2,500 copies of new novels.

12. Charlie Sandles interview, ASCA-2, vol. 9, TX, pt. 8: 3447.

13. "The Negro Excitements," (Raymond, MS) *Hinds County Gazette,* Jan. 7, 1857; Charles Joyner, "Folklore," in *Dictionary of Afro-American Slavery,* ed. Randall M. Miller and John David Smith (Westport, CT: Greenwood Press, 1988), 256; William H. Wiggins Jr., *O Freedom! Afro-American Emancipation Celebrations* (Knoxville: University of Tennessee Press, 1987), 26; Roger D. Abrahams, *Singing the Master: The Emergence of African American Culture in the Plantation South* (New York: Penguin Books, 1992), 30–31.

14. Frederick Douglass, *Narrative of the Life of Frederick Douglass, an American Slave,* 6th, ed. (London: H. G. Collins, 1851), 68–71.

15. Michael Tadman, "The Persistent Myth of Paternalism: Historians and the Nature of Master-Slave Relations in the American South," *Sage Race Relations Abstract* 23 (Feb. 1998): 7–23, esp. 16–17.

16. See, for example, in addition to William Freehling's work cited above, Steven Nissenbaum, *The Battle for Christmas* (New York: Alfred A. Knopf, 1996), 258–300; Restad, *Christmas in America,* 75–90; Eugene D. Genovese, *Roll, Jordan, Roll: The World the Slaves Made* (1972; paper ed., New York: Vintage Books, 1976), 573–76; Kenneth M. Stampp, *The Peculiar Institution: Slavery in the Ante-Bellum South* (New York: Vintage Books, 1956), 169–70: Charles Joyner, *Down by the Riverside: A South Carolina Slave Community* (Urbana: University of Illinois Press, 1984), 101–2, 134–37; David J. Anderson, "Nostalgia for Christmas in Postbellum Plantation Reminiscences," *Southern Studies* 21 (Fall/Winter 2014): 39–73.

17. Anderson, "Nostalgia," 40.

18. Robert E. May, *John A. Quitman: Old South Crusader* (Baton Rouge: Louisiana State University Press, 1985).

19. Shauna Bigham and Robert May, "The Time o' All Times? Masters, Slaves, and Christmas in the Old South," *Journal of the Early Republic* 18 (Summer 1998): 263–88.

20. Robert E. May, " 'Christmas Gif', Empty Chairs, and Confederate Defeat," *North & South* 8 (Jan. 2006): 52–58.

1. TIME AND PUNISHMENT

1. "A Typical Negro," *Harper's Weekly,* July 4, 1863, p. 429; Kathleen Collins, "The Scourged Back," *History of Photography* 9 (1985): 43–45. Collins explains that Gordon might have suffered from a physical condition exacerbating the extent of his scarring.

2. Stuart B. Schwartz, *Sugar Plantations in the Formation of Brazilian Society: Bahia, 1550-1835* (New York: Cambridge University Press, 1985), 101–3; *Le Code Noir ou Edit Du Roy . . . Pour le Gouvernement & l'Administration de Justice & la Police des Isles Françoise de l'Amerique . . .* (1685), trans. John Garrigus, http://www2.latech .edu/~bmagee/louisiana_anthology/texts/louis_xiv/louis_xiv—code_noir _english.html; David Barry Gaspar, "Sugar Cultivation and Slave Life in Antigua before 1800," in *Cultivation and Culture: Labor and the Shaping of Slave Life in the Americas,* ed. Ira Berlin and Philip D. Morgan (Charlottesville: University Press of Virginia, 1993), 120–22; *An Act for the Protection, Subsisting, and for the Better Order and Government, of Slaves* (St. Iago de la Vega [Jamaica]: Alexander Aikman and Son, 1808), 14.

3. "An Act for making more effectual provision against Invasions and Insurrections," Feb. 1727, in *The Statutes at Large: Being a Collection of all the Laws of Virginia, from the First Session of the Legislature in the Year 1619,* comp. William Waller Hening, vol. 4 (Richmond, VA: Samuel Pleasants, 1814), 202; Charles Carter to Landon Carter, Dec. 19, 1773, quoted in Albert H. Tillson Jr., *Accommodating Revolutions: Virginia's Northern Neck in an Era of Transformations, 1760–1810* (Charlottesville: University of Virginia Press, 2010), 113; "Negro Life Before the Revolution," quoting letter to the editor of the *Pee Dee Times,* June 4, 1860, in *Charleston Tri-Weekly Courier,* June 9, 1860.

4. Joyce E. Chaplin, "Slavery and the Principle of Humanity: A Modern Idea in the Early Lower South," *Journal of Social History* 24 (Winter 1990): 299–315, esp. 299–300, 309; Frank Klingberg, *An Appraisal of the Negro in Colonial South Carolina: A Study in Americanization* (Washington, D.C.: Associated Publishers, 1941), 24n, 55, 58n, 93; Teresa S. Moyer, *Ancestors of Worthy Life: Plantation Slavery and Black Heritage at Mount Clare* (Gainesville: University Press of Florida, 2015), 73; Peter H. Wood, *Black Majority: Negroes in Colonial South Carolina from 1670 through the Stono Rebellion* (New York: Alfred A. Knopf, 1975), 182; Ras Michael Brown, *African-Atlantic Cultures and the South Carolina Lowcountry* (New York: Cambridge University Press, 2012), 81; Cheryll Ann Cody, "There Was No 'Absalom' on the Ball Plantations: Slave-Naming Practices in the South Carolina Low Country, 1720–1865," *American Historical Review* 92 (June 1987): 563–96, esp. 573, 575–76; John C. Inscoe, "Carolina Slave Names: An Index to Acculturation," *JSH* 49 (Nov. 1983): 527–54, esp. 538; Iman Makeba Laversuch, "Runaway Slave Names Recaptured: An Investigation of the Personal First Names of Fugitive Slaves Advertised in the *Virginia Gazette* Between 1736 and 1776," *Names* 54 (Dec. 2006): 331–62, esp. 336.

5. Philip Vickers Fithian Diary, Dec. 18, 25, 26, 1773, in *Philip Vickers Fithian: Journal and Letters, 1767–1774 . . . ,* ed. John Rogers Williams (Princeton, NJ: The University Library, 1900), 63, 70–74; Bruce David Forbes, *Christmas: A Candid History* (Berkeley: University of California Press, 2007), 27.

6. Philip Vickers Fithian Diary, Dec. 24, 25, 1773, in Williams, ed., *Fithian: Journal and Letters,* 70, 71; Lorena S. Walsh, "Slave Life, Slave Society, and Tobacco Production in the Tidewater Chesapeake, 1620–1820," in Berlin and Morgan, eds., *Cultivation and Culture,* 177. Christmas Boxes, also a custom in the British colony of Jamaica, were containers masters gave slaves at the holiday with small sums of money inside. Roderick A. McDonald, *The Economy and Material Culture of Slaves: Goods and Chattels on the Sugar Plantations of Jamaica and Louisiana* (Baton Rouge: Louisiana State University Press, 1993), 37.

7. Charles Ball, *Slavery in the United States: A Narrative of the Life and Adventures of Charles Ball* (1836; rpt., Detroit: Negro Histories Press, 1970), 206–8; Jennifer Oast, *Institutional Slavery: Slaveholding Churches, Schools, Colleges, and Businesses in Virginia, 1680–1860* (New York: Cambridge University Press, 2016), 154; Thomas Jefferson to Jeremiah A. Goodman, Dec. 23, 1814, in *The Papers of Thomas Jefferson: Retirement Series,* vol. 8, ed. J. Jefferson Looney (Princeton, NJ: Princeton University Press, 2011), 157–58.

8. John Pierpont Journal, Dec. 25, 1805, quoted in Abe C. Ravitz, "John Pierpont and the Slaves' Christmas," *Phylon* 21 (No. 4, 1960): 383–86, esp. 384;

G. S. S., "Sketches of the South Santee," *American Monthly Magazine* 8 (Oct., Nov. 1836): 313–19, 431–42, esp. 433–34.

9. Ulrich B. Phillips, "A Jamaica Slave Plantation," *American Historical Review* 3 (Apr. 1914): 543–58, esp. 553; Nicholas P. Cushner, "Slave Mortality and Reproduction on Jesuit Haciendas in Colonial Peru," *Hispanic American Historical Review* 55 (May 1975): 177–99, esp. 184; Richard B. Sheridan, "From Chattel to Wage Slavery in Jamaica, 1740–1760," *Slavery & Abolition* 14 (Apr. 1993): 13–40, esp. 16–17; Robin Blackburn, *The Making of New World Slavery: From the Baroque to the Modern, 1492–1800* (1997; rpt., London: Verso, 1998), 429; Michael Iyanaga, "Why Saints Love Samba: A Historical Perspective on Black Agency and the Rearticulation of Catholicism in Bahia, Brazil," *Black Music Research Journal* 35 (Spring 2015): 119–47, esp. 136; Langford Lovell to "My Dear Sir," in Lovell, *A Letter to a Friend Relative to the Present State of the Island of Domínica* (Winchester: James Robbins, 1818), 7.

10. "An Act for making more effectual provision against Invasions and Insurrections," 202–3; H. M. Henry, *The Police Control of the Slave in South Carolina* (Emory, VA: privately published, 1914), 42.

11. William Stephens to the Trustees from Savannah, Dec. 31, 1741, in *Colonial Records of the State of Georgia,* vol. 23, comp. Allen D. Candler (Atlanta: Chas. P. Byrd, 1914), 189–90; "An Act for the better security of the inhabitants by obliging the male white persons to carry fire arms to places of public worship," February 27, 1770, in Candler, comp., *Colonial Records of the State of Georgia,* vol. 19 (1911), 137–40.

12. Brian Schoen, *The Fragile Fabric of Union: Cotton, Federal Politics, and the Global Origins of the Civil War* (Baltimore: Johns Hopkins University Press, 2009), 2; James L. Huston, *Calculating the Value of the Union: Slavery, Property Rights, and the Economic Origins of the Civil War* (Chapel Hill: University of North Carolina Press, 2003), 26–27; Edward E. Baptist, *The Half Has Never Been Told: Slavery and the Making of American Capitalism* (New York: Basic Books, 2014), 350; William Kauffman Scarborough, *Masters of the Big House: Elite Slaveholders of the Mid-Nineteenth-Century South* (Baton Rouge: Louisiana State University Press, 2003), 631, 76.

13. James Oakes, *The Ruling Race: A History of American Slaveholders* (1982; rpt., New York: Vintage Books, 1983), 38–39; Charles Joyner, *Down by the Riverside: A South Carolina Slave Community* (Urbana: University of Illinois Press, 1984), 31, 53; William Dusinberre, *Them Dark Days: Slavery in the American Rice Swamps* (New York: Oxford University Press, 1996), 12, 286; Bruce Levine, *The Fall of the House of Dixie: The Civil War and the Social Revolution That Transformed the South* (New York: Random House, 2013), 6–7.

14. "An Act Concerning Crimes and Punishments," in *The Laws of Maryland . . .*, rev. Virgil Maxcy, 3 vols. (Baltimore: Philip H. Nicklin, 1811), 3:458–79, esp. 473; William D. Crump, ed., *The Christmas Encyclopedia* (2001; 3rd ed., Jefferson, NC: McFarland, 2013), 425; "An Act Reorganizing the Comptroller's and Treasurer's departments," Mar. 3, 1848 (Sec. 9), *Alabama Legislative Acts, December 1847 through March 1848,* p. 114, digital.archives.alabama.gov.; Titles 123 and 139, *An Alphabetical Digest of the Public Statute Law of South-Carolina,* vol. 2 (Charleston, SC: John Hoff, 1814), 97, 175.

15. "Sketches of South-Carolina. Number Three. 'Merry Christmas,'" *Knickerbocker* 21 (Mar. 1843): 222–29 (quotation on 223).

16. Robert Mitchell to John Page, Dec. 25, 1804, in *Calendar of Virginia State Papers and Other Manuscripts,* ed. H. W. Flournoy, vol. 9 (Richmond, VA: James E. Goode, 1890), 430; (Philadelphia) *Pennsylvania Inquirer and National Gazette,* Jan. 4, 1843; John Pierpont Jr. to his father, Dec. 26, 1853, quoted in George H. Gibson, "The Georgia Letters of John Pierpont, Jr., to His Father, pt. I," *GHQ* 55 (Winter 1971): 543–82, esp. 570–71. According to Mary Theobald and Libbey Oliver, biblically oriented sects in Virginia's Shenandoah Valley, like Scotch-Irish Presbyterians, Baptists, and Quakers, hardly kept Christmas. They also note that holiday gun firing represented a rare early Virginia Christmas custom not transplanted from England. Mary Miley Theobald and Libbey Hodges Oliver, *Four Centuries of Virginia Christmas* (Richmond, VA: Dietz Press, 2000), 57–58, 22.

17. (Austin, TX) *South-Western American,* Dec. 29, 1852; James Hamilton Couper to his wife, Dec. 24, 1835, in R. P. Brooks, ed., "Letters of James Hamilton Couper to His Wife," *GHQ* 14 (June 1930): 150–73, esp. 164; Charles Heinrich Journal, Jan. 1, 1855, in John Quincy Wolf, ed., "Journal of Charles Heinrich, 1849–1856," *Arkansas Historical Quarterly* 24 (Autumn 1965): 241–83 (quotation on 269); Charles Lyell, *A Second Visit to the United States of North America,* vol. 1 (London: John Murray, 1849), 293; Elizabeth Reid Murray, *Wake: Capital County of North Carolina,* vol. 1 (Raleigh, NC: Capital County Publishing, 1983), 368; Thomas B. Chaplin Journal, Dec. 25, 1850, in *Tombee: Portrait of a Cotton Planter with the Journal of Thomas B. Chaplin (1822–1890),* ed. Theodore Rosengarten (New York: William Morrow, 1986), 515; John A. Selden Journal, Dec. 26, 1858, in "The Westover Journal of John A. Selden, Esqr., 1858–1862," ed. John Spencer Bassett and Sidney Bradshaw Fay, *Smith College Studies in History* 6 (July 1921): 281.

18. Mary A. Livermore, *The Story of My Life . . .* (Hartford, CT: A. D. Worthington, 1897), 210; Marilyn Elizabeth Perry, "Livermore, Mary," *American National Biography Online;* Susan Bradford Eppes Diary, Dec. 23, 1855, in Eppes, *Through Some Eventful Years* (Macon, GA: J. W. Burke, 1926), 64; Henry W. Ravenel Diary, Dec. 25, 26, 1860, in *The Private Journal of Henry William Ravenel, 1859-1887,* ed. Arney Robinson Childs (Columbia: University of South Carolina Press, 1947), 45; Thomas Porcher Ravenel Diary, Dec. 27, 1850, Thomas Porcher Ravenel Papers, South Carolina Historical Society, RSP, Series B, Reel 1.

19. Susan Dabney Smedes, *Memorials of a Southern Planter,* ed. Fletcher M. Green (New York: Alfred A. Knopf, 1965), xi, 148; James Hammond Diary, Dec. 25, 1837, SCL, RSP, Series A, pt. 1, Reel 1; Basil Armstrong Thomasson Diary, Dec. 24, 1854, in *North Carolina Yeoman: The Diary of Basil Armstrong Thomasson, 1853-1862* (Athens: University of Georgia Press, 1996), 58; Susannah Warfield Diary, Feb. 25, 1845, Maryland Historical Society, RSP, Series D, Reel 12 (masquerade party).

20. Jeff Strickland, *Unequal Freedoms: Ethnicity, Race, and White Supremacy in Civil War–Era Charleston* (Gainesville: University Press of Florida, 2015), 33; Reuben Davis, *Recollections of Mississippi and Mississippians* (1889; rpt., Hattiesburg:

University and College Press of Mississippi, 1972), 45; Susan Bradford Eppes Diary, Dec. 23, 1855, in Eppes, *Through Some Eventful Years* (Macon, GA: J. W. Burke, 1926), 64; *Macon (GA) Telegraph,* Dec. 24, 1827, p. 243; Israel Gibbons, "Christmas Day in New Orleans," quoted in Gibbons, *Crescent-Shrine; Or, Gleams of Light on All Sorts of Subjects from the Columns of the "New Orleans Crescent"* (New Orleans: J. O. Nixon, 1866), 149–50; Lawrence J. Haughton to William Shepard Pettigrew, Dec. 20, 1827, in *The Pettigrew Papers,* ed. Sarah McCulloh Lemon, vol. 2, *1819–1843* (Raleigh: North Carolina Department of Cultural Resources, 1988), 89; Charles Heinrich Journal, Jan. 1, 1855, in Wolf, ed., "Journal of Charles Heinrich," 269; Jacques D. Bagur, *Antebellum Jefferson, Texas: Everyday Life in an East Texas Town* (Denton: University of North Texas Press, 2012), 541; Jacqueline Jones, *Saving Savannah: The City and the Civil War* (New York: Knopf, 2008), 71.

21. Jeremiah Gage to Mary Gage, Dec. 21, 1857, Civil War Archive, University of Mississippi, clio.lib.olemiss.edu/cdm/compoundobject/collection /civil_war/id/1525/rec/6; Sarah E. Watkins to her daughter Letitia, Dec. 28, 1856, in *Letters from Forest Place: A Plantation Family's Correspondence, 1846–1861,* ed. E. Grey Dimond and Herman Hattaway (Jackson: University Press of Mississippi, 1993), 95–97, 96n.

22. William Bush to James Hammond, Dec. 22, 1833, James Hammond Papers, SCL, RSP, Series A, pt. I, Reel 7; Bennet H. Barrow Plantation Journal (edited typescript), Dec. 22, 1836, Dec. 25, 1837, Dec. 22, 1839, Dec. 23, 25, 1846, HT, RSP, Series H, Reel 19; James Battle Avirett, *The Old Plantation: How We Lived in Great House and Cabin Before the War* (New York: F. Tennyson Neely, 1901), 176; David S. Cecelski, "Oldest Living Confederate Chaplain Tells All? Or, James B. Avirett and the Rise and Fall of the Rich Lands," *Southern Cultures* 3 (Winter 1997): 5–24, esp. 5–10; Basil Armstrong Thomasson Diary, Dec. 25, 1860, in Escott, ed., *Diary of Basil Armstrong Thomasson,* 295.

23. John A. Quitman Daybook, Dec. 21, 1839, Dec. 26, 1843, LSU; Annie Rosalie Quitman Diary, Nov. 6, 1852, LSU; Louisa Quitman to John A. Quitman, Dec. 27, 1840, Quitman Family Papers, SHC; Eliza Quitman to F. Henry Quitman, Nov. 8, 1849, letter in the possession of Mrs. Earl B. Shaw Jr., Signal Mountain, TN.

24. Robert E. May, *John A. Quitman: Old South Crusader* (Baton Rouge: Louisiana State University Press, 1985), 26–27; James E. Bagwell, *Rice Gold: James Hamilton Couper and Plantation Life on the Georgia Coast* (Macon, GA: Mercer University Press, 2000), 15–18.

25. Henry W. Ravenel Diary, Dec. 25, 1859, in *Private Journal,* 3; Henry W. Huntington to William N. Mercer, Dec. 27, 1836, William N. Mercer Papers, HT, RSP, Series H, Reel 24; John A. Selden Journal, Dec. 26, 1858, in Bassett and Fay, eds., "Westover Journal of John A. Selden," 318; Ann Blount Pettigrew to Ebenezer Pettigrew, Dec. 31, 1829, in Lemon, ed., *Pettigrew Papers,* 2:128–29; Louisa Maxwell Holmes Cocke Diary, Dec. 25, 1840, Cocke Family Papers, University of Virginia, *American Women's Diaries: Southern Women,* Readex Film Products, Reel 3; *Huntsville (AL) Republican,* Dec. 25, 1817, p. 2.

26. Annie Rosalie Quitman Diary, Dec. 24, 1853, LSU; Henry Metcalfe to Cousin Mary, Dec. 23, 1857, Moses and St. John Richardson Liddell Family

Papers, LSU, in "Slavery, Abolition, & Social Justice," Adam Matthew Digital Collections; *Savannah Morning News,* Dec. 22, 1851; Murray, *Wake,* 368–69.

27. Penne L. Restad, *Christmas in America: A History* (New York: Oxford University Press, 1995), 8–10, 30–33 (quotation on 33), 57–69; Forbes, "Christmas," 79–85, 50–52; "Holiday Greens," *Harper's Weekly,* Jan. 17, 1874, p. 59.

28. Robert E. Lee to "dear Custis and William," Dec. 24, 1846, quoted in Bernice-Marie Yates, *The Perfect Gentleman,* vol. 1, *The Life and Letters of George Washington Custis Lee* (Fairfax, VA: Xulon Press, 2003), 87–91 (quotation on 87); Mahala Eggleston Roach Diary, Christmas 1852, quoted in Harnett T. Kane, *The Southern Christmas Book: The Full Story from Earliest Times to Present: People, Customs, Conviviality, Carols, Cooking* (New York: David McKay, 1958), 190; *NODP,* Dec. 28, 1851; Annie Rosalie Quitman Diary, Dec. 25, 1853, Dec. 24, 1855, LSU; Annie Rosalie Quitman Diary, Dec. 25, 1857, Quitman Family Papers, SHC; Annie Rosalie Quitman to F. Henry Quitman, Dec. 29, 1857, Quitman Family Papers, Mississippi Department of Archives and History, Jackson; Dolly S. L. Burge Diary, Dec. 24, 25, 1852, in James I. Robertson Jr., ed., "The Diary of Dolly Hunt Burge, Part III," *GHQ* 44 (Dec. 1960): 455; Murray, *Wake,* 368.

29. Antonia Quitman to Eliza Quitman, Dec. 20, 1847, M. L. McMurran to Eliza Quitman, Dec. 20, 1847, Quitman Family Papers, SHC; Mahala Eggleston Roach Diary, Christmas 1851 and Christmas 1860, quoted in Kane, *Southern Christmas Book,* 189, 196; Eppes Diary, Dec. 23, 1855, Dec. 12, 1857, in Eppes, *Some Eventful Years,* 64, 82; Elizabeth Silverthorne, *Plantation Life in Texas* (College Station: Texas A&M University Press, 1986), 135; *Charleston Mercury,* Dec. 27, 1856.

30. Roxana Chapin Gerdine to Emily McKinstry Chapin, Jan. 1, 1860, Civil War Archive, University of Mississippi, clio.lib.olemiss.edu/cdm /compoundobject/civil_war/id/1634/rec/30; Julia Floyd Smith, *Slavery and Rice Culture in Low Country Georgia, 1750–1860* (Knoxville: University of Tennessee Press, 1985), 117.

31. Henry W. Huntington to William N. Mercer, Dec. 20, 1836, William N. Mercer Papers, HT, RSP, Series H, Reel 24; Avirett, *Old Plantation,* 57, 173–76; Esther S. Reynolds, *Memories of Mulberry* (Brooklyn, NY: Eagle Press, 1913), 9.

32. (Frankfort) *Kentucky Commonwealth,* Mar. 13, 1839, quoted in (New York) *Emancipator,* Apr. 4, 1839; *Macon (GA) Telegraph,* Dec. 24, 1827; *New Orleans Daily Crescent,* Jan. 8, 1857; T. B. Thorpe, "Christmas in the South," *Frank Leslie's Illustrated Newspaper,* Dec. 26, 1855, p. 62; Louis Sweet to James Gordon Bennett, Apr. 22, 1858, *New York Herald,* May 3, 1858, p. 2.

33. F. G. De Fontaine, "A Plantation Xmas: How the Day Was Spent in the South 'Before the War Came,'" ca. 1891, American Press Association, and reprinted in the *Atkinson Daily Globe,* Jan. 1, 1892, and other papers; R. Lockwood Tower, ed., *A Carolinian Goes to War: The Civil War Narrative of Arthur Middleton Manigault* (Columbia: University of South Carolina Press, 1983), 116n; "Christmas in Alabama," *NODP,* Dec. 24, 1893, p. 19; Elizabeth W. Allston Pringle, *Chronicles of Chicora Wood* (New York: Charles Scribner's Sons, 1922), 152–53; Avirett, *Old Plantation,* 57; John Williamson Palmer, "Of Maryland Homes and Ways," *Century Magazine* 27 (Dec. 1894): 260; Ralph B. Flanders, "Two Plantations and a County of Antebellum Georgia," *GHQ* 12 (Mar. 1928): 12; Kane, *Southern*

Christmas Book, 64; "Rules on the Rice Estate of P. C. Weston; South Carolina, 1856," *De Bow's Review* 22 (Jan. 1857): 40.

34. Abigail Mason to Mary Mason Brooks, Dec. 29, 1832, in Bessie M. Henry, "A Yankee Schoolmistress Discovers Virginia," *Exxex Institute Historical Collection* 101 (Jan. 1965): 121–32 (quotation on 129); Charles Lanman, *Adventures in the Wilds of the United States and British North American Provinces,* 2 vols. (Philadelphia: John W. Moore, 1856), 2:273–74; Charles Parker Gizzard, "A Glimpse of the South in the Spring of 1855" (handwritten travel journal), Beinecke Rare Book and Manuscript Library, Yale University, New Haven, CT; Frederick Law Olmsted, *A Journey in the Seaboard Slave States, with Remarks on their Economy* (New York: Dix & Edwards, 1856), 101.

35. Frederick Douglass, *Narrative of the Life of Frederick Douglass, an American Slave. Written by Himself,* 6th ed. (London: H. G. Collins, 1851), 68; *Slave and Freeman: The Autobiography of George L. Knox,* ed. Willard B. Gatewood Jr. (Lexington: University Press of Kentucky, 1979), 260; *Douglass' Monthly* 3 (Apr. 1861): 446; Mary B. Harlan, *Ellen; or the Chained Mother, And Pictures of Kentucky Slavery. Drawn from Real Life* (Cincinnati: privately published, 1853), 31–32; Richard Hildreth, *The Slave: Or Memoirs of Archy Moore* (Boston: John H. Eastburn, 1836), 84; Booker T. Washington, "Christmas Days in Old Virginia," in *The Booker T. Washington Papers,* vol. 1, *The Autobiographical Writings,* ed. Louis R. Harlan (Urbana: University of Illinois Press, 1972): 394; statistics by Shauna Bigham for Shauna Bigham and Robert E. May, "'The Time O' All Times'? Masters, Slaves, and Christmas in the Old South," *Journal of the Early Republic* 18 (Summer 1998): 278; *John Washington's Civil War: A Slave Narrative,* ed. Crandall Shifflett (Baton Rouge: Louisiana State University Press, 2008), 3.

36. Peter Kolchin, *American Slavery, 1619-1877* (New York: Hill and Wang, 1993), 115–16; Silverthorne, *Plantation Life in Texas,* 135.

37. Scholars' accounts of the length of slave Christmases vary. See, for example, David K. Wiggins, "Recreation, Slave," in *Dictionary of Afro-American Slavery,* ed. Randall M. Miller and John David Smith (Westport, CT: Greenwood Press, 1988), 622; Charles Sydnor, *Slavery in Mississippi* (New York: D. Appleton-Century, 1933), 21; Stephen Nissenbaum, *The Battle for Christmas* (New York: Alfred A. Knopf, 1996), 165; Eugene D. Genovese, *Roll, Jordan, Roll: The World the Slaves Made* (1972; paper ed., New York: Vintage Books, 1976), 573.

38. Oakes, *Ruling Race,* 38.

39. George Benaugh, Proctor, University of Alabama promissory note, Jan. 1, 1858, University Libraries Division of Special Collection, University of Alabama Digital Collections, acumen.lib.49.edu/u0003/0001603/000001 /0001/?pages=1&limit=40; Natalie De lage Sumter Diary [typescript copy], Dec. 27, 1840, SCL, RSP, Series A, pt. 2, Reel 4; Ordinance of Sept. 23, 1850, in (Austin) *Texas State Gazette,* Oct. 5, 1850, p. 6.

40. W. H. Venable, "Down South Before the War: Records of a Ramble to New Orleans in 1858," *Ohio Archaeological and Historical Quarterly* 2 (1889): 462; Charles B. Dew, *Bond of Iron: Master and Slave at Buffalo Forge* (New York: W. W. Norton, 1994), 30–32, 78.

41. Calvin Schermerhorn, *Money over Mastery: Family over Freedom: Slavery in the Antebellum Upper South* (Baltimore: Johns Hopkins University Press, 2011),

186–87; Robert S. Starobin, *Industrial Slavery in the Old South* (New York: Oxford University Press, 1970), 95; *Charleston Mercury* quoted in *Newark (OH) Advocate,* Jan. 11, 1861; Joseph Clarke Robert, *The Tobacco Kingdom: Plantation, Market, and Factory in Virginia and North Carolina* (Gloucester, MA: Peter Smith, 1965), 201; Joseph P. Reidy, *From Slavery to Agrarian Capitalism in the Cotton Plantation South: Central Georgia, 1800-1880* (Chapel Hill: University of North Carolina Press, 1992), 27.

42. Contract quoted in Jonathan D. Martin, *Divided Mastery: Slave Hiring in the American South* (Cambridge, MA: Harvard University Press, 2004), 53; Katherine C. Mooney, *Race Horse Men: How Slavery and Freedom Were Made at the Racetrack* (Cambridge, MA: Harvard University Press, 2014), 50; Robert S. Starobin, "Disciplining Industrial Slaves in the Old South," *JNH* 53 (Apr. 1968): 111–28, esp. 116; Starobin, *Industrial Slavery,* 95–96.

43. Bennet H. Barrow Journal, Jan. 1, 1841, Jan. 1, 1840, HT, RSP, Series H, Reel 19; Andrew Pickens Calhoun to John C. Calhoun, Dec. 30, 1840, in *The Papers of John C. Calhoun,* ed. Clyde N. Wilson (Columbia, SC: University of South Carolina Press, 1981), 15:404–5; John Niven, *John C. Calhoun and the Price of Union: A Biography* (Baton Rouge: Louisiana State University Press, 1988), 243.

44. Solomon Northup, *Twelve Years a Slave,* in *Puttin' On Ole Massa: The Slave Narratives of Henry Bibb, William Wells Brown, and Solomon Northup,* ed. Gilbert Osofsky (New York: Harper & Row, 1969), 342.

45. Everard Green Baker Diary, Dec. 28, 1852, SHC, RSP, Series J, pt. 6, Reel 16.

46. McDonald, *Economy,* 7, 53; John C. Rodrique, *Reconstruction in the Cane Fields* (Baton Rouge: Louisiana State University Press, 2001), 10–19; Richard Follett, *The Sugar Masters: Planters and Slaves in the Louisiana Cane World, 1820-1860* (Baton Rouge: Louisiana State University Press, 2005), 135; Clement Eaton, *The Growth of Southern Civilization, 1790-1860* (New York: Harper & Row, 1961), 134–35.

47. Deer Range Plantation Journal, Dec. 26, 1858, quoted in William K. Scarborough, "Slavery—The White Man's Burden," in *Perspectives and Irony in American Slavery,* ed. Harry P. Owens (Oxford: University Press of Mississippi, 1976), 121–22; Octave Colomb Plantation Journal, Dec. 23–26, 1851, Dec. 23–25, 1852, Jan. 19–23, 1853, Dec. 27–29, 1854, Dec. 24–27, 1855, Dec. 24–27, 1856, Dec. 24–26, 1857, Dec. 25–26, 1858, Dec. 24–31, 1859, Dec. 25–27, 1860, HT, RSP, Series H, Reel 20.

48. Caroline Gilman, *Recollections of a Southern Matron* (New York: Harper & Brothers, 1838), 102; Letter to General John H. Howard, Sept. 20, 1851, in [Mrs. Henry Rowe Schoolcraft], *Letters on the Condition of the African Race in the United States. By a Southern Lady* (Philadelphia: T. K. and P. G. Collins, 1852), 13; "Holydays," James Henry Hammond Plantation Manual, photocopy courtesy Elizabeth Laney, Park Interpreter, Redcliffe Plantation State Historic Site, Beech Island, SC; Richard J. Arnold Plantation Journal, Dec. 24–27, 1847, in Charles Hoffmann and Tess Hoffman, *North by South: The Two Lives of Richard James Arnold* (Athens: University of Georgia Press, 1988), 130–31; David Rees Plantation Journal, HT, RSP, Series H, Reel 30.

49. John Nevitt Record Book, Dec. 24–27, 1827, Dec. 24–28, 1828, Dec. 24–28, 1829, Dec. 24–28, 1830, Dec. 24–28, 1831, SHC, RSP, Series J, Reel

3; Bonavenura Plantation Book, Dec. 24–27, 1850, Louisiana State Museum, RSP, Series H, Reel 1.

50. John P. Thomas Diary, Dec. 28 for the years 1838, 1843, 1833, 1829, 1831, and Dec. 27, 1829, SCL, RSP, Series A, pt. 2, Reel 5.

51. Northup, *Twelve Years a Slave 341;* David Harris quoted in Walter Edgar, *South Carolina: A History* (Columbia: University of South Carolina Press, 1998), 315; Bennet H. Barrow Journal, Jan. 2, 1846, HT, RSP, Series H, Reel 19; Abraham Lincoln, "Fragment on Slavery" (July 1, 1854?], in *The Collected Works of Abraham Lincoln,* ed. Roy P. Basler, 9 vols. (New Brunswick, NJ: Rutgers University Press, 1953–55), 2:222.

52. Genovese, *Roll, Jordan, Roll,* 573–74. Genovese's conclusions, in turn, have guided later scholars. William Blair, for instance, only cited Genovese for his own generalization that slave Christmases lasted "from as little as three days to the more typical week—sometimes longer." William Blair, *Cities of the Dead: Contesting the Memory of the Civil War in the South* (Chapel Hill: University of North Carolina Press, 2004), 15, 210n.

53. *Alexandria (VA) Gazette,* Dec. 29, 1828, Dec. 25, 1855 (quoting *Fredericksburg News*); (Natchez) *Mississippi Free Trader,* Oct. 20, 1849 ("March of Gen. Quitman"); *Richmond Whig,* Dec. 25, 1855 ("ye olden tyme"); *Charleston Courier,* Dec. 25, 1857, Dec. 25, 1858; W. Gilmore Simms, "Maize-in-Milk: A Christmas Story of the South," *Godey's Lady's Book* 34 (Feb. 1847): 62–67, (Mar. 1847): 146–52, (Apr. 1847): 199–204, (May 1847): 249–58, esp. 152.

54. Nissenbaum, *Battle for Christmas,* 165.

55. "The Holly Back-Log," *Youth's Companion,* Dec. 22, 1887, 575; Ruth McEnery Stuart, "Christmas Gifts," *Lippincott's Monthly Magazine* 47 (Jan. 1891): 104; Rebecca Cameron, "Christmas at Buchoi, A North Carolina Rice Plantation," *Ladies Home Journal* Christmas issue, 1891, reprinted in *The North Carolina Booklet* 13 (July 1913): 3–10, esp. 4, 10; LaSalle Corbell Pickett, *Yule Log* (Washington, D.C.: Neale, 1900), 17–18. An 1889 article, with no specifics, claimed there was "one [master] on record" who adhered to Yule log customs, letting a wood-chopper trick him into extralong Christmas slave holidays by soaking a tree trunk in a swamp. W. T. Coleman, "A Virginia Plantation," *The Chatauquan* 9 (Apr. 1889): 412–15 (quotation on 414).

56. Kane, *Southern Christmas Book,* 67–68; Theobald and Oliver, *Four Centuries,* 83. Penne Restad's *Christmas in America* perpetuates such mythology, citing Kane's *Southern Christmas Book* as its first source on the Yule log. Restad, *Christmas in America,* 76, 190n.

57. Paul Clark, "Historic Site to Offer Glimpse of an 1830-Style Christmas," *Asheville Citizen,* Nov. 30, 1999, Sec. B, p. 1, Gannett Newsstand:search .proquest.com.ezproxy.lib.purdue.edu; "Christmas in the Quarters: An Activity Book," Redcliffe Plantation (SC) State Historic Site; Elizabeth L. Laney to Robert E. May, June 15, 2017, email; Elizabeth A. Fenn, " 'A Perfect Equality Seemed to Reign': Slave Society and Jonkonnu," *North Carolina Historical Review* 65 (Apr. 1988): 127–53, esp. 137.

58. Booker T. Washington, *Up from Slavery: An Autobiography* (1901), in *The Booker T. Washington Papers,* vol. 1, *The Autobiographical Writings,* ed. Louis R. Harlan (Urbana: University of Illinois Press, 1972), 286; Jenny Fillmer, "Traditions

Run Deep in Ozarks Christmas," *Springfield (MO) News Leader,* Dec. 25, 2003, A-1, Gannett Newsstand: search.proquest.com.ezproxy.lib.purdue.edu.

59. (Lewis Clarke), *Narrative of the Sufferings of Lewis Clarke, during a Captivity of More Than Twenty-Five Years Among the Algerines of Kentucky, One of the So Called Christian States of North America* (Boston: David H. Ela, 1845) 69; Carver Clark Gayton, *When Owing a Shilling Costs a Dollar: The Saga of Lewis G. Clarke, Born a "White" Slave* (Bloomington, IN: Xlibris, 2014), 9; Lewis Evans interview, Hector Godbold interview, Madison Griffin interview, ASCA, South Carolina, vol. 2, SC, pt. 2: 32, 143, 212; Peter Clifton interview, ASCA, vol. 2, SC, pt. 1: 207; Wes Brady interview, ASCA, vol. 4, TX, pt. 1: 135; Andy Marion interview, ASCA, vol. 3, SC, pt. 3: 162, 201; Frances Patterson interview, ACSA-1, vol. 9, MS, pt. 4: 1680.

60. Ball, *Narrative,* 207–8; Louis J. Stewart, "A Contingency Theory Perspective on Management Control System Design among U.S. Ante-Bellum Slave Plantations," *Accounting Historical Journal* 37 (June 2010): 91–120, esp. 113.

61. Thomas G. Clemson to John C. Calhoun, Dec. 27, 1840, in Wilson, ed., *Papers of John C. Calhoun,* 15:404–5; Niven, *Calhoun,* 224, 242; *Tallahassee Floridian* quoted in *Savannah (GA) Daily Morning News,* Apr. 16, 1857; *Southern Cultivator* 8 (Nov. 1850): 162–64 (quotations on 162).

62. Ebenezer Pettigrew to Mary Williams Bryan, Dec. 29, 1840, in *The Pettigrew Papers,* ed. Sarah McCulloh Lemon, vol. 2, *1819–1843* (Raleigh: North Carolina Department of Cultural Resources, 1988), 454; Thomas B. Chaplin Journal, Dec. 27, 1847, Dec. 25, 27, 1850, Dec. 28, 1852, in Rosengarten, *Tombee,* 448, 515, 592; Louis Manigault quoted in Dusinberre, *Them Dark Days,* 186.

63. Enclosure in James R. Sparkman to Benjamin Allston, Mar. 10, 1858, in James H. Easterby, ed. *The South Carolina Rice Plantation as Revealed in the Papers of Robert F. W. Allston* (Chicago: University of Chicago Press, 1945), 345.

64. Pringle, *Chronicles,* 152; Reynolds, *Memories of Mulberry,* 7, 10, 11; Douglass, *Narrative,* 68; Lanman, *Adventures in the Wilds,* 2:275–76.

65. Silverthorne, *Plantation Life in Texas,* 135; Madison Griffin interview, ASCA, vol. 2, SC, pt. 2: 212; Dwight L. Smith, "An Antebellum Boyhood: Samuel Escue Tillman on a Middle Tennessee Plantation," *Tennessee Historical Quarterly* 47 (Spring 1988): 3–9, esp. 7–8; Ada Bacot Diary, Dec. 24, 1860, SCL, *American Women's Diaries* (microfilm).

66. William Ethelbert Ervin Diary, Dec. 31, 1843, SHC, RSP, Series J, Reel 17; Louis Hughes, *Thirty Years a Slave, From Bondage to Freedom ...* (Milwaukee: South Side Printing, 1897), 15; northerner quoted in the *Georgia Journal* and reprinted in *Washington (D.C.) National Intelligencer,* Oct. 25, 1819; John Blackford Journal, Dec. 25, 1838, in *Ferry Hill Plantation Journal,* Jan. 4, 1838–Jan. 15, 1839, ed. Fletcher M. Green (Chapel Hill: University of North Carolina Press, 1961), 124; [David Brown], *The Planter: Or, Thirteen Years in the South. By a Northern Man* (Philadelphia: H. Hooker, 1853), 69.

67. Olmsted, *Journey in the Seaboard Slave States,* 89; Edmund Kirke, *Among the Pines: Or South in Secession-Time* (New York: J. R. Gilmore, 1862), 81; John Edmund Stealey III, "Slavery and the Western Virginia Salt Industry," *JNH* 59 (Apr. 1974): 105–31, esp. 109.

68. Addie Vinson interview, ASCA, vol. 13, GA, pt. 4: 108.

69. C. G. Parsons, *Inside View of Slavery: Or a Tour Among the Planters* (Boston: John P. Jewett, 1855), 13–19, 24–25, 40–47; Austin Willey, *The History of the Antislavery Cause in State and Nation* (Portland, ME: Brown Thurston and Hoyt, Fogg and Donham, 1886), 177.

70. Augusta Rohrbach, *Truth Stranger Than Fiction: Race, Realism and the U.S. Literary Marketplace* (New York: Palgrave, 2002), 46–48.

71. (Charles Friend) White Hill Plantation Books cited in Wilma King, *Stolen Childhood: Slave Youth in Nineteenth-Century America* (Bloomington: Indiana University Press, 1995), 59; Flanders, "Two Plantations," 12; Collie Rolley interview, ASCA-1, vol. 9, MS, pt. 4: 1885–86.

72. Speech of Matthew Gaines in *Houston (TX) Age,* reprinted in *San Francisco Daily Evening Bulletin,* July 21, 1871; Toler incident in Ervin L. Jordan Jr., *Black Confederates and Afro-Yankees in Civil War Virginia* (Charlottesville: University Press of Virginia), 1995), 111–12; Liese M. Perrin, "Resisting Reproduction: Reconsidering Slave Contraception in the Old South," *Journal of American Studies* 35 (No. 2, 2001): 255–74 (quotations on 264).

73. Ezekiel Birdseye letter quoted in *Abolitionist in the Appalachian South: Ezekiel Birdseye on Slavery, Capitalism, and Separate Statehood in East Tennessee, 1841–1846,* ed. Durwood Dunn (Knoxville: University of Tennessee Press, 1997), 131–33; James L. Smith, *Autobiography of James L. Smith, Including, Also, Reminiscences of Slave Life, Recollections of the War, Education of Freedmen, Causes of the Exodus, etc.* (Norwich, CT: Bulletin Company, 1881), 25–26; Isaac Williams Narrative in *A North-Side View of Slavery: The Refugee: Or the Narratives of Fugitive Slaves in Canada Related by Themselves . . . ,* ed. Benjamin Drew (Cleveland: John P. Jewett, 1856), 55–56; Robert F. W. Allston Diary, Jan. 14, 1860, in Easterby, ed., *South Carolina Rice Plantation,* 454.

74. Truman Case to "Friend Johnson," Oct. 8, 1849, in the *Anti-Slavery Bugle,* reprinted in (Boston) *The Liberator,* Nov. 23, 1849, p. 186.

75. Slave patrols, which existed throughout the South, consisted of small groups of white men who held legal authority and responsibility to scour roads and pathways looking for escaped or potentially rebellious slaves. Patrollers had authority to whip apprehended blacks caught traveling without written permission from their owners.

76. *Slave Life in Georgia: A Narrative of the Life, Sufferings, and Escape of John Brown, a Fugitive Slave Now in England,* ed. L. A. Chamerovzow (London: n.p., 1855), 31–39; *Trial and Imprisonment of Jonathan Walker, at Pensacola, Florida, for Aiding Slaves to Escape from Bondage . . .* (1845; rpt., Boston: Anti-Slavery Office, 1848), 9–51 (prison journal quotations on 45, 50); Max L. Grivno, *Historic Resource Study: Ferry Hill Plantation* (Hagerstown, MD: U.S. Department of Interior, National Park Service, Chesapeake & Ohio Canal National Historical Park, 2007), 46; Anthony E. Kaye, *Joining Places: Slave Neighborhoods in the Old South* (Chapel Hill: University of North Carolina Press, 2007), 165. Newspaper reports confirm many of the details about Walker's internment, which became something of a cause célèbre for antislavery northerners. See, for example, *Newark (NJ) Sentinel of Freedom,* Oct. 1, 1844, p. 1.

77. B. B. Edwards, ed., *Memoir of the Rev. Elias Cornelius* (Boston: Perkins & Marvin, 1833), 101–2; Bennet H. Barrow Journal, Dec. 23–25, 1839, HT, RSP,

Series H, Reel 19; Francis Terry Leak Plantation Journal, Dec. 24, 20, 1858, SHC, RSP, Series J, pt. 6, Reel 25.

78. William H. Holcombe, "Sketches of Plantation-Life," *Knickerbocker Magazine* 57 (June 1861): 619–33 (quotation on 626).

2. Purchased at Little Cost

1. Junius Quattlebaum interview, ASCA, vol. 3, SC, pt. 3, pp. 285–86.

2. Quattlebaum interview, 283; Rose Thomas interview, ASCA-2, vol. 9, TX, pt. 8: 3825; Sarah Wilson interview, ASCA-2, vol. 109, TX, pt. 9: 4224; Prince Johnson interview, ASCA, vol. 7, MS, pt. 2: 76–80 (quotation on 80); C. Vann Woodward, "History from Slave Sources," *American Historical Review* 79 (Apr. 1974): 470–81; Paul D. Escott, *Slavery Remembered: A Record of Twentieth-Century Slave Narratives* (Chapel Hill: University of North Carolina Press, 1979), 3–17. Only a few FWP interviewers were African American. Escott, *Slavery Remembered,* 9.

3. Frank Gill interview, ASCA, vol. 6, AL, pt. 1: 151; Carrie Hudson interview, ASCA, vol. 12, GA, pt. 2: 216; Solomon Northup, *Twelve Years a Slave,* in *Puttin' On Ole Massa: The Slave Narratives of Henry Bibb, William Wells Brown, and Solomon Northup,* ed. Gilbert Osofsky (New York: Harper & Row: 1969), 342–44; Pierce Butler to his manager, quoted in *Major Butler's Legacy: Five Generations of a Slaveholding Family,* ed. Malcolm Bell Jr. (Athens: University of Georgia Press, 1987), 228; Everard Green Baker Diary, Dec. 25, 1852, SHC, RSP, Series J, pt. 6, Reel 16; Wade Hampton II to Mary, Nov. 1855, quoted in Rod Andrew Jr., *Wade Hampton: Confederate Warrior to Southern Redeemer* (Chapel Hill: University of North Carolina Press, 2008), 17.

4. Kathleen M. Hilliard, *Masters, Slaves, and Exchange: Power's Purchase in the Old South* (New York: Cambridge University Press, 2014), 137 (quotation on 134); Thomas Ruffin, *State v. Boyce,* quoted in William W. Fisher III, "Ideology and Imagery in the Law of Slavery," in Paul Finkelman, ed., *Slavery and the Law* (Lanham, MD: Rowman & Littlefield, 2002), 48.

5. C. F. Sturgis, *Melville Letters; Or, The Duties of Masters to Their Servants* (Charleston, SC: Southern Baptist Publication Society, 1851), 79; overseer quoted in Stephen Nissenbaum, *The Battle for Christmas* (New York: Alfred A. Knopf, 1996), 273.

6. Elisha Doc Garey interview, ASCA, vol. 12, GA, pt. 2: 5.

7. Charles Lanman, *Adventures in the Wilds of the United States and British North American Provinces,* vol. 2 (Philadelphia: John W. Moore, 1856), 275; Mrs. Henry Rowe Schoolcraft to John H. Howard, Sept. 20, 1851, in [Mrs. Henry Rowe Schoolcraft], *Letters on the Condition of the African Race in the United States. By a Southern Lady* (Philadelphia: T. K. and P. G. Collins, 1852), 13; Mary B. Harlan, *Ellen; or the Chained Mother, and Pictures of Kentucky Slavery. Drawn from Real Life* (Cincinnati: Applegate, 1853), 32.

8. "Sketches of South-Carolina. Number Three. 'Merry Christmas,'" *Knickerbocker* 21 (Mar. 1843): 222–29 (quotation on 227); Paul Harvey, *Moses, Jesus, and the Trickster in the Evangelical South* (Athens: University of Georgia Press, 2012), 101–3; Jake Terriell interview, ASCA-2, vol. 90, SC, pt. 8: 3772; anonymous ex-slave and later preacher quoted in ASCA, vol. 19, 148;

statistics compiled by Purdue University doctoral student Shauna Bigham for Shauna Bigham and Robert May, "The Time O' All Times? Masters, Slaves, and Christmas in the Old South," *Journal of the Early Republic* 18 (Summer 1998): 263–88 (esp. 268n); Jay Furman, ed., *Slavery in the Clover Bottom: John McCline's Narrative of His Life during Slavery and the Civil War* (Knoxville: University of Tennessee Press, 1988), 24; Irving F. Lowery, *Life on the Plantation in Ante-bellum Days, Or a Story Based on Facts* (Columbia, SC: State Company, 1911), 65; David T. Bailey, *Shadow on the Church: Southwestern Evangelical Religion and the Issue of Slavery, 1783–1860* (Ithaca, NY: Cornell University Press, 1985), 195; Albert J. Raboteau, *Slave Religion: The "Invisible Institution" in the Antebellum South* (1978; rpt., New York: Oxford University Press, 1980), 239–43. The one spiritual is suspect because its lyrics surfaced late, in James Weldon Johnson, ed., *The Books of American Negro Spirituals,* a two-volume1940 collection. If the song was authentic, it suggests slaves only had a rudimentary comprehension of Jesus's story, since it seems to conflate Jesus's birth with the exodus of Jews from Egypt. Olli Alho, *The Religion of the Slave: A Study of the Religious Tradition and Behaviour of Plantation Slaves in the United States1830–1865* (Helsinki: Academia Scientiarum Fennica, 1976), 82, 252n.

9. Martha Haines Butt, *Antifanaticism: A Tale of the South* (Philadelphia: Lippincott, Grambo, 1853), 151–59 (quotation on 159). Stowe's novel sold over 300,000 copies by the end of 1853. Butt was one of many southern authors publishing novels specifically written to rebut it. Kimberley Wallace-Sanders, *Mammy: A Century of Race, Gender, and Southern Memory* (Ann Arbor: University of Michigan Press, 2008), 24–25; Antoinette G. van Zelm, "Martha Haines Butt (1833–1871), https:www.encyclopediavirginia.org/Butt_Martha_Haines_1833-1871.

10. Roxana Chapin Gerdine to Emily McKinstry Chapin, Jan. 1, 1860, Civil War Archive, University of Mississippi, clio.lib.olemiss.edu/cdm/compoundobject/civil_war/id/1634/rec/30; Annie Rosalie Quitman Diary, Dec. 25, 1857, Dec. 25, 1858, Quitman Family Papers, SHC; Jacob Stroyer, *My Life in the South* (1879; 4th ed., Salem, MA: Newcomb & Gauss, 1898), 45.

11. Dolly Lunt Burge Diary, Dec. 25, 1853, "The Diary of Dolly Hunt Burge, pt. IV, ed. James I. Robertson Jr., *GHQ* 45 (Mar. 1961): 59; Julius Nelson interview, ASCA, vol. 15, pt. 2: 145.

12. Ruth McEnery Stuart, "Christmas Gifts" (*Lippincott's Monthly Magazine,* Jan. 1891), in *Christmas Stories from Louisiana,* ed. Dorothy Dodge Robbins and Kenneth Robbins (Jackson: University Press of Mississippi, 2009), 119–36, esp. 120–21.

13. Eliza Ripley, *Social Life in Old New Orleans: Being Recollections of My Girlhood* (New York: D. Appleton, 1912), 258; Cornelia Branch Stone, "Vivid Reminiscences of the Old Plantation," *Confederate Veteran* 20 (Dec. 1912): 568–69; Susan Bradford Eppes Diary, Dec. 22, 1857, in Eppes, *Through Some Eventful Years* (Macon, GA: J. W. Burke, 1926), 82; Lowery, *Life on the Old Plantation,* 67–68.

14. Annie Stanton and William Henry Towns interviews, ASCA, vol. 6, AL, pt. 1: 354, 391; Prince Johnson interview, ASCA, vol. 7, MS, pt. 2: 80; John Washington Narrative, in *John Washington's Civil War: A Slave Narrative,* ed. Crandall Shifflett (Baton Rouge: Louisiana State University Press, 2008), 3.

15. Hilliard, *Masters, Slaves, and Exchange,* 135–36; Furman, ed., *Slavery in the Clover Bottoms,* 24; William H. Holcombe, "Sketches of Plantation-Life," *Knickerbocker Magazine* 57 (June 1861): 619–33 (quotation on 625).

16. Hughes, *Thirty Years a Slave, 15;* Furman, ed., *Slavery in the Clover Bottoms,* 24.

17. Hilliard, *Masters, Slaves, and Exchange,* 136; Julia Floyd Smith, *Slavery and Rice Culture in Low Country Georgia, 1750–1860* (Knoxville: University of Tennessee Press, 1985), 117; Ulrich B. Phillips, ed., *Plantation and Frontier Documents, 1649–1863 . . . ,* 2 vols. (Cleveland: A. H. Clark, 1909), 1:148; John A. Selden Diary, Dec. 25, 1858, in "The Westover Journal of John A. Selden, Esqr., 1858–1862," ed. John Spencer Bassett and Sidney Bradshaw Fay, *Smith College Studies in History* 6 (July 1921): 281; John W. Milliken Plantation Journal, Dec. 25, 1854, quoted in Rosser Howard Taylor, "The Gentry of Ante-Bellum North Carolina," *North Carolina Historical Review* 17 (Apr. 1940): 114–31 (quotation on 127); Martha Forman Diary, Dec. 25, 1817, Maryland Historical Society, RSP, Series D, Reel 12; John P. Thomas Diary, Dec. 25, 1828; *Narrative of James Williams. An American Slave; Who Was for Several Years a Driver on a Cotton Plantation in Alabama* (New York: American Anti-Slavery Society, 1838), 64–65; Andrew Goodman interview, ASCA-2, vol. 4, TX, pt. 2: 1524.

18. Caroline Kiger to Basil Kiger, Dec. 22, 1852, Kiger Family Papers, Natchez Trace Collection, Center for American History, University of Texas; Thomas B. Chaplin Journal, Dec. 24, 1849, in *Tombee: Portrait of a Cotton Planter; with the Journal of Thomas B. Chaplin (1822–1890),* 480; Wade Hampton II to Mary Hampton, Dec. 26, 1850, Hampton Family Papers, SCL; Frank Gill interview, ASCA, vol. 6, AL, pt. 1: 151.

19. Mary Scott interview, ASCA, vol. 3, SC, pt. 4: 85; John Washington Narrative, in Shifflett, ed., *John Washington's Civil War,* 3; John P. Thomas Diary, Dec. 23, 1843, SCL, Series A, pt. 2, RSP; Booker T. Washington, "Christmas Days in Old Virginia," in *The Booker T. Washington Papers,* vol. 1, *Autobiographical Writings,* ed. Louis R. Harlan (Urbana: University of Illinois Press, 1972), 396.

20. Hilliard, *Masters, Slaves, and Exchange,* 132; "Narrative of Nehemiah Caulkins," *Monthly Offering* 2 (Jan./Feb. 1842): 10; *Narrative of Nehemiah Caulkins, An Extract from "American Slavery, As It Is"* (New York: American and Foreign Anti-Slavery Society, 1849), iv; Mary A. Livermore, *The Story of My Life . . .* (Hartford, CT: A. D. Worthington, 1897), 210; Bert Mayfield interview in ASCA, vol. 16, KY: p. 13; Harry Smith, *Fifty Years of Slavery in the United States of America* (1891; rpt., Mount Pleasant, MI: Clarke Historical Society, 1990), 37; Sam Polite interview in ASCA, vol. 1, SC, pt. 1: 272.

21. Correspondent of the *Salem (MA) Register,* quoted in E. S. Abdy, *Journal of a Residence and Tour in the United States of North America, From April 1833, to October, 1834,* vol. 3 (London: John Murray, 1835), 340–41.

22. John Nevitt Diary, Dec. 26, 1829, SHC, RSP, Series J, pt. 6, Reel 3; John P. Thomas Diary, Dec. 25, 1828, Dec. 23, 1843, RSP, Series A, pt. 2, Reel 5; James H. Hammond Diary, Dec. 25, 1831, SCL, RSP, South Carolina, Series A, Reel 1; Peter Clifton interview, ASCA, vol. 2, SC, pt. 1: 207; Frances Lewis interview in Ronnie W. Clayton, *Mother Wit: The Ex-Slave Narratives of the Louisiana Writers' Project* (New York: Peter Lang, 1990), 159; Thomas L. Webber,

Deep Like the Rivers: Education in the Slave Quarter Community, 1831–1865 (New York: W. W. Norton, 1978), 131, 301n.

23. Hilliard, *Masters, Slaves, and Exchange,* 144–45, 148; Ron J. Jackson Jr. and Lee Spencer White, *Joe: The Slave Who Became an Alamo Legend* (Norman: University of Oklahoma Press, 2015), 99–100; Wilma King, *Stolen Childhood: Slave Youth in Nineteenth-Century America* (1995; 2nd ed., Bloomington: Indiana University Press, 2011), 140; "Interview with Bert Mayfield," *Federal Writers' Project: Slave Narrative Project, vol. 7, Kentucky, Boogie-Woods with Combined Interviews of Others,* https://www.loc.gov/item/mesn070/; Annie Rosalie Quitman Diary, Dec. 25, 1853, John Quitman Papers, Louisiana and Lower Mississippi Valley Collections, LSU; James Redpath, *The Roving Editor: Or, Talks with Slaves in the Southern States* (New York: A. B. Burdick, 1859), 137–38.

24. Letter dated Jan. 31, 1860, in *New York Herald,* Feb. 19, 1860, p. 2; A Mississippi Planter, "Management of Negroes upon Southern Estates," *De Bow's Southern and Western Review* 10 (June 1851): 621–25.

25. Frances Lewis interview in Clayton, *Mother Wit,* 159; Lowery, *Life on the Old Plantation,* 65; Martha Bradley and Gertha Couric interviews, ASCA, vol. 6, AL, pt. 1: 11 and 46, respectively.

26. "Christmas in the Enslaved Community," listing for 1790, https://www.monticello.org/site/research-and-collections/christmas; Abigail Mason to Mary Mason Brooks, Dec. 29, 1832, in Bessie M. Henry, "A Yankee Schoolmistress Discovers Virginia," *Essex Institute Historical Collections* 101 (Jan. 1965): 121–32 (quotation on 129); Stroyer, *My Life in the South,* 45.

27. *Washington v. Emery,* in Hamilton C. Jones, Reporter, *Reports of Cases in Equity, Argued and Determined in The Supreme Court of North Carolina, From June Term, 1858, To August Term, 1859, Inclusive,* vol. 4 (Salisbury, NC: [n.p.], 1859), 32–39 (quotation on 37); William Kauffman Scarborough, *The Allstons of Chicora Wood: Wealth, Honor, and Gentility in the South Carolina Lowcountry* (Baton Rouge: Louisiana State University Press, 2011), 44; John P. Thomas Diary, Dec. 25, 1831, RSP, Series A, pt. 2; Hilliard, *Masters, Slaves, and Exchange,* 146.

28. Hilliard, *Masters, Slaves, and Exchange,* 146, 142; Richard Follett, *The Sugar Masters: Planters and Slaves in Louisiana's Cane World, 1820–1860* (Baton Rouge: Louisiana State University Press, 2005), 157–58; "The Farm and Farming of the Rev. J. H. Turner," *Farmers' Register* 10 (Mar. 1842): 127–30.

29. James H. Hammond Diary, Dec. 25, 1832, SCL, RSP, South Carolina, Series 1, Reel 1.

30. Louis Hughes, *Thirty Years a Slave, From Bondage to Freedom . . .* (Milwaukee: South Side Printing, 1897), 15; Ralph B. Flanders, "Two Plantations and a County of Antebellum Georgia," *GHQ* 12 (Mar. 1928): 11–12; Northup, *Twelve Years a Slave,* 342–44.

31. *The State* v. *Jacob Boyce,* December 1849, North Carolina Supreme Court, Raleigh, http://www.slavery.amdigital.co.uk. Bill Cecil-Fronsman notes that the Perquimans County case may have represented a case of common white southerners in the area venting their resentment of the slaveholding aristocracy. Bill Cecil-Fronsman, *Common Whites: Class and Culture in Antebellum North Carolina* (Lexington: University Press of Kentucky, 1992), 86.

32. Edmund Ruffin Diary, Dec. 26, 1859, *The Diary of Edmund Ruffin,* vol. 1, *Toward Independence, October 1856–April, 1861,* ed. William Kauffman Scarborough (Baton Rouge: Louisiana State University Press 1972), 385; Sarah Wilson interview, ASCA-2, vol. 109, TX, pt. 9: 4224; Adele Petigru Allston to Benjamin Allston, Jan. 1, 1857, in *The South Carolina Rice Plantation as Revealed in the Papers of Robert F. W. Allston,* ed. J. H. Easterby (Chicago: University of Chicago Press, 1945), 135–36.

33. Susan Dabney Smedes, *Memorials of a Southern Planter,* ed. Fletcher M. Green (1887; rpt., New York: Alfred A. Knopf, 1965), 149; James E. Bagwell, *Rice Gold: James Hamilton Couper and Plantation Life on the Georgia Coast* (Macon, GA: Mercer University Press, 2000), 17; Louis Cain interview, ASCA, vol. 4, TX, pt. 1: 186.

34. Northup, *Twelve Years a Slave,* 342; Basil Hall, *Travels in North America, in the Years 1827 and 1828,* vol. 3 (Edinburgh: Cadell, 1830), 224.

35. John Nevitt Diary, Dec. 27, 1828, Dec. 26, 1829, SHC, RSP, Series J, pt. 6, Reel 3; Stroyer, *My Life in the South,* 45; Matthew Mulcahy, *Hubs of Empire: The Southeastern Lowcountry and British Caribbean* (Baltimore: Johns Hopkins University Press, 2014), 133; Roswell King Jr. to Pierce Butler, June 1823, quoted in Bell, ed., *Major Butler's Legacy,* 236; James Battle Avirett, *The Old Plantation: How We Lived in Great House and Cabin Before the War (New York: F. Tennyson Neely, 1901),* 175. For mention of an abstemious master, see, for example, James Lucas interview, ASCA, vol. 7, MS, pt. 2: 92.

36. Peter Clifton interview, ASCA, vol. 2, SC, pt. 2: 207; Noel Leo Erskine, *Plantation Church: How African American Religion Was Born in Colonial Slavery* (New York: Oxford University Press, 2014), 55; Ezra Martin interview in "A Slave-Time Christmas," *Macon (GA) Telegraph,* Dec. 27, 1898, p. 7; Will Adams interview, ASCA, vol. 4, TX, pt. 1: 2; James Boyd interview, ASCA, vol. 4, pt. 1: 118.

37. Adele Allston to Robert F. W. Allston quoted in Scarborough, *Allstons of Chicora Wood,* 45; Dena J. Epstein, "Slave Music in the United States before 1860: A Survey of Sources (Part 2), *Notes for the Music Library Association* 20 (Summer 1964): 382; Hillary A. Herbert quoted in *NODP,* Dec. 24, 1893, p. 19.

38. Robert F. W. Allston Diary, Dec. 1859 (exact date unclear), in Easterby, ed., *South Carolina Rice Plantation,* 453; John Blassingame, *The Slave Community: Plantation Life in the Ante-Bellum South* (New York: Oxford University Press, 1972), 19–20; John Pierpont journal quoted in Abe C. Ravitz, "John Pierpont and the Slaves' Christmas," *Phylon* 21 (No. 4, 1960): 383–86.

39. Lanman, *Adventures,* 132; Blassingame, *Slave Community,* 55; Roxana Chapin Gerdine to Emily McKinstry Chapin, Jan. 1, 1860, Civil War Archive, University of Mississippi, clio.lib.olemiss.edu/cdm/compoundobject /civil_war/id/1634/rec/30; [Virginia Clay-Clopton], *A Belle of the Fifties: Memoirs of Mrs. Clay, of Alabama, Covering Social and Political Life in Washington and the South, 1853-66* (New York: Doubleday, Page, 1905), 217. The term "juba" probably derived from the recently deceased northern black minstrel performer "Juba" (William Henry Lane), famous for his "Ethiopian" dances. Eric Lott, *Love and Theft: Blackface Minstrelsy and the American Working Class* (New York: Oxford University Press, 1993), 113–15; T. Allston Brown and Charles Day, "Black

Musicians and Early Ethiopian Minstrelsy," *Black Perspective in Music* 3 (Spring 1975): 77–99, esp. 81–82.

40. John P. Thomas Diary, Dec. 27, 1828; Hillary A. Herbert quoted in *NODP,* Dec. 24, 1893, p. 19; Gus Feaster interview, ASCA, vol. 2, SC, pt. 2: 69, Elvira Boles interview, ASCA, vol. 4, TX, pt. 1: 107; James Lucas interview, ASCA, vol. 7, MS, pt. 2: 92.

41. Ripley, *Social Life in Old New Orleans,* 256–58.

42. Allston Basil Kiger to his wife, Oct. 29, 1852, quoted in Christopher Morris, *Becoming Southern: The Evolution of a Way of Life, Warren County and Vicksburg, Mississippi, 1770*-1860 (New York: Oxford University Press, 1995), 69, 224n; Natalie Delage Sumter Diary, December 26, 1840 (typescript copy), SCL, RSP, Series A, pt. 2, Reel 4; Richard J. Arnold Plantation Journal, Dec. 24–29, 1847, in Charles Hoffmann and Tess Hoffman, *North by South: The Two Lives of Richard James Arnold* (Athens: University of Georgia Press, 1988), 130–31; T. B. Thorpe, "Christmas in the South," *Frank Leslie's Illustrated Newspaper,* Dec. 26, 1847, p. 62.

43. Richard H. Steckel, "Slave Marriage and the Family," *Journal of Family History* 5 (Winter 1980): 406–21, esp. 411; Annie Rosalie Quitman Diary, Jan. 10, 1857, Quitman Family Papers, Southern Historical Collection, University of North Carolina; Charles Parker Gizzard, "A Glimpse of the South in the Spring of 1855" (handwritten travel journal), Beinecke Rare Book and Manuscript Library, Yale University, p. 70.

44. Gordon Bluford interview, ASCA, vol. 2, SC, pt. 1: 63; Washington, "Christmas Days in Old Virginia," 396.

45. Henry W. Ravenel Diary, Dec. 28, 1859, in Childs, ed., *Private Journal,* 4.

46. Sally Strong Baxter Hampton to her father, Dec. 1860, quoted in Andrew, *Wade Hampton,* 19–20; Chaplin Journal, Dec. 26, 1849, Dec. 25, 1850, Rosengarten, ed., *Tombee,* 481, 516; John Houston Bills Diary, Dec. 26, 1856, quoted in Ted Ownby, *American Dreams in Mississippi: Consumers, Poverty & Culture* (Chapel Hill: University of North Carolina Press, 1999), 50.

47. Redpath, *Roving Editor,* 92; Charles Thompson quoted in William Still, *The Underground Rail Road: A Record of Facts, Authentic Narratives, Letters, &c. . . .* (Philadelphia: Porte & Coates, 1872), 146; Bennet H. Barrow Plantation Journal (edited typescript), Dec. 28, 1842, HT, RSP, Series H, Reel 19; James H. Hammond Diary, Dec. 25, 1845, RSP, South Carolina, Series A, Reel 1; Hilliard, *Masters, Slaves, and Exchange,* 143.

48. Sam Polite interview, ASCA, vol. 3, SC, pt. 3: 273; Fayette Stephens interview, ASCA-2, vol. 9, TX, pt. 8: 3728; Gordon Bluford interview, ASCA, vol. 2, SC pt. 1: 63; Marilda Pethy interview, ASCA, vol. 11, MO: 277–78; Sylvia Durant interview, ASCA, vol. 2, SC, vol. 2, pt. 1: 343.

49. Jeff Forret, *Slave Against Slave: Plantation Violence in the Old South* (Baton Rouge: Louisiana State University Press, 2015), 58–59, 191, 274–75, 304, 77, 85–86.

50. Francis Fedric, *Slave Life in Virginia and Kentucky, or, Fifty Years of Slavery in the Southern States of America* (London: Wertheim, Macintosh, and Hunt, 1863), 29.

51. Will Adams interview, ASCA, vol. 4, TX, pt. 1: 2.

52. Stroyer, *My Life in the South,* 45; Campbell Davis interview, ASCA, vol. 4, TX, pt. 1: 286; *Wilkinson (MS) Whig,* quoted in *Sunbury (PA) American,* Mar. 10,

1849, p. 1, and *Water-Cure Journal, and Herald of Reforms,* June 1, 1849, p. 165; Don S. McKinney, "Moral Agency in Nineteenth Century Slave Culture: Perspectives on the Literature of the Slave Community," *Western Journal of Black Studies* 15 (Spring 1991): 24–30, esp. 30. The same bee lines appear in a different context in escaped slave William Wells Brown's later, important 1853 novel, *Clotel; or the President's Daughter: A Narrative of Slave Life in The United States* (London: Partridge & Oakey, 1853), 137–38. Brown's version has a "cruel master" surnamed Peck give each slave a dram of whiskey before making the toast request, assuming they will give compliant remarks and impress a group of visiting northerners with their contentment at his ownership. All the slaves comply, suggesting their contentment, until Jack, supposedly the "most witty slave on the farm," speaks the bee verse.

53. Wade Hampton to Mary Hampton, Dec. 26, 1853, Hampton Family Papers, SCL; Henry W. Ravenel Diary, Dec. 28, 1859, in Childs, ed., *Private Journal,* 4.

54. Solomon Northup quoted in Walter Johnson, *River of Dark Dreams: Slavery and Empire in the Cotton Kingdom* (Cambridge, MA: Harvard University Press, 2013), 227; Roswell King to Pierce Butler, Jan. 18, 1818, quoted in Bell, *Major Butler's Legacy,* 219; John P. Thomas Diary, Dec. 28, 1838.

55. Roxana Gerdine to Emily McKinstry Chapin, Dec. [no exact date], Civil War Archive, University of Mississippi, clio.lib.olemiss.edu/cdm/compoundobject/civil_war/id/1629/rec/9; Sarah (Haynesworth) Gayle Diary, Dec. 25, 1834, University of Alabama Library, *American Women's Diaries* (Southern), Readex Film Products; Charles A. Slack to John Slack, Dec. 25, 1846, quoted in Follett, *Sugar Masters,* 164; Daniel R. Hundley, *Social Relations in Our Southern States,* ed. William J. Cooper Jr. (1860; rpt. with a new introduction by Cooper, Baton Rouge: Louisiana State University Press, 1979), 359–60.

56. *Washington (D.C.) Sentinel,* quoted in *Albany Evening Journal,* reprinted in (Salem, OH) *Anti-Slavery Bugle,* July 19, 1856, p. 1; George Fitzhugh, *Cannibals All! or Slaves without Masters,* ed. C. Vann Woodward (1857; rpt., Cambridge, MA: Harvard University Press, 1960), 18; Thomas Frean, "A PARODY ON 'MASSACHUSETTS VS. SOUTH CAROLINA,'" republished from *South Carolinean* in *Boston Atlas,* Apr. 11, 1845; Solon Robinson, "Wages of Labor," in *Charleston Mercury,* republished in *Edgefield (SC) Advertiser,* Jan. 9, 1851, p. 1. See also Louis Sweet, letter dated Nashville, Apr. 22, 1858, in (Boston) *The Liberator,* May 7, 1858, p. 75, and South Carolina slave owner William Elliott's allusion to the "christmas jubilee" in his pseudonymous assertion that blacks lacked the self-restraint to survive emancipation. "Agricola," "Slavery. No. 5," in *Columbia (SC) Telescope,* Sept. 17, 1833, p. 1.

57. W. Gilmore Simms, "Maize-in-Milk: A Christmas Story of the South," *Godey's Lady's Book* 34 (Feb. 1847), 62–67, (Mar. 1847), 146–52, (Apr. 1847), 199–204, (May 1847), 249–58; Drew Gilpin Faust, *A Sacred Circle: The Dilemma of the Intellectual in the Old South, 1840–1860* (1977; rpt., Philadelphia: University of Pennsylvania Press, 1986), 27–28, 126; John McCardell, *The Idea of a Southern Nation: Southern Nationalists and Southern Nationalism, 1830–1860* (New York: W. W. Norton, 1979), 145–51 (quotation on 151).

58. Simms, "Maize-in-Milk," 62–66, 148–49, 201–2 (quotations on 44, 204, 201, 66).

59. Simms, "Maize-in-Milk," 249–58.

60. Susan Bradford Eppes Diary, Dec. 26, 1859, in Eppes, *Through Some Eventful Years,* 121; Sally Strong Baxter Hampton to her father, Dec. 1860, quoted in Andrew, *Wade Hampton,* 19–20.

61. *New York Tribune* correspondent quoted in *New York Evening News* and reprinted in *New York Evangelist,* Dec. 11, 1845, p. 198; *Albany Evening Journal* quoted in (Salem, OH) *Anti-Slavery Bugle,* July 19, 1856, p. 1.

62. Louis Cain interview, ASCA, vol. 4, Texas, pt. 1, p. 186; Natalie Delage Sumter Diary, December 26, 1840 (typescript copy), SCL, RSP, Series A, pt. 2, Reel 4.

63. Henry W. Huntington to William N. Mercer, Dec. 27, 1836, William N. Mercer Papers, HT, RSP, Series H, Reel 24.

3. Human Trafficking on Jesus's Birthday

1. *Macon (GA) Telegraph,* Dec. 24, 1827.

2. *A Codification of the Statute Law of Georgia, Including the English Statutes of Force: In Four Parts* (1845; 2nd ed., Augusta, GA: Charles E. Grenville, 1848), 772; Posey Account Book, Jan. 1, 1854, Maryland Historical Society, RSP, Series D, Reel 10.

3. John Nevitt Diary, Dec. 24, 1831, RSP, Series J, Reel 3; Minute Book, Citizens Bank of Louisiana, Dec. 24, 1847, Reel 15, Dec. 26, 1854, Dec. 24, 1855, Dec. 26, 1856, Reel 16, Dec. 26, 1859, Dec. 24, 1860, Dec. 26, 1861, Reel 17, HT, RSP, Series H, Reel 17; John Porter to John McDonough, Dec. 25, 1830, Andrew Dumford to McDonough, Dec. 24, 1843, Dec. 25, 1844, 1845, John McDonough Papers, HT, RSP, Series H, Reel 7; Bennet H. Barrow Plantation Journal (edited typescript), Dec. 25, 1842, HT, RSP, Series H, Reel 19; entry Dec. 25, 1839, Land Transaction Register, Robert Ruffin Barrow Papers, HT, Series H, Reel 19, RSP; Freight charge receipt, Dec. 24, 1852, Lestan Prudhomme Papers, HT, RSP, Series H, Reel 21.

4. *Irish v. Wright et al.,* in *New Orleans Commercial Bulletin,* July 8, 1844; John Tyler to James Madison, Oct. 28, 1811, in *The Letters and Times of the Tylers,* ed. Lyon G. Tyler, vol. 1 (New York: Da Capo Press, 1970), 2540–55; Deed of Sale, Dec. 24, 1836, Everett Family Papers, HT, RSP, Series H, Reel 27; Louisa Maxwell Holmes Cocke Diary, Dec. 25, 1837, Cocke Family Papers, University of Virginia, *American Women's Diaries: Southern Women,* Readex Film Products, Reel 3; (Austin, TX) *Southern Intelligencer,* Dec. 30, 1857, p. 2.

5. *Chicago Times* correspondent's letter, Jan. 12, 1853, quoted in *Syracuse (NY) Evening Chronicle,* Mar. 7, 1853, p. 2.

6. Dale Edwyna Smith, *The Slaves of Liberty: Freedom in Amite County, Mississippi, 1820–1868* (New York: Garland, 1999), 45–47; *Irish v. Wright et al., New Orleans Commercial Bulletin,* July 8, 1844; R. J. M. Blackett, *The Captives Quest for Freedom: Fugitive Slaves, the 1850 Fugitive Slave Law, and the Politics of Slavery* (New York: Cambridge University Press, 2018), 276–77.

7. Martha A. M. Lide Receipt to Ezra J. Pugh and John A. Miller, Dec. 28, 1851, Miscellaneous Collections, SCL, RSP, Series A, pt. 2, Reel 18; Citizens Bank of Louisiana Minute Book, Dec. 23, 1851, HT, RSP, Reel 15.

8. Wilma A. Dunaway, *The African-American Family in Slavery and Emancipation* (New York: Cambridge University Press, 2003), 59; John Thompson, *The Life of John Thompson, A Fugitive Slave; Containing His History of 25 Years in Bondage and His Providential Escape* (Worcester, MA: John Thompson, 1856), 28.

9. Lydia Maria Child to the editor (with an unnamed relative's letter quoted at length), in *New York Independent,* Apr. 5, 1866, p. 1; *The Life of Samuel Hall, a Slave for Forty-Seven Years* (Washington, IA: Journal Print, 1912), 28, docssouth.unc .edu/neh/hall/hall.htm.

10. Kate Clifford Larson, *Bound for the Promised Land: Harriet Tubman, Portrait of an American Hero* (New York: Ballantine Books, 2004), 110-15.

11. http://www.rootsweb.ancestry.com/~scsumter/wills/volume2/mwills /millerjohnb.htm; John Hightower to Henry Clayton sale document, Dec. 29, 1856, Henry De Lamar Clayton, Sr. Papers, William Stanley Hoole Special Collections Library, University of Alabama Digital Collections, acumen.lib .ua.edu/u0003/0313/0000886/0001/?page=1&limit=40; Slave Bill of Sale by Thomas W. Coleman, Christian County, Kentucky, to Robert D. Winder, Dec. 24, 1833, Slavery Manuscript Series, HT, RSP, Series H, Reel 20.

12. William Wikoff to Daniel Wikoff, "Christmas Day, 1810," Robert Ruffin Barrow Papers, HT, RSP, Series H, Reel 18.

13. James L. Petigru to Adele Petigru Allston, Dec. 21, 1858, Petigru to Robert F. W. Allston, Dec. 29 (continued on Dec. 30), 1858, in James H. Easterby, ed., *The South Carolina Rice Plantation as Revealed in the Papers of Robert F. W. Allston* (Chicago: University of Chicago Press, 1945), 148, 149; James Walker to James K. Polk, Jan. 1, 1847, in *Correspondence of James K. Polk,* vol. 12, *January–July 1847* (Knoxville: University of Tennessee Press, 2013), 23-25.

14. Richard T. Earle to James Hollyday, Jan. 24, 1824, Hollyday Family Papers, Maryland Historical Society, RSP, Series D, Reel 4; James Hamilton Couper to his wife, Dec. 24, 1835, in Brooks, ed., "Letters of James Hamilton Couper," 150-73 (quotation on 163); James E. Bagwell, *Rice Gold: James Hamilton Couper and Plantation Life on the Georgia Coast* (Macon. GA: Mercer University Press, 2000), 28-31; Anna King to Thomas Butler King, Dec. 27, 1844, in *Anna: The Letters of a St. Simons Island Plantation Mistress, 1817-1859* (Athens: University of Georgia Press, 2002), 31; William A. Whittle to Lewis Whittle, Dec. 21, 1858, Lewis Neale Whittle Papers, SHC; Maud C. Fentress to David Fentress, Dec. 25, 1860 (typed transcript), University of North Texas Libraries, Special Collections, Denton, TX, http:/texashistory.unt.edu/ark:/67531.

15. Robert J. Gage quoted in Lacy K. Ford Jr., *Origins of Southern Radicalism: The South Carolina Upcountry, 1800-1860* (New York: Oxford University Press, 1988), 37; William Ethelbert Ervin Diary, Dec. 23, 1846, SHC, RSP, Series J, Reel 17; James Henry Hammond to Harry Hammond, December 28, 1856, James H. Hammond Papers, SCL, RSP, Series A, pt. 1, Reel 10.

16. Francis Terry Lake Plantation Journal, Dec. 24, 1852, Jan. 1, 1853, SHC, RSP, Series J, Reel 24.

17. Larry E. Rivers, "Slavery and the Political Economy of Gadsden County, Florida: 1823-1861," *Florida Historical Quarterly* 70 (July 1991): 1-19, esp. 16; T. H. N. letter, Dec. 25, 1852, in *Philadelphia Presbyterian,* Jan. 15, 1853; Midori Takagi, *Rearing Wolves to Our Own Destruction: Slavery in Richmond, Virginia,*

1783–1865 (Charlottesville: University Press of Virginia, 1999), 38–39; Thomas W. McCue to Samuel Dixon, Dec. 24, 1847, James McDowell Papers, SHC; Orville Vernon Burton, *In My Father's House Are Many Mansions: Family and Community in Edgefield, South Carolina* (Chapel Hill: University of North Carolina Press, 1985), 174.

18. A. J. McElveen to Z. B. Oakes, Dec. 23, 29, 1854, Dec. 30, 1856, in *Broke by the War: Letters of a Slave Trader,* ed. Edmund L. Drago (Columbia: University of South Carolina Press, 1991), 109–10, 138; Anthony E. Kaye, *Joining Places: Slave Neighborhoods in the Old South* (Chapel Hill: University of North Carolina Press, 2007), 27–28; Steve Deyle, *Carry Me Back: The Domestic Slave Trade in American Life* (New York: Oxford University Press, 2005), 125.

19. *Richmond Daily Dispatch,* May 14, 1861, p. 1; Vicksburg (MS) *Register,* Dec. 22, 1836, p. 2. There were additional such notices on page 3.

20. *Richmond Enquirer,* Dec. 25, 1854.

21. Jennifer Oast, *Institutional Slavery: Slaveholding Churches, Schools, Colleges, and Businesses in Virginia, 1680–1860* (New York: Cambridge University Press, 2016), 109.

22. "Days of Slavery: Incidents of Those Times Recalled by Ex-Slaves," *Syracuse (NY) Sunday Herald,* Nov. 1, 1896, p. 9; Dunaway, *African-American Family,* 41; John J. Zaborney, *Slaves for Hire: Renting Enslaved Laborers in Antebellum Virginia* (Baton Rouge: Louisiana State University Press, 2012), 10, 58 (Kelly quotation), 61, 66; Linda Brent [Harriet Brent Jacobs], *Incidents in the Life of a Slave Girl,* ed. Lydia Maria Child (1861; paper ed. with new introduction and notes by Walter Teller, New York: Harcourt Brace Jovanovich, 1973), 13. For other Christmas Day contracts, see, for instance, Aaron Astor, *Rebels on the Border: Civil War Emancipation, and the Reconstruction of Kentucky and Missouri* (Baton Rouge: Louisiana State University Press, 2012), 26; J. Winston Coleman Jr., *Slavery Times in Kentucky* (Chapel Hill: University of North Carolina Press, 1940), 125.

23. *The Liberty Almanac for 1847* (New York: William Harned, [1846?], unpaged; (Boston) *The Liberator,* July 21, 1854, p. 15; (Salem, OH) *Anti-Slavery Bugle,* Jan. 26, 1856, p. 2.

24. *Thirty Years a Slave, From Bondage to Freedom. The Institution of Slavery as Seen on the Plantation and in the Home of the Planter. Autobiography of Louis Hughes* (Milwaukee: South Side Printing, 1897), 5, 15.

25. J. Vance Lewis, "Out of the Ditch: A True Story of an Ex-Slave," p. 8, in "Documenting the American South," University Library, University of North Carolina, docsouth.edu/neh/lewisj.html; "Marse Tom's Chrismus Gif'," *Galveston (TX) Daily News,* Dec. 25, 1892, p. 12; *Unwritten History of Slavery: Autobiographical Accounts of Negro Ex-Slaves* [typescript], Social Science Source Documents No. 1 (Fisk University: Social Science Institute, 1945), 226; "Relatives Fight for the Property of Mrs. Henrietta Daniels," *NYT,* Nov. 22, 1883, p. 1.

26. Robert Russa Moton, *Finding a Way Out: An Autobiography* (Garden City, NY: Doubleday, Page), 6.

27. William R. Smith speech, Jan. 25, 1861, in Smith, comp. and ed., *The History and Debates of the People of Alabama, Begun and held in the City of Montgomery, on the Seventh Day of January, 1861* . . . (Montgomery, AL: White, Pfister, 1861), 201. Smith's remarks came in the context of applauding the long-outlawed African

slave trade for having beneficially civilized African blacks, though he stated opposition to its relegalization as policy.

28. Robert E. Lee to his wife, Dec. 27, 1856, quoted in Douglas Southall Freeman, *R. E. Lee: A Biography,* vol. 1 (New York: Charles Scribner's Sons, 1945), 370–73.

29. Susan Bradford Eppes Diary, Mar. 9, Dec. 22, 1854, and narrative material, in Eppes, *Through Some Eventful Years* (Macon, GA: J. W. Burke, 1926), 46, 53, 30.

30. LaSalle Corbell Pickett, *Yule Log* (Washington, D.C.: Neale, 1900), 33–34.

4. GAMING THE SYSTEM

1. James Battle Avirett, *The Old Plantation: How We Lived in Great House and Cabin Before the War* (New York: F. Tennyson Neely, 1901), 178.

2. Louise-Clarke Pyrnelle, *Diddie, Dumps, and Tot, or Plantation Child-Life* (New York: Harper & Brothers, 1882), 29, v; "Marse Tom's Chrismus Gif'," *Galveston (TX) Daily News,* Dec. 25, 1891, p. 12; F. G. de Fontaine, "A Plantation Xmas," American Associated Press 1901, reprinted in *Atchison (KS) Daily* Globe, Jan. 1, 1892; James C. Plummer, "In the Quarter," *Milwaukee Sentinel,* Dec. 18, 1887. For more on Pyrnelle, see Paula T. Connolly, *Slavery in American Children's Literature, 1790–2010* (Iowa City: University of Iowa Press, 2013), 103; Joyce Kelley, "Louise Clarke Pyrnelle," *Encyclopedia of Alabama,* http://www .encyclopediaofalabama.org/article/h-2525.

3. Susan Dabney Smedes, *Memorials of a Southern Planter,* ed. Fletcher M. Green (1887; rpt., New York: Alfred A. Knopf, 1965), 150; Joel Chandler Harris, *On the Plantation: A Story of a Georgia Boy's Adventures during the War* (New York: D. Appleton, 1905), 119–20; A. M. Paynter, "Christmas in the Old Southern Home," *Christian Observer,* Dec. 13, 1899, p. 19.

4. Elizabeth W. Allston Pringle, *Chronicles of Chicora Wood* (New York: Charles Scribner's Sons, 1922), 151–52.

5. Charlemae Rollins, comp., *Christmas Gif'* (Chicago: Follett Publishing, 1963), page 8 of foreword [pages unnumbered]; Louisa Davis interview, ASCA, vol. 2, SC, pt. 1: 301–2; Booker T. Washington, *Up from Slavery: An Autobiography* (1901), in *The Booker T. Washington Papers,* vol. 1, *The Autobiographical Writings,* ed. Louis R. Harlan (Urbana: University of Illinois Press, 1972), 286; Julia Peterkin, *A Plantation Christmas* (1929; rpt., Boston: Houghton Mifflin, 1934), 24–25; Elizabeth Robeson, "Life Out of Darkness: The Recovery of Julia Peterkin, Forgotten Pulitzer Prize Winner," *Readex Report,* 8, Issue 1, www .readex.com/readex-report/life-out-darkness-recover-julia-peterkin-forgotten -pulitzer-prize-winner.

6. Penne L. Restad, *Christmas in America: A History* (New York: Oxford University Press, 1995), 66. For a suggestion that eventually southern white elite families adopted Christmas Gif' for themselves, see Elizabeth Findley Shores, *Earline's Pink Party: The Social Rituals and Domestic Relics of a Southern Woman* (Tuscaloosa: University of Alabama Press, 2017), 74.

7. Ella Gertrude Clanton Diary, Dec. 25, 1851, in *The Secret Eye: The Journal of Ella Gertrude Clanton Thomas, 1848–1889,* ed. Virginia Ingraham Burr (Chapel Hill: University of North Carolina Press, 1990), 94.

8. De Fontaine, "A Plantation Xmas"; Smedes, *Memorials of a Southern Planter*, 150.

9. Pyrnelle, *Diddie, Dumps, and Tot*, v–vi; Avirett, *The Old Plantation*, dedication page (unnumbered), v–ix.

10. Stephen Nissenbaum, *The Battle for Christmas* (New York: Alfred A. Knopf, 1996), 271, 279.

11. Betty Wood, *Women's Work, Men's Work: The Informal Slave Economies of Low-country Georgia* (Athens: University of Georgia Press, 1995), 203n; Sarah Wilson interview, ASCA-2, vol. 10, TX, pt. 9: 4223; Annie Rosalie Quitman Diary, Dec. 25, 1853, John Quitman Papers, Louisiana and Lower Mississippi Valley Collections, LSU; Kathleen M. Hilliard, *Masters, Slaves, and Exchange: Power's Purchase in the Old South* (New York: Cambridge University Press, 2014), 5, 15, 21ff, 33, 55.

12. Joseph B. Cobb, "The Old Negress and Her Son," in *Mississippi Scenes; Or, Sketches of Southern and Western Life and Adventure . . .* (Philadelphia: A. Hart, 1851), 85–86; John B. Padgett, "Joseph Beckham Cobb," *The Mississippi Writers Page*, mwp.olemiss.edu/dir/cobb_joseph_beckham/; Dwight L. Smith, "An Antebellum Boyhood: Samuel Escue Tillman on a Middle Tennessee Plantation," *Tennessee Historical Quarterly* 47 (Spring 1988): 3–9, esp. 8; William Faulkner, *The Sound and the Fury* (1929; rpt., New York: Random House, 1956), 106–7. Contrarily, white memoirist Esther Reynolds claimed that white children wanted to "catch" family servants, but that the latter were simply quicker. Reynolds, *Memoirs of Mulberry* (Brooklyn, NY: Eagle Press, 1913), 9.

13. Peter Bruner, *A Slave's Adventures toward Freedom: Not Fiction but the True Story of a Struggle* (Oxford, OH: n.p., 1918), 16–22. For the legitimacy of this text as nonfiction, see http://docsouth.unc.edu/neh/bruner/summary.html.

14. Frances J. B. Robertson Diary, Alabama Department of History, Montgomery, *American Women's Diaries* (Southern), Readex Film Productions, p. 354; Daniel R. Hundley, *Social Relations in Our Southern States,* ed. William J. Cooper Jr. (1860; rpt., Baton Rouge: Louisiana State University Press, 1979), 360–61; Annie Rosalie Quitman Diary, Quitman Family Papers, SHC; Richard Follett, *The Sugar Masters: Planters and Slaves in Louisiana's Cane World, 1820–1860* (Baton Rouge: Louisiana State University Press, 2005), 164. Stephen Nissenbaum argues that aggressive shouting by slaves to arouse the big house at the "crack of dawn" was "a ritually sanctioned way for slaves to get away with rousing white people from a night's sleep." Nissenbaum, *Battle for Christmas,* 280.

15. Abraham Lincoln, Address at Cooper Institute, New York City, Feb. 27, 1860, in *The Collected Works of Abraham Lincoln,* ed. Roy P. Basler, 9 vols. (New Brunswick, NJ: Rutgers University Press, 1953–1955), 3:540.

16. Sterling Stuckey, *Slave Culture: Nationalist Theory and the Foundations of Black America* (New York: Oxford University Press, 1987), 67; Nissenbaum, *Battle for Christmas,* 283–85; Marvin L. Michael Kay and Lorin Lee Cary, *Slavery in North Carolina, 1748-1775* (Chapel Hill: University of North Carolina Press, 1995), 183; Linda Brent (Harriet Jacobs), *Incidents in the Life of a Slave Girl,* ed. Lydia Maria Child (1861; new ed., New York: Harcourt Brace Jovanovich, 1973), 121; Dougald MacMillan, "John Kuners," *Journal of American Folklore* 39 (Jan.–Mar. 1926): 53–57; Margaret M. Mulrooney, *Race, Place, and Memory: Deep*

Currents in Wilmington, North Carolina (Gainesville: University Press of Florida, 2018), 67–68. Generally the holiday was called Jonkonnu in Jamaica and one of the other names in the United States. Mulrooney notes that antebellum Kuners in Wilmington performed a skit at the Market House to conclude their procession, which referenced the biblical story of Noah and Ham that some southerners used to justify slavery on religious grounds. Mulrooney, *Race, Place, and Memory,* 69–70.

17. C. Nigel Bolland, "Creolisation and Creole Societies: A Cultural Nationalist View of Caribbean Social History," *Caribbean Quarterly* 44 (Mar. 1998): 24; Douglas B. Chambers, *Murder at Montpelier: Igbo Africans in Virginia* (Jackson: University Press of Mississippi, 2005), 181–82; Kay and Cary, *Slavery in North Carolina,* 183–84; David S. Cecelski, *The Waterman's Song: Slavery and Freedom in Maritime North Carolina* (Chapel Hill: University of North Carolina Press, 2001), 14–19, 27–28, 141; Michael Craton, "Decoding Pitchy-Patchy: The Roots, Branches and Essence of Junkanoo," *Slavery & Abolition* 16 (Apr. 1995): 14–44, esp. 14, 29. Blacks may have originated and performed John Canoe in Jamaica by the mid-1680s. Elizabeth A. Fenn, "'A Perfect Equality Seemed to Reign': Slave Society and Jonkonnu," *North Carolina Historical Review* 65 (Apr. 1988): 127–53, esp. 127–32.

18. Matthew Gregory Lewis Journal, Jan. 1, 1816, in Lewis, *Journal of a Residence among the Negroes in the West Indies* (1834; new ed., London: John Murray, 1861), 23–24. Banjees were stringed musical instruments of African derivation related to the later banjo.

19. Stuckey, *Slave Culture,* 106; Kay and Cary, *Slavery in North Carolina,* 183; "Scenes in North Carolina," (Boston) *The Liberator,* May 26, 1837, p. 85.

20. Warren quoted in Dorothy Spruill Redford with Michael D'Orso, *Somerset Homecoming: Recovering a Lost Heritage* (New York: Doubleday, 1988), 157–58; Brent, *Incidents,* 121.

21. Rebecca Cameron, "Christmas at Buchoi, a North Carolina Rice Plantation," *The North Carolina Booklet* 13 (July 1913), 3–10 (quotations on 8), reprinted from *Ladies Home Journal* Christmas issue 1891.

22. Rev. Moses Ashley Curtis quoted in Bertram Wyatt-Brown, *Southern Honor: Ethics and Behavior in the Old South* (New York: Oxford University Press, 1982), 444. My argument here is based on Bolland, "Creole Societies," 24; Nissenbaum, *Battle for Christmas,* 290–91; Elizabeth Maddock Dillon, *New World Drama: The Performative Commons in the Atlantic World, 1649–1849* (Durham, NC: Duke University Press, 2014), 203–5; Fenn, "Perfect Equality," 132n.

23. Warren's account in *Somerset Homecoming,* 158; Cameron, "Christmas at Buchoi," 9.

24. Cameron, "Christmas at Buchoi," 9; Brent, *Incidents,* 122.

25. "Scenes in North Carolina," *The Liberator.*

26. Anthony E. Kaye, "The Problem of Autonomy: Toward a Postliberal History," in *New Directions in Slavery Studies: Commodification, Community, and Comparison,* ed. Jeff Forret and Christine E. Sears (Baton Rouge: Louisiana State University Press, 2015), 150–75.

27. Swithin Wilmot, "The Politics of Protest in Free Jamaica—The Kingston John Canoe Christmas Riots, 1840 and 1841," *Caribbean Quarterly* 36 (Dec.

1990): 65–70 (quotation on 65); Raymond Gavins, "North Carolina Black Folklore and Song in the Age of Segregation: Toward Another Meaning of Survival," *North Carolina Historical Review* 66 (Oct. 1989): 412–42, esp. 416–18.

5. WINTERS OF THEIR DISCONTENT

1. "News from Washington" dated Dec. 15, 1861, in *New York Herald,* Dec. 16, 1861, p. 1.

2. James W. King to Jenny, Dec. 26, 1861, in *Conspicuous Gallantry: The Civil War and Reconstruction Letters of James W. King, 11th Michigan Volunteer Infantry,* ed. Eric R. Faust (Kent, OH: Kent State University Press, 2015), 28.

3. James Henry Hammond Diary, Dec. 25, 1831, SCL, RSP, Series A, pt. 1, Reel 1; Lewis W. Paine, *Six Years in a Georgia Prison . . .* (New York: privately published, 1851), 185; Bennet H. Barrow Plantation Journal (edited typescript), Dec. 24, 1836, Dec. 23, 26, 1837, Dec. 23, 1839, Dec. 24, 1840, HT, RSP, Series H, Reel 19; Letter II, Sept. 20, 1851, in [Mrs. Henry Rowe Schoolcraft], *Letters on the Condition of the African Race in the United States* (Philadelphia: T. K. and P. G. Collins, 1852), 13; Stephanie M. H. Camp, *Closer to Freedom: Enslaved Women and Everyday Resistance in the Plantation South* (Chapel Hill: University of North Carolina Press, 2004), 31.

4. Charlie Sandles interview, ASCA-2, vol. 9, TX, pt. 8: 3447; Andy Marion interview, ASCA, vol. 3, SC, pt. 3: 169; Solomon Northup, *Twelve Years a Slave,* in *Puttin' On Ole Massa: The Slave Narratives of Henry Bibb, William Wells Brown, and Solomon Northup,* ed. Gilbert Osofsky (New York: Harper & Row, 1969), 342–43, 347.

5. Paine, *Six Years,* 185; T. H. N. letter from Lexington, Dec. 25, 1852, (Philadelphia) *Presbyterian,* Jan. 15, 1853, p. 1; Northup, *Twelve Years a Slave,* 347.

6. Frederick Law Olmsted, *A Journey in the Seaboard Slave States, With Remarks on Their Economy* (New York: Dix & Edwards, 1856), 74–75.

7. Ira Berlin, *Slaves without Masters: The Free Negro in the Antebellum South* (1974; rpt., New York: Vintage Books, 1976), 136.

8. Northern traveler's letter from Savannah, Jan. 1, 1847, in *The Knickerbocker* 29 (Mar. 1847): 197–99; Benjamin L. C. Wailes Diary [typescript copy], Dec. 26, 1857, David M. Rubenstein Rare Book and Manuscript Library, Duke University; William Gilmore Simms, "Home Sketches or Life Along the Highways and Byways of the South," *Literary World,* Jan. 3, 1852, pp. 1–3.

9. Franklin (TN) *Western Weekly Review,* Jan. 2, 1852, quoted in Lisa C. Tolbert, *Constructing Townscapes: Space and Society in Antebellum Tennessee* (Chapel Hill: University of North Carolina Press, 1999), 263n.

10. Citizens of Wilkinson County, to Mississippi Assembly, ca. 1852, in *The Southern Debate over Slavery,* vol. 1, *Petitions to Southern Legislatures, 1778–1864* (Urbana: University of Illinois Press, 2001), 219–21 (quotations on 221); *Tallahassee Floridian* quoted in *Savannah (GA) Daily Morning News,* Apr. 16, 1857, p. 1; John T. O'Brien, "Factory, Church, and Community: Blacks in Antebellum Richmond," *JSH* 44 (Nov. 1978): 509–36, esp. 514.

11. Berlin, *Slaves without Masters,* 136; "The Negro Excitement," (Raymond, MS) *Hinds County Gazette,* Jan. 7, 1857; letter dated Perry County, Ala., Dec. 24, 1841, in (Boston) *The Liberator,* Jan. 22, 1841, p. 16.

12. Richard C. Wade, *Slavery in the Cities: The South 1820–1860* (1964; rpt., New York: Oxford University Press, 1967), 188; Ulrich Bonnell Phillips, "Historical Notes of Milledgeville, Ga.," *Gulf States Historical Magazine* 2 (Nov. 1903): 161–71, esp. 167.

13. Robert Nesbit to Robert F. W. Allston, Dec. 26, 1837, in *The South Carolina Rice Plantation as Revealed in the Papers of Robert F. W. Allston*, ed. James H. Easterby (Chicago: University of Chicago Press, 1945), 76.

14. John Nevitt Diary, Dec. 27, 1831, SHC, RSP, Series J, pt. 6, Reel 3; Louis Manigault to Charles Manigault, Dec. 28, 1852, quoted in William Dusinberre, *Them Dark Days: Slavery in the American Rice Swamps* (New York: Oxford University Press, 1996), 186; Marion Lumpkin Cobb to Callie King, undated [1856?], Joseph Henry Lumpkin Family Papers, Hargrett Rare Book and Manuscript Library, University of Georgia, http://dlg.galileo.usg.edu /hargrett/lumpkin/jhl0032.php; Henry W. Huntington to William N. Minor, William N. Minor Papers, HT, RSP, Series H, Reel 24.

15. Gerald Horne, *The Counter-Revolution of 1776: Slave Resistance and the Origins of the United States of America* (New York: New York University Press, 2014), 68.

16. "An Act for the Better Ordering and Governing of Negroes and Slaves," in *Statutes at Large of South Carolina*, ed. David J. McCord, vol. 7 (Columbia, SC: A. S. Johnston, 1840), 352; 1726 Virginia law quoted in Rhys Isaac, *The Transformation of Virginia, 1740–1790* (1982; rpt., New York: W. W. Norton, 1988), 106; South Carolina Assembly petition to William Bull, quoted in Peter H. Wood, *Black Majority: Negroes in Colonial South Carolina from 1670 through the Stono Rebellion* (New York: Alfred A. Knopf, 1975), 320n.

17. Jeffrey Robert Young, *Domesticating Slavery: The Master Class in Georgia and South Carolina, 1670–1837* (Chapel Hill: University of North Carolina Press, 1999), 53; Walter Edgar, *South Carolina: A History* (Columbia: University of South Carolina Press, 1998), 209–10; Sylviane A. Diouf, *Slavery's Exiles: The Story of the American Maroons* (New York: New York University Press, 2014), 257–58.

18. Report of committee, enclosed in (Governor) Charles G. Montagu to the Earl of Hillsborough, Apr. 19, 1769, in *The Colonial Records of North Carolina*, vol. 8, *1769 to 1771* (Raleigh, NC: Josephus Daniels, 1890), 554–66 (quotations on 558); Philip J. Schwarz, *Twice Condemned: Slaves and the Criminal Laws of Virginia, 1705–1865* (Baton Rouge: Louisiana State University Press, 1988), 179–80. The Virginia affair occurred in 1769. Firearms allowed whites to get the best of the slaves, with authorities executing the ringleader and some of his comrades.

19. Waldemar Westergaard, ed., "Account of the Negro Rebellion on St. Croix, Danish West Indies, 1759," *JNH* 11 (Jan. 1926): 50–61, esp. 53–56; Thelma Peterson Peters, "The American Loyalists and the Plantation Period in the Bahama Islands" (Ph.D. diss., University of Florida, 1960), 131–32; K. O. Laurence, "The Tobago Slave Conspiracy of 1801," *Caribbean Quarterly* 28 (Sept. 1982): 1–9, esp. 1–3; Ada Ferrer, *Freedom's Mirror: Cuba and Haiti in the Age of Revolution* (New York: Columbia University Press, 2014), 208–9; Stuart B. Schwartz, *Sugar Plantations in the Formation of Brazilian Society: Bahia, 1550–1835* (New York: Cambridge University Press, 1985), 480–82; Flavio dos Santos Gomes and H. Sebrina Gledhill, "A 'Safe Haven': Runaway Slaves, Macambos, and Borders in Colonial Amazonia, Brazil," *Hispanic American Historical*

Review 82 (Aug. 2002): 469–98, esp. 484–85; Bernard Moitt, "Slave Resistance in Guadeloupe and Martinique, 1791–1848," *Journal of Caribbean History* 25 (Jan. 1991): 136–59, esp. 149. Bermuda experienced a Christmas season slave insurrection scare in 1673. Horne, *Counter-Revolution*, 25.

20. David Barry Gaspar, "Sugar Cultivation and Slave Life in Antigua before 1800," in *Cultivation and Culture: Labor and Slave Life in the Americas, ed.* Ira Berlin and Philip D. Morgan (Charlottesville: University Press of Virginia, 1993), 121; Manisha Sinha, *The Slave's Cause: A History of Abolition* (New Haven, CT: Yale University Press, 2016), 213; Noel Leo Erskine, *Plantation Church: How African American Religion Was Born in Colonial Slavery* (New York: Oxford University Press, 2014), 92; Ousmane K. Power-Greene, *Against Wind and Tide: The African American Struggle against the Colonization Movement* (New York: New York University Press, 2014), 64–65.

21. Lacy K. Ford, *Deliver Us from Evil: The Slavery Question in the Old South* (New York: Oxford University Press, 2009), 67; James H. Dormon, "The Persistent Specter: Slave Rebellion in Territorial Louisiana," *Louisiana History* 18 (Autumn 1977): 389–404, esp. 404; Daniel Rasmussen, *American Uprising: The Untold Story of America's Largest Slave Revolt* (New York: Harper, 2011); Joanna Bowen Gillespie, *The Life and Times of Martha Laurens Ramsay, 1759–1811* (Columbia: University of South Carolina Press, 2001), 181; Jon F. Sensbach, *A Special Canaan: The Making of an Afro-Moravian World in North Carolina, 1763–1840* (Chapel Hill: University of North Carolina Press, 1998), 261; John Hope Franklin and Loren Schweninger, *Runaway Slaves: Rebels on the Plantation* (New York: Oxford University Press, 1999), 12.

22. Lionel H. Kennedy and Thomas Parker et al., *An Official Report of the Trials of Sundry Negroes, Charged With an Attempt to Raise an Insurrection In The State Of South-Carolina . . .* (Charleston, SC: James R. Schenck, 1822), 20, 22, 23, 24, 91, 95; Douglas R. Egerton, *He Shall Go Out Free: The Lives of Denmark Vesey* (1999; rev. ed., Lanham, MD: Rowman & Littlefield, 2004), 71, 194.

23. William W. Freehling, *Prelude to Civil War: The Nullification Controversy in South Carolina, 1816–1836* (New York: Harper & Row, 1965), 61.

24. Henry O. Wagoner to Frederick Douglass, Nov. 27, 1851, in *The Frederick Douglass Papers,* Series 3: Correspondence, vol. 1, ed. John R. McKivigan (New Haven, CT: Yale University Press, 2009), 501–2.

25. Margaret (Elizabeth Margaret Chandler?), "Christmas," *The Genius of Universal Emancipation and Quarterly Anti-Slavery Review* 14 (Jan. 1834): 18; Thomas Hill, "The Mother's Prayer," in *Christmas and Poems on Slavery for Christmas, 1843* (Cambridge, MA: privately published "For the Massachusetts Anti-Slavery Fair," 1843), 5–6; Allen Carden, *Freedom's Delay: America's Struggle for Emancipation, 1776–1865* (Knoxville: University of Tennessee Press, 2014), 149; Sybil R. Willingham, "Christmas Songs as Propaganda," *UDC Magazine* (Nov. 2007): 12–13.

26. (Boston) *The Liberator,* July 28, 1854, p. 117; Lydia Maria Child to Henry Wise, Dec. 17, 1859, in *Correspondence between Lydia Maria Child, and Gov. Wise and Mrs. Mason, of Virginia* (New York: American Anti-Slavery Society, 1860), 18–28, esp. 26; Paul Finkelman, "Manufacturing Martyrdom: The Antislavery Response to John Brown's Raid" and Wendy Hamand Venet, " 'Cry Aloud and Spare Not': Northern Antislavery Women and John Brown's Raid," both in

Finkelman, ed., *His Soul Goes Marching On: Responses to John Brown and the Harpers Ferry Raid* (Charlottesville: University Press of Virginia, 1995), 41–66, 98–115, esp. 47, 54–58, 106–11; (Boston) *The Liberator,* Dec. 28, 1860, p. 207.

27. John T. Cumbler, *From Abolition to Rights for All: The Making of a Reform Community in the Nineteenth Century* (Philadelphia: University of Pennsylvania Press, 2008), 47–49; Lee Chambers-Schiller, "'A Good Work among the People': The Political Culture of the Boston Antislavery Fair," in *The Abolitionist Sisterhood: Women's Political Culture in Antebellum America,* ed. Jean Fagan Yellin and John C. Van Horne (Ithaca, NY: Cornell University Press, 1994), 250, 250n; *Fourteenth Annual Report Presented to the Massachusetts Anti-Slavery Society, By its Board of Managers, January 24, 1849* (Boston: Andrew & Prentiss, 1849), 62.

28. (Boston) *The Liberator,* Dec. 14, 1838, p. 199, Nov. 6, 1840, p. 179, May 5, 1843, p. 69, Dec. 26, 1845, p. 206, July 13, 1849, p. 110, Dec. 28, 1860, p. 206; (Philadelphia) *Pennsylvania Inquirer and Daily Courier,* Dec. 22, 1841, p. 2; (Rochester, NY) *North Star,* Jan. 5, 1849, p. 2, Aug. 24, 1849, p. 3, Oct. 24, 1850, p. 2.

29. *The American Anti-Slavery Almanac for 1836* . . . (Boston: Webster and Southard, 1835), 18; (Boston) *The Liberator,* Mar. 5, 1836, p. 37, Feb. 14, 1840, p. 26; *Remarks of Henry B. Stanton in the Representatives' Hall, on the 23d and 24th of February, 1837, Before the Committee of the House of Representatives of Massachusetts* . . . , 2nd. ed. (Boston: Isaac Knapp, 1837), 38n (American traveler's letter dated Dec. 29, 1836); Lydia Maria Child, *Anti-Slavery Catechism* (Newburyport, MA: C. Whipple, 1836), 23; *Frederick Douglass' Paper,* Oct. 29, 1852; B. W. Higman, "Slavery Remembered: The Celebration of Emancipation in Jamaica," *Journal of Caribbean History* 12 (Jan. 1979): 55–74, esp. 56. When a northern antislavery account of peaceful post-emancipation Christmases in the British islands implied that a single instance of slave inebriation could be attributed to the bad holiday habits of whites, proslavery southern polemicist John Jacobus Flournoy rebutted, tracing black alcohol proclivities to practices in ancient Egypt. James A. Thome and Horace Kimball, *Emancipation in the West Indies. A Six Months' Tour in Antigua, Barbadoes, and Jamaica in the Year 1837* (New York: American Anti-Slavery Society, 1838), 102; J. J. Flourney, *A Reply to a Pamphlet, Entitled* . . . (Athens, GA: n.p., 1838), 62–63.

30. "The Negro Excitements," (Raymond, MS) *Hinds County Gazette,* Jan. 7, 1857, p. 2; *Richmond Enquirer,* quoted in *NYT,* Dec. 18, 1856, p. 1; Judith Kelleher Schaefer, *Becoming Free, Remaining Free: Manumission and Enslavement in New Orleans, 1846-1862* (Baton Rouge: Louisiana State University Press, 2003), 84; Douglas R. Egerton, "The Slaves' Election: Frémont, Freedom, and the Slave Conspiracy of 1856," *Civil War History* 61 (Mar. 2015): 35–63. "Black Republican," an epithet used by the Republican Party's opponents (especially southerners but also northern Democrats), appealed to the racism of many voters but had little to do with the skin color of Republican voters, candidates, or party activists. The term implied the party was dedicated to blacks at the expense of whites.

31. David Walker, *Appeal, in Four Articles; Together with a Preamble to the Coloured Citizens of the World, But in Particular, and Very Expressly, to Those of the United States of America* (Boston: David Walker, 1829); Elizabeth R. Varon, *Disunion: The Coming of the American Civil War, 1789-1859* (Chapel Hill: University of North Carolina

Press, 2008), 63–65; Walker quoted in Bruce Levine, *Half Slave and Half Free: The Roots of Civil War* (New York: Hill and Wang, 1992), 147; Diouf, *Slavery's Exiles,* 273–74; Charles L. Pettigrew to Ebenezer Pettigrew, Dec. 20, 1830, in *The Pettigrew Papers,* , ed. Sarah McCulloh Lemon, vol. 2, *1819-1843* (Raleigh: North Carolina Department of Cultural Resources, 1988), 152–53; *Roanoke Advertiser* quoted in (Boston) *The Liberator,* Jan. 15, 1831, p. 11; Hiram White account in *American Slavery as It Is: Testimony of a Thousand Witnesses* (New York: American Anti-Slavery Society, 1839), 67–68.

32. Daniel Walker Howe, *What Hath God Wrought: The Transformation of America, 1815-1848* (New York: Oxford University Press, 2007), 428–30; James Lal Penick Jr., *The Great Western Land Pirate: John A. Murrell in Legend and History* (Columbia: University of Missouri Press, 1981), 3, 9, 14–27, 48–54, 106–51; Joshua D. Rothman, *Harsh Times and Fever Dreams: A Story of Capitalism and Slavery in the Age of Jackson* (Athens: University of Georgia Press, 2012), 62, 78, 87 ("mass hysteria"), 373n; Clement Eaton, *The Freedom-of-Thought Struggle in the Old South* (1940; rev. ed., New York: Harper & Row, 1964), 95–99.

33. Rothman, *Harsh Times,* 272 ("approach of Christmas"); *Jackson Mississippian,* Dec. 25, 1835, p. 3; report from New Orleans in (Washington) *Daily National Intelligencer,* Jan. 12, 1836, p. 3; report from Alexandria, LA, (Little Rock) *Arkansas Gazette,* Feb. 2, 1836, p. 3; *Richmond Enquirer,* Jan. 14, 1836, p. 2; *St. Francisville Journal* quoted in (Cincinnati) *Philanthropist,* Apr. 8, 1836, p. 1. Reports differed over the East Feliciana informant's gender, the race of the two executed men, and the name of the plantation owner in question.

34. *New Orleans Tropic,* Nov. 17, 1842, quoted in (Worcester) *Massachusetts Spy,* Dec. 7, 1842, p. 2; *New York Daily Tribune,* Nov. 29, 1842, p. 2; (Cincinnati) *Philanthropist,* Dec. 7, 1842, p. 2; A. P. P., "Slavery" (about article in Oct. 1842 *Southern Review*), *Christian Examiner and General Review* 34 (Mar. 1843): 29–51, esp. 29, 40–41.

35. *Norfolk Herald,* quoted in *New York Daily Tribune,* Jan. 11, 1845; *Holly Springs Gazette,* Dec. 13, 1844, p. 2; Ellen Kenton McCauley Wallace Journal, Nov. 20, Dec. 7, 8, 1846, cited and quoted in Gary R. Matthews, *More American Than Southern: Kentucky, Slavery, and the War for an American Ideology, 1828-1861* (Knoxville: University of Tennessee Press, 2014), 154, 298n.

36. *Richmond (VA) Enquirer, Nashville (TN) Union, Richmond (VA) Whig, Richmond (VA) Dispatch,* and *Alexandria (VA) Sentinel* reports in *NYT,* Dec. 18, 1856, p. 8; Harvey Wish, "The Slave Insurrection Panic of 1856," *JSH* 5 (May 1939), 206–22.

37. *Nacogdoches Chronicle* quoted in (Austin) *Texas State Times,* Jan. 17, 1857, p. 2; (Milledgeville, GA) *Federal Union,* Dec. 23, 1856, quoted in *Plantation and Frontier Documents: 1649-1863 . . . ,* ed. Ulrich B. Phillips, vol. 2 (Cleveland: Arthur H. Clark, 1909), 116; Schaefer, *Becoming Free,* 84.

38. Mary Sharpe Jones to Mary Jones, Dec. 27, 1856, in *The Children of Pride: A True Story of Georgia and the Civil War,* ed. Robert Manson Myers (New Haven, CT: Yale University Press, 1972), 282; Jacqueline Jones, *Saving Savannah: The City and the Civil* War (New York: Knopf, 2008), 71–72; report dated Louisville, Dec. 16, 1856, in *New York Herald,* Dec. 18, 1856, p. 4; Marion Brunson Lucas, *A History of Blacks in Kentucky: From Slavery to Segregation, 1760-1891* (1992;

rpt., Frankfort: Kentucky Historical Society, 2003), 59–60; Egerton, "Slaves' Election," 48.

39. Ella Gertrude Clanton Thomas Diary, Jan. 1, 1857, in *The Secret Eye: The Journal of Ella Gertrude Clanton Thomas, 1848-1889,* ed. Virginia Ingraham Burr (Chapel Hill: University of North Carolina Press, 1990), 152–53; Daniel W. Cobb Diary, Jan. 11, 1857, in *Cobb's Ordeal: The Diaries of a Virginia Farmer, 1842-1872,* ed. Daniel W. Crofts (Athens: University of Georgia Press, 1997), 88; *Nashville (TN) Union* report in *NYT,* Dec. 18, 1856, p. 8; *Livingston (AL) Messenger,* Dec. 24, 1856, quoted in *NYT,* Jan. 9, 1857, p. 3; report dated Louisville, Dec. 20, in *NYT,* Dec. 23, 1856, p. 1; Lucas, *Blacks in Kentucky,* 60; Schaeffer, *Becoming Free,* 84; Charles B. Dew, "Black Ironworkers and the Slave Insurrection Panic of 1856," *JSH* 41 (Aug. 1975): 321–38, esp. 328–31.

40. Egerton, "Slaves' Election," 37; *Athens (GA) Southern Watchman,* Jan. 1, 1857, quoted in Phillips, ed., *Plantation and Frontier Documents,* 116–17.

41. Sarah E. Watkins to Letitia Watkins, Dec. 28, 1856, in *Letters from Forest Place: A Plantation Family's Correspondence, 1846-1861,* ed. E. Grey Dimond and Herman Hattaway (Jackson: University Press of Mississippi, 1993), 96.

42. Willard B. Gatewood Jr., ed., *Slave and Freeman: The Autobiography of George L. Knox* (Lexington: University Press of Kentucky, 1979), 44–46.

43. Wish, "Slave Insurrection Panic," 222; Egerton, "Slaves' Election," 48; Dew, "Black Ironworkers," 333–37.

44. Ella Gertrude Clanton Thomas Diary, Jan. 1, 1857, Dec. 25, 1858, in Burr, ed., *Secret Eye,* 152–53, 166.

45. Edmund Ruffin Diary, Dec. 25, 1856, in *The Diary of Edmund Ruffin,* vol. 1: *Toward Independence, October 1856-April 1861,* ed. William K. Scarborough (Baton Rouge: Louisiana State University Press, 1972), 18–19.

46. *Nashville Union* quoted in *NYT,* Dec. 18, 1856, p. 8; *Athens (GA) Southern Watchman,* Jan. 1, 1857, quoted in Phillips, ed., *Plantation and Frontier Documents,* 116–17; "Misplaced Sympathy," *New Orleans Daily Crescent,* Jan. 8, 1857, p. 2.

47. Susan Bradford Eppes Diary, Dec. 26, 1859, in Eppes, *Through Some Eventful Years* (Macon, GA: J. W. Burke, 1926), 121.

48. Alfred Huger to Joseph Holt, Jan. 3, 1860, quoted in Stephen A. Channing, *Crisis of Fear: Secession in South Carolina* (New York: W. W. Norton, 1970), 42–43; Clarence L. Mohr, *On the Threshold of Freedom: Masters and Slaves in Civil War Georgia* (Baton Rouge: Louisiana State University Press, 1986), 8; William L. Barney, *The Secessionist Impulse: Alabama and Mississippi in 1860* (Princeton, NJ: Princeton University Press, 1974), 165–66; *Bolivar (MO) Courier,* Jan. 7, 1860, quoted in *Charleston (SC) Tri-Weekly Courier,* Jan. 24, 1860.

49. Douglas R. Egerton, *Year of Meteors: Stephen Douglas, Abraham Lincoln and the Election That Brought on the Civil War* (New York: Bloomsbury Press, 2010), 230–31; Randolph B. Campbell, *A Southern Community in Crisis: Harrison County, Texas, 1850-1880* (Austin: Texas State Historical Association, 1983), 188; correspondent's letter, Dec. 22, 1860, in *San Antonio Ledger and Texan,* Dec. 22, 1860, p. 3; William W. Freehling, *The Road to Disunion,* vol. 2, *Secessionists Triumphant* (New York: Oxford University Press, 2007), 460 ("fanatical").

50. Robert F. W. Allston to C. Williams, Dec. 25, 1860, in Easterby, ed., *South Carolina Rice Plantation,* 170; (Anonymous), "An Englishman in South

Carolina: December, 1860, and July, 1862," *Continental Monthly,* pt. 1, vol. 2 (Dec. 1862): 692; pt. 2, vol. 3 (Jan. 1863): 111.

51. Andrew J. Torget, "The Problem of Slave Flight in Civil War Texas," in *Lone Star Unionism, Dissent, and Resistance: Other Sides of Civil War Texas, ed.* Jesús F. de la Teja (Norman: University of Oklahoma Press, 2016), 40; Charles A. Hentz Diary, *"Early January 1861,"* in *A Southern Practice: The Diary and Autobiography of Charles A. Hentz, M.D.,* ed. Steven M. Stowe (Charlottesville: University of Virginia Press, 2000), 81; Sallie McNeill Diary, Dec. 26, 1860, in *The Uncompromising Diary of Sallie McNeill, 1858-1867,* ed. Ginny McNeill Raska and Mary Lynne Gasaway Hill (College Station: Texas A&M University Press, 2009), 92; Mary Petigru to Adele Petigru, Dec. 27, 1860, in Easterby, ed., *South Carolina Rice Plantation,* 151; Eliza Ripley, *Social Life in Old New Orleans: Being Recollections of My Girlhood* (New York: D. Appleton, 1912), 262.

52. John A. Selden Diary, Dec. 25, 1860, in *The Westover Journal of John A. Selden, Esqr., 1858-1862,* ed. John Spencer Bassett and Sidney Bradshaw Fay, *Smith College Studies in History* 6 (July 1921): 318.

53. Stephen A. West, *From Yeoman to Redneck in the South Carolina Upcountry, 1850-1915* (Charlottesville: University of Virginia Press, 2008), 61; correspondent's letter dated Charleston, Dec. 23, 1860, *New-York Daily Tribune,* Dec. 28, 1860, p. 6; letter dated Dec. 15 in "SIGNS OF SHOT-GUNS AND PISTOLS," *New-York Daily Tribune,* Jan. 5, 1861, p. 6; Samuel Andrew Agnew Diary, Dec. 24, 25, 1860, quoted in Armistead L. Robinson, *Bitter Fruits of Bondage: The Demise of Slavery and the Collapse of the Confederacy* (Charlottesville: University of Virginia Press, 2005), 38.

54. Robert Cartmell Diary, Dec. 25, 1860, quoted in Gary T. Edwards, "'Negroes . . . and All Other Animals': Slaves and Masters in Antebellum Madison County," *Tennessee Historical Quarterly* 57 (Spring 1988): 24–35, esp. 29; Catherine Cooper Hopley, *Life in the South; from the Commencement of the War, By a Blockaded British Subject . . . ,* vol. 1 (London: Chapman and Hall, 1863), 156–65.

55. (Houston, TX) *Weekly Telegraph,* Jan. 8, 1861, p. 2; *Montgomery Mail* quoted in *Bangor (ME) Daily Whig and Courier,* Dec. 21, 1860; correspondent's letter from Columbus, GA, Dec. 28, 1860, in *New-York Daily Tribune,* Jan. 3, 1861, p. 8; William C. Davis, *"A Government of Our Own:" The Making of the Confederacy* (Baton Rouge: Louisiana State University Press, 1994), 39–40. Reportedly, the Alabama scare spilled over into southern Georgia with rumors that some slave plotters had crossed state lines to avoid arrest, leading to several "barbarous [preventative] executions." Correspondent's letter from Columbus, GA, Dec. 28, 1860, in *New-York Daily Tribune,* Jan. 3, 1861, p. 8.

56. *NYT,* Dec. 29, 1856, p. 4.

57. Elizabeth A. Fenn, "'A Perfect Equality Seemed to Reign': Slave Society and Jonkonnu, *North Carolina Historical Review* 65 (Apr. 1988): 127–53, esp. 148, 148n; (Boston) *The Liberator,* Jan. 23, 1857, p. 187; Julia Floyd Smith, *Slavery and Rice Culture in Low Country Georgia, 1750-1860* (Knoxville: University of Tennessee Press, 1985), 191. In the 1823 incident, the innkeeper died two days after the assault. Fenn, "Perfect Equality," 148.

58. Cases of Charles Thompson, Anna Scott, and others in William Still, *The Underground Rail Road: A Record of Facts, Authentic Narratives, Letters, &c. . . .*

(Philadelphia: Porte & Coates, 1872), esp. 146 and 336; R. C. Smedley, *History of the Underground Railroad in Chester and the Neighboring Counties of Pennsylvania* (Lancaster, PA: Office of the Journal, 1883), 207; Still manuscript journal, Historical Society of Pennsylvania, online/digital-history-projects /uncovering-william-stills-underground-railroad.

59. James Redpath, *The Roving Editor: Or, Talks with Slaves in the Southern States* (New York: A. B. Burdick, 1859), 136–37.

60. Freddie L. Parker, ed., *Stealing a Little Freedom: Advertisements for Slave Runaways in North Carolina, 1791–1840* (New York: Garland, 1994), xvii *and passim.*

61. Still, *Underground Rail Road,* 336; C. G. Parsons, *Inside View of Slavery: Or a Tour Among the Planters* (Boston: John P. Jewett, 1855), 44; D. A. Dunkley, *Agency of the Enslaved: Jamaica and the Culture of Freedom in the Atlantic World* (Lanham, MD: Lexington Books, 2013), 33–34. The 2 percent figure for North Carolina slaves choosing the twelve-day Christmas season to escape almost certainly is on the low side, since the same volume has advertisements lacking date specificity that might mask Dec. 20–31 escapes–for example: "In December last a Negro of mine called Jim . . . ran off" (389).

62. John Andrew Jackson, *The Experience of a Slave in South Carolina* (London: Passmore & Alabaster, 1862), 7–28 (escape account 23–28); William Craft, *Running a Thousand Miles for Freedom; Or, The Escape of William and Ellen Craft from Slavery* (London: William Tweedie, 1860), 31.

63. (Brandon, VT) *Voice of Freedom,* Jan. 28, 1847, p. 1; Henry Bibb Narrative, in Osofsky, ed., *Puttin' On Ole Massa,* 82–87.

64. James L. Smith, *Autobiography of James L Smith, Including, Also, Reminiscences of Slave Life, Recollections of the War, Education of Freedmen, Causes of the Exodus, etc.* (Norwich, CT: Bulletin, 1881), 37; John Thompson, *The Life of John Thompson, A Fugitive Slave; Containing His History of 25 Years in Bondage and His Providential Escape* (Worcester, MA: John Thompson, 1856), 65–66; *Life of Isaac Mason as a Slave* (Worcester, MA: n.p., 1893), 25–40 (quotation on 37).

65. [J. W. Loguen?], *The Rev. J. W. Loguen, As a Slave and as a Freeman. A Narrative of Real Life* (Syracuse, NY: J. G. K. Truair, 1859), 260–336, esp. 232, 234, 261, 262, 271, 274; Angela F. Murphy, *The Jerry Rescue: The Fugitive Slave Law, Northern Rights, and the American Sectional Crisis* (New York: Oxford University Press, 2016), 79–83.

66. *Cincinnati Gazette* article republished in (Washington, D.C.) *Southern Press,* Jan. 18, 1851, p. 3, and many northern newspapers; *Winchester Virginian,* Jan. 10, 1855, quoted in (Boston) *The Liberator,* Jan. 19, 1855, p. 11.

67. *Charleston City Gazette,* Jan. 15, 1790, in *Fugitive Slave Advertisements in the City Gazette: Charleston, South Carolina, 1787–1797,* ed. Thomas Brown and Leah Sims (Lanham, MD: Lexington Books, 2015), 34; *Hancock (GA) Advertiser* quoted in (Boston) *The Liberator,* May 14, 1831, p. 85; *North Carolina Minerva and Raleigh Register,* Jan. 5, 1821, *and North Carolina State Gazette,* Jan. 17, 1817, quoted in Parker, ed., *Stealing a Little Freedom,* 125, 264; image of Grigsby ad in Franklin and Schweninger, *Runaway Slaves,* 58. Franklin and Schweninger also allude to Christmas escapes on 60, 64, 79, and 146.

68. *New York Weekly Herald,* Dec. 28, 1850, p. 412; *NYT,* Nov. 2, 1859, p. 2; *Charleston Mercury,* Nov. 4, 1859; Christopher Phillips, *Freedom's Port: The African*

American Community of Baltimore, 1790–1860 (Urbana: University of Illinois Press, 1997), 125; Joseph P. Reidy, *From Slavery to Agrarian Capitalism in the Cotton Plantation South: Central Georgia, 1800–1880* (Chapel Hill: University of North Carolina Press, 1992), 27; Larry Eugene Rivers, *Rebels and Runaways: Slave Resistance in 19th-Century Florida* (Urbana: University of Illinois Press, 2012), 54.

69. "Englishman in South Carolina," pt. 1, pp. 691–94, pt. 2, p. 110.

70. "Englishman in South Carolina," pt. 1, pp. 692, 693.

6. RANSACKING THE GARRET

1. *Richmond Examiner,* Dec. 28, 1863.

2. Willie Lee Rose, *Rehearsal for Reconstruction: The Port Royal Experiment,* introduction by C. Vann Woodward (New York: Vintage Books, 1964), xiii in Woodward's introduction ("big gun-shoot"), 9, 16; David Silkenat, *Driven from Home: North Carolina's Civil War Refugee Crisis* (Athens: University of Georgia Press, 2016), 188–89.

3. Louisa Quitman Lovell to Joseph Lovell, Dec. 22, 1861, Quitman Family Papers, SHC; Henry William Ravenel Diary, Dec. 28, 1861, in *The Private Journal of Henry William Ravenel, 1859–1887,* ed. Arney Robinson Childs (Columbia: University of South Carolina Press, 1947), 110; Ella Gertrude Clanton Thomas Diary, Dec. 31, 1861, in *The Secret Eye: Journal of Ella Gertrude Clanton Thomas, 1848–1889* (Chapel Hill: University of North Carolina Press, 1990), 199; Mary Chesnut Diary, December 25, 1861, in *A Diary from Dixie,* ed. Ben Ames Williams (1949; rpt., Cambridge, MA: Harvard University Press, 1980), 176; Anya Jabour, *Topsy-Turvey: How the Civil War Turned the World Upside Down for Southern Children* (Columbia: University of Missouri Press, 2010), 94. Chesnut's diary entry was actually a rewritten entry she did in the 1880s on the basis of a diary volume that has since disappeared. Editorial note in C. Vann Woodward and Elisabeth Muhlenfeld, eds., *The Private Mary Chesnut: The Unpublished Civil War Diaries* (New Haven, CT: Yale University Press), 218.

4. *Richmond Whig and Public Advertiser,* Dec. 24, 1861, p. 2, Dec. 27, 1861, p. 3; *Charleston Mercury,* Dec. 23, 1861, p. 2; *Macon Telegraph,* Dec. 27, 1861, p. 1; *San Antonio Daily Ledger and Texan,* Dec. 24, 1861, p. 2; "Texas Items," *Houston Weekly Telegraph,* Jan. 15, 1861, p. 1.

5. *Edgefield (SC) Advertiser,* Dec. 25, 1861, p. 2; *Charleston Mercury,* Jan. 3, 1862, p. 1, Dec. 25, 1861, p. 1; letter dated Dec. 26, 1861, in *Charleston Daily Courier,* Jan. 4, 1862, p. 1.

6. "Merry Christmas," *Shreveport Semi-Weekly News,* Dec. 24, 1861, p. 2; *Charleston Mercury,* Dec. 25, 1861, p. 2; correspondent's letter dated Nashville, Dec. 26, 1861, in *Charleston Daily Courier,* Dec. 30, 1861, p. 1.

7. John B. Jones Diary, Dec. 25, 1862, in *A Rebel War Clerk's Diary,* ed. Earl Schenck Miers (New York: Sagamore Press, 1958), 140; *Mobile Register and Advertiser,* Dec. 25, 1862, p. 2; *Richmond Whig & Public Advertiser,* Jan. 2, 1863, p. 3; *Griffin (GA) Confederate States,* Dec. 25, 1862, p. 3; Sam Richards Diary, Dec. 27, 1862, in *Sam Richards's Civil War Diary: A Chronicle of the Atlanta Home Front,* ed. Wendy Hamand Venet (Athens: University of Georgia Press, 2009), 145.

8. Stephen H. Boineau to Charles Heyward, Dec. 24, 28, 1863, in *Twilight on the South Carolina Rice Fields: Letters of the Heyward Family, 1862–1871,* ed. Margaret

Belser Hollis and Allen H. Stokes (Columbia: University of South Carolina Press, 2010), 46–47, 48; *Mobile Daily Advertiser,* Dec. 25, 1863, p. 1.

9. [Sally A. Putnam], *Richmond during the War; Four Years of Personal Observation* (New York: G. W. Carleton, 1867), 89; Sallie McNeill Diary, Dec. 16, 1861, in Raska and Hill, eds., *Uncompromising Diary,* 113; Mary Eliza Powell Dulany Diary, Dec. 25, 1861, in *In the Shadow of the Enemy: The Civil War Journal of Ida Powell Dulany,* ed. Mary L. Mackall, Steven F. Meserve, and Anne Mackall Sasscer (Knoxville: University of Tennessee Press, 2009), 44; Kate Stone Diary, Jan. 6, 1862, in *Brokenburn: The Journal of Kate Stone, 1861-1868,* ed. John Q. Anderson (1955; rpt. with new introduction by Drew Gilpin Faust, Baton Rouge: Louisiana State University Press, 1995), xvii, 77–78; Ravenel Diary, Dec. 25, 1861, Dec. 23, 25, 1862, Dec. 25, 1864, Dec. 25, 1859, in Childs, ed., *Private Journal,* 110, 167, 205, 3, 4.

10. *Augusta (GA) Daily Chronicle & Sentinel,* Dec. 19, 1861, p. 3; Charles Colcock Jones to Charles C. Jones Jr., Dec. 25, 1861, in *The Children of Pride: A True Story of Georgia and the Civil War,* ed. Robert Manson Myers, 3 vols. (paper ed., New York: Popular Library, 1972), 2:827; Antonia Quitman Lovell to Louisa Quitman Lovell, Dec. 18, 1861, Quitman Family Papers, SHC; *Jackson Weekly Mississippian,* Dec. 25, 1861, p. 3; A. Wilson Greene, *Civil War Petersburg: Confederate City in the Crucible of War* (Charlottesville: University of Virginia Press, 2006).

11. Everard Green Baker Diary, Dec. 28, 1861, SHC, RSP, Series J, pt. 6, Reel 16; *Shreveport (LA) Semi-Weekly News,* Dec. 10, 1861, p. 2; *Augusta (GA) Daily Constitutionalist,* Dec. 15, 1861, p. 3.

12. Emory M. Thomas, *The Confederate Nation: 1861-1865* (New York: Harper & Row, 1979), 155; Gary W. Gallagher, *The Confederate War* (Cambridge, MA: Harvard University Press, 1997), 29.

13. Tally N. Simpson to Anna Talullah Simpson, Dec. 25, 1862, in *Far, Far from Home: The Wartime Letters of Dick and Tally Simpson, 3rd South Carolina Volunteers,* ed. Guy R. Everson and Edward H. Simpson Jr. (New York: Oxford University Press, 1994), 168–69; "Bettie" to William Beverley Pettit, Dec. 25, 1862, in *Civil War Letters of Arabella and William Beverley Pettit of Fluvanna County, Virginia, March 1862-March 1865,* ed. Charles W. Turner, vol. 1 (Roanoke: Virginia Lithography & Graphics, 1988 [?]), 82–83; Francis Butler Simkins and James Welch Patton, *The Women of the Confederacy* (Richmond, VA: Garrett and Massie, 1936), 218.

14. Margaret Preston, "A Christmas Carol for 1862," quoted in Stacey Jean Klein, *Margaret Junkin Preston: Poet of the Confederacy, A Literary Life* (Columbia: University of South Carolina Press, 2007), 49; Henry Timrod, "Christmas," in *War Songs and Poems of the Southern Confederacy, 1861-1865 . . . ,* comp. H. M. Wharton (n.p.: n.p., 1904), 325–28 (quotations on 325, 326).

15. "The Fiend Unbound," *Charleston Mercury,* Dec. 25, 1863, p. 2; "What We Sing On Christmas Day, 1864," *Macon Daily Telegraph,* Dec. 26, 1864, p. 2.

16. *Mobile Register and Advertiser,* Dec. 17, 1862, p. 2; *Augusta (GA) Daily Constitutionalist,* Dec. 24, 1862, p. 3; Jacob Kent Langhorne to his mother, Dec. 20, 1862, www.vmi.edu/uploaded/Files/Archives/Manuscripts/00361Langhorne/Langhorne_VMI_fulltext; *Charleston Mercury,* Feb. 9, 1864, p. 1; letter from Florence, Jan. 18, 1864, in *Memphis Daily Appeal,* Jan. 28, 1864.

17. *Southern Illustrated News,* Dec. 13, 1862, p. 2; *Mobile Daily Advertiser,* Dec. 25, 1863, p. 2; *Daily Richmond Examiner,* Dec. 24, 1864, p. 2.

18. John F. Shaffner to Carrie Fries, Dec. 26, 1862, quoted in Gallagher, *Confederate War,* 74; *Augusta (GA) Daily Constitutionalist,* Dec. 25, 1863, p. 2, Dec. 25, 1864, p. 3; Caroline Gilman to her daughter Eliza, Dec. 25, 1864, in "Letters of a Confederate Mother: Charleston in the Sixties," in *Atlantic Monthly* 137 (Apr. 1916): 509–10.

19. Thomas P. Lowry, *Confederate Heroines: 120 Southern Women Convicted by Union Military Justice* (Baton Rouge: Louisiana State University Press), 7; William F. Robert to Jefferson Davis, Dec. 25, 1864, quoted in calendar, *The Papers of Jefferson Davis,* vol. 11, ed. Lynda Lasswell Crist (Baton Rouge: Louisiana State University Press, 2003), 252; Reuben F. Thomas to "Friend George," Mar. 15, 1863, Charles Boyle to "Dear Home," Dec. 25, 1863, in *Yankee Correspondence: Civil War Letters between New England Soldiers and the Home Front,* ed. Nina Silber and Mary Sievens (Charlottesville: University of Virginia Press, 1996), 43, 104–5. The already freed Virginia slave had been running an errand for her master in Portsmouth when it came under Yankee control.

20. Cornelia Peake McDonald Diary, Dec. 23, 24, 25, 1862, in *A Woman's Civil War: A Diary, with Reminiscences of the War, from March 1862,* ed. Minrose C. Gwin (Madison: University of Wisconsin Press, 1992), 101–4.

21. Mary S. Mallard Journal, Dec. 25, 1864, in Myers, ed., *Children of Pride,* 2:1237; William Harman to Henry A. Wise, Dec. 29, 1862, OR, Ser. 1, vol. 18, p. 809; Simkins and Patton, *Women of the Confederacy,* 44–45; Sarah E. Watkins to Letitia Walton, Dec. 25, 1862, in *Letters from Forest Place: A Plantation Family's Correspondence, 1846-1861,* ed. E. Grey Dimond and Herman Hattaway (Jackson: University Press of Mississippi, 1993), 303; C. M. Cole's mother (not further identified) to her cousin "Blanche," Nov. 2 and Dec. 28, 1862 (combined letter), in *Confederate Veteran* 13 (June 1905): 262–65.

22. "Correspondent's Letter," Dec. 31, 1863, *The New South,* Jan. 2, 1864, digital.tcl.sc.edu/cdm/compoundobject/collection/NSN/id/172/rec17; *Milwaukee Daily Sentinel,* Jan. 11, 1864; (Concord) *New Hampshire Statesman,* Jan. 15, 1864; Cornelius L. Burckmyer to Charlotte Rebecca Boyce Burckmyer, Dec. 25, 1863, in *The Burckmyer Letters, March, 1863-June, 1865,* ed. Charlotte R. Holmes (Columbia, SC: State Company, 1926), 237, 238.

23. George C. Rable, *God's Almost Chosen Peoples: A Religious History of the American Civil War* (Chapel Hill: University of North Carolina Press, 2010), 351; Sarah Morgan Diary, Dec. 25, 1863, in *Sarah Morgan: The Civil War Diary of Sarah Morgan,* ed. Charles R. East (New York: Simon & Schuster, 1992), 584–85; Walter Q. Gresham to Matilda Gresham, Dec. 26, 1863, in Matilda Gresham, *Life of Walter Quintin Gresham, 1832-1895,* vol. 1 (Chicago: Rand McNally, 1919), 283; Benjamin A. Fordyce to his wife and children, Dec. 30, 1863, in *Echoes from the Letters of a Civil War Surgeon,* ed. Lydia P. Hecht (n.p.: Bayou Publishing, 1996), 124–26.

24. Letter of Missouri Reddick, Dec. 24, 1863, quoted in Brian Steel Wills, *The War Hits Home: The Civil War in Southeastern Virginia* (Charlottesville: University of Virginia Press, 2001), 198–99; Emilie Riley McKinley Diary, Jan. 6, 1864, in *From the Pen of a She-Rebel: The Civil War Diary of Emilie Riley McKinley,* ed. Gordon A. Cotton (Columbia: University of South Carolina Press, 2001), 62.

25. William T. Sherman to Abraham Lincoln, Dec. 22, 1864, in *Sherman's Civil War: Selected Correspondence of William T. Sherman, 1860-1865,* ed. Brooks D. Simpson and Jean V. Berlin (Chapel Hill: University of North Carolina Press, 1999), 772; Fanny Yates Cohen Journal, Dec. 21–25, 1864, in Spencer B. King Jr., ed., "Fanny Cohen's Journal of Sherman's Occupation of Savannah," *GHQ* 41 (Dec. 1957): 407–16, esp. 410–13.

26. Cohen Journal, Dec. 23, 1864, in King, ed., "Fanny Cohen's Journal," 411; James W. King to Sarah Jane "Jenny" Babcock, Dec. 24, 1862, in Faust, ed., *Conspicuous Gallantry,* 75–76.

27. General Orders No. 118, New Orleans, Dec. 24, 1862, in OR, Ser. 1, vol. 15; Report from New York, Jan. 6, in *Daily Cleveland Herald,* Jan. 7, 1863; Peggy Robbins, "Peace on Earth—But Not in Vicksburg," *Civil War Times Illustrated* 38 (Dec. 1999): 50; General Orders No. 532, Vicksburg, Dec. 29, 1863, in *The War of the Rebellion,* Ser. 2, vol. 6, p. 776; Emilie Riley McKinley Diary, Jan. 6, 1864, in Cotton, ed., *Pen of a She-Rebel, 62.*

28. Fanny Yates Cohen Journal, Dec. 25, 22, 1864, in King, ed., "Fanny Cohen's Journal," 412–13, 411.

29. James Oakes, *Freedom National: The Destruction of Slavery in the United States, 1861-1865* (New York: W. W. Norton, 2013), 137–38, 189; Eric Foner, *The Fiery Trial: Abraham Lincoln and American Slavery* (New York: W. W. Norton, 2010), 174–75, 228–39, 299, 383.

30. John M. Sacher, " 'Twenty-Negro,' or Overseer Law: A Reconsideration," *Journal of the Civil War Era* 7 (June 2017): 269–92, esp. 270, 283–84.

31. Oakes, *Freedom National,* 88–105 (quotations on 89); Ira Berlin, "Who Freed the Slaves? Emancipation and Its Meaning," in *Union and Emancipation: Essays on Politics and Race in the Civil War Era,* ed. David W. Blight and Brooks D. Simpson (Kent, OH: Kent State University Press, 1997), 105–21 (esp. 110–11); Foner, *Fiery Trial,* 167; Bob Luke and John David Smith, eds., *Black Soldiers in Blue: African American Troops in the Civil War Era* (Chapel Hill: University of North Carolina Press, 2002), 13–42; John David Smith, *Soldiering for Freedom: How the Union Army Recruited, Trained, and Deployed the U.S. Colored Troops* (Baltimore: Johns Hopkins University Press, 2014), 5, 24; Lorenzo Thomas to Edwin M. Stanton, Dec. 27, 1864, OR, Ser 3, vol. 4, pp. 1017–18. The initial Confederate draft law of April 1862 excepted professions deemed essential to the war effort, like telegraph operators and railroad workers, from draft liability. A revision that fall allowed men who either owned or supervised twenty slaves to escape the draft. Additionally, Confederate draft legislation allowed persons to hire substitutes, favoring wealthy citizens.

32. S. L. W. to the editors of the *Memphis Daily Appeal,* Nov. 29, 1862, in *Memphis Daily Appeal,* Dec. 15, 1862; Eugene D. Genovese, *Roll, Jordan, Roll: The World the Slaves Made* (1972; paper ed., New York: Vintage Books, 1976), 122–25.

33. R. S. Ripley to Robert E. Lee, Dec. 25, 1861, Lee to Ripley, Dec. 27, 1861, OR, Ser 1, vol. 6, pp. 352–53, 358; Office of Agent of Impressment for the District of Augusta to the "Slaveholders of the District of Augusta," Jan. 6, 1865, in *Augusta (GA) Daily Constitutionalist,* Jan. 7, 1865, p. 2.

34. Charles Colcock Jones to Charles C. Jones Jr., Dec. 25, 1861, and unnumbered prologue, in Myers, ed., *Children of Pride,* 2:826–27, 1:prologue;

Susan Bradford Eppes Diary, Dec. 25, 1861, in Eppes, *Through Some Eventful Years* (Macon, GA: J. S. W. Burke, 1926), 168.

35. Joel Chandler Harris, *On the Plantation: A Story of a Georgia Boy's Adventures during the War* (New York: D. Appleton, 1905), 118–21; Samuel Porcher Gaillard Plantation Journal, Dec. 24, 1863, SCL, RSP, Series A, pt. 2, Reel 2; Lucy Pier Stevens Diary, Dec. 25, 26, 1863, in *Another Year Finds Me in Texas: The Civil War Diary of Lucy Pier Stevens,* ed. Vicki Adams Tongate (Austin: University of Texas Press, 2016), 241–42; Stephen H. Boineau to Charles Heyward, Dec. 24, 1863, in Hollis and Stokes, eds., *Twilight,* 46–47; Gerry Van Der Heuvel, *Crowns of Thorns and Glory: Mary Todd Lincoln and Varina Howell Davis: The Two First Ladies of the Civil War* (New York: E. P. Dutton, 1988), 173.

36. Margaret Preston Junkin War Journal, Dec. 24, 1862 (remembering Christmas 1861), in Elizabeth Preston Allan, *Life and Letters of Margaret Junkin Preston* (Boston: Houghton, Mifflin, 1903), 157; Kate Stone Diary, Dec. 22, 1861, Jan. 6, 1862, in Anderson, ed., *Brokenburn,* 73–75, 77; Louisa Quitman to Joseph Lovell, Jan. 1, 1862, Quitman Family Papers, SHC; Harriet E. Powe to Sallie (?), Dec. 27, 1861, William Drayton Rutherford Papers, SCL, digital .tcl.sc.edu/cdm/compoundobject/collection/WDRP/id/1254/rec/2.

37. Fannie to her husband, Dec. 28, 1862, in Randolph B. Campbell and Donald K. Pickens, eds., "'My Dear Husband': A Texas Slave's Love Letter, 1862," *JNH* 65 (Autumn 1980): 363–64; Charles B. Dew, *Bond of Iron: Master and Slave at Buffalo Forge* (New York: W. W. Norton, 1994), 319; John A. Cobb to Howell Cobb, Dec. 20, 1862, in R. P. Brooks, ed., "Howell Cobb Papers," *GHQ* 6 (Dec. 1922): 362.

38. Greene, *Civil War Petersburg,* 63; Moses Liddell to his wife, Dec. 12, 1861, LSU, "Slavery, Abolition & Social Justice," http://www.slavery.amdigital .co.uk.ezproxy.lib.purdue.edu/Contents/DocumentDetailsSearch.aspx ?documentid=254488&prevPos=254488&previous=5&vpath=searchresults& searchmode=true&pi=1; Louisa Quitman to Joseph Lovell, Jan. 1, 1862, Quitman Family Papers, SHC; Augustus Benners Diary, Dec. 26, 1861, in *Disunion, War, Defeat, and Recovery in Alabama: The Journal of Augustus Benners, 1850–1885,* ed. Glenn Linden and Virginia Linden (Macon, GA: Mercer University Press, 2007), 73.

39. Booker T. Washington, "Christmas Days in Old Virginia," in *The Booker T. Washington Papers,* vol. 1, *The Autobiographical Writings,* ed. Louis R. Harlan (Urbana: University of Illinois Press, 1972), 394; James Hammond Diary, Dec. 25, 1861, Dec. 26, 27, 1862, Dec. 25, 27, 1863, James Hammond Papers, SCL, RSP, Series A, pt. I, Reel 1; Dolly Lunt Burg Diary, Dec. 24, 25, 1864, in James I. Robertson Jr., ed., "The Diary of Dolly Lunt Burge," pt. 7, *GHQ* 45 (Dec. 1961): 376.

40. Wayne K. Durrill, *War of Another Kind: A Southern Community in the Great Rebellion* (New York: Oxford University Press, 1990), 164; W. Sweet to Adele Allston, Dec. 28, 1864, in Easterby, ed. *South Carolina Rice Plantation,* 323; Philip N. Racine, *Living a Big War in a Small Place: Spartanburg, South Carolina during the Confederacy* (Columbia: University of South Carolina Press, 2013), 54, 72, 79, 107n.

41. Stephanie McCurry, *Confederate Reckoning: Power and Politics in the Civil War* (Cambridge, MA: Harvard University Press, 2010), 233–36; Joe Gray Taylor,

"Slavery in Louisiana during the Civil War," *Louisiana History* 8 (Winter 1967): 27–33, esp. 28–29.

42. Durrill, *War of Another Kind,* 164; Robert D. Reid, "The Negro in Alabama during the Civil War," *JNH* 35 (July 1950): 265–88, esp. 274.

43. LaSalle Corbell Pickett, *Yule Log* (Washington, D.C.: Neale, 1900), 47–68; Barbara L. Bellows, *Two Charlestonians at War: The Civil War Odysseys of a Lowcountry Aristocrat and a Black Abolitionist* (Baton Rouge: Louisiana State University Press, 2018), 214–15; Steven V. Ash, *A Year in the South, 1865: The True Story of Four Ordinary People Who Lived through the Most Tumultuous Twelve Months in American History* (New York: Palgrave Macmillan, 2002), 121.

44. H. Tompkins to the Provost Marshal of the District of Nashville, Feb. 27, 1864, John W. Horner to W. R. Rowley, Feb. 27, 1864, in *Freedom: A Documentary History of Emancipation, 1861–1867,* Series 1, vol. 1, *The Destruction of Slavery,* ed. Ira Berlin et al. (New York: Cambridge University Press, 1985), 318–19; Everard Green Baker Diary, Dec. 26, 1863; Chandra Manning, *Troubled Refuge: Struggling for Freedom in the Civil War* (New York: Alfred A. Knopf, 2016), 73.

45. *Richmond Daily Dispatch,* Jan. 5, 1863, p. 2; *Memphis Daily Appeal,* Jan. 20, 1863, p. 2; *Augusta (GA) Daily Chronicle & Sentinel,* Apr. 7, 1863, p. 3. At the time, the *Memphis Daily Appeal* was published in Jackson, having been uprooted from its host city after Union forces occupied Memphis in June 1862. R. A. Halley, "A Rebel Newspaper's War Story: Being a Narrative of the War History of the *Memphis Appeal,*" *American Historical Magazine and Tennessee Historical Society Quarterly* 8 (Apr. 1903): 124–53, esp. 125, 134.

46. Mary Chesnut Diary, Sept. 21, 27, Oct. 9, 10, 1861, in Woodward and Muhlenfield, eds., *Private Mary Chesnut,* 162, 174, 175 (quotation on 164); Mary Chesnut Diary, December 25, 1861, in Williams, ed., *Diary from Dixie,* 176.

47. Arabella Pettit to William Beverley Pettit, Nov. 16, 1862, in Turner, ed., *Civil War Letters of Arabella Speairs and William Beverley Pettit,* 68; B. A. Smith to John J. Pettus quoted in Herbert Aptheker, "Notes on Slave Conspiracies in Confederate Mississippi," *JNH* 29 (Jan. 1944): 77, 77n; Mary Jane Lipscomb to Jefferson Davis, Nov. 15, 1862, in *The Papers of Jefferson Davis,* jeffersondavis.ric.edu/Content.aspx?id=112.

48. Pre. Soniat to General, Dec. 20, 1862, Affidavit of Gustave Chabaud and J. Burcard, Dec. 22 [21], 1862, in Berlin et al., eds., *Freedom,* Series 1, vol. 1, pp. 231, 233–35; James G. Hollandsworth Jr., *The Louisiana Native Guards: The Black Military Experience during the Civil War* (Baton Rouge: Louisiana State University Press, 1995), 1–38; Susan Eva O'Donovan, *Becoming Free in the Cotton South* (Cambridge, MA: Harvard University Press, 2007), 87; "To the People of Louisiana," Dec. 24, 1862, enclosed in Nathaniel P. Banks to Henry W. Halleck, Dec. 24, 1862, OR, Ser. 1, vol. 15, pp. 618–19.

49. Silkenat, *Driven from Home,* 197–98; Harriott Kinloch Middleton to Susan Middleton (in Columbia, SC), Dec. 25, 1863, in *Flat Rock of the Old Time: Letters from the Mountains to the Lowcountry, 1837–1939,* ed. Robert B. Cuthbert (Columbia: University of South Carolina Press, 2016), 23, 245n (quotations on 46); Henry Nutt to Zebulon Vance, Dec. 12, 1864, in *North Carolina Civil War Documentary,* ed. W. Buck Yearns and John G. Barrett (Chapel Hill: University of North Carolina Press, 1980), 257–58; Gideon Lincecum to William

P. Doran, Dec. 27, 1864, in *Gideon Lincecum's Sword: Civil War Letters from the Texas Home Front,* ed. Jerry Bryan Lincecum, Edward Hake Phillips, and Peggy A. Redshaw (Denton: University of North Texas Press, 2001), 296–97 (see also 6, 19, 31, 39–42); Carl H. Moneyhon, "White Society and African-American Soldiers," in *"All Cut to Pieces and Gone to Hell": The Civil War, Race Relations, and the Battle of Poison Spring,* ed. Mark K. Christ (Little Rock, AR : August House, 2003), 47.

50. James A. Seddon to Joseph E. Brown, Dec. 26, 1862, OR, Ser. 4, vol. 2, p. 262; McCurry, *Confederate Reckoning,* 292–93.

51. Charles Boyle to "Dear Home," Dec. 25, 1863, in Silber and Sievens, eds., *Yankee Correspondence,* 104–5.

52. Bell Irvin Wiley, "Billy Yank and the Black Folk," *JNH* 36 (Jan. 1951): 35–52, esp. 36.

53. *NYT,* Jan. 14, 1862, p. 5; Robert F. Engs, *Freedom's First Generation: Black Hampton, Virginia, 1861–1890* (New York: Fordham University Press, 2004), 20, 22.

54. Fortress Monroe correspondent of the *Boston Traveler* quoted in "Christmas among the Contrabands," *Daily Cleveland Herald,* Jan. 4, 1862; Engs, *Black Hampton,* 34–35; "Christmas Eve at Beaufort," *Lowell (MA) Daily Citizen and News,* Feb. 12, 1862.

55. Sarah Wadley quoted in Jabour, *Topsy-Turvey,* 76; John B. Jones Diary, Dec. 25, 1862, in Miers, ed., *Rebel War Clerk's Diary,* 141.

56. Andrew Ward, *The Slaves' War: The Civil War in the Words of Former Slaves* (New York: Houghton Mifflin Harcourt, 2008), 163; Stephen F. Fleharty letter, Dec. 31, 1862, in *"Jottings from Dixie": The Civil War Dispatches of Sergeant Major Stephen F. Fleharty,* ed. Philip J. Reyburn and Terry L. Wilson (Baton Rouge: Louisiana State University Press, 1999), 89–91; Thomas J. Davis to "Mr. Lincoln & Co.," Dec. 29, 1862, in *The Bedax Tigers: From Shiloh to the Surrender with the 18th Wisconsin Volunteers,* ed. Thomas P. Nanzig (Lanham, MD: Rowman & Littlefield, 2002), 127; Rose, *Rehearsal for Reconstruction,* 102.

57. Rose, *Rehearsal for Reconstruction,* 75–79.

58. Thomas Wentworth Higginson, Camp Diary, Dec. 25, 26, 1862, in Higginson, *Army Life in a Black Regiment* (New York: Collier Books, 1962), 55–56; Dudley Taylor Cornish, *The Sable Arm: Negro Troops in the Union Army, 1861–1865* (1956; rpt., New York: W. W. Norton, 1966), 80–90.

59. Charlotte L. Forten, "New-Year's Day on the Islands of South Carolina in 1863," in *The Freedmen's Book,* ed. Lydia Maria Child (Boston: Ticknor and Fields, 1865), 251–53; Laura M. Towne Diary, Dec. 25, 1862, in *Letters and Diary of Laura M. Towne: Written from the Sea Islands of South Carolina, 1862–1884,* ed. Rupert Sargent Holland (1912; rpt., New York: Negro Universities Press, 1969), 96–97.

60. Herbert Aptheker, "The Negro in the Union Navy," *JNH* 32 (Apr. 1947): 169–200; James H. Willbanks, ed., *America's Heroes: Medal of Honor Recipients from the Civil War to Afghanistan* (Santa Barbara, CA: ABC-CLIO, 2011), 23–24; William Francis Allen Journal, Dec. 25, 1863, in *A Yankee Scholar in Coastal South Carolina: William Francis Allen's Civil War Journal* (Columbia: University of South Carolina Press, 2015), 65. See also the *Boston Recorder,* Jan. 15, 1864, p. 10, for a Union assistant surgeon's account of Christmas night 1863 at Robert E. Lee's occupied Arlington estate in Virginia, where black children being educated

by a missionary at a schoolhouse there put on an exhibition including a ten-year-old boy's rendition of Patrick Henry's "Give me liberty or give me death."

7. Sanitizing the Past

1. Letter from Quitman, Georgia, Aug. 25, 1865, in *Letters from the Commercial Correspondent of an Association of Cotton Manufacturers* (Boston: George C. Rand & Avery, 1865), 5; "Quondam" Dec. 12 letter from Milledgeville, *NYT,* Dec. 27, 1865, p. 1; Adele Allston to Adele Horst, Dec. 15, 1865, in *The South Carolina Rice Plantation as Revealed in the Papers of Robert F. W. Allston* (Chicago: University of Chicago Press, 1945), 215–16; letter from New Orleans, Oct. 21, 1865, in *Boston Daily Advertiser,* Nov. 2, 1865; Circular No. 2, Office Acting Assistant Commissioner, Freedmen's Bureau in Georgia, in *Augusta (GA) Daily Chronicle & Sentinel,* Oct. 7, 1865; *Richmond Whig and Public Advertiser,* Oct. 20, 1865, p. 2; Jacksonville, Florida, report in *Alexandria Gazette and Virginia Advertiser,* Nov. 23, 1865.

2. Eric Foner, *Reconstruction: America's Unfinished Revolution, 1863–1877* (New York: Harper & Row, 1988), 68; Circular No. 2, Oct. 8, 1865, Acting Assistant Commissioner for Georgia, Freedmen's Bureau, in *Augusta (GA) Daily Chronicle & Sentinel,* Oct. 7, 1865, p. 2; Oliver Otis Howard Circular, Nov. 11, 1865, in *Jackson Daily Mississippian,* Nov. 12, 1865; Davis Tillson report to Oliver Howard, Nov. 1, 1866, in *Sen. Ex. Doc.* 6, 39 Cong., 2 Sess., 48–50; E. A. Kozlay report as Acting Subassistant Commissioner, Orangeburg, SC, to Headquarters, South Carolina Freedmen's Bureau Assistant Commissioner, dated Orangeburg, SC, Jan. 29, 1866, in *Freedom: A Documentary History of Emancipation, 1861–1867,* Series 3, vol. 2, *Land and Labor, 1866–1867,* ed. René Hayden et al. (Chapel Hill: University of North Carolina Press, 2013), 387–90; Oliver Otis Howard speech at African church in Richmond, summarized in *Richmond Whig and Public Advertiser,* Oct. 3, 1865, p. 4; Steven Hahn, "'Extravagant Expectations' of Freedom: Rumour, Political Struggle, and the Christmas Insurrection Scare of 1865 in the American South," *Past and Present* 157 (Nov. 1997): 122–58.

3. Nancy Cohen-Lack, "A Struggle for Sovereignty: National Consolidation, Emancipation, and Free Labor in Texas, 1865," *JSH* 58 (Feb. 1992): 57–98, esp. 71; Sidney Andrews letter, Sept. 12, 1865, in Andrews, *The South Since the War: As Shown by Fourteen Weeks of Travel and Observation in Georgia and the Carolinas* (Boston: Ticknor and Fields, 1866), 35–36 (quotation on 36); *Vicksburg Journal* quoted in *Natchez Daily Courier,* Dec. 27, 1865; *Memphis Daily Appeal,* Nov. 30, 1865, p. 2; correspondent's letter from Milledgeville, GA, Dec. 12, 1865, in *NYT,* Dec. 27, 1865, p. 1; W. H. Wilder to J. Madison Wells, Dec. 14, 1865, in *Washington (D.C.) Daily National Intelligencer,* Dec. 14, 1865; telegraph report from Washington, D.C., Dec. 15, 1865, in *Richmond Daily Dispatch,* Dec. 16, 1861, p. 2; Dan T. Carter, "The Anatomy of Fear: The Christmas Day Insurrection Scare of 1865," *JSH* 42 (Aug. 1976): 345–64, esp. 346–49, 351–62.

4. Report from Augusta, GA, dated Dec. 20, 1865, in *Washington (D.C.) Daily National Intelligencer,* Dec. 28, 1865; *Augusta (GA) Daily Constitutionalist,* Dec. 15, 1865, p. 2.

5. Tallahassee, Florida, correspondent letter, Nov. 7, 1865, in *NYT,* Nov. 26, 1865, p. 1; Humphreys Nov. 8 proclamation and correspondent's letter dated Jackson, Nov. 3, in *Natchez Daily Courier,* Nov. 9, 1865; *Jackson Daily Mississippian,*

Nov. 12, 1865; *Richmond Daily Dispatch,* Dec. 13, 1865, p. 2; Samuel Porcher Gaillard Plantation Journal, Dec. 20, 1865, SCL, RSP, Series A, pt. 2, Reel 2; Susan Eva O'Donovan, *Becoming Free in the Cotton South* (Cambridge, MA: Harvard University Press, 2007), 154.

6. *Natchez Daily Courier,* Dec. 27, 1865; *Washington (D.C.) Daily National Intelligencer,* Dec. 27, 29, 1865; *Pittsburgh Gazette* account of Alexandria disturbance in *Daily Cleveland Herald,* Dec. 28, 1865; (Boston) *The Congregationalist,* Jan. 12, 1866, p. 8; William Blair, *Cities of the Dead: Contesting the Memory of the Civil War in the South* (Chapel Hill: University of North Carolina Press, 2004), 29–30.

7. Various reports in *Washington (D.C.) Daily National Intelligencer,* Dec. 28, 1865; *Edgefield (SC) Advertiser,* Dec. 27, 1865, p. 2; "Christmas," *Jacksonville Florida Union,* Dec. 30, 1865, p. 2; report of General and Assistant Freedmen's Bureau Commissioner for Alabama Wager Swayne, Oct. 31, 1866, in *Sen. Ex. Doc.* 6, 39 Cong., 2 Sess., 3; Circular No. 3 with sample contract, issued by the Assistant Commissioner of the South Carolina Freedmen's Bureau, Feb. 5, 1866, in Hayden et al., *Freedom: A Documentary History of Emancipation,* Series 3, vol. 2: p. 111; Carter, "Anatomy of Fear," 362–64.

8. John T. Trowbridge, *The South: A Tour of Its Battle-Fields and Ruined Cities, a Journey Through the Desolated States, and Talks with the People* . . . (Hartford, CT: L. Stebbins, 1866), 332–33; Henry William Ravenel Diary, Dec. 25, 1865, in *The Private Journal of Henry William Ravenel, 1859–1887* (Columbia: University of South Carolina Press, 1947), 259; Dolly Lunt Burge Diary, Dec. 24, 25, 1865, in James I. Robertson Jr., ed., "The Diary of Dolly Lunt Burge," pt. 7, *GHQ* 45 (Dec. 1961): 381–82; Jane Taylor deposition, May 13, 1919, quoted in *Voices of Emancipation: Understanding Slavery, the Civil War, and Reconstruction through the U.S. Pension Bureau Files,* ed. Elizabeth A. Regosin and Donald R. Shaffer (New York: New York University Press, 2008), 156–62.

9. Leon F. Litwack, *Been in the Storm So Long: The Aftermath of Slavery* (New York: Vintage Books, 1979), 184–85; correspondent's report, Aug. 8, 1866, in *NYT,* Aug. 14, 1866, p. 4.

10. O'Donovan, *Becoming Free,* 128; Charles B. Dew, *Bond of Iron: Master and Slave at Buffalo Forge* (New York: W. W. Norton, 1994), 349; Wilmer Shields to William N. Mercer, Dec. 19, 1865, quoted in Michael Wayne, *The Reshaping of Plantation Society: The Natchez District, 1860–1880* (Baton Rouge: Louisiana State University Press, 1983), 111; John C. Rodrique, *Reconstruction in the Cane Fields: From Slavery to Free Labor in Louisiana's Sugar Parishes, 1862–1880* (Baton Rouge: Louisiana State University Press, 2001), 71.

11. Adele Petigru Allston to Benjamin Allston, Dec. 27, 1866, in Easterby, ed., *South Carolina Rice Plantation,* 226; Freedmen's Bureau subassistant commissioner Nov. 10, 1868, report, quoted in "Memorial of the colored men of the second congressional district of Georgia, setting forth their grievances and asking protection," Dec. 4, 1868, in *House Misc. Doc.,* 40 Cong., 3 Sess., #52, p. 94.

12. Sallie McNeill Diary, Jan. 4, 1867, in *The Uncompromising Diary of Sallie McNeill, 1858–1867* (College Station: Texas A&M University Press, 2009), 135–36; Betsey Bittersweet letter of Jan. 1, 1868, quoted in Anne Sarah Rubin, *A Shattered Nation: The Rise and Fall of the Confederacy, 1861–1868* (Chapel Hill: University

of North Carolina Press, 2005), 227; "Quince" (William G. Simms) correspondent's letter, Dec. 25, [1867], in *Charleston Tri-Weekly Courier,* Jan. 4, 1867, p. 1; Mary C. Simms Oliphant, Alfred Taylor Odell, and T. C. Duncan Eaves, eds., *The Letters of William Gilmore Simms,* vol. 5 (Columbia: University of South Carolina Press, 1956), 104n.

13. Henry William Ravenel Diary, Dec. 25, 1872, in Childs, ed., *Private Journal of Henry William Ravenel,* 362; *Sonoma (CA) Democrat,* Apr. 8, 1876.

14. Jefferson Davis to A. Dudley Mann, Dec. 31, 1882, in *The Papers of Jefferson Davis,* ed. Lynda Lasswell Crist, vol. 14 (Baton Rouge: Louisiana State University Press, 2015), 163–64.

15. Peter Kolchin, "Reexamining Southern Emancipation in Comparative Perspective," *JSH* 81 (Feb. 2015): 7–40; *Edgefield Advertiser,* Dec. 27, 1865, p. 2.

16. (Boston) *The Congregationalist,* Jan. 12, 1866, p. 8; *Ogdensburg (NY) Daily Journal,* Dec. 28, 1865, p. 2; *Northern New York Journal,* Jan. 9, 1866, p. 2.

17. Black victim quoted in O'Donovan, *Becoming Free,* 154. Occasional apprehensions about Christmas black insurrections continued in some southern circles for a few years afterward, but nothing like the 1865 panic. See, for example, Stephen Ward Angell, *Bishop Henry McNeal Turner and African-American Religion in the South* (Knoxville: University of Tennessee Press, 1992), 64.

18. Mrs. A. C. Carmichael, *Domestic Manners and Social Condition of the White, Coloured, and Negro Population of the West Indies,* 2 vols. (London: Whittaker, Treacher, 1833), 2:142–48, 192, 288–92 (quotations on 292; flour throwing on 193, 288). See *Charleston Courier,* Apr. 12–Aug. 16, 1844; (Washington, D. C.) *National Intelligencer,* Nov. 19, 1833; (Washington, D.C.) *Globe,* Jan. 3–July 7, 1834, for advertisements of Carmichael's *Domestic Manners.*

19. Marli F. Weiner, *Mistress and Slaves: Plantation Women in South Carolina, 1830–1880* (Urbana: University of Illinois Press, 1998), 100; Jan Bakker, "Another Dilemma of an Intellectual in the Old South: Caroline Gilman, the Peculiar Institution, and Greater Rights for Women in the Rose Magazines," *Southern Literary Journal* 17 (Fall 1984): 12–25; Elizabeth Moss, *Domestic Novelists in the Old South: Defenders of Southern Culture* (Baton Rouge: Louisiana State University Press, 1992), 1–2, 7, 37–38, 67, 69–71, 221.

20. Caroline Gilman, *Recollections of a Southern Matron* (New York: Harper & Brothers, 1838), 98–103 (quotation on 101–2).

21. Irwin Russell, "Christmas-Night in the Quarters," *Scribner's Monthly* 15 (Jan. 1878): 445–48; G. William Nott, "Irwin Russell, First Dialect Author," and Joel Chandler Harris, "Introduction," in *Christmas-Night in the Quarters* (Richmond, VA: Dietz Press, 1917 [?]), v–xiii, xv–xvi.

22. Catherine Ann Ware Warfield, *The Romance of Beauseincourt: An Episode Extracted from the Retrospect of Miriam Monfort* (New York: G. W. Carleton, 1867), 125–27. In a bizarre plot twist, a chained bear kept as a plantation pet bursts free during the Christmas celebration and mauls the master, with male field hands witnessing the incident helplessly and rescue being provided by a family dog that attacks the bear's throat, allowing the master to fatally stab the bear with his Bowie knife. Warfield imparts a racialist moral to the incident, saying that the contrast in master-slave reactions evidenced the difference between white "promptness, energy, and forethought" and blacks' sluggishness.

Warfield, *Romance,* 127–30. For more on Warfield and a slightly different interpretation of the tale, see Bertram Wyatt-Brown, *The House of Percy: Honor, Melancholy, and Imagination in a Southern Family* (New York: Oxford University Press, 1994), 112–18.

23. Mary Tucker Magill, *The Holcombes: A Story of Virginia Home-Life* (Philadelphia: J. B. Lippincott, 1871), unpaged dedication, v; Warfield, *Romance of Beauseincourt,* 126.

24. Magill, *Holcombes,* 51–83 (quotation on 77).

25. John Marchmont (Celina E. Means), *Thirty-Four Years: An American Story of Southern Life* (Philadelphia: Claxton, Remsen and Haffelfinger, 1878), vii ("To The Public"), 70–96 (quotations on 78–83); George Armstrong Wauchope, *The Writers of South Carolina . . .* (Columbia, SC: State Company, 1910), 62.

26. Louise-Clarke Pyrnelle, *Diddie, Dumps, and Tot, or Plantation Child-Life* (New York: Harper & Brothers, 1882), 29–43.

27. R. Bruce Bickley Jr., "Joel Chandler Harris (1845–1908)," in *New Georgia Encyclopedia Companion to Georgia Literature,* ed. Hugh Ruppersburg (Athens: University of Georgia Press, 2007), 205–12; Edward L. Ayers, *The Promise of the New South: Life after Reconstruction* (New York: Oxford University Press, 1992), 341–43; *Uncle Remus, His Songs and Sayings: The Folklore of the Old Plantation* (New York: D. Appleton, 1880); Paula T. Connolly, *Slavery in American Children's Literature, 1790–2010* (Iowa City: University of Iowa Press, 2013), 111–13, 231n; Michael Price, "Back to the Briar Patch: Joel Chandler Harris and the Literary Defense of Paternalism," *GHQ* 81 (Fall 1997): 686–712; David W. Blight, *Race and Reunion: The Civil War in American Memory* (Cambridge, MA: Harvard University Press, 2001), 227–31.

28. This argument derives mostly from the obvious empathy Harris displayed for slaves on the Turner plantation, his own deprived background that might have inclined him to favor underdogs, his relatively progressive racial views for his day, and the fact that his trickster characters like Brer Rabbit got the upper hand over more powerful opponents like Brer Fox (as in the second of the stories in the first of his Uncle Remus volumes—"The Wonderful Tar-Baby Story").

29. Joel Chandler Harris, *Nights with Uncle Remus: Myths and Legends of the Old Plantation* (Boston: Houghton Mifflin, 1883), 386–404 (quotations on 386, 402, 397).

30. Joel Chandler Harris, "The Baby's Christmas," in *Tales of the Home Folks in Peace and War* (Boston: Houghton, Mifflin, 1898), 377–417 (quotations on 385, 411); Harris, *On the Plantation: A Story of a Georgia Boy's Adventures During the War* (New York: D. Appleton, 1892), 104–23 (quotations on 119–21).

31. Alice M. Bacon, "Christmas Days at the School," *Southern Workman,* Feb. 1, 1886, p. 17; Susan Dabney Smedes, *Memorial of a Southern Planter,* ed. Fletcher M. Green (1887; rpt., New York: Alfred A. Knopf, 1965), ix, 148–53. Yet other mid-1880s southern white glorifications of antebellum slave Christmas experiences included novelist and ex-Confederate officer John Esten Cooke's "Christmas Time in Old Virginia," *Magazine of American History* 10 (Dec. 1883): 443–59; and Montgomery M. Folsom's "Christmas at Brockton Plantation," *Southern Bivouac,* New Series 1 (Jan. 1886): 483–89.

32. James Lane Allen, "Mrs. Stowe's 'Uncle Tom' at Home in Kentucky," *Century Illustrated Magazine* 34 (Oct. 1887): 852–67, esp. 866; James H. Jones to the mayor of New Orleans, and editorial comment, in *Galveston (TX) Daily News,* Dec. 20, 1889, p. 4. For Jones's relationship with Davis at the end of the Civil War and prior to Davis's death, see Felicity Allen, *Jefferson Davis: Unconquerable Heart* (Columbia: University of Missouri Press, 1999), 8; William J. Cooper Jr., *Jefferson Davis, American* (New York: Alfred A. Knopf, 2000), 644.

33. Ruth McEnery Stuart, "Christmas Gifts" (*Lippincott's Monthly Magazine,* Jan. 1891), in *Christmas Stories from Louisiana,* ed. Dorothy Dodge Robbins and Kenneth Robbins (Jackson: University Press of Mississippi, 2009), 119–36; Stuart, *A Golden Wedding and Other Tales* (New York: Harper & Brothers, 1893), 129–54; "Negro and Indian Students to Present Plays on Lincoln's Birthday," *NYT,* Feb. 4, 1901, p. 7; Rebecca Cameron, "Christmas at Buchoi, a North Carolina Rice Plantation," *Ladies Home Journal* Christmas issue, 1891, reprinted in *The North Carolina Booklet* 13 (July 1913), 3–10. Reprintings of Stuart's 1893 collection included two by Harper & Brothers in 1900 and 1901, one by Garrett Press (New York, 1969), and one by Books for Libraries Press (Freeport, NY, 1972).

34. Cameron, "Christmas at Buchoi" (*North Carolina Booklet*), 5–8.

35. Albert B. Shepard, "Christmas Eve on the Old Plantation," and Marie L. Points, "Henriette's Christmas," both in *NODP,* Dec. 27, 1891, p. 20.

36. William P. Trent, *William Gilmore Simms* (Boston: Houghton Mifflin, 1892), 96–99 (quotations on 99).

37. "Marse Tom's Christmas Gif'," *Galveston (TX) Daily News,* Dec. 25, 1891, p. 12.

38. "How They Hung Their Stockings," *NODP,* Dec. 24, 1893, p. 19; Bowman Matthews, "Beauchamp of Oakhurst: A Christmas Story of the South in Other Days," *NODP,* Dec. 25, 1893, p. 9; John Williamson Palmer, "Old Maryland Homes and Ways," reprinted from *Century Magazine,* in "A Plantation Christmas," *NODP,* Dec. 2, 1894, p. 15; "Christmas and New Year Days," *NODP,* Dec. 22, 1895, p. 18; Elizabeth M. Gilmer, "Uncle Isom as Santa Claus," *NODP,* Dec. 24, 1899, p. 10.

39. Sallie May Dooley, *Dem Good Ole Times* (New York: Doubleday, Page, 1906), 107–33, esp. 107–19 (quotations on 119, 117); Ruth McEnery Stuart, "Duke's Christmas," in Stuart, *Solomon Crow's Christmas Pockets and Other Tales* (1896; rpt., Freeport, NY: Libraries Press, 1969), 165–89 (quotations on 180–81, 188).

40. Varina Davis, "Christmas in the Confederate White House," *New York World,* Dec. 13, 1896, http://www.civilwar.org/education/history/on-the-homefront/culture/christmas.html; Carol K. Bleser, "The Marriage of Varina Howell and Jefferson Davis: 'I gave the best and all my life to a girdled tree,'" *JSH* 65 (Feb. 1999): 3–40, esp. 37.

41. Thomas Nelson Page, *Social Life in Old Virginia Before the War* (New York: Charles Scribner's Sons, 1897), 81–101; Page, "Social Life in Old Virginia Before the War: All the Year and Christmas," *Christian Union,* Dec. 19, 1891, pp. 1212–21.

42. Ruth McEnery Stuart, "An Old-Time Christmas Gift," *St. Nicholas,* 25 (Dec. 1897): 94–103 (quotations on 94, 102); Stuart, "A Christmas Gift That

Went . . . A-Begging," *Milwaukee Journal,* Dec. 18, 1897; Stuart, *George Washington Jones: A Christmas Gift That Went A-Begging* (1903; rpt., Freeport, NY: Books for Libraries Press, 1972), esp. 17–19, 123.

43. See W. Fitzhugh Brundage, *The Southern Past: A Clash of Race and Memory* (Cambridge, MA: Harvard University Press, 2005), 12–16, 21–33; Caroline E. Janney, *Burying the Dead but Not the Past: Ladies' Memorial Associations and the Lost Cause* (Chapel Hill: University of North Carolina Press, 2008); Karen L. Cox, *Dixie's Daughters: The United Daughters of the Confederacy and the Preservation of Confederate Culture* (Gainesville: University Press of Florida, 2003); Keith S. Hébert, *The Long Civil War in the North Georgia Mountains: Confederate Nationalism, Sectionalism and White Supremacy in Bartow County, Georgia* (Knoxville: University of Tennessee Press, 2017), 176–78; Laura Lyons McLemore, "Gray Ghost: Creating a Collective Memory of a Confederate Texas," in *Lone Star Unionism, Dissent, and Resistance: Other Sides of Civil War Texas,* ed. Jesús F. de la Teja (Norman: University of Oklahoma Press, 2016), 15–36, esp. 24–26.

44. Eugenia J. Bacon, *Lyddy: A Tale of the Old South* (New York: Continental Publishing, 1898), preface, 29–31 (quotation on 30); Lucinda H. MacKethan, "Reading Marlboro Jones: A Georgia Slave in Civil War Virginia," in *Virginia's Civil War,* ed. Peter Wallenstein and Bertram Wyatt-Brown (Charlottesville: University of Virginia Press, 2005), 165–75, esp. 172–73.

45. Mrs. A. M. Paynter, "Christmas in the Old Southern Home," *Christian Observer,* Dec. 13, 1899, p. 19.

46. Belle Kearney, *A Slaveholder's Daughter* (St. Louis: St. Louis Christian Advocate, 1900), unpaged biographical note, 4–6, 249–50; LaSalle Corbell Pickett, *Yule Log* (Washington, D.C.: Neale, 1900), quotations on 11, 34; Georgia Bryan Conrad, *Reminiscences of a Southern Woman, Reprinted from the "Southern Workman"* (Hampton, VA: Hampton Institute Press, 1900), 5, 15, 18, 20.

47. James Battle Avirett, *The Old Plantation: How We Lived in Great House and Cabin Before the War* (New York: F. Tennyson Neely, 1901); David S. Cecelski, "Oldest Living Confederate Chaplain Tells All? Or, James B. Avirett and the Rise and Fall of the Rich Lands," *Southern Cultures* 3 (Winter 1997): 5–24; Comer L. Peek, *Lorna Carswell: A Story of the South* (New York: Broadway Publishing, 1903), 1, 9, (quotations on 148–49); "New Books," *Florida Magazine* 7 (No. 1): 176; Francis L. Fleming to Comer L. Peek, Sept. 16, 1903, quoted along with other endorsements and a review in *Confederate Veteran* 12 (Oct. 1904): 467.

48. H. M. Hamill, *The Old South: A Monograph* (Nashville, TN: Smith & Lamar, 1904), 38–40 (quotations on 40); Obituaries to Hamill in *Confederate Veteran* 23 (Mar. 1915), 139–40; Margaret Devereux, *Plantation Sketches* (Cambridge, MA: Riverside Press, 1906), unpaged "To My Grandchildren" (first quotation), 1–2, 36–37 (second, third, and fourth quotations), 119 (fifth quotation).

49. Eliza Ripley, *Social Life in Old New Orleans: Being Recollections of my Girlhood* (New York: D. Appleton, 1912), 219, 256–62; Cornelia Branch Stone, "Vivid Reminiscences of the Old Plantation," *Confederate Veteran* 20 (Dec. 1912): 568–71; Esther S. Reynolds, *Memories of Mulberry* (Brooklyn, NY: Eagle Press, 1913), 9–12; *Minutes of the Twenty-Fourth Annual Convention of the United Daughters of the Confederacy, Held in Chattanooga, Tennessee, November 14–17, 1917* (Richmond, VA: Richmond Press, 1918), 331–33, 8–9, 138, 141, 148.

50. Eugenia Dunlap Potts, "Slavery," read March 14, 1909, in *Historic Papers on the Causes of the Civil War* (Lexington, KY: Ashland Printing, 1909 [?]), 12–13; Virginia Frazer Boyle, "Christmas Gif'!': A Memory of the Old South," *Century Illustrated Monthly Magazine* 83 (Dec. 1911), 305–9; "The Confederate Memorial Association," *Confederate Veteran* 17 (Jan. 1909): 310; Mildred Lewis Rutherford, *The South in History and Literature* . . . (Atlanta: Franklin Turner, 1907), 669.

51. Edna Turpin, "Abram's Freedom," *Atlantic Monthly* 110 (Jan. 1912): 311–21; Turpin, *Abram's Freedom* (Boston: Pilgrim Press, 1913); Mrs. F. C. Roberts, "Christmas in the Confederacy," *Carolina and the Southern Cross* 1 (Jan. 1914): 4.

52. Mildred Lewis Rutherford, *"The Civilization of the Old South: What Made It: What Destroyed It: What Has Replaced It," Address Delivered by Miss Mildred Lewis Rutherford* . . . (Athens, GA: McGregor, 1916), 15 (quotations), 17, 35, 46.

53. Archibald Rutledge, *Plantation Game Trails* (Boston: Houghton Mifflin, 1921), 290–300 (quotation on 294); Elizabeth W. Allston Pringle, *Chronicles of Chicora Wood* (New York: Charles Scribner's Sons, 1922), 150–56; Patience Pennington (pseud.), *A Woman Rice Planter* (New York: Macmillan, 1913), 271–74; Harry McBrayer Bayne, "Rutledge, Archibald Hamilton," in *The New Encyclopedia of Southern Culture,* vol. 9, ed. M. Thomas Inge (Chapel Hill: University of North Carolina Press, 2008), 408–9. *A Woman Rice Planter* was itself reprinted many times by Macmillan in the nineteenth century and by the Reprint Company and University of South Carolina Press in the late twentieth century.

54. Harriet Beecher Stowe, "Christmas Day North and South," *Christian Union,* Dec. 18, 1872, pp. 505–6; Anne Rowe, *The Enchanted Country: Northern Writers in the South, 1865–1910* (Baton Rouge: Louisiana State University Press, 1978), 1–21. Rowe argues that Stowe's transformation was foreshadowed in *Uncle Tom's Cabin* passages that romanticized the South and southern aristocrats and depicted "the happy-go-lucky darkie." For northern complicity in celebratory mythologies about slavery and the Lost Cause, see John David Smith, *An Old Creed for the New South: Proslavery Ideology and Historiography, 1865–1918* (1985; rpt. of 1991 edition, Athens: University of Georgia Press, 2008), 42–52; Karen L. Cox, *Dreaming of Dixie: How the South Was Created in American Popular Culture* (Chapel Hill: University of North Carolina Press, 2011); Rollin G. Osterweis, *The Myth of the Lost Cause, 1865–1900* (Hamden, CT: Archon Books, 1973), 30–32.

55. Sinclair was born in Baltimore, but his family moved to New York City and he attended the College of the City of New York and Columbia University. He wrote the novel while living on a rented farm in Princeton, New Jersey, and can hardly be classed as a southerner. Lauren Coodly, *Upton Sinclair: California Socialist, Celebrity Intellectual* (Lincoln: University of Nebraska Press, 2013), 19–35.

56. Upton Sinclair, *Manassas: A Novel of the War* (New York: Macmillan, 1904), 19; [Thomas J. Hudson], *Centennial History of Arkansas,* ed. Dallas T. Herndon, vol. 1 (Chicago: S. J. Clarke, 1922), 5 (foreword by Dallas T. Herndon), 443–44. See also John Hugh Reynolds, *Makers of Arkansas History* (1905; rpt., New York: Silver, Burdett, 1905), 181.

57. [No author listed], "Her Old Clock," *Youth's Companion,* Dec. 21, 1882, pp. 549–50; M. B. Williams, "Uncle Jake's Story," *Youth's Companion,* Dec. 17, 1885, pp. 534–35; Williams, "A Christmas of the Past," *Youth's Companion,* Dec.

20, 1888, pp. 644–45; Sarah Winter Kellogg, "Sidney's Body-Servant," *Youth's Companion,* Dec. 23, 1893, pp. 651–52.

58. "Under the Confederacy," *The American: A National Weekly Journal of Politics, Literature, Science, Art, and Finance,* Dec. 25, 1880, 168–69; N. T. M., "Mammy's C'ris'mus," *Catholic World* 52 (Jan. 1891): 529–39 (quotations on 533, 537).

59. F. G. de Fontaine, "A Plantation Xmas," in *Atchison (KS) Daily Globe,* Jan. 1, 1892; *Edwardsville (IL) Intelligencer,* Dec. 30, 1891, p. 2; *Deer Lake (MT) New Northwest,* Jan. 9, 1892, p. 1; Jean Folkerts, "Felix Gregory de Fontaine (1834–11 December 1896)," in *American Newspaper Journalists, 1690-1872,* ed. Perry J. Ashley, vol. 43 in *Dictionary of Literary Biography* (Detroit: Gale Resources, 1985), 147–51.

60. "Andy's Christmas Gift to the Rebels," *Milwaukee Daily Sentinel,* Dec. 28, 1868; James C. Plummer, "In the Quarter," *Milwaukee Sentinel,* Dec. 18, 1887.

61. Charles Hallock, "Holumdays in Old Dixie," *Forest and Stream,* Dec. 23, 1899, pp. 507–8; Hallock, *An Angler's Reminiscences: A Record of Sport, Travel, and Adventure, With Autobiography of the Author* (Cincinnati: Sportsmen's Review, 1913), 1.

62. John Tebbel and Mary Ellen Zuckerman, *The Magazine in America, 1741-1990* (New York: Oxford University Press, 1991), 22–23, 50; Eric Fettmann, "Harper's Weekly," in *Encyclopedia of the American Civil War: A Political, Social, and Military History,* 5 vols. (Santa Barbara, CA: ABC-CLIO, 2000), 2:931–33.

63. "Christmas in Virginia," *Harper's Weekly,* Dec. 30, 1871, p. 1220.

64. "Christmas in the South," *Harper's Weekly,* Dec. 12, 1885, p. 827.

65. Lillie Devereux Blake, "Looking Backward to Two Christmas Days of Long Ago," *NYT,* Dec. 18, 1904, First Sunday Magazine Section, p. 4.

66. William Ludwell Sheppard, "Holiday Festivities at the South—An Egg-Nogg Party in Richmond, Virginia—The Critical Moment," *Frank Leslie's Illustrated Weekly,* Dec. 29, 1892, p. 470; "Topics and Pictures Fifty Years Ago," *Leslie's Weekly,* Dec. 26, 1907, p. 628; Sheppard, "Christmas in the South—A Suggestive Visit to the Old Family," *Harper's Weekly,* Dec. 12, 1885, p. 832; Sheppard, "A Christmas Gift to 'Ole Marster and Missus,'" *Harper's Weekly,* Dec. 22, 1883, p. 820; Karal Ann Marling, *Merry Christmas! Celebrating America's Greatest Holiday* (Cambridge, MA: Harvard University Press, 2000), 256–57; Timothy G. Young, *Drawn to Enchant: Original Children's Book Art in the Betsy Beinecke Shirley Collection* (New Haven, CT: Yale University Press, 2007), 212.

67. Unsigned letter to *New York Tribune,* reprinted in *Galveston (TX) Daily News,* Mar. 25, 1895, p. 6; Dianne Swann-Wright, *A Way Out of No Way: Claiming Family and Freedom in the New South* (Charlottesville: University of Virginia Press, 2002), 96.

68. "Ex-Slaves Pray We Stay at Peace," *NYT,* Dec. 25, 1940, p. 20; "Lord Sent It, But Devil Was Bearer," *Chicago Defender,* Jan. 1, 1921, p. 1; "Ex-Slaves Sing, Dance and Feast in Atlanta," *NYT,* Dec. 25, 1930, p. 14.

69. "Funds Yet Needed for These Baskets," *Athens Banner-Herald,* Dec. 20, 1926, p. 1; "The Ex-Slave Christmas Fund," *Athens Banner-Herald,* Dec. 22, 1927, p. 4; Daniel Vivian, "Plantation Life: Varieties of Experience on the Remade Plantations of the South Carolina Lowcountry," in *Leisure, Plantations, and the Making of the New South: The Sporting Plantations of the South Carolina Lowcountry and Red Hills Region, 1900-1940,* ed. Julia Brock and Daniel Vivian (Lanham, MD: Lexington Books, 2015), 21–56, esp. 43–44.

70. Ellen Call Long, "Princesse Achille Murat: A Biographical Sketch" (first published in 1867), *Florida Historical Quarterly* 2 (July 1909): 27-38, esp. 36; "A Former Slave's Gratitude," *NODP* quoted in *New York Evening Post,* Supplement, Jan. 8, 1881, p. 3; *San Francisco Evening Bulletin,* Feb. 4, 1881, p. 4; *Central City (CO) Daily Register-Call,* May 2, 1881, p. 3.

71. "Mourned by a Slave Many Years," correspondent's report in the *Boston Traveller,* Jan. 1, 1890, quoted in *NYT,* Jan. 5, 1890, p. 6, and *St. Paul Daily News,* Feb. 1890, p. 4.

72. "Former Slave Santa Claus at Soldiers' Home in Atlanta," *Sacramento Union,* Dec. 25, p. 18; "Ex-Slave Gives Old Vets Xmas Party," *Los Angeles Herald,* Jan. 6, 1920, A-6; "A Slave-Time Christmas," *Macon (GA) Telegraph,* Dec. 27, 1898, p. 7; "Negro Plays Santa to Old Confederates," *NYT,* Dec. 25, 1919, p. 11; "Black Confederate Soldiers," www.scv-kirby-smith.org/Black%20 Confederate.htm; "Confederate Heritage Month," Robert E. Lee Camp 1640, Sons of Confederate Veterans, Apr. 1, 2015, https://www.facebook.com/RELeeCamp1640 /posts/8353695531847920:0; Sonny Perdue, "Confederate History Month Proclamation," Mar. 5, 2008, in *The Confederate and Neo-Confederate Reader: The "Great Truth" about the "Lost Cause,"* ed. James W. Loewen and Edward H. Sebesta (Jackson: University Press of Mississippi, 2010), 382-83; Calvin E. Johnson Jr., "April Is Confederate History Month in Dixie," Mar. 20, 2008, spofga.org /flag/2008/march/calvin_johnson.php; Chaplain's Corner, "All It Took Was a Yopp!": (R. de T. Lawrence), *Bill Yopp: 10-Cent Bill* (Clarkston, GA: Charles W. Hampton, 1969). To be fair, some African Americans have claimed ownership of Yopp's story, and some of Yopp's descendants attended Governor Perdue's signing event. See, for instance "Laurens County African American History," laurenscountyafricanamericanhistory.blogspot.com.

73. Stowe, "Christmas Day," 505; Henry Churton (Albion W. Tourgée), *Toinette: A Tale of Transition* (New York: J. B. Ford, 1875), esp. 7-38 (quotations on 16, 18, 23); Sharon D. Kennedy-Nolle, *Writing Reconstruction: Race, Gender, and Citizenship in the Postwar South* (Chapel Hill: University of North Carolina Press, 2015), 76-122.

74. Henrietta Matson, *The Mississippi Schoolmaster* (Boston: Congregational Sunday-School and Publishing Society, 1893), 31-34 (quotation on 31-32); *Nashville Union and American,* Nov. 4, 1870, p. 4; "New Appointments. 1877-1878," *American Missionary* 32 (Feb. 1878): 44 (listing Henrietta Matson of North Bloomfield, Ohio, as a new instructor at Fisk University); Henrietta Matson listing, Twelfth U.S. Census, 1900, Population, Tennessee, Davidson County.

75. Gilmer, "Uncle Isom"; J. G. Clinkscales, *On the Plantation: Reminiscences of His Childhood* (Spartanburg, SC: Band & White, 1916), unpaged foreword, 7-8, 52-56 (quotation on 55).

76. David W. Blight, "If You Don't Tell It Like It Was, It Can Never Be as It Ought to Be," in *Slavery and Public History: The Tough Stuff of American Memory,* ed. James Oliver Horton and Lois E. Horton (New York: New Press, 2006), 19-33, esp. 26-27; Smith, *Old Creed,* 197-238, esp. 200-201.

77. Mitch Kachun, *Festivals of Freedom: Memory and Meaning in African American Emancipation Celebrations, 1808-1915* (Amherst: University of Massachusetts Press, 2003), 148-50; J. W. Hood, "The Mission of Methodism to All Classes,"

in *Proceedings, Sermons, Essays, and Addresses of the Centennial Methodist Conference Held in Mt. Vernon Place Methodist Episcopal Church, Baltimore, MD., December 9–17, 1884,* ed. H. K. Carroll, W. P. Harrison, and J. H. Bayliss (New York: Phillips & Hunt, 1885), 475–79 (quotation on 478); Bettye Collier-Thomas, comp. and ed., *African-American Christmas Stories* (New York: Henry Holt, 1997). As late as 1974, a writer for the African American paper *Milwaukee Star-Times* reproached those blacks preferring "not to talk about the past" in a piece urging the value of learning about southern plantation traditions including Christmas Gif' as a means toward racial self-fulfillment. "A Plantation Xmas," *Milwaukee Star-Times,* Dec. 5, 1974, p. 16.

78. James H. W. Howard, *Bond and Free; A True Tale of Slave Times* (Harrisburg, PA: Edwin K. Meyers, 1886), 28, 42; Ronald A. Tyson, "James H. W. Howard," in *African American Authors, 1745–1945: A Bio-Bibliographical Critical Sourcebook* (Westport, CT: Greenwood Press, 2000), 244.

79. Jack Thorne (pseud. for David Bryant Fulton), *Hanover; Or, Persecution of the Lowly: Story of the Wilmington Massacre* (n.p.: M. C. L. Hill, 1901), 72–76 (quotations on 72); Margaret M. Mulrooney, *Race, Place, and Memory: Deep Currents in Wilmington, North Carolina* (Gainesville: University Press of Florida, 2018), 152–54 and passim; William L. Andrews, "Fulton, David Bryant," https://www.ncpedia.org/biography/fulton-david-bryant.

80. T. Thomas Fortune, "The Graveyard 'Possum," in *After War Times: An African American Childhood in Reconstruction Days,* ed. Daniel R. Weinfeld (Tuscaloosa: University of Alabama Press, 2014), xi–xiii, 18 ("gala").

81. Booker T. Washington, "Christmas Days in Old Virginia," *Suburban Life* 5 (Dec. 1907): 336–37, reprinted in *The Booker T. Washington Papers, vol. 1, The Autobiographical Writings,* ed. Louis R. Harlan (Urbana: University of Illinois Press, 1972), 394–97; Washington, *The Story of the Negro: The Rise of the Race from Slavery,* vol. 1 of 2 vols., extract in *The Booker T. Washington Papers,* vol. 1, *The Autobiographical Writings,* 414–15.

82. Irving F. Lowery, *Life on the Old Plantation in Ante-bellum Days, or A Story Based on Facts* (Columbia, SC: State Company, 1911), 13, 15, 29, 64–68 (quotations on 65, 67, 68, 65).

83. Merl R. Eppse, *The Negro, Too, in American History* (Nashville, TN: National Publication, 1943), xi, 68; Cheryl Knott, "A Race Against Obscurity: Merl R. Eppse and *The Negro, Too, in American History,*" in *Writing History from the Magazines: African Americans and the Quest for Freedom,* ed. Claire Parfait, Hélène Le Dantec-Lowry, and Clair Bourhis-Mariotti (New York: Routledge, 2017), 26–42.

84. "Days of Slavery," *Syracuse Sunday Herald,* Nov. 1, 1896, p. 9.

85. Fannie Barrier Williams, "After Many Days: A Christmas Story," *Colored American Magazine* 6 (Dec. 1902): 140–53.

86. "A Christmas Morning Long Ago," *New York Age,* Dec. 24, 1914, p. 1.

87. John B. Gordon, "Boyhood in the South," *The Youth's Companion,* Jan. 11, 1900, pp. 15–16.

EPILOGUE

1. In 2000, *Southern Living* ranked nineteenth, with 2,540,821 paid subscribers, ahead of such mainstays as *Martha Stewart Living, U.S. News & World Report,*

Parenting Magazine, and the *National Enquirer.* adage.com/datacenter/datapopup
.php?article_id=106282.

2. Cassandra M. Vanhooser, "An 1863 Homecoming," *Southern Living* 33
(Dec. 1998): 36; "A Plantation Christmas," *Southern Living* 28 (Nov. 1993):
141–54.

3. Jennifer L. Eichstedt and Stephen Small, *Representations of Slavery: Race and
Ideology in Southern Plantation Museums* (Washington, D.C.: Smithsonian Institution Press, 2002), 1.

4. Mark St. John Erickson, "Plantations Outfitted in Their Christmas Best," *Daily Press,* Dec. 12, 1999, articles.dailypress.com/1999-12-12
/entertainment/9912100120_1_sherwood-forest-plantation-christmas-new
-holiday-traditions; Krys Stefansky, "Holiday Home Tours: Decked Halls
Open to the Public, *Virginian-Pilot* online, Dec. 2, 2012, pilotonline.com/life
/holiday-home-tours-deecked-halls-open-t-the-public/article_595b7807-4;
www.oakalleyplantation.com/2016_Bonfire_Party; www.oakalleyplantation
.com/events/annual-christmas-bonfire-party. For the concept of heritage tourism, see Tanya Shields, "Magnolia Longing: The Plantation Tour as Palimp-
sest," *Souls: A Critical Journal of Black Politics, Culture and Society* 19 (No. 1, 2017):
6–23, esp. 10.

5. www.edmondstonalston.com/visit/special-events.html; www.crafted
charlestontours.com/blog/74-christmas; bellegroveplantation.com/7800;
www.edgewoodplantation.com/events.htm; "Grand Illumination at Middleton Place," www.charlestoncvb.com/events/grand-illumination-at-middleton
-place-8410/.

6. James Oliver Horton, "Slavery in American History: An Unfortunate
National Dialogue," in *Slavery and Public History: The Tough Stuff of American Memory,*
ed. James Oliver Horton and Lois E. Horton (New York: New Press, 2006), 35–55
(quotation on 48).

7. "One Hundred Years of Christmas," Historic Latta Plantation, https://
www.lattaplantgation.org/new-events/2016/11/25/hundred-years-christmas
("holiday cheer"); "Christmas at Mount Vernon,"www.mountvernon./org
/plan-your-visit/activities-tours/christmas-at-mount-vernon; David Nicholson,
"Day-tripping: Enjoy Virginia's Elegant Plantations during the Holiday Season," www.daily-press.com/features/home-garden/dp-fea-day-trip-plantations
-at-christmas-20141130-story.htmn; "Candlelight Open House Kicks Off the
Holiday Season," www.gcnews.com/candlelight-open-house-kicks-off-the
-holiday-season/; www.wafb.com/story/1568366/nottoway-plantation-christmas
-candlelight-tours; Joanne Sasvari, "Nottoway Is a White House with a Dark
Past," culturelocker.com/satory/2014/Louisiana-Nottoway.html.

8. Texas Historical Commission site, www.the.texas.gov/historic-sites
/varner-hogg-plantation-state-historic-site/varner-hogg-planttion-history;
Amanda McVay, "Varner-Hogg Plantation by Candlelight," www.the.texas
.gov/blog/varner-hogg-plantation-candlelight.

9. E. Arnold Modlin Jr., "Tales Told on the Tour: Mythic Representations
of Slavery by Docents at North Carolina Plantation Museums," *Southeastern
Geographer* 48 (Nov. 2008): 265–87, esp. 265–66; "Christmas at Mount Vernon"; "Grand Illumination at Middleton Place"; "Middleton Place Grand

Illumination," discoversouthcarolina.com/products/1988; Historic Rosedale Plantation Candlelight Christmas, Dec. 6, 2015, www.meetup.com/ghosts -26/events/226997096/; "Christmas 1860 at the Edmondston-Alston House," www.craftedcharlestontours.com/blog/74-christmas-1860-at-the-edmondston -alston-house.

10. Nicholson, "Day-tripping"; "Bacon's Castle Christmas," https://video .com/82210061; "One Hundred Years of Christmas" (advertising 2017 festivities at Latta Plantation); www.historicaljonesboro.org/Events.htm; www .historicaljonesboro.org/indexhome.htm; www.historicaljonesboro.org /About.htm.

11. Tara McPherson, *Reconstructing Dixie: Race, Gender, and Nostalgia in the Imagined South* (Durham, NC: Duke University Press, 2003), 43; Eichstedt and Small, *Representations of Slavery,* 17, 258; Niels Eichhorn, "The Plantation Tour Disaster: Teaching Slavery, Memory, and Public History," in *Muster: Reflections on Popular Culture Brought to You by the Journal of the Civil War Era,* Dec. 5, 2016, https:// journalofthecivilwarera.org/2016/12/plantation-tour-disaster-teaching-slavery -memory-public-history/; *Erickson,* "Plantations Outfitted"; "Callaway Plantation," www.exploregeorgia.org/listing/688-callaway-plantation/map); www .news-reporter.com/news/2012-11-22/News/Christmas/tours_at_Callaway _Plantation_set_Decembe.html; Shields, "Magnolia Longing," 11–12, 14– 18. Eichstedt and Small looked at 122 white-centric sites in their three states.

12. Robin Miller, "Merry Christmas from 1857," *Alexandria (LA) Town Talk,* Dec. 19, 1999, Sec. E, p. 1; Brett and Michelle Darnell to President and Mrs. Madison, Dec. 10, 2012, https//virginiaplantation.wordpress.com/2012/12/10 /candlelight-tour-at-montpelier; www.instantdeviephotography.com/journal /belle-grove-plantation.

13. "38th Annual Hofwyl Plantation Christmas," www.gastateparks.org /info/223740?c=13520913; Jean Cleveland, "Hofwyl-Broadfield Plantation," www.georgiaencyclopedia.org/articles/history-archaelogoy/holfyl-broadfield -plantation; "Holidays at Darshana," www.darshanahallplantation.com /holidays.html; O. C. Stonestreet, "Darshana Hall Plantation Is Worth a Visit," Dec. 28, 2008, www. statesville.com/news/darshana-hall-plantation-is =worth-a-visit/article_26e72c3f-4f11–5509-a597–7943c57fd24.html; Sasvari, "Nottoway"; www.wafb.com/story/1568366/nottoway-plantation-christmas -candlelight-tours; www.oakleyplantation.com/events/annual-christmas -bonfire-party; "Seasonal Fun and Activities: Christmas and Holiday Events 2016," www.fredericksburgparent.net/read/seasonal-fam/3966-christmas -and-holiday-events; https://www.irisinn.com/blog/2013/12/candlelight -christmas-tours-at-montpelier; "Celebrate Christmas at Montpelier with a Special Candlelight Tour," www.readthehook.com/69525/christmas-candlelight -tours-montpelier.

14. [Anon.], *Monmouth Plantation: A Dream in Time* (Los Angeles: Timothy Perior, 1989); msbusiness.com./2012/02/bank-to-take-over-histori -monmouth-in-foreclosure-proceedings-2/; Lindsley Shelton, "Monmouth Changing Hands," www.natchezdemocrat.com/2012/03/3/monmouth -changing-hands/; www.monmouthhistoricinn.com/historical-overview .html; monmouthhistoricinn.com/timeline.html; "Monmouth Historic Inn,"

bnblist.com/mississippi-bed-and-breakfast-directory/monmouth-historic
-inn-natchez-mis.

15. "Historical Overview," www.monmouthhistoricinn.com/historical
-overview.html; http://www.monmouthhistoricinn.com/timeline.html.

16. "Monmouth Historic Inn"; "St. Pius X Christmas Gala," Oct. 3, 2006, st
.piusxchristmasgala.blogspot.com/2006/10/two-nights-of-romantic-monmouth
.html; www.inspirems.co/2/post/2014/12/monmouth-historic-inn-html.

17. J. P. White, "Christmas at the Plantation," *North American Review* 278
(Nov./Dec. 1993): 4–9 (quotations on 5, 6).

18. Paul Clark, "Historic Site to Offer Glimpse of a 1830-Style Christmas,"
Asheville Citizen, Nov. 30, 1999, Sec. B:1, proquest.com.ezproxy.lib.purdue.edu.

19. "Food for Thought," *Black News,* Dec. 26, 1973, p. 24; Barbara Omolade,
"Christmas on the Plantation," *Black News,* Jan. 1, 1981, p. 26; "Janey, Flip Flop
Byrne Is in Serious Trouble," *Chicago Metro News,* Dec. 15, 1979, p. 4; Willie
Dixon Jr., "Christmas in the Quarters," *Chicago Metro News,* Dec. 24, 1983, p. 6;
Colson Whitehead, *The Underground Railroad* (New York: Random House Large
Print, 2016), 44.

20. Patricia C. McKissack and Frederick L. McKissack, *Christmas in the Big
House, Christmas in the Quarters* (New York: Scholastic Press, 1994); Paul Erickson, *1853: Daily Life on a Southern Plantation* (New York: Lodestar Books, 1998), 8,
17, 19, 32 (quotation on 32). A third children's literature title from the 1990s—
Irene Smalls's picture book *Irene Jennie and the Christmas Masquerade: The Johnkankus*
(Boston: Little, Brown, 1996)—undercut stereotypes by having "Koners" sing
about stingy masters, and portraying a slave girl distraught because her parents had been rented out to labor at a holiday party at another plantation. But
it also had the master benevolently excuse the parents from cleanup after the
party so they could enjoy part of Christmas with their daughter.

21. Chuck Mobley, "House Slaves Also Had Something to Look Forward to during Christmas," *Savannah Morning News,* Dec. 18, 2006, https:
search-proquest-com.ezproxy.lib.purdue.edu/docview/381893999/fulltext
/5FD666D331A54591PQ/1?accountid=13360; "1774: A Stratford Hall Christ-
mastide," www.stratfordhall.org/events/1774-a-stratford-hall-christmastide/;
7DF5E7265DF4521PQ/1?accountid=13360; Rachel Murdy, "Christmas in
the Quarters," posted Dec. 14, 2011, on southcarolinaparks.com/sc-parks
-insider/Blog/7145, and many other web announcements such as "Christmas in the Quarters," Dec. 19, 2015, scliving.coop/events/christmas-in-the
-quarters2/; "Christmas in the Quarters: An Activity Book," courtesy of Elizabeth L. Laney, park interpreter, Redcliffe Plantation State Historic Site; Fielding Freed, director of Historic House Museums, Historic Columbia email to
the author, June 13, 2017.

22. Edward Bacon to Thomas Jefferson, Nov. 17, 1808, Jefferson to Jeremiah Goodman, Dec. 23, 1814, Joel Yancey to Jefferson, Dec. 24, 1818, Mary
Jefferson Randolph to Virginia Jefferson Randolph, Dec. 27, 1821, https://
www.monticello.org/site/research-and-collections/christmas; Brent Staples,
"The Legacy of Monticello's Black First Family," *NYT,* July 5, 2018, p. A18;
"Christmas Open House Guidelines 2015," courtesy of Christian J. Cotz, director of Education and Visitor Engagement, James Madison's Montpelier.

23. Jeremy Borden, "Tour Looks at a Slave's Christmas," *Washington Post,* Dec. 8, 2013, Sec. LE, p. 1, http://search.proquest.com.ezproxy.lib.purdue .edu/newsstand/docview/1466015569/3.

24. "Booker T. Washington National Monument: An Old Virginia Christmas of 1864," https://www.nps.gov/bowa/planavisit/upload/Christmas-event -flyer-20140final.pdf; "Christmas Event at BTW Monument Draws 700 visitors," *Franklin (TN) News-Post,* Dec. 26, 2013, http://www.thefranklinnewspost .com/smith_mountain_lake/christmas-event-at-btw-monument-draws-visitors /article_d8a9d1d2–6a02–57b5–91b6–8a8a389d1955.html; Amy Sowder, "Hear the Leaves Drop, Creeks Run in Rural Virginia," *Fort Myers (FL) News Press,* Nov. 24, 2007, http://search.proquest.com.ezproxy.lib.purdue.edu/gannettnews /docview/382460929/fulltext/93630A38716840CBPQ/1?accountid=13360.

25. "Plantation Puts On Its Christmas Best," Nov. 30, 2005, www .heraldtribune.com/article/LK/20051130/News/605245648/SH/; www.Flpub licarchaelogy.or/civilwar/industry-and-economy/gamble-plantation-eden ton; Ted Ungar, "Gamble Plantation," District 4 Report, dep.state.fl.us; https://www.facebook.com/pages/Gamble-Plantation-Historic-State-Park /107949225892700.

26. Miles E. Johnson, "Historic Virginia Mansion Hosts 'Plantation Christmas' Because Nothing Says 'Festive' Like Slavery," *Mother Jones,* Dec. 15, 2015, www.motherjones.com/politics/2015/12/george-mason-mansion-celebrate -plantation-christmas.

27. Brandon Byrd, "Ghosts of Slavery's Christmas," Dec. 22, 2016, *Black Perspectives,* www.aalhs.org/ghosts-of-slaverys-christmas; "African-Americans," https://bellemeadeplantation.com/african-americans/.

28. "Celebrate the Holidays at Louisiana's Grand Plantations," www .louisianatravel.com/articles/celebrate-holidays-louisianas-plantations.

29. Felicity Allen, *Jefferson Davis: Unconquerable Heart (Columbia: University of Missouri Press, 1999),* 26, 414–15, 525–16, 549; Bell Irvin Wiley, *Confederate Women* (Westport, CT: Greenwood Press, 1975), 129–30, 134.

30. Ed Brandt, "Bring Back Slavery," (Norfolk, VA) *New Journal and Guide,* Oct. 9, 1965, p. 8. Brandt quoted from Francis Butler Simkins, Spoptswood Hunnicutt, and Sidman P. Poole, *Virginia: History, Government, Geography* (New York: Charles Scribner's Sons, 1964), 371.

31. www.oakalleyplantation.org/learn-explore/history//enslaved.

32. Libby Swope Siersema, "Antebellum Christmas," *Atlanta Journal Constitution,* Dec. 3, 2009, http://www.accessatlanta.com/lifestyles/holiday/antebellum -christmas/OF8oh5B0qiMB7rcwhJ3xuK/; "Historic Rosedale Plantation Candlelight Christmas"; https://www.historicrosedale.org/about-2.

33. David W. Blight, "If You Don't Tell It Like It Was, It Can Never Be as It Ought to Be," in Horton and Horton, ed., *Slavery and Public History,* 19–33 (quotations on 20); Modlin, "Tales Told on the Tour," 284.

INDEX

Individual magazines, newspapers, and plantations and historic homes are grouped under entries for magazines and periodicals; newspapers; and plantations and mansions, respectively. Italicized page numbers refer to illustrations.